JONATHAN AGNEW'S
Cricket Year

WITH CONTRIBUTIONS BY

Tony Cozier   John Emburey   Simon Hughes   Vic Marks
Christopher Martin-Jenkins   Marcus Trescothick

29TH EDITION

September 2009 to September 2010

PUBLISHING

Edited by Mark Baldwin
with contributions by
Chris Adams
Qamar Ahmed
Paul Bolton
Tony Cozier
Mark Eklid (*Derby Telegraph*)
John Emburey
Gulu Ezekiel
Richard Gibson
Andrew Hignell
Paul Hiscock
Simon Hughes
Martin Johnson
Richard Latham
Vic Marks

Christopher Martin-Jenkins
Martyn Moxon
Mark Pennell
Mark Ramprakash
Chris Rogers
Emily Salvidge
Will Smith
Vikram Solanki
Richard Thomas
Marcus Trescothick
Simon Walter (*Southampton Echo*)
Tim Wellock
Andy Wilson

With special thanks to testmatchextra.com

First published in 2010 by
TME Publishing
78 Loughborough Road
Quorn, Loughborough
Leicestershire LE12 8DX

Copyright © Jonathan Agnew 2010

The right of Jonathan Agnew to be identified as the author of this work has been asserted by him in accordance with the Copyright, Designs and Patents Act 1988.

A copy of the CIP entry for this book is available from the British Library.

ISBN: 978-0-9566542-0-5

10 9 8 7 6 5 4 3 2 1

This book is produced using paper that is made from wood grown in managed, sustainable forests. It is natural, renewable and recyclable. The logging and manufacturing processes conform to the environmental regulations of the country of origin.

Project editor: Julian Flanders
Design: Kathie Wilson
Statistics and county information: Peter Griffiths at cricketarchive.com
All pictures © Graham Morris (www.cricketpix.com), except page 165 (left) © Hannah Bills; page 128 © Gloucestershire CCC; pages 40, 42, 43, 44, 47, 174 and 240 © PA Images; and pages 206–7 © Sussex CCC.

Printed and bound in the UK by Butler Tanner and Dennis, Frome

For full scorecards and day-to-day match reports and details of every game played in the 2010 County Championship, Friends Provident t20 and Clydesdale Bank 40, and for full listings of averages and other statistical details, please go to www.cricketarchive.com

CONTENTS

IN MY VIEW

by Jonathan Agnew

It was ten years ago that a senior High Court Judge, Malik Muhammad Qayyum, delivered a damning report into corruption in Pakistan cricket. Several senior players stood accused of match fixing and while only two, Salim Malik and Ata-ur-Rehman, were found guilty of that particular charge and banned for life, familiar names such as Wasim Akram, Waqar Younis, Mushtaq Ahmed and Inzamam-ul-Haq were all fined and warned as to their future conduct.

A decade later, and Pakistan's cricket is strongly linked with corruption once again. This time it is not specifically an allegation of match fixing, rather spot betting which, to the layman, might appear less serious than altering the outcome of a match, and yet its impact on the game is equally damaging. The integrity of the cricket currently played by Pakistan is highly questionable, and while none of the allegations made against Salman Butt, Mohammad Asif and Mohammad Aamer had been substantiated at the time of writing, their defence to the charge of bowling no-balls to order in the Lord's Test will be interesting, indeed. We have all seen the video of Mazhar Majeed, who was an agent to some of Pakistan's players, sitting behind a mountain of money and secretly filmed as he specified three deliveries – the first ball of the third over, the last ball of the tenth over and then the third ball of the following day's third over – would be no-balls. He even confidently predicted which bowler would deliver them. We then watched the video replays of those deliveries; each one a no-ball with the young, some might say naive Aamer, overstepping by as much as two feet which bewildered the commentators on both television and radio.

Whatever the outcome of the inquiry, the damage to Pakistan cricket has already been done. The extra-ordinary rant by the chairman of the Pakistan Cricket Board, Ijaz Butt, in which he claimed that England's players had deliberately thrown the third one-day international at The Oval, was more than just foolish; it said everything that is wrong with the administration of cricket in that country. It goes without saying that Butt has to go before any credible clean up on the scale that will satisfy the cricketing world can begin.

There have been calls for Pakistan to be banned from international cricket while it gets its house in order, but I do not believe that will benefit anybody. The country needs all the help it can get at the moment with teams unable to tour there because of security concerns. Giles Clarke and David Collier at the England and Wales Cricket Board have every right to be extremely affronted by Mr Butt's behaviour having been so accommodating to his team this summer, but surely it is far better that the ICC is closely involved with the necessary restructuring and that the PCB is seen to be

Above Mohammad Aamer – superb talent or naïve youngster? – celebrates taking the wicket of Jonathan Trott during the third Test at The Oval.

Right Captain Salman Butt, pictured in the Long Room at Lord's, has much to ponder as the future of Pakistan cricket hangs in the balance.

taking action, and is properly monitored. This also involves the punishment of any player found to have been guilty of corruption, and for this a life ban is the only way to restore the public's faith in cricket. There have been calls for young players like Aamer to be treated leniently should they be found guilty, but I cannot see any merit in that. Every international cricketer is fully briefed and shown an ICC film highlighting the perils of becoming embroiled in corruption before he takes the field for the first time. There is not a cricketer playing the game who could claim not to be fully aware of the consequences of involvement with bookmakers. There are no excuses.

However, this is not a problem entirely for Pakistan to confront. Thus far, the only cricketer to be actually charged with fraud is an Essex county cricketer called Mervyn Westfield who, it is alleged, acted dishonestly in a match against Durham in 2009. It is for everyone involved with cricket at every level – the players, umpires, administrators and even the commentators and correspondents – to police the sport and report anything that appears suspicious to the ICC. Only when it becomes impossible for the few rotten apples that exist within the game to continue playing dishonestly can we all be sure that cricket is clean.

What a shame that corruption should be the major talking point rather than England's superb year. Unbeaten in their four Test and five ODI series during the last 12 months, the team continues to make encouraging progress under the shrewd and calm leadership of Andrew Strauss and the coach Andy Flower. The captaincy has had a dramatic impact on Strauss's batting, particularly in one-day cricket, to

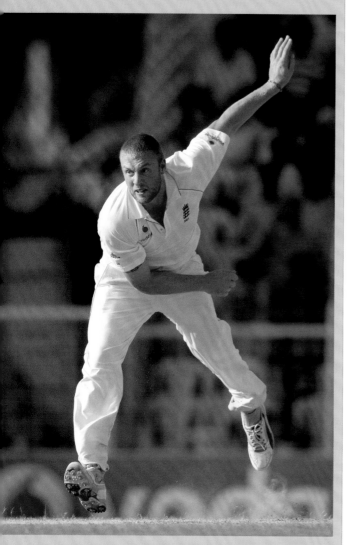

Steven Finn (holding the ball) is hoping to reproduce the sort of attritional bowling that made his hero, Glenn McGrath, one of the world's best-ever bowlers.

Andrew Flintoff's Test match career was, statistically, only a great one between 2004 and 2006 – as the chart below clearly shows. For most of his 11 years as a Test player his performances were modest, figures-wise, though his value to the side in terms of presence and the balance he brought as a genuine all-rounder are incalculable.

the extent that he appears to have reinvented himself into a cavalier shot-player. It makes it all the more remarkable that he was overlooked for the job when the selectors preferred Kevin Pietersen, who ended the season dropped from the England team, and without a county club. By his high standards, the last 12 months – in which he failed to score a Test century – have been very disappointing. England fans will be hoping that he responds positively and scores a mountain of runs against Australia.

I am not alone in setting off for the Ashes with a confident spring in my step. It has been a very long time – 24 years – since Mike Gatting's team last won in Australia, but there is good reason for that. In Shane Warne, Glenn McGrath, Adam Gilchrist and Matthew Hayden, Australia were blessed with a group of extraordinarily talented cricketers whose skill and

THE THREE STAGES OF ANDREW FLINTOFF'S TEST CAREER

Period	Tests	Runs	Avg	100s	Wkts	Avg	5WI	SR
July 1998 to December 2003	29	1,209	25.72	2	52	45.55	0	94.7
January 2004 to June 2006	33	1,918	39.95	3	134	25.80	2	50.8
July 2006 to August 2009	17	718	27.61	0	40	39.57	1	80.2
Career	79	3,845	31.77	5	226	32.78	3	66.1

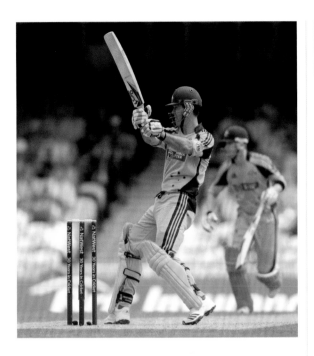

Ricky Ponting's skills as captain and most experienced batsman will be tested to the full as England head Down Under for another Ashes tour.

Andrew Strauss leads a confident England team to Australia, but does he have what it takes to be the first England captain in 24 years to return with the Ashes?

attitude helped to lift those less gifted players around them. Now they have all left the stage and, of that special category, only Ricky Ponting remains. He turns 37 during the winter, and one wonders how the strain of leading a less talented team might impact on his own game. Time will tell.

England, meanwhile, have exciting competition for places within their batting line-up and, in Graeme Swann, boast the leading spin bowler in the world. Traditional and old fashioned – on the field, at least – Swann has demonstrated that there is still a leading part in the game for the orthodox finger spinner. Australia will look to target him because of the invaluable containing role he performs in a four-man attack, and that will be one of the particularly fascinating elements of this Ashes contest. James Anderson will be hoping he can swing the Kookaburra ball with the same deadly effect he enjoyed with the Duke this summer, while the three leggy young pacemen, Stuart Broad, Steven Finn and Chris Tremlett, must focus on developing the metronomic accuracy that made McGrath – similarly tall – such a wonderful bowler.

The one area that England is lacking is a bruising, aggressive and hostile fast bowler; someone to rough up the batsmen and blow away the tail. Who can I be talking about? Andrew Flintoff, of course, who finally

gave up his dream of becoming a true freelance of Twenty20 cricket when confronted with the news that he would need yet another big knee operation. An inspirational figure on the field, Flintoff did more than anyone – with both bat and ball – to win the Ashes in 2005, and his genuinely fast bowling was a vital ingredient in the 2009 series victory against Australia, too. His final tally of runs scored and wickets taken do not accurately assess his contribution; he was, for a start, a very unlucky bowler. What he would have given for some of Ian Botham's knack of inducing a loose drive to extra cover, or another hook sent down deep square leg's throat. Flintoff beat the bat over and over again, while bowlers at the other end benefitted from the pressure he created. But more than any of that, he created a buzz of excitement whenever he walked out to bat or was thrown the ball. Spectators would rush back to their seats and even the most tedious of games would come back to life once again. Only very few sportsmen are blessed with that ability. It makes talk of degrees of 'greatness' irrelevant; they are special. And when fit and firing against the Australians, Andrew Flintoff was certainly special.

Jonathan Agnew
Leicestershire, October 2010

ENGLAND v. PAKISTAN
by Jonathan Agnew

Cricketing relations between England and Pakistan have always been rocky. Ever since the Pakistani umpire, Idris Baig, was allegedly debagged and soaked with water by an MCC touring team of the mid-1950s, tempers have run high resulting in a series of notoriously ugly flashpoints.

Somehow, the two teams have continued to play against each other despite the deep-rooted mistrust lurking just beneath the surface, but Pakistan's visit to England in the summer of 2010 might turn out to be one tour too many. Dogged by accusations of corruption, this was the most ill tempered and damaging tour since Bodyline nearly 80 years ago.

The tour did not begin promisingly when Pakistan's captain, Shahid Afridi, suddenly resigned after the first of two Tests against Australia which, because of the security concerns in Pakistan, were played in England. Salman Butt, the quietly spoken opening batsman, was suddenly propelled into leading his country, and although he seemed a little reluctant at first, he managed at Headingley to lead his team to their first victory over Australia since 1995. His seam bowlers, Mohammad Asif and Mohammad Aamer looked especially potent as Australia were bundled out for just 88 in their first innings, and there appeared to be the genuine prospect of a close and interesting series against England to follow.

Eoin Morgan, England's Irish wizard, unleashes his powerful reverse sweep to hit Pakistan leg spinner Danish Kaneria for four during the first Test at Trent Bridge. Morgan went to complete a maiden Test hundred and set up a crushing England victory.

Jimmy Anderson holds the ball aloft as he salutes the crowd in now traditional fashion after taking his fifth wicket in Pakistan's first innings of the opening Test, at Trent Bridge. He has just dismissed Mohammad Aamer, and will go on to claim 11 wickets in the match.

The first Test at Trent Bridge set the pattern. The ball swung prodigiously – not through the recently perfected, mechanical reverse swing, but the traditional, orthodox and mysterious art of real swing bowling. No batsman on either side was comfortable, illustrating a serious deficiency in the technique of modern cricketers, and England's top order regularly found itself needing to be bailed out.

At Nottingham it was Eoin Morgan who produced a steely, defiant innings of 130 – his first contribution of note in Test cricket – and one that presumably came about only through an injury to Ian Bell. It was a gritty knock; ideal for the situation that stood at 118 for 4 when he joined Paul Collingwood. Together they added 219 although Collingwood – who scored 82 – was horribly missed by wicketkeeper Kamran Akmal, whose exhibition behind the wickets was truly dreadful. Later in the series it was announced by the ICC that Akmal's recent performances in Test cricket were the subject of investigation by its Anti Corruption Unit.

Morgan reached his first Test century with a six, but England lost their last six wickets for 23 and were bowled out for 354. Anderson and Finn quickly found the same assistance, and Pakistan were 108 for 8 before Umar Gul smashed 65 not out to avoid the follow-on. England's batsmen struggled against the swinging ball once again in their second innings, floundering on 98 for 6 before Prior came to the rescue with a bristling 102 not out. The last four wickets added 164 as, supported by Swann and Broad, Prior steered England to a lead of 434 and by the close of the third day, Pakistan were already 15 for 3.

Anderson completed the rout by lunchtime the following day as Pakistan were blown away for a spineless 80, with the swing bowler taking 6 for 17 to give him match figures of 11 for 71.

The chaos surrounding the administration of Pakistan cricket was evident as, first, the team's senior spinner Danish Kaneria was dropped from the tour and banished to his county, Essex. Even more remarkable was the announcement that Mohammad Yousuf, who was one of a number of Pakistan players to be punished and suspended by the Board – in Yousuf's case, for life – following the 'dysfunctional' tour of Australia, was bundled on to the next flight from Lahore. There was even talk of him playing in the second Test, despite landing in Birmingham only late on the previous afternoon.

Common sense prevailed, however, and while Yousuf was given time to get over his jetlag, and reacquaint himself with his bat, Pakistan dropped Kamran Akmal in favour of Zulquarnain Haider and reinforced the batting order by restoring Shoaib Malik – another player who had been banned for a year. In fewer than 40 overs, Pakistan were routed for 72, their lowest score against England, with Anderson and Broad taking four wickets each. England's reply was somewhat laboured, with Trott scoring 55 having been dropped on eight, and Pietersen, whose place was starting to be the subject of debate, a thoroughly unconvincing 80. He was dropped badly on nine, again on 20 and once

FIRST TEST – ENGLAND v. PAKISTAN
29 July–1 August 2010 at Trent Bridge

ENGLAND

	First Innings		Second Innings	
AJ Strauss (capt)	c Kamran Akmal b Mohammad Aamer	45	c Kamran Akmal b Mohammad Aamer	0
AN Cook	c Imran Farhat b Mohammad Aamer	8	c Kamran Akmal b Mohammad Asif	12
IJL Trott	lbw b Mohammad Aamer	38	b Umar Gul	26
KP Pietersen	b Mohammad Asif	9	c Kamran Akmal b Umar Gul	22
PD Collingwood	lbw b Mohammad Asif	82	lbw b Umar Gul	1
EJG Morgan	lbw b Mohammad Asif	130	run out	17
*MJ Prior	run out	6	not out	102
GP Swann	lbw b Mohammad Asif	2	lbw b Danish Kaneria	28
SCJ Broad	b Umar Gul	3	c Imran Farhat b Shoaib Malik	24
JM Anderson	lbw b Mohammad Asif	0	c Kamran Akmal b Shoaib Malik	2
ST Finn	not out	0	not out	9
Extras	b 5, lb 14, w 5, nb 7	31	b 4, lb 11, w 1, nb 3	19
	(all out 104.1 overs)	354	(9 wkts dec 75.3 overs)	262

	First Innings				Second Innings			
	O	M	R	W	O	M	R	W
Mohammad Aamer	24	7	41	3	16	3	35	1
Mohammad Asif	27	9	77	5	17	1	56	1
Umar Gul	18.1	5	61	1	15	2	41	3
Danish Kaneria	21	0	100	0	12	0	71	1
Shoaib Malik	11	2	39	0	10.3	0	31	2
Azhar Ali	1	0	9	0	-	-	-	-
Umar Amin	1	0	3	0	5	1	13	0
Imran Farhat	1	0	5	0	-	-	-	-

Fall of Wickets
1-42, 2-93, 3-116, 4-118, 5-337, 6-344, 7-351, 8-354, 9-354
1-2, 2-18, 3-65, 4-66, 5-72, 6-98, 7-147, 8-203, 9-213

PAKISTAN

	First Innings		Second Innings	
Imran Farhat	b Anderson	19	c Strauss b Anderson	15
Salman Butt (capt)	c Prior b Anderson	1	c Collingwood b Broad	8
Azhar Ali	c Prior b Anderson	14	lbw b Broad	0
Umar Amin	c Swann b Finn	2	lbw b Anderson	1
Umar Akmal	c Swann b Finn	4	(6) lbw b Anderson	4
Shoaib Malik	c Strauss b Anderson	38	(7) c Collingwood b Anderson	9
*Kamran Akmal	c Collingwood b Finn	0	(8) lbw b Finn	0
Mohammad Aamer	c Swann b Anderson	25	(5) c Pietersen b Finn	4
Umar Gul	not out	65	c Collingwood b Anderson	9
Danish Kaneria	b Broad	7	not out	16
Mohammad Asif	run out	0	c Swann b Anderson	0
Extras	b 5, lb 2	7	b 4, lb 8, w 1, nb 1	14
	(all out 54 overs)	182	(all out 29 overs)	80

	First Innings				Second Innings			
	O	M	R	W	O	M	R	W
Anderson	22	7	54	5	15	8	17	6
Broad	17	4	59	1	8	2	23	2
Finn	13	5	50	3	6	3	28	2
Swann	2	1	12	0	-	-	-	-

Fall of Wickets
1-5, 2-32, 3-35, 4-41, 5-45, 6-47, 7-105, 8-108, 9-147
1-10, 2-10, 3-11, 4-31, 5-37, 6-41, 7-41, 8-50, 9-65

Umpires: EAR de Silva (Sri Lanka) & AL Hill (New Zealand)
Toss: England
Man of the Match: JM Anderson

SECOND TEST – ENGLAND v. PAKISTAN
6–9 August 2010 at Edgbaston

PAKISTAN

	First Innings		Second Innings	
Imran Farhat	c Prior b Broad	0	b Swann	29
Salman Butt (capt)	c Swann b Finn	7	c Strauss b Anderson	0
Azhar Ali	lbw b Broad	0	b Swann	19
Shoaib Malik	c Prior b Anderson	3	c Prior b Finn	3
Umar Akmal	lbw b Finn	17	lbw b Swann	20
Umar Amin	c Collingwood b Broad	23	st Prior b Swann	14
*Zulqarnain Haider	c Prior b Broad	0	c Strauss b Swann	88
Mohammad Aamer	c Cook b Anderson	12	c Strauss b Broad	16
Umar Gul	c Pietersen b Anderson	0	(10) not out	13
Saeed Ajmal	not out	5	(9) c Collingwood b Swann	50
Mohammad Asif	c Pietersen b Anderson	0	c Pietersen b Broad	14
Extras	lb 4, nb 1	5	b 16, lb 14	30
	(all out 39.3 overs)	72	(all out 117.5 overs)	296

	First Innings				Second Innings			
	O	M	R	W	O	M	R	W
Anderson	14.3	6	20	4	28	13	62	1
Broad	17	7	38	4	28.5	8	66	2
Finn	8	3	10	2	16	5	57	1
Swann	-	-	-	-	37	20	65	6
Collingwood	-	-	-	-	7	2	14	0
Pietersen	-	-	-	-	1	0	2	0

Fall of Wickets
1-8, 2-9, 3-12, 4-29, 5-33, 6-36, 7-63, 8-64, 9-67
1-1, 2-53, 3-54, 4-76, 5-82, 6-101, 7-153, 8-268, 9-269

ENGLAND

	First Innings			
AJ Strauss (capt)	c Zulqarnain Haider b Mohammad Aamer	25	not out	53
AN Cook	c Umar Akmal b Mohammad Asif	17	b Mohammad Aamer	4
IJL Trott	c sub (Yasir Hameed) b Umar Amin	55	not out	53
KP Pietersen	c and b Saeed Ajmal	80		
PD Collingwood	c Imran Farhat b Saeed Ajmal	28		
EJG Morgan	c Zulqarnain Haider b Mohammad Asif	6		
*MJ Prior	lbw b Saeed Ajmal	15		
GP Swann	c and b Saeed Ajmal	4		
SCJ Broad	c sub (Yasir Hameed) b Saeed Ajmal	0		
JM Anderson	lbw b Mohammad Aamer	0		
ST Finn	not out	0		
Extras	b 10, lb 9, w 1, nb 1	21	b 5, nb 3	8
	(all out 83.1 overs)	251	(1 wkt 36.3 overs)	118

	First Innings				Second Innings			
	O	M	R	W	O	M	R	W
Mohammad Aamer	20	4	57	2	11	1	31	1
Mohammad Asif	20	5	41	2	6	0	20	0
Umar Gul	9	1	24	0	-	-	-	-
Saeed Ajmal	26.1	5	82	5	14.3	1	42	0
Umar Amin	8	2	28	1	-	-	-	-
Shoaib Malik	-	-	-	-	5	0	20	0

Fall of Wickets
1-44, 2-44, 3-177, 4-205, 5-220, 6-243, 7-248, 8-248, 9-251
1-7

Umpires: SJ Davis (Australia) & M Erasmus (South Africa)
Toss: Pakistan
Test debut: Zulqarnain Haider
Man of the Match: GP Swann

England won by 354 runs

England won by 9 wickets

Graeme Swann appeals during his second-innings haul of 6 for 65 in England's second Test win against Pakistan at Edgbaston. It was a victory that put them 2-0 up in the four-match series.

more on 36 before giving Saeed Ajmal a return catch. The spinner ran through the tail, but with increasing suspicion about the degree of flexibility in his elbow whenever he delivered his doosra.

Despite losing their last five wickets for eight runs, England established a lead of 179 and before long, Pakistan were plummeting towards defeat on 101 for 6, when the debutant, Haider, was given out lbw first ball. Sensibly, this decision was reviewed and Haider was duly reprieved; he went on to score 88 and showed great character, too, which frustrated England to the point of Broad throwing the ball at him, for which he was heavily fined. Ajmal chipped in with 50 to leave England needing 118 to win. Cook – another England batsman whose place was by now in serious jeopardy – was bowled by Aamer for seven, but Strauss and Trott both eased to half-centuries to complete another shortened Test match with a nine-wicket win.

A feisty individual named Wahab Riaz was introduced to the Pakistan team for the third Test at the Oval, and made an immediate impact, taking 5 for 63 with his energetic left-arm pace bowling. England's top order failed again, with Cook and Pietersen both scoring six and were reduced to 74 for 6 and 94 for 7, before Prior embarked on his second rescue act of the series. He scored 84 not out, adding 129 with Broad and steering England to 233, which was at least 100 runs below par. As nightwatchman, Wahab scored 27 as Pakistan battled to establish a match-winning lead. He almost ran out Yousuf first ball – the old campaigner survived to make 56 while Azhar Ali, one of the promising new generation, scored a lovely unbeaten 92.

Strauss and the night-watchman Anderson were both dismissed before Pakistan's lead of 75 was overcome while Cook was battling to save his international future. In fact, he batted very freely; adding 116 with Trott before being gifted his hundred in the most bizarre circumstances. Playing the ball defensively to the bowler, Mohammad Asif, Cook made no attempt to leave his crease, and was astonished to see Asif hurl the ball aggressively, but wildly over his head, over the wicketkeeper's head and into the boundary to take Cook

Alastair Cook drives beautifully for four past Umar Akmal, the close offside fielder, as the England opener revives his Test career with a determined and characterful century in the third Test against Pakistan at The Oval.

to 100. Ajmal ran through the lower order as England lost seven wickets for 28, leaving Pakistan 148 to win.

Anyone with a keen interest in Pakistan cricket would be aware that this could easily prove to be too much, and Yasir Hameed fell to Anderson in the first over for a duck. Farhat and Butt added 52, and Pakistan looked all but home on 103 for 2. Four wickets then fell for 28 runs, leaving Pakistan needing 16 to win with four wickets in hand and, well as Swann bowled, Umar Akmal and Mohammad Aamer saw them nervously but securely over the line.

And so to the final Test of the series at Lord's, during the course of which the *News of the World* published allegations that the newspaper claimed resulted from a meeting with one of its undercover reporters, and an agent to some of Pakistan's players, Mazhar Majeed. This is now at the centre of a criminal investigation and, at the time of writing, none of the allegations – which have been denied by Mr Majeed, Salmon Butt, Mohammad Asif and Mohammad Aamer – has been substantiated.

However, the film produced by the *News of the World* clearly shows Mr Majeed handling a large amount of money – supposedly £150,000 – and apparently predicting that three specific deliveries bowled by Aamer and Asif during the course of the match would be no-balls. In every case, these predictions turned out to be correct, including the first delivery of the third over of the match, which was bowled by Aamer. I was commentating at the time, and the size of the no-ball immediately took me and Phil Tufnell by surprise. Why let go of the ball when you are so obviously over the line? At the time, the match simply proceeded with no one any the wiser of what would happen on Saturday night and Sunday morning when the *News of the World* published its story.

The Test should have been remembered for the highest eighth-wicket partnership ever recorded. Trott and Broad, whose 169 is the second highest score by a No. 9 in Tests, added 332 in 426 minutes in England's first innings after successive ducks by Pietersen, Collingwood and Morgan – who all fell to Aamer – reduced England

THIRD TEST – ENGLAND v. PAKISTAN
18–21 August 2010 at The Oval

ENGLAND

	First Innings		Second Innings	
AJ Strauss (capt)	c Kamran Akmal b Wahab Riaz	15	c Yasir Hameed b Mohammad Aamer	4
AN Cook	c Kamran Akmal b Mohammad Asif	6	c Kamran Akmal b Wahab Riaz	110
IJL Trott	c Yasir Hameed b Wahab Riaz	12	(4) c Azhar Ali b Mohammad Aamer	36
KP Pietersen	c Kamran Akmal b Wahab Riaz	6	(5) b Saeed Ajmal	23
PD Collingwood	b Mohammad Aamer	5	(6) c Kamran Akmal b Mohammad Aamer	3
EJG Morgan	c Kamran Akmal b Wahab Riaz	17	(7) b Saeed Ajmal	5
*MJ Prior	not out	84	(8) c Kamran Akmal b Mohammad Aamer	5
GP Swann	c Umar Akmal b Mohammad Asif	8	(9) b Saeed Ajmal	6
SCJ Broad	lbw b Wahab Riaz	48	(10) c Mohammad Asif b Mohammad Aamer	6
JM Anderson	lbw b Mohammad Asif	0	(3) c Kamran Akmal b Saeed Ajmal	11
ST Finn	lbw b Saeed Ajmal	0	not out	1
Extras	b 10, lb 11, w 6, nb 5	32	lb 5, w 2, nb 5	12
	(all out 62.3 overs)	233	(all out 77 overs)	222

	First Innings				Second Innings			
	O	M	R	W	O	M	R	W
Mohammad Aamer	15	4	49	1	19	5	52	5
Mohammad Asif	20	5	68	3	16	7	45	0
Wahab Riaz	18	6	63	5	8	1	40	1
Saeed Ajmal	9.3	1	32	1	31	7	71	4
Imran Farhat	-	-	-	-	3	0	9	0

Fall of Wickets
1-9, 2-35, 3-40, 4-47, 5-67, 6-74, 7-94, 8-213, 9-214
1-4, 2-40, 3-156, 4-194, 5-195, 6-202, 7-206, 8-210, 9-220

PAKISTAN

	First Innings		Second Innings	
Imran Farhat	b Anderson	11	lbw b Swann	33
Yasir Hameed	c Prior b Finn	36	c Swann b Anderson	0
Wahab Riaz	lbw b Swann	27		
Salman Butt (capt)	c Prior b Swann	17	(3) c Collingwood b Swann	48
Mohammad Yousuf	c and b Swann	56	(4) b Anderson	33
Azhar Ali	not out	92	(5) run out	5
Umar Akmal	run out	38	(6) not out	16
*Kamran Akmal	c Morgan b Broad	10	(7) lbw b Swann	0
Mohammad Aamer	c Prior b Broad	6	(8) not out	4
Saeed Ajmal	b Anderson	0		
Mohammad Asif	c Anderson b Swann	8		
Extras	lb 4, w 1, nb 2	7	b 4, lb 2, w 2, nb 1	9
	(all out 100.2 overs)	308	(6 wkts 41.4 overs)	148

	First Innings				Second Innings			
	O	M	R	W	O	M	R	W
Anderson	24	6	79	2	14	5	39	2
Broad	25	4	72	2	6	0	35	0
Finn	20	4	74	1	3	0	18	0
Swann	27.2	9	68	4	18.4	4	50	3
Collingwood	4	0	11	0	-	-	-	-

Fall of Wickets
1-48, 2-48, 3-76, 4-110, 5-179, 6-236, 7-251, 8-269, 9-270
1-5, 2-57, 3-103, 4-124, 5-131, 6-132

Umpires: SJ Davis (Australia) & AL Hill (New Zealand)
Toss: England
Test debut: Wahab Riaz
Man of the Match: Mohammad Aamer

Pakistan won by 4 wickets

to 47 for 5. When Swann was dismissed for another 0, England were 102 for 7. It was not until the score reached 434 that Pakistan claimed their next wicket.

There was nothing in the *News of the World* story, or anywhere else, which suggests that this partnership was anything but entirely bona fide and genuine. However, in the light of the spot fixing allegations, everyone involved with the game found themselves wondering about what was genuine, and what might not be so. Such is the damaging impact of corruption on sport.

With 32 overs remaining on the third day, Pakistan had already been bundled out for a pitiful 74 – their lowest total at Lord's. Swann claimed 4 for 12 and Finn 3 for 38, but the application and effort of the visitors was woeful. By the close, Pakistan were 41 for 4, still 331 runs behind, having lost 14 wickets for 115 runs in the day. Another four-day defeat loomed.

When everyone reconvened at Lord's the following morning the atmosphere was one of absolute depression and dismay. Anger, too, while the *News of the World* story was making headlines all over the world. Pakistan's players arrived late, and chose not to warm up or practice, but remained in their dressing room. Pakistan

Matt Prior, one of the most fluent batsmen in the game, turns a ball off his pads for more runs during the third Test against Pakistan at Edgbaston.

FOURTH TEST – ENGLAND v. PAKISTAN
26–29 August 2010 at Lord's

SERIES AVERAGES
England v. Pakistan

ENGLAND

	First Innings	
AJ Strauss (capt)	b Mohammad Asif	13
AN Cook	c Kamran Akmal b Mohammad Aamer	10
IJL Trott	c Kamran Akmal b Wahab Riaz	184
KP Pietersen	c Kamran Akmal b Mohammad Aamer	0
PD Collingwood	lbw b Mohammad Aamer	0
EJG Morgan	c Yasir Hameed b Mohammad Aamer	0
*MJ Prior	c Kamran Akmal b Mohammad Aamer	22
GP Swann	c Azhar Ali b Mohammad Aamer	0
SCJ Broad	lbw b Saeed Ajmal	169
JM Anderson	c Yasir Hameed b Saeed Ajmal	6
ST Finn	not out	0
Extras	b 4, lb 17, w 7, nb 14	42
	(all out 139.2 overs)	446

	First Innings			
	O	M	R	W
Mohammad Aamer	28	6	84	6
Mohammad Asif	29	6	97	1
Wahab Riaz	27.2	4	92	1
Saeed Ajmal	44	5	126	2
Yasir Hameed	1	1	0	0
Imran Farhat	10	1	26	0

Fall of Wickets
1-31, 2-39, 3-39, 4-39, 5-47, 6-102, 7-102, 8-434, 9-446

PAKISTAN

	First Innings		Second Innings (following on)	
Imran Farhat	c Prior b Anderson	6	c Cook b Broad	5
Yasir Hameed	c Swann b Broad	2	lbw b Anderson	3
Salman Butt (capt)	b Swann	26	lbw b Swann	21
Mohammad Yousuf	b Broad	0	c Trott b Finn	10
Azhar Ali	c Cook b Swann	10	b Swann	12
Umar Akmal	b Finn	6	not out	79
*Kamran Akmal	c Prior b Finn	13	c Prior b Anderson	1
Mohammad Aamer	lbw b Finn	0	b Swann	0
Wahab Riaz	lbw b Swann	2	c Pietersen b Swann	0
Saeed Ajmal	not out	4	run out (Broad)	8
Mohammad Asif	c and b Swann	0	c Collingwood b Swann	1
Extras	lb 4, nb 1	5	b 1, lb 2, w 3, nb 1	7
	(all out 33 overs)	74	(all out 36.5 overs)	147

	First Innings				Second Innings			
	O	M	R	W	O	M	R	W
Anderson	10	6	10	1	13	4	35	2
Broad	6	4	10	2	6	1	24	1
Finn	9	4	38	3	4	0	23	1
Swann	8	3	12	4	13.5	1	62	5

Fall of Wickets
1-9, 2-9, 3-10, 4-46, 5-53, 6-57, 7-57, 8-70, 9-74
1-7, 2-9, 3-41, 4-41, 5-63, 6-64, 7-65, 8-73, 9-97

Umpires: BF Bowden (New Zealand) & AL Hill (New Zealand)
Toss: Pakistan
Man of the Match: SCJ Broad
Men of the Series: Mohammad Aamer & IJL Trott

ENGLAND

Batting	M	Inns	NO	Runs	HS	Av	100	50	c/st
IJL Trott	4	7	1	404	184	67.33	1	2	1/-
MJ Prior	4	6	2	234	102*	58.50	1	1	12/1
SCJ Broad	4	6	0	250	169	41.66	1	-	-/-
EJG Morgan	4	6	0	175	130	29.16	1	-	1/-
AJ Strauss	4	7	1	155	53*	25.83	-	1	5/-
AN Cook	4	7	0	167	110	23.85	1	-	3/-
KP Pietersen	4	6	0	140	80	23.33	-	1	5/-
PD Collingwood	4	6	0	119	82	19.83	-	1	8/-
ST Finn	4	6	5	10	9*	10.00	-	-	-/-
GP Swann	4	6	0	48	28	8.00	-	-	9/-
JM Anderson	4	6	0	19	11	3.16	-	-	1/-

Bowling	Overs	Mds	Runs	Wkts	Av	Best	5/inn	10m
GP Swann	106.5	38	269	22	12.22	6-65	2	-
JM Anderson	140.5	55	316	23	13.73	6-17	2	1
ST Finn	79	24	298	13	22.92	3-38	0	-
SCJ Broad	113.5	30	327	14	23.35	4-38	0	-

Also bowled: PD Collingwood 11-2-25-0, KP Pietersen 1-0-2-0.

PAKISTAN

Batting	M	Inns	NO	Runs	HS	Av	100	50	c/st
Zulqarnain Haider	1	2	0	88	88	44.00	-	1	2/-
Umar Gul	2	4	2	87	65*	43.50	-	1	-/-
Umar Akmal	4	8	2	184	79*	30.66	-	1	2/-
Mohammad Yousuf	2	4	0	99	56	24.75	-	1	-/-
Danish Kaneria	1	2	1	23	16*	23.00	-	-	-/-
Saeed Ajmal	3	5	2	67	50	22.33	-	1	-/-
Azhar Ali	4	8	1	152	92*	21.71	-	1	2/-
Salman Butt	4	8	0	128	48	16.00	-	-	-/-
Imran Farhat	4	8	0	118	33	14.75	-	-	3/-
Shoaib Malik	2	4	0	53	38	13.25	-	-	-/-
Yasir Hameed	2	4	0	41	36	10.25	-	-	4/-
Umar Amin	2	4	0	40	23	10.00	-	-	-/-
Wahab Riaz	2	3	0	29	27	9.66	-	-	-/-
Mohammad Aamer	4	8	1	67	25	9.57	-	-	-/-
Kamran Akmal	3	6	0	24	13	4.00	-	-	17/-
Mohammad Asif	4	7	0	23	14	3.28	-	-	1/-

Bowling	Overs	Mds	Runs	Wkts	Av	Best	5/inn	10m
Mohammad Aamer	133	30	349	19	18.36	6-84	2	-
Wahab Riaz	53.2	11	195	7	27.85	5-63	1	-
Saeed Ajmal	125.1	19	353	12	29.41	5-82	1	-
Umar Gul	42.1	8	126	4	31.50	3-41	-	-
Mohammad Asif	135	33	404	12	33.66	5-77	1	-
Umar Amin	14	3	44	1	44.00	1-28	-	-
Shoaib Malik	26.3	2	90	2	45.00	2-31	-	-
Danish Kaneria	33	0	171	1	171.00	1-71	-	-

Also bowled: Yasir Hameed 1-1-0-0, Azhar Ali 1-0-9-0, Imran Farhat 14-1-40-0.

England won by an innings and 225 runs

England won series 3-1

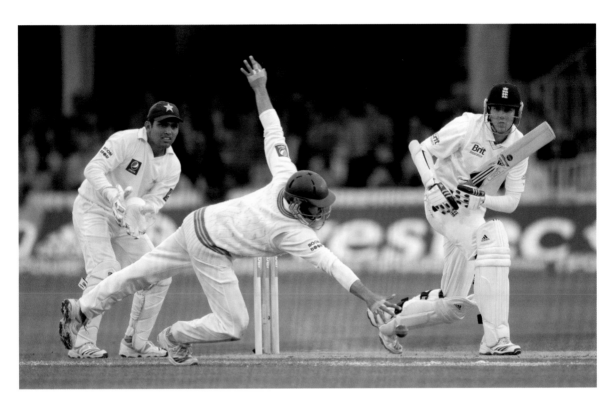

Stuart Broad's remarkable 169 from No. 9 in the final Test against Pakistan at Lord's was a brilliant batting performance sadly overshadowed by the spot-fixing allegations which broke in the following 24 hours. Broad, though, will always remember his maiden Test hundred and his world-record eighth-wicket Test match partnership with Jonathan Trott.

duly collapsed again, losing their last six wickets for 106, and because of the betting allegations, the presentations were conducted inside the MCC pavilion out of the public gaze rather than the usual position outside on the grass. Mohammad Aamer was awarded Pakistan's Player of the Series, and the expression on the face of ECB chairman, Giles Clarke, as he made the presentation is one of the images of the summer – the other being the photograph of the Pakistan management sitting on their balcony, intently reading the *News of the World*.

Following a week of uncertainty, it was announced by the ICC that Butt, Asif and Aamer would be temporarily suspended from all cricket, and this ended mounting speculation about the fate of the one-day series. The three cricketers were interviewed by Scotland Yard, and eventually returned home to prepare their defence against charges that will be brought against them by the ICC. With a waning appetite for the continuation of the tour, England nevertheless won the two Twenty20 matches before poor crowds in Cardiff, and recorded victories at Durham and Leeds in the 50-overs variety despite encouraging performances by Pakistan, who were now led once again by Afridi.

But the third match at The Oval was the focal point of yet another flashpoint. It was won by Pakistan, who defended 242 thanks to some inspired reverse swing bowling at pace by Gul. He took 4 for 6 in 18 balls as England's lower order was swept away, only for the ICC to announce the following day that the match was being investigated because of certain 'scoring patterns'. The ICC failed to reveal the team involved, but privately disclosed that it was Pakistan.

The information had been supplied to the ICC by another tabloid newspaper, but the basic framework of Pakistan's innings was absolutely routine. Using the tried and trusted formula of doubling the score at 30 overs to predict the likely total, Pakistan were 121 for 5 and finished with 241. The investigations continue.

Then, just when things could not have got any worse, the chairman of the Pakistan Cricket Board, Ijaz Butt, launched an outrageous attack on the integrity of England's players, including the claim that they had been paid by bookmakers to throw The Oval match. It was clearly nonsense, and a disgraceful slur from a fellow member of the ICC. Butt's outburst seriously jeopardised the fourth match at Lord's, which at the start of the day

SIMON HUGHES writes…

A Strange Scene Witnessed at Lord's

There have been many words written already about the Lord's Test between England and Pakistan. It is amazing what reams and reams of coverage are generated by a couple of apparently innocent no-balls.

Incidentally, I once bowled a no-ball at Lord's and felt the full wrath of my seniors. It just happened to be the ball with which I had Geoff Boycott caught behind for what would have been a duck. The rest of my Middlesex teammates were furious, and my father, who was watching and was always on at me about my no-ball habit, didn't speak to me for three days.

A sportsman's ultimate aim is to achieve the respect of his peers (and father), to feel a significant part of the team. But one of the less-documented aspects of the spot-fixing allegations is that the traditional respect of one's elders in Pakistan society can be dangerously abused. The language used on the telephone by the alleged fixer Mahzar Majeed to the 18-year-old Mohammed Aamer, while he was in bed, was reminiscent of the scene from the movie *Slumdog Millionaire* as the leader of a begging establishment treats his young recruits like scum.

The revelations, moreover, have made me look again at a strange scene I witnessed during the Lord's Test. I had got to the ground early on the Friday morning, sensing it could be Aamer's day (there had been just 12 overs' play the previous afternoon and England were one wicket down overnight). I was intending to watch Aamer practice and then have a casual chat with him. Except that he didn't practice. Instead, he and three other members of the Pakistan touring squad were strolling around the boundary.

They weren't running, but walking and talking, while the rest of the Pakistan team practised elsewhere on the field. Odd. The other three were Mohammed Asif, Salman Butt and the coach Waqar Younis. I went to approach Waqar to ask if I could have a quick chat with Aamer but he made it clear they were having a private conversation, so I kept my distance. I kept my eye on them though, imagining they were talking bowling tactics.

The particularly strange thing was they circuited the boundary three, maybe four times. I have never seen a group do that before. It doesn't take that long to discuss how to take wickets (which, to be honest in those conditions required simply bowling straight and pitching it up as Aamer proved).

Butt, and Waqar, did a lot of talking. Asif and Aamer did a lot of listening. So, as a result, I have a lot of questions. Why weren't the rest of the team involved, especially other bowlers? Why wasn't it in the dressing room? Why so early in the morning? What was Waqar's role? And, of course, what were they talking about?

It is amazing how subsequent events make you look at something you saw in a totally different light. It is easy, now, to imagine they were discussing the 'arrangements' for the day and what were the ultimate rewards (and risks). Certainly, the impression was of the 'masters' (i.e. captain and coach) giving their subordinates their 'orders'.

The extravagant extent to which Aamer overstepped the line suggested (a) he was totally committed to his alleged order because (b) he didn't want to incur the displeasure of the people who had allegedly given him them.

Respect for one's peers, or elders, is good. Total indoctrination is bad.

Calm before the storm: Mohammad Asif and his Pakistan teammates cheerfully ignore the sign to keep off the grass as they walk across the Lord's outfield towards net practice at the Nursery End ahead of the final Test against England.

was given only a 50 per cent chance of being played. Common sense prevailed and after England published a strongly-worded statement, which included the threat of legal action against Mr Butt, the game went ahead albeit, in Strauss's words 'through gritted teeth'. England looked distracted, too, and lost the game by 38 runs to leave the series level with only the last game to play. Word emerged of a public tussle in then nets between Trott and Wahab Riaz, which was dealt with by the match referee before the game. Frankly, no one could wait for this ghastly tour to end.

Perversely, the bad blood and the tight series did wonders for ticket sales at the Rose Bowl where host county Hampshire, only a few days before, had been fearful of a flop. Morgan scored a brilliant hundred to lift England from 106 for 4 to 256 for 6 and after nine overs Pakistan had made a good reply, on 57 for no wicket. The tenth over – the final in the Power Play – was blocked out and there appeared to be no effort to strike another boundary for 24 overs. Subsequently the match petered out as Pakistan were bowled out for 135 in 37 overs. It was a confusing but fitting end to a visit by Pakistan that left many questions unanswered, and cricket at its lowest ebb.

TWENTY20 INTERNATIONALS

Match One
5 September 2010 at Cardiff
Pakistan 126 for 4 (20 overs)
England 129 for 5 (17.1 overs)
England won by 5 wickets

Match Two
7 September 2010 Day/Night at Cardiff
Pakistan 89 all out (18.4 overs)
(TT Bresnan 3 for 10)
England 90 for 4 (14 overs)
England won by 6 wickets

ONE-DAY INTERNATIONALS

Match One
10 September 2010 at Chester-le-Street
England 274 for 6 (41 overs) (SM Davies 87, IJL Trott 69, Saeed Ajmal 4 for 58)
Pakistan 250 for 9 (41 overs)
(Kamran Akmal 53)
England won by 24 runs

It's all over, with Tim Bresnan bowling Pakistan last man Shoaib Akhtar in the second Twenty20 international at Cardiff.

Match Two
12 September 2010 at Headingley
Pakistan 294 for 8 (50 overs) (Kamran Akmal 74, Asad Shafiq 50, SCJ Broad 4 for 81)
England 295 for 6 (49.3 overs) (AJ Strauss 126, IJL Trott 53)
England won by 4 wickets

Match Three
17 September 2010 Day/Night at The Oval
Pakistan 241 all out (49.4 overs) (Fawad Alam 64)
England 218 all out (45.4 overs) (AJ Strauss 57, EJG Morgan 61, Umar Gul 6 for 42)
Pakistan won by 23 runs

Match Four
20 September 2010 Day/Night at Lord's
Pakistan 265 for 7 (50 overs) (Mohammad Hafeez 64, GP Swann 4 for 37)
England 227 all out (46.1 overs) (AJ Strauss 68, Umar Gul 4 for 32)
Pakistan won by 38 runs

Match Five
22 September 2010 Day/Night at the Rose Bowl
England 256 for 6 (50 overs) (EJG Morgan 107*)
Pakistan 135 all out (37 overs)
England won by 121 runs
England won the series 3-2

PAKISTAN VIEW
by Qamar Ahmed

There has never been a dull moment in Pakistan cricket. For right reasons or wrong they have rarely failed to attract the spotlight. That has been the past, and nor do I see any noticeable difference in the present regime to say that the game in Pakistan seems to be moving in the right direction.

In a flawed system, in which the chairman of the Pakistan Cricket Board (PCB) is nominated by the head of the state and who in turn has the authority to hire and fire using his dictatorial and discretional powers, transparency in the running of the affairs of the game is neither expected nor has ever been evident.

That is the reason why, in the last two and half years since Ijaz Butt was given the responsibility of chairman, the standing committee of sports from the senate to the parliament has at various times summoned him and his cronies to answer allegations of maladministration, financial irregularities, corruption, lack of discipline, controversies involving team members and bias in team selection.

The end result of those meetings was recommendations made to the head of state to remove Butt from the chairmanship of the PCB for being economical with the truth in answering the allegations. But those recommendations have subsequently fallen on deaf ears and have been allowed to fizzle out.

Much of the controversy involving Pakistan and its players towards the end of their tour of England therefore, I feel, stems from that arrogance and incompetence within the corridors of power at the PCB. Over the years, indeed, it has affected the game in Pakistan at every level.

The controversy which marred Pakistan's 2010 tour of England, in which allegations of spot-fixing surfaced through the sting operation of a Sunday tabloid, was

A Sunday morning storm has just broken over Lord's and, reading the 29 August edition of the *News of the World*, the Pakistan tour manager Yawar Saeed (right) and his assistant manager Shafqat Rana catch up with all the grisly details of the spot-fixing allegations against their fast bowlers, Mohammad Asif and Mohammad Aamer, and captain, Salman Butt.

Two of the Pakistan players caught in the eye of the spot-fixing storm: Mohammad Aamer (left) and captain, Salman Butt.

embarrassing yet certainly not an isolated incident but the continuation of what had gone before it. The Shakoor Rana and Mike Gatting affair of 1987, the ball tampering row of 1992, and the forfeiture of the Test at The Oval in 2006 had previously marred Pakistan v England series, but PCB officials have clearly not learned from them.

If only those lessons had been learnt, the recent controversy in which Pakistan captain Salman Butt and his colleagues Mohammad Asif and Mohammad Aamer, two very fine bowlers, were suspended by the ICC for allegedly bowling 'no-balls to order' might have been avoided.

Another fast bowler, Wahab Riaz, was investigated by Scotland Yard police and yet the whole affair might not have created as much fuss or bad blood as it did if PCB chairman Butt had not then behaved so irresponsibly in making unwarranted allegations that insinuated involvement by the England players in match fixing.

That Butt then had to bow down to the inevitable outcry and withdraw his comments, made seemingly in a moment of madness, not only shamed those of us who had been present in England but also disgraced all those who love the game of cricket in Pakistan. The chairman of the PCB should, instead, have acknowledged the fact that if it were not for the ICC and the efforts of the England and Wales Cricket Board, the Pakistan team could not have played a 'home' Test series against Australia on the grounds of England.

By doing what he did, Butt has certainly not done any favours to the game or to himself, and his actions may yet end up isolating Pakistan cricket from the rest of the world. Butt has sadly failed in his duties from the day the Sri Lankan visiting team was attacked by terrorists at Lahore during the second Test of March 2009.

Nor did he take serious note of allegations made against some of the Pakistan players after the team had lost a Test in suspicious circumstances at Sydney early in January

2010. He initially banned Shoaib Malik from national cricket for a year, Younis Khan, Mohammad Yousuf and Rana Naved-ul-Hasan for indefinite periods and imposed heavy fines on Shahid Afridi, Kamran Akmal and Umar Akmal, but later withdrew all charges and made a U-turn on the issue with hardly any explanation.

Had Pakistan's administration and leadership been what it should have been then things may not have turned out as bleakly as they did during the tour of England.

Because of security reasons, Pakistan cannot now host any visiting team, and this is a situation that I see lasting for at least the next five years. And, in a situation as grim as this, I suppose Pakistan cricket has first got to put its house in order instead of playing a blame game which will only make their national teams 'untouchables' as far as the rest of the world is concerned.

For this to happen they need to clean up the whole sorry mess and end the unprofessional approach which has contributed so much to it. Only then can Pakistan keep clear of the controversies that have plagued them in recent years.

Qamar Ahmed is one of Pakistan's most respected cricket writers.

SIMON HUGHES pays tribute to the rise and rise of
England off-spinner Graeme Swann…

Swann Displays New Art of the Possible

The Graeme Swann story – as a world-class spinner – began on a baking hot afternoon in Chennai in the middle of December 2008. Called up to bowl his first over in Test cricket enterprisingly early by Kevin Pietersen (the 13th over of the innings), he began nervously with a long hop which was despatched for four by Gautam Gambhir.

But he immediately recovered his composure to trap Gambhir lbw with his third ball and, after a deafening din had accompanied Sachin Tendulkar's first run, he snared Rahul Dravid, again lbw, with his sixth. It was some start. A masterclass from Tendulkar in how to play the turning ball quickly brought him back to terra firma but Swann was off and spinning.

He then contributed usefully in the West Indies, but perhaps the turning point in his first year as a Test cricketer came at Lord's, in early May 2009, against the same opponents. Encouraged by the England spin coach Mushtaq Ahmed to play his natural game with the bat and go for his shots, he contributed a breezy 63, and then sent back the world's most obdurate batsman, Shivnarine Chanderpaul, twice for the sum total of four runs.

It wasn't just the dismissals of Chanderpaul that were significant, but how he got them. In the first innings he produced the perfect spinning delivery to take the edge as the left-hander pushed forward. In the second innings, Chanderpaul received what looked like an identical ball and allowed for the spin. It didn't turn, took the inside edge and he was caught at silly point off his front pad.

Those two wickets revealed the essence of Swann's game.

He looks to spin most deliveries, but with subtle changes of seam position some balls turn and others don't. Against left-handers, he is especially dangerous in this way.

Interestingly, 26 of his first 62 Test wickets were lbws (including those first two in Chennai). His lbw tally now stands at 38, which is all but a third of all his 113 Test victims. The increasing acceptance of Hawkeye has persuaded umpires to give far more lbws against batsmen propping forward to spinners. It must make old off spinners like Geoff Miller and John Emburey wince, having spent their lives screaming themselves hoarse for rejected lbws.

Swann, half a century later, eclipsed Jim Laker's previous record tally for an England spinner of 48 wickets in a calendar year by taking 54 wickets in 2009. In the first eight months of 2010, too, his strike rate did not slacken. His 113 wickets from 24 Tests have come at the impressive average of 26.55 runs apiece, and following England's series victory against Pakistan he was ranked second in the world among Test bowlers.

All this is, of course, a product of 10 years' hard labour on the county circuit, which should not be underestimated or ignored. Swann initially earned international recognition when he was only 20 but, as he admits himself, he wasn't good enough or mature enough to seize that opportunity. His single one-day international appearance, during England's 1999-2000 tour to South Africa, came at Bloemfontein. He bowled five wicketless overs, for 24 runs, and did not bat. He has learnt his craft since on the docile surfaces of Northampton and Trent Bridge (having moved to Nottinghamshire in 2005) and there is no shame in that.

It is rare for a spinner to properly know his game before his late 20s, but at the age of 31 he knows it now, and has become, in a very short space of time, vital to England's resources – while re-invigorating the art of old-fashioned spin at the same time.

As the second decade of the 21st century begins to take shape, every hard-bitten old tweaker will drink to that.

Above Graeme Swann in action – after a long apprenticeship in county cricket the off spinner is now a master of his craft.

Left Swann appeals for the wicket of Shahadat Hossain during the second Test against Bangladesh at Old Trafford.

MARCUS TRESCOTHICK, the 2005 Ashes winner, salutes the growing maturity of England's James Anderson…

Mature Anderson Can Lead Ashes Challenge

James Anderson can be a key figure in this winter's Ashes series even though conditions in Australia will not be in his favour. In the Test series against Pakistan last summer the Lancashire bowler proved that he is as good as anyone in the world when the ball is swinging. I would bracket him with Pakistan's Mohammad Asif in that respect.

Although Jimmy's record is nowhere near as good away from home where the ball doesn't move in the air as much, I believe he now ready to start putting that right. The reason I say that is that I regard him as ten times the bowler he was when I last played international cricket. I think he has learned from the experience of touring and now knows what is required on the various types of pitches he has to bowl on abroad. He is a much more canny bowler these days with a greater variety of delivery. It wouldn't surprise me if he caused the Aussies a lot of problems.

I think England now have the seam attack to give us a great chance of retaining the Ashes. Steve Finn, the 2010 Young Cricketer of the Year, has all the attributes to do well in Aussie conditions. His height will make him an awkward customer on bouncy pitches and I really like the way he is progressing. Stuart Broad caused my Somerset team a lot of problems when we played at Trent Bridge last season, working up some serious pace and it was a real challenge batting against him. He will also appreciate the extra bounce on the hard wickets Down Under.

With Tim Bresnan and Ajmal Shahzad, and Chris Tremlett added to the Ashes mix, England have a very strong group of seamers to pick from, plus the leading spinner in the world in Graeme Swann.

England head for Australia on the back of a comprehensive 3-1 series victory against Pakistan. And, while I wouldn't go as far as to say we are favourites for once to win Down Under, I think we have a major advantage in that our current Test team virtually picks itself. I remember how important it was to us in 2005 to go into the Ashes battles with a winning side and one in which all the players felt comfortable with one another. We have to keep our guys fit over the next couple of months, but if we do I think we are more than capable of handling the current Australia squad.

Marcus Trescothick, the Somerset captain, played 76 Tests and 123 one-day internationals for England between 2000 and 2006. He captained England twice in Tests and a further ten times in ODIs.

Left Jimmy Anderson in full flow during England's second Test against Pakistan at Edgbaston.

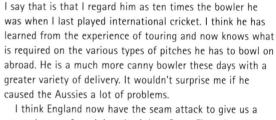

Right Anderson grabs a souvenir stump after his 6 for 17 blows Pakistan away at Trent Bridge in the first Test.

RICHARD GIBSON speaks to England Test wicketkeeper MATT PRIOR, who certainly showed in 2010 that he is made of the right stuff...

The Gloveman Who Can Take a Punch

If he were a boxer you get the feeling that Matt Prior's routine response to a right hook would be to stagger to his feet in just enough time for the obligatory eight count. For when donning a different pair of sporting gloves over the past three years as an international wicketkeeper, he has become accustomed to taking the blows and clambering off the canvas.

Since winning his first Test cap back in 2007, just about every aspect of Prior's game has been under scrutiny but it has predominantly been for his work behind rather than in front of the stumps. Yet, having temporarily lost his place to Tim Ambrose, his return has been one of triumphalism.

Nothing has been lost from his batting in the five-day game – of England's batsmen only Andrew Strauss scored more than Prior in the 2009 Ashes and he was outstanding again in last summer's Test series against Pakistan – and little was missed in the way of chances in the field either; in fact, the glovework which condemned him to one of his international exiles has become exemplary.

In fact, Prior's present problems are now confined to the shorter forms of the game, just months away from the World Cup. The 28-year-old does not currently hold a place in the England Twenty20 or 50-over teams despite ripples of support stirred by his latest riposte to setback.

'Someone said to me recently that they don't know anyone who can get knocked down as much as me, and that I seem to come back stronger time and again,' said Prior, who was sacrificed at limited-overs level on the back of Craig Kieswetter's rise to prominence upon qualification earlier this year. 'I wish I hadn't been forced into the position so often but it is the nature of the business we are in.

'International sport is about being pushed to the limit by your rivals and that competition has to be healthy. I have always enjoyed pressure situations, I genuinely have, whether it be in a game or in a scenario where I have had to fight my way back into a team, whatever.

'When you get left out for a certain reason it is simply another challenge to prove people wrong. I have never been one to blame others, I just take it on the chin and hope I am honest enough to say when I have not got it right. Being honest with yourself helps you to move forward and improve.'

Matt Prior reverse sweeps Shoaib Malik during the first Test between England and Pakistan at Trent Bridge.

England's short leg fielder Alastair Cook watches anxiously as Matt Prior completes a reflex catch at the second attempt after Pakistan captain Salman Butt edges a ball from Graeme Swann during the third Test at The Oval.

While missing out on the World Twenty20 success hurt, it also offered a rare chance to address the areas brought up in his most recent England appraisal: that they wanted the wanted their wicketkeeper to be an aggressor against the new ball. Ironically, he had only concentrated on becoming a middle-order batsman as a response to James Foster's selection the previous summer.

But the latest reinvention – including the development of aerial leg-side strokes – provided some outstanding statistics. In the 2010 domestic 20-over competition, Prior's strike-rate of 169 outstripped all of his English rivals and was not matched by anyone who registered more than 400 runs in the competition. There were also 18 sixes to boot.

'I am far from giving up on anything, as I showed by the way I played when I went back to play for Sussex in the Twenty20 competition,' Prior said. 'What I won't be doing is looking either too far in front of me or over my shoulder and worrying about what might happen. If I perform to my best I am confident of playing in all forms of the game again in the future.

'As a 19-year-old it was my role to smash the new ball and take the attack to the bowlers but I almost put that side of my game away for a while and ended up playing punchier, more compact shots.

'But when I talked to Brendon McCullum about opening the batting in Twenty20 cricket, when he was with Sussex last summer, he helped redress the balance by reminding me of the enjoyment of hitting the ball and not over-analysing.'

That is undoubtedly when Prior – one of only half-a-dozen wicketkeepers in history to score 1,500 Test runs at an average in excess of 40 – is at his best.

Richard Gibson is a former cricket correspondent of the Press Association.

JOHN EMBUREY assesses the merits of England's new batting star
Eoin Morgan and picks out temperament as the left-hander's key attribute…

Morgan's the Man for the Job

There is no doubt in my mind that Eoin Morgan has what it takes to go all the way in the game. By that, of course, I mean that he can become a top-class Test match batsman as well as a limited-overs player already good enough to win match after match for England.

I am sure that Andy Flower, the England team director, sees Morgan as a real long-term prospect in Test cricket as well as the one-day stuff. Indeed, I reckon that Flower sees more than a little bit of himself in Morgan's left-handedness, his method and his calmness and composure at the crease.

Morgan played his first two Tests against Bangladesh at the start of last summer, and did OK without going on to get a big score. In one innings, he got himself out playing at a ball away from his body, and getting an edge to the keeper. Bowlers will try to work Morgan out in the longer form of the game, of course, and they will post a slip cordon and try to get him nicking off by pushing ball after ball across him. But, then again, they will have to get their length consistently right because Morgan – like a lot of left-handers – is a devastating cutter.

Though he tailed off towards the end of the Test series against Pakistan, Morgan showed with his magnificent 130 in the first match at Trent Bridge that he can flourish at that level. Meanwhile, his unbeaten match-winning hundred in the first of England's five NatWest Series games against Australia, was the perfect showcase of his talent for identifying what needs to be done to win a match and then executing it with the minimum of fuss.

It reminded me of an innings I saw Stephen Fleming, the former New Zealand captain, play for Middlesex back in 2001 when we were chasing down a sizeable target to beat Gloucestershire at Bristol. Fleming worked out exactly what he had to do in each session, in terms of the runs he himself had to score as the man leading the chase, and he was totally clinical about the process.

Morgan has this same ability. In fact, I don't think there is a better cricketer than him on the English circuit in temperament. At the crease he shows hardly any emotion, and he knows instinctively where fielders are and what he has to do to pace his innings correctly. He never seems flustered, whatever the situation.

The two players he has been compared to, in one-day international terms, are Michael Bevan of Australia and Neil Fairbrother of England. Both of them were magnificent one-day batsmen, seemingly equal to any task, but neither made it at Test level and that's

A job well done: Eoin Morgan acknowledges the applause as he walks off at the close of play at Trent Bridge with a maiden Test hundred to his name.

There is no need to run for this shot as Eoin Morgan hits Australian seamer James Hopes for six in the fourth one-day international at The Oval. England won the series 3-2, and Morgan was one of the stars of the victory.

where I think Morgan has the ability to achieve far more. He never looks as if he is under pressure and he can dominate bowling attacks with almost surgical flair and range of strokes.

John Emburey played 64 Tests and 61 ODIs for England, and took 1,608 first-class wickets – most of them for Middlesex, where he has also served as head coach and director of cricket.

ENGLAND v. AUSTRALIA ODIs
by Jonathan Agnew

Following the low-key Test series against Bangladesh, this five-match contest against Australia was an uplifting if entirely irrelevant distraction. It is a measure of the amount of cricket the authorities cram into every available opportunity that these games represented less than a third of the one-day internationals played between the two countries in England over the next three summers.

Whether the public tires of too much of a good thing remains to be seen, and will probably depend on England's success over the old enemy. With the Ashes around the corner, it was impossible not to have half an eye on the prospects of both teams from that perspective. Ricky Ponting expressed the view before a ball was bowled that only the winning team would take anything from the one-day series into the Ashes which, from his stand point was just as well because his unhappy record against England in this country now includes Australia's first defeat in a five-match series of one-day internationals here for 13 years.

It was a shame that every game followed the same formula, with Australia batting first on each occasion, irrespective of which captain won the toss. It should also be mentioned that Australia were understandably short of match practice. Eoin Morgan's first century for his adopted country steered England to victory in the opening game at the Rose Bowl – and a beautifully paced innings it was, too, after Australia set England 268 to win.

After England's dramatic escape in the 2009 Ashes, Cardiff would not be high on the list of Ponting's favourite venues. This time, England completed a very straightforward win with 28 balls and four wickets in hand after Cameron White hit 86 not out. Morgan struck another half-century, while Andrew Strauss's 51 from 56 balls was our first glimpse of his new attacking style which would silence most of the debate about his position as captain of England in the 2011 World Cup. Graeme Swann finished the match with a six, having put on 32 in 31 balls with Tim Bresnan.

The most exciting match took place at Old Trafford where, set 213 to win the

Eoin Morgan played superbly during the series, driving powerfully and scoring runs quickly. His maiden century in the first ODI at the Rose Bowl illustrating his growing maturity as a top class batsman.

England complete victory at Old Trafford, after Tim Bresnan has hit Australia's James Hopes for four.

series, England lost six wickets for 18 runs, including Strauss for 87. They collapsed from the absolute safety of 185 for 4 to a perilous 203 for 9 at which point Bresnan showed great calm and dragged his team over the line in the final over.

As that match suggested, Australia were starting to warm up by now, and they completed a much needed and emphatic win in the fourth match with Ponting (92) and Michael Clarke (99 not out) sharing a stand of 155 from 154 balls. Australia's total of 290 for 5 was well beyond England, who lost four wickets for 13 in 12 balls to lose by 78 runs.

The gloss was rather taken off England's success in the series by their defeat in the fifth and final game at Lord's, this time by 42 runs. Australia plundered 130 from their last 11 overs, with Shaun Marsh (59) and Mike Hussey (79 from 60 balls) tearing England's attack to shreds. Shaun Tait then grabbed two early wickets and Ryan Harris dismissed Craig Kieswetter for his fourth consecutive low score as England were bowled out for 235.

ONE-DAY INTERNATIONALS

Match One
22 June 2010 Day/Night at the Rose Bowl
Australia 267 for 7 (50 overs) (MJ Clarke 87*)
England 268 for 6 (46 overs) (EJG Morgan 103*)
England won by 4 wickets

Match Two
24 June 2010 Day/Night at Cardiff
Australia 239 for 7 (50 overs) (SR Watson 57, CL White 86*, SCJ Broad 4 for 44)
England 243 for 6 (45.2 overs) (AJ Strauss 51, EJG Morgan 52)
England won by 4 wickets

Match Three
27 June 2010 at Old Trafford
Australia 212 all out (46 overs) (SR Watson 61, GP Swann 4 for 37)
England 214 for 9 (49.1 overs) (AJ Strauss 87)
England won by 1 wicket

Match Four
30 June 2010 Day/Night at The Oval
Australia 290 for 5 (50 overs) (RT Ponting 92, MJ Clarke 99*)
England 212 all out (42.4 overs) (MH Yardy 57, RJ Harris 5 for 32)
Australia won by 78 runs

Match Five
3 July 2010 at Lord's
Australia 277 for 7 (50 overs) (TD Paine 54, SE Marsh 59, MEK Hussey 79, SCJ Broad 4 for 64)
England 235 all out (46.3 overs) (PD Collingwood 95, SW Tait 4 for 48)
Australia won by 42 runs
England won the series 3-2

MARTIN JOHNSON, of the *Sunday Times*, turns his humorous attentions towards the Australians in a special scene-setter ahead of an Ashes winter...

The Ashes is the Perfect Winter Warmer

Australia's gargantuan capacity for blowing its own trumpet is even more entertaining when you consider that their biggest contribution to global technology is the rotary clothes line, but on the last five occasions they've received a visit from the England cricket team they've gleefully employed it for their favourite national sport of hanging the Poms out to dry.

The last time England won the Ashes in Australia, there was still a grassy Hill at the Sydney Cricket Ground, *Neighbours* had only been going for about 12 months, and tours lasting anything up to five months involved up-country games in such remote places that a visit to a portaloo (or the 'outside dunny' as the Aussies call it) involved warnings to check for not very pleasant spiders lurking under the seat before lowering your underwear.

However, 24 years of losing in Australia hasn't deterred increasingly large numbers of English fans from making the trip – and why not? It's a pretty nice place to visit, and whatever the reason for England's dismal record since Mike Gatting's team won in 1986-87, you certainly can't put it down to lack of support. There will be the usual invasion this winter, and the odds against taking a stroll down the High Street in Adelaide and bumping into someone from Milton Keynes wearing a Barmy Army T-shirt will be no better than even money.

It's all a far cry from the way we used to follow the Ashes in Australia, and some can still recall the days when marriages were threatened by the 2 a.m. crackle of a crystal set buried beneath the pillow. 'For heaven's sake, turn that thing off.' 'But darling, Larwood's just coming in to bowl at Bradman.' 'Right, that's it, I'm off to the spare room.'

Nowadays, you can get to Sydney in about 20 hours, catch the Test match, and be there and back in a week with half the skin peeling away from your nose, and a newly acquired fondness for ostrich steaks and tasteless lager. And even if you can't get away, it will be wall-to-wall, and ball-by-ball, on the telly.

In that respect, some of the romance has gone from a winter trip Down Under. Once upon a time the players congregated at Tilbury for the boat to Fremantle, honing team spirit with three weeks of deck quoits, and the first thing into the suitcase was a tuxedo for all those cocktail parties and civic receptions in places so remote that the local newspaper was a single sheet of paper pinned to a wooden board outside a corked hat shop. I came across one once, travelling somewhere in Queensland, and under the headline 'Local News' was the single entry: 'There is no local news this week'.

By comparison, a modern Ashes tour is the equivalent of a weekend break, jetting in and out of the major venues, and with no time for the players to do their bit for mother country relations by listening to some local mayor droning on somewhere in Crocodile Dundee country. On Gatting's 1986-87 tour, England's first stop was in the rum-producing town of Bundaberg, with no less than 34 internal flights on Biggles-type aircraft, flitting in and out of places where even the lizards wore sun block, and the flies were the size of cocker spaniels.

There was the trip to Kalgoorlie, for instance, where the locals were celebrating the installation

Australia might be winning but Brett Lee still has to listen to the Barmy Army in full voice at Brisbane during the 2006-07 Ashes.

Above left The England players go into a huddle during the traditional tour opener at Lilac Hill at the start of the 2006-07 Ashes tour.

Above right The shadows lengthen towards the end of the Masters match between England and Australia at the Chateau Tanunda ground on the eve of the second Ashes Test of the 2006-07 series in Adelaide.

of their first traffic light, which was hardly necessary as there were so many brothels the cars were moving pretty slowly in any event. England were there to play a Western Australian Country XI, and, as ever on these occasions, the local tannoy announcer – who'd been rehearsing his big moment for months – was worth double the tiny amount of admission money.

'Opening the bowling from the northern end is Norman 'Stormy' Gale,' he boomed, with scant regard for the fact that Norman was halfway through a 60-yard run-up. 'C'mon Stormy, let's see you put the wind up the Poms!' Stormy rather spoiled it though by losing his undercarriage in his delivery stride, ricking his back, and having to be helped from the field.

Not long afterwards, at some agricultural college during another up-country game in Queensland, the northern end was called the 'Piggery End', with the England openers coming out to bat from behind the hot dog stand, where trying to get one into your mouth without the added protein supplied by a thousand flies was more or less impossible. Memories will never fade for the players on duty that day, nor indeed will the smell.

Then there was a trip to another remote outpost in South Australia, Wudinna, on a flight so hairy that Bill Athey, who opened the batting in the Test series, fell onto the tarmac upon arrival and gave it a Papal kiss. These small places loved nothing more than a visit from the Poms,

although it did occasional border on the farcical, such as when the major of Bendigo (on the 1990-91 tour) presented the 'general' of the Barmies with an official crest in an on-field ceremony during the game, and received a Barmy T-shirt in return.

The Barmies weren't around in 1986-87, which is why many of us look back fondly upon that particular tour as the last one unaccompanied by a load of beery oiks labouring under the misconception that hours of brain-dead monotone chanting is in some way adding to the richness of the entertainment. They're even more irritating than those golf watchers who shout 'go in the hole!' for whom a suitable punishment would be a similar shout from the bloke in charge of the firing squad just before they were executed.

This time, there is a strong belief that England can win in Australia for the first time since the Barmy-less tour of 1986-87, but I seem to remember a similar mood before Brisbane last time out. That was when we all turned out to be Barmy.

Please Lord, not again. There is nothing worse than being an Englishman Down Under when the Australians are beating us at cricket, and becoming more insufferably smug with each victory. Which is why, if I had a time machine, I'd set the dial to 1932-33. It's hard to imagine now that Douglas Jardine was pilloried for the way he stuffed them on their own turf. Nowadays, he'd have been knighted.

CHRISTOPHER MARTIN-JENKINS writes...
England Against Australia Now too Close to Call

The first act of the longest dress rehearsal in cricket history was as interesting as expected. Strictly speaking, the NatWest Series between England and Australia was preparation for the World (50-over) Cup on the subcontinent in early 2011, but, of course, there were points to be made by individuals and by both teams that are relevant to the Ashes tour that precedes it. England's series win and Australia's great improvement in the last two games underlined that there is not going to be much between them in any format.

That Australia had more players unavailable because of injury underpinned Ricky Ponting's confidence that he will again get his revenge for last year's narrow defeat when the Ashes are at stake again. Peter Siddle, Ben Hilfenhaus and Mitchell Johnson will, he hopes, be back in contention come the new Australian season and Shaun Tait, Ryan Harris and Doug Bollinger emphasised that Australia have as much fast bowling depth as England. Tait has said that he will not play any more first-class cricket, but anyone can change his mind and Andrew Hilditch, the selection boss, or Ponting must surely be tempted to persuade him to have another go.

If so, England might be the mugs. Tait made all the difference to the Australia attack when he came into the team, fit and focused enough to bowl at 100 mph at Lord's. He bowled Andrew Strauss with a corker in the final game, very quick and swinging in to hit the left-hander's off stump, but by then Strauss the batsman had underlined the mental strength that will make England better led this winter than they were in Australia last time.

Strauss made a nonsense of the idle speculation that he might not remain as captain of the 50-over team, while Eoin Morgan emphasised his talent and added more fuel to the debate about whether a place should be found for him in the Test team immediately, even if all the established batsmen are fit.

Sheer pace from Shaun Tait beats the immaculate forward defensive of Andrew Strauss, and rearranges the England captain's furniture at Lord's.

It's been a tough couple of years for Australia captain Ricky Ponting. With a number of top players retiring, his own form taking a dive and then a Test series defeat in India, his captaincy has recently been called into question.

Of the bowlers, Stuart Broad produced some good spells and Graeme Swann's quality and intelligence once again stood out. James Anderson's tendency to blow a bit hot and cold was emphasised and his generally rather expensive figures (having been left out of the World Twenty20 eleven to accommodate Ryan Sidebottom) underlined that an opportunity was missed not to give at least one or two chances to the up-and-coming swing bowling of Ajmal Shahzad.

Australia were rusty, inevitably, before the NatWest matches but they looked more like the real 'green and gold' deal in the two games in London that completed the series.

As usual, both sides learned some lessons, or should have done. England's main mistake, in this case a trick missed by Strauss, was to take the foot off the pedal in that notorious middle phase of a 50-over innings, when traditionally on good pitches batsmen mark time and place the ball about the field for four or five an over at around the 30-over mark. At Lord's especially, Strauss was too content to push his fielders back instead of keeping the early pressure on by leaving men inside the circle to make Mike Hussey and Shaun Marsh take risks.

Swann was on top on a pitch allowing him some turn but the two left-handers were able to relax a little and to lay the base of a fine partnership that accelerated the scoring rate dramatically when they chose to take the batting powerplay earlier than England had expected. Marsh did particularly well, scoring his first 15 runs at a rate only of a run every two balls, but then unleashing a volley of boundaries that brought him 35 from 14 balls. All of a sudden England's grip was utterly loosened and Australia were back in the game.

Australia also learned that Michael Clarke, conveniently absent with a back strain for the last game, finds it hard to step on the gas like Hussey and Marsh. It is illogical that Clarke has been the Twenty20 Australia captain.

The essential orthodoxy of Marsh's strokeplay suggested a proper Test batsman, potentially as good as his durable father, Geoff. The contrast between Marsh and the much less orthodox Morgan is clear, but Morgan's talent and temperament surely give him every chance of making it as a Test player too.

This is an abridged version of an article that first appeared on testmatchextra.com.

ENGLAND IN BANGLADESH
ENGLAND v. BANGLADESH
by Jonathan Agnew

The prospect of a hectic international calendar, culminating in the Ashes and the World Cup, prompted England's captain, Andrew Strauss, to miss England's tour of Bangladesh.

It was unusual but, especially as the ICC's unfathomable scheduling also had Bangladesh playing two Tests at the start of the English summer, it was also entirely understandable, and several of the journalists and commentators who criticised Strauss for his decision also took the opportunity to spend some welcome time at home. Whether the rest does Strauss good in the long term remains to be seen, but on the evidence of his performances in one-day cricket at the end of the summer, he certainly appeared to be fit and fresh.

So Alastair Cook, who has been viewed as Strauss's likely successor for some time, took over for the short tour of Bangladesh, and was overall viewed as a success. England won both Tests and the one-day series – although they were pushed harder in the shorter form of the game – and Cook hit centuries in both Tests, with Collingwood making 145 in the first, and Bell 138 in the second, in which Tim Bresnan also scored 91.

This series marked the first appearances of Steven Finn, the 6 foot 7 inch-tall pace bowler from Middlesex who, not surprisingly, found the desperately slow pitches in Bangladesh offered him nothing whatsoever.

Alastair Cook scored hundreds in each of the two Tests in Bangladesh in which he captained England in the absence of the resting Andrew Strauss. More important for Cook was the fact that England also won the short series 2-0.

FIRST TEST – BANGLADESH v. ENGLAND
12–16 March 2010 at Chittagong

ENGLAND

	First Innings		Second Innings	
AN Cook (capt)	c & b Mahmudullah	173	c Aftab Ahmed b Mahmudullah	39
MA Carberry	lbw b Mahmudullah	30	lbw b Abdur Razzak	34
IJL Trott	c Mushfiqur Rahim b Rubel Hossain	39	c Junaid Siddique b Shakib Al Hasan	14
KP Pietersen	b Abdur Razzak	99	lbw b Shakib Al Hasan	32
PD Collingwood	c Tamim Iqbal b Abdur Razzak	145	c Mahmudullah b Abdur Razzak	3
IR Bell	c Rubel Hossain b Shakib Al Hasan	84	not out	39
*MJ Prior	not out	0	c Shahadat Hossain b Shakib Al Hasan	7
GP Swann			c Junaid Siddique b Shakib Al Hasan	32
SCJ Broad				
TT Bresnan				
ST Finn				
Extras	b 6, lb 9, w 3, nb 11	29	b 5, lb 2, nb 2	9
	(6 wkts dec 138.3 overs)	599	(7 wkts dec 49.3 overs)	209

	First Innings				Second Innings			
	O	M	R	W	O	M	R	W
Shahadat Hossain	17	2	73	0	6	0	19	0
Rubel Hossain	19	0	97	1	6	1	28	0
Shakib Al Hasan	34.3	4	133	1	16.3	1	62	4
Naeem Islam	12	1	42	0	3	0	14	0
Mahmudullah	23	1	78	2	8	0	26	1
Abdur Razzak	31	1	157	2	10	2	53	2
Aftab Ahmed	1	0	2	0	–	–	–	–
Tamim Iqbal	1	0	2	0	–	–	–	–

Fall of Wickets
1-72, 2-149, 3-319, 4-412, 5-596, 6-599
1-65, 2-87, 3-126, 4-130, 5-131, 6-144, 7-209

BANGLADESH

	First Innings		Second Innings	
Tamim Iqbal	b Bresnan	86	b Swann	14
Imrul Kayes	c Prior b Broad	4	c Prior b Finn	23
Junaid Siddique	c & b Broad	7	c Collingwood b Swann	106
Aftab Ahmed	c Bell b Swann	1	c Prior b Bresnan	26
Mahmudullah	c Collingwood b Swann	51	b Bresnan	5
Shakib Al Hasan (capt)	b Swann	1	lbw b Swann	4
Shahadat Hossain	c Collingwood b Finn	14	(10) c Prior b Bresnan	12
*Mushfiqur Rahim	c sub b Swann	79	(7) b Swann	95
Naeem Islam	run out	38	(8) c Carberry b Swann	36
Abdur Razzak	not out	0	(9) lbw b Broad	1
Rubel Hossain	b Swann	0	not out	0
Extras	b 1, lb 12, w 1, nb 1	15	b 2, lb 7	9
	(all out 90.3 overs)	296	(all out 124 overs)	331

	First Innings				Second Innings			
	O	M	R	W	O	M	R	W
Broad	21	4	70	2	24	7	65	1
Bresnan	25	10	72	1	24	7	63	3
Swann	29.3	8	90	5	49	11	127	5
Finn	14	5	48	1	18	7	47	1
Pietersen	1	0	3	0	7	1	15	0
Trott	–	–	–	–	2	0	5	0

Fall of Wickets
1-13, 2-27, 3-51, 4-145, 5-149, 6-159, 7-183, 8-296, 9-296
1-33, 2-45, 3-99, 4-105, 5-110, 6-277, 7-294, 8-301, 9-327

Umpires: AL Hill (New Zealand) & RJ Tucker (Australia)
Toss: Bangladesh
Test debuts: MA Carberry & ST Finn
Man of the Match: GP Swann

England won by 181 runs

SECOND TEST – BANGLADESH v. ENGLAND
20–24 March 2010 at Mirpur

BANGLADESH

	First Innings		Second Innings	
Tamim Iqbal	c Prior b Tredwell	85	c Broad b Swann	52
Imrul Kayes	c Finn b Broad	12	b Broad	4
Junaid Siddique	lbw b Swann	39	c & b Tredwell	34
Jahurul Islam	lbw b Swann	0	b Swann	43
Mahmudullah	c Collingwood b Finn	59	c Prior b Bresnan	6
Shakib Al Hasan (capt)	lbw b Tredwell	49	st Prior b Tredwell	96
*Mushfiqur Rahim	c Prior b Bresnan	30	b Broad	3
Naeem Islam	not out	59	(9) c Pietersen b Tredwell	3
Abdur Razzak	lbw b Swann	3	(10) lbw b Finn	8
Shafiul Islam	c Prior b Bresnan	53	(8) c Trott b Tredwell	28
Rubel Hossain	c Prior b Swann	17	not out	0
Extras	b 1, lb 10, nb 2	13	lb 3, w 5	8
	(all out 117.1 overs)	419	(all out 102 overs)	285

	First Innings				Second Innings			
	O	M	R	W	O	M	R	W
Broad	18	5	69	1	16	2	72	2
Bresnan	21	7	57	2	13	2	34	1
Swann	36.1	5	114	4	30	7	73	2
Finn	10	2	61	1	9	3	21	1
Tredwell	31	5	99	2	34	8	82	4
Collingwood	1	0	8	0	–	–	–	–

Fall of Wickets
1-53, 2-119, 3-122, 4-167, 5-226, 6-254, 7-301, 8-314, 9-388
1-23, 2-86, 3-110, 4-130, 5-156, 6-169, 7-232, 8-258, 9-275

ENGLAND

	First Innings		Second Innings	
AN Cook (capt)	c Imrul Kayes b Abdur Razzak	21	not out	109
IJL Trott	b Shakib Al Hasan	64	run out	19
KP Pietersen	c Imrul Kayes b Shakib Al Hasan	45	not out	74
PD Collingwood	lbw b Rubel Hossain	0		
IR Bell	c Jahurul Islam b Shakib Al Hasan	138		
*MJ Prior	b Shakib Al Hasan	62		
TT Bresnan	st Mushfiqur Rahim b Abdur Razzak	91		
GP Swann	run out (Shakib Al Hasan)	6		
SCJ Broad	lbw b Mahmudullah	3		
JC Tredwell	st Mushfiqur Rahim b Abdur Razzak	37		
ST Finn	not out	0		
Extras	b 9, lb 12, w 1, nb 7	29	b 2, lb 4, nb 1	7
	(all out 173.3 overs)	496	(1 wkt 44 overs)	209

	First Innings				Second Innings			
	O	M	R	W	O	M	R	W
Shafiul Islam	14	3	45	0	6	0	22	0
Abdur Razzak	39.3	8	132	3	15	0	67	0
Shakib Al Hasan	66	27	124	4	8	0	31	0
Mahmudullah	20	4	53	1	7	1	38	0
Rubel Hossain	26	4	88	1	4	0	26	0
Naeem Islam	7	0	29	0	4	0	19	0
Tamim Iqbal	1	0	4	0	–	–	–	–

Fall of Wickets
1-29, 2-105, 3-107, 4-174, 5-272, 6-415, 7-426, 8-434, 9-481
1-42

Umpires: AL Hill (New Zealand) & RJ Tucker (Australia)
Toss: Bangladesh
Test debuts: Jahurul Islam & JC Tredwell
Man of the Match: Shakib Al Hasan
Man of the Series: GP Swann

England won by 9 wickets

England won the series 2-0

ONE-DAY INTERNATIONALS

Match One

28 February 2010 Day/Night at Mirpur
Bangladesh 228 all out (45.4 overs) (Tamim Iqbal 125)
England 229 for 4 (46 overs) (AN Cook 64,
PD Collingwood 75*)
England won by 6 wickets

Match Two

2 March 2010 at Mirpur
Bangladesh 260 for 6 (50 overs) (Imrul Kayes 63,
Mushfiqur Rahim 76)
England 261 for 8 (48.5 overs) (AN Cook 60, EJG Morgan 110*)
England won by 2 wickets

Match Three

5 March 2010 at Chittagong
England 284 for 5 (50 overs) (C Kieswetter 107)
Bangladesh 239 for 9 (50 overs) (TT Bresnan 4 for 28)
England won by 45 runs
England won the series 3-0

SERIES AVERAGES
Bangladesh v. England

BANGLADESH

Batting	M	Inns	NO	Runs	HS	Av	100	50	c/st
Tamim Iqbal	2	4	0	237	86	59.25	-	3	1/-
Mushfiqur Rahim	2	4	0	207	95	51.75	-	2	1/2
Junaid Siddique	2	4	0	186	106	46.50	1	-	2/-
Naeem Islam	2	4	1	136	59*	45.33	-	1	-/-
Shafiul Islam	1	2	0	81	53	40.50	-	1	-/-
Shakib Al Hasan	2	4	0	150	96	37.50	-	1	-/-
Mahmudullah	2	4	0	121	59	30.25	-	2	2/-
Jahurul Islam	1	2	0	43	43	21.50	-	-	1/-
Aftab Ahmed	1	2	0	27	26	13.50	-	-	1/-
Shahadat Hossain	1	2	0	26	14	13.00	-	-	1/-
Imrul Kayes	2	4	0	43	23	10.75	-	-	2/-
Rubel Hossain	2	4	2	17	17	8.50	-	-	1/-
Abdur Razzak	2	4	1	12	8	4.00	-	-	-/-

Bowling	Overs	Mds	Runs	Wkts	Av	Best	5/inn	10m
Shakib Al Hasan	125	32	350	9	38.88	4-62	-	-
Mahmudullah	58	6	195	4	48.75	2-78	-	-
Abdur Razzak	95.3	11	409	7	58.42	3-132	-	-
Rubel Hossain	55	5	239	2	119.50	1-88	-	-

Also bowled: Aftab Ahmed 1-0-2-0, Naeem Islam 26-1-104-0, Shafiul Islam 20-3-67-0,
Shahadat Hossain 23-2-92-0, Tamim Iqbal 2-0-6-0.

ENGLAND

Batting	M	Inns	NO	Runs	HS	Av	100	50	c/st
IR Bell	2	3	1	261	138	130.50	1	1	1/-
AN Cook	2	4	1	342	173	114.00	2	-	-/-
TT Bresnan	2	1	0	91	91	91.00	-	1	-/-
KP Pietersen	2	4	1	250	99	83.33	-	2	-/-
PD Collingwood	2	3	0	148	145	49.33	1	-	4/-
JC Tredwell	1	1	0	37	37	37.00	-	-	1/-
MJ Prior	2	3	1	69	62	34.50	-	1	9/1
IJL Trott	2	4	0	136	64	34.00	-	1	1/-
MA Carberry	1	2	0	64	34	32.00	-	-	1/-
GP Swann	2	2	0	38	32	19.00	-	-	-/-
SCJ Broad	2	1	0	3	3	3.00	-	-	2/-
ST Finn	2	1	1	0	0*	-	-	-	1/-

Bowling	Overs	Mds	Runs	Wkts	Av	Best	5/inn	10m
GP Swann	144.5	31	404	16	25.25	5-90	2	1
JC Tredwell	65	13	181	6	30.16	4-82	0	-
TT Bresnan	83	26	226	7	32.28	3-63	0	-
ST Finn	51	17	177	4	44.25	1-21	0	-
SCJ Broad	79	18	276	6	46.00	2-70	0	-

Also bowled: PD Collingwood 1-0-8-0, KP Pietersen 8-1-18-0, IJL Trott 2-0-5-0.

James Tredwell, the Kent off spinning all-rounder, made his Test debut against Bangladesh in Mirpur – taking six wickets and scoring 37 in his only innings.

FIRST TEST – ENGLAND v. BANGLADESH
27–31 May 2010 at Lord's

ENGLAND

	First Innings		Second Innings	
AJ Strauss (capt)	b Mahmudullah	83	c Mushfiqur Rahim b Shakib Al Hasan	82
AN Cook	lbw b Shahadat Hossain	7	lbw b Mahmudullah	23
IJL Trott	c Imrul Kayes b Shahadat Hossain	226	not out	36
KP Pietersen	b Shakib Al Hasan	18	not out	10
IR Bell	b Rubel Hossain	17		
EJG Morgan	c Mushfiqur Rahim b Shahadat Hossain	44		
*MJ Prior	run out	16		
TT Bresnan	c Junaid Siddique b Shahadat Hossain	25		
GP Swann	c Rubel Hossain b Shakib Al Hasan	22		
JM Anderson	b Shahadat Hossain	13		
ST Finn	not out	3		
Extras	lb 10, w 8, nb 13	31	lb 5, w 1, nb 6	12
	(all out 125 overs)	505	(2 wkts, 35.1 overs)	163

	First Innings				Second Innings			
	O	M	R	W	O	M	R	W
Shahadat Hossain	28	3	98	5	2	0	19	0
Robiul Islam	22	2	107	0	1	0	12	0
Shakib Al Hasan	27	3	109	2	16	1	48	1
Rubel Hossain	23	0	109	1	1	0	8	0
Mahmudullah	23	3	59	1	15.1	1	71	1
Mohammad Ashraful	2	0	13	0	-	-	-	-

Fall of Wickets
1-7, 2-188, 3-227, 4-258, 5-370, 6-400, 7-463, 8-478, 9-498
1-67, 2-147

BANGLADESH

	First Innings		Second Innings (following on)	
Tamim Iqbal	run out	55	c Trott b Finn	103
Imrul Kayes	c Strauss b Finn	43	c Bell b Finn	75
Junaid Siddique	c Prior b Finn	58	c Bresnan b Finn	74
Jahurul Islam	c Prior b Anderson	20	c and b Trott	46
Mohammad Ashraful	lbw b Finn	4	c Prior b Anderson	21
Shakib Al Hasan (capt)	c Strauss b Anderson	25	(7) c Morgan b Finn	16
*Mushfiqur Rahim	b Finn	16	(8) c Prior b Finn	0
Mahmudullah	b Anderson	17	(9) c Prior b Bresnan	19
Shahadat Hossain	b Anderson	20	(6) b Bresnan	0
Rubel Hossain	c Cook b Bresnan	9	c Strauss b Bresnan	4
Robiul Islam	not out	9	not out	0
Extras	lb 4, w 1, nb 2	7	b 4, lb 2, w 2, nb 1	9
	(all out 93 overs)	282	(all out 110.2 overs)	382

	First Innings				Second Innings			
	O	M	R	W	O	M	R	W
Anderson	31	6	78	4	29	8	84	1
Bresnan	24	5	76	1	26.2	9	93	3
Finn	25	5	100	4	24	6	87	5
Swann	11	6	19	0	27	5	81	0
Trott	2	0	7	0	4	0	16	1

Fall of Wickets
1-88, 2-134, 3-179, 4-185, 5-191, 6-221, 7-234, 8-255, 9-266
1-185, 2-189, 3-289, 4-321, 5-322, 6-347, 7-354, 8-361, 9-381

Umpires: BF Bowden (New Zealand) & EAR de Silva (Sri Lanka)
Toss: Bangladesh
Test debuts: Robiul Islam & EJG Morgan
Man of the Match: ST Finn

SECOND TEST – ENGLAND v. BANGLADESH
4–6 June 2010 at Old Trafford

ENGLAND

	First Innings	
AJ Strauss (capt)	c Imrul Kayes b Shafiul Islam	21
AN Cook	c Junaid Siddique b Abdur Razzak	29
IJL Trott	b Shafiul Islam	3
KP Pietersen	st Mushfiqur Rahim b Shakib Al Hasan	64
IR Bell	b Shakib Al Hasan	128
EJG Morgan	c Jahurul Islam b Shahadat Hossain	37
*MJ Prior	c Jahurul Islam b Shakib Al Hasan	93
GP Swann	lbw b Abdur Razzak	20
A Shahzad	c Abdur Razzak b Shakib Al Hasan	5
JM Anderson	not out	2
ST Finn	lbw b Shakib Al Hasan	0
Extras	b 6, lb 5, w 4, nb 2	17
	(all out 121.3 overs)	419

	First Innings			
	O	M	R	W
Shahadat Hossain	21	3	84	1
Shafiul Islam	21	2	63	2
Mahmudullah	12	1	31	0
Shakib Al Hasan	37.3	4	121	5
Abdur Razzak	30	3	109	2

Fall of Wickets
1-44, 2-48, 3-83, 4-153, 5-223, 6-376, 7-399, 8-414, 9-419

BANGLADESH

	First Innings		Second Innings (following on)	
Tamim Iqbal	c Prior b Anderson	108	c Prior b Anderson	2
Imrul Kayes	c Shahzad b Finn	36	c Shahzad b Finn	9
Junaid Siddique	c Prior b Swann	1	c Pietersen b Anderson	6
Jahurul Islam	b Shafiul Islam	5	(5) c Prior b Finn	0
Mohammad Ashraful	c Morgan b Shahzad	11	(4) c Trott b Anderson	14
Shakib Al Hasan (capt)	c Anderson b Swann	10	b Shahzad	1
*Mushfiqur Rahim	c Anderson b Swann	11	c sub (KR Brown) b Finn	13
Mahmudullah	b Shahzad	8	c Prior b Finn	38
Shafiul Islam	b Shahzad	4	(10) c Strauss b Finn	4
Abdur Razzak	not out	0	(9) c Morgan b Swann	19
Shahadat Hossain	lbw b Swann	0	not out	4
Extras	b 4, lb 7, w 8, nb 3	22	b 13	13
	(all out 54.1 overs)	216	(all out 34.1 overs)	123

	First Innings				Second Innings			
	O	M	R	W	O	M	R	W
Anderson	14	4	45	1	10	3	16	3
Finn	8	1	39	1	10	2	42	5
Swann	22.1	4	76	5	7.1	0	34	1
Shahzad	10	2	45	3	7	2	18	1

Fall of Wickets
1-126, 2-153, 3-169, 4-169, 5-185, 6-200, 7-210, 8-214, 9-216
1-2, 2-14, 3-18, 4-21, 5-37, 6-39, 7-76, 8-97, 9-119

Umpires: BF Bowden (New Zealand) & EAR de Silva (Sri Lanka)
Toss: England
Test debut: A Shahzad
Man of the Match: IR Bell
Men of the Series: ST Finn & Tamim Iqbal

England won by an innings and 80 runs

England won series 2-0

England won by 8 wickets

Jonathan Trott cuts late but effectively on his way to a mammoth 226 in the first Test at Lord's to set up England's 8-wicket victory – the first of the summer.

However, come the first Test on his home ground at Lord's two months later, and he showed everyone just what a tremendous prospect he is.

After Trott piled up 226 in England's first innings, Finn took 4 for 100 and then, as Bangladesh followed on a massive 223 behind, 5 for 87. He produced sharp bounce, bowled with commendable accuracy for a 21-year-old and appeared unflappable – even when Tamim Iqbal, the left-handed opening batsman, flayed England's bowlers all over Lord's during his 100-ball innings of 103. Supported by Imrul Kayes and Junaid Siddique, Tamim's stirring knock at least ensured that England had to bat again, and they achieved their victory target of 160 with 8 wickets in hand.

The most notable statistic to emerge from the second Test at Old Trafford was that Bangladesh were bowled out twice in two successive sessions. Between tea and the close of the second day, they lost 10 wickets for 120

runs, thus wrecking the opportunity another brilliant hundred from Tamim had presented them to avoid following on. They were then skittled for 123 the following morning.

A fine 128 from Bell and 93 by Prior enabled England to recover on the first day from a disappointing 223 for 5 to 419, with the left-arm spinner Shakib taking 5 for 121. Then the left-handed Tamim hammered 108 from 114 balls before edging Anderson to Prior behind the wicket. Ajmal Shahzad, in his first Test appearance, took 3 for 10 in four overs and after changing ends, and Swann captured five wickets for 50 as Bangladesh were dismissed for 216 – 203 runs behind England's total of 419, which included a century by Bell. Finn then ran through the visitors' second innings, claiming 5 for 42 to finish with 15 wickets for 268 in the two matches. For this he was named Man of the Series, and a new Test career was born.

SERIES AVERAGES
England v. Bangladesh

ENGLAND

Batting	M	Inns	NO	Runs	HS	Av	100	50	c/st
IJL Trott	2	3	1	265	226	132.50	1	-	3/-
IR Bell	2	2	0	145	128	72.50	1	-	1/-
AJ Strauss	2	3	0	186	83	62.00	-	2	4/-
MJ Prior	2	2	0	109	93	54.50	-	1	10/-
KP Pietersen	2	3	1	92	64	46.00	-	1	1/-
EJG Morgan	2	2	0	81	44	40.50	-	-	3/-
TT Bresnan	1	1	0	25	25	25.00	-	-	1/-
GP Swann	2	2	0	42	22	21.00	-	-	-/-
AN Cook	2	3	0	59	29	19.66	-	-	1/-
JM Anderson	2	2	1	15	13	15.00	-	-	2/-
A Shahzad	1	1	0	5	5	5.00	-	-	2/-
ST Finn	2	2	1	3	3*	3.00	-	-	-/-

Bowling	Overs	Mds	Runs	Wkts	Av	Best	5/inn	10m
A Shahzad	17	4	63	4	15.75	3-45	-	-
ST Finn	67	14	268	15	17.86	5-42	2	-
IJL Trott	6	0	23	1	23.00	1-16	-	-
JM Anderson	84	21	223	9	24.77	4-78	-	-
GP Swann	67.2	15	210	6	35.00	5-76	1	-
TT Bresnan	50.2	14	169	4	42.25	3-93	-	-

BANGLADESH

Batting	M	Inns	NO	Runs	HS	Av	100	50	c/st
Tamim Iqbal	2	4	0	268	108	67.00	2	-	-/-
Imrul Kayes	2	4	0	163	75	40.75	-	1	2/-
Junaid Siddique	2	4	0	139	74	34.75	-	2	2/-
Mahmudullah	2	4	0	82	38	20.50	-	-	-/-
Abdur Razzak	1	2	1	19	19	19.00	-	-	1/-
Jahurul Islam	2	4	0	71	46	17.75	-	-	2/-
Shakib Al Hasan	2	4	0	52	25	13.00	-	-	-/-
Mohammad Ashraful	2	4	0	50	21	12.50	-	-	-/-
Mushfiqur Rahim	2	4	0	40	16	10.00	-	-	2/1
Shahadat Hossain	2	4	1	24	20	8.00	-	-	-/-
Rubel Hossain	1	2	0	13	9	6.50	-	-	1/-
Shafiul Islam	1	2	0	8	4	4.00	-	-	-/-
Robiul Islam	1	2	2	9	9*	-	-	-	-/-

Bowling	Overs	Mds	Runs	Wkts	Av	Best	5/inn	10m
Shafiul Islam	21	2	63	2	31.50	2-63	0	-
Shahadat Hossain	51	6	201	6	33.50	5-98	1	-
Shakib Al Hasan	80.3	8	278	8	34.75	5-121	1	-
Abdur Razzak	30	3	109	2	54.50	2-109	0	-
Mahmudullah	350.1	5	161	2	80.50	1-59	0	-
Rubel Hossain	24	0	117	1	117.00	1-109	0	-

Also bowled: Mohammad Ashraful 2-0-13-0, Robiul Islam 23-2-119-0.

ONE-DAY INTERNATIONALS

Match One
8 July 2010 Day/Night at Trent Bridge
Bangladesh 250 for 9 (50 overs) (Junaid Siddique 51, Raqibul Hasan 76)
England 251 for 4 (45.1 overs) (AJ Strauss 50, IR Bell 84*)
England won by 6 wickets

Match Two
10 July 2010 at Bristol
Bangladesh 236 for 7 (50 overs) (Imrul Kayes 76)
England 231 all out (49.3 overs) (IJL Trott 94)
Bangladesh won by 5 runs

Match Three
12 July 2010 at Edgbaston
England 347 for 7 (50 overs) (AJ Strauss 154, IJL Trott 110)
Bangladesh 203 all out (45 overs) (RS Bopara 4 for 38)
England won by 144 runs
England won the series 2-1

Andrew Strauss hits Bangladesh left-arm spinner Abdur Razzak for six during the second one-day international at Bristol.

ICC WORLD TWENTY20

ENGLAND TRIUMPH IN THE CARIBBEAN
by Jonathan Agnew

England's unexpected success in the ICC World Twenty20 realised one niggling ambition for those who run English cricket – as well as for the players themselves. In winning England's first 'global event', Paul Collingwood's team finally secured the stated aim of successive ECB and TCCB blueprints for the game, which were often published more in hope than realistic expectation. In reality, this was long overdue with England's previous appearance in a World Cup one-day final having been almost 20 years ago, in 1992.

This was an outstanding team performance, and one that drew admiring comments from everyone who watched England narrowly escape early embarrassment by Ireland in a preliminary group match that was eventually washed out before the Irish could embark on what appeared to be a generous target using the Duckworth-Lewis method. That safely negotiated, England never looked back, and their comfortable win over Australia in the final really was the icing on the cake.

The skill of the bowlers over that of their competitors stood out significantly. Subtle changes of pace have now been extended to bouncers and are highly effective. Such is the deception that the ball appears to the batsman to have been hurled into the pitch at full speed only for the ball to arrive long after the pull shot has been completed. Ryan Sidebottom – whose inclusion ahead of James Anderson at the start of the tournament surprised many of us – and Stuart Broad were both brilliant exponents of this new art, which is

testimony to excellent planning by the coaching staff followed by hours spent in the nets getting it right.

England's success was also due to some outstanding performances by their two spinners, Graeme Swann and Michael Yardy. They flourished on the disappointingly slow pitches that made strokeplay difficult. In the key Super Eight stage match against South Africa, for example, the two slow bowlers took 5 for 55 from their combined eight overs, and their partnership is a reason for so many seasoned pundits suddenly backing England to win the World Cup proper in similar conditions on the subcontinent in the spring of 2011.

Kevin Pietersen was Man of the Tournament for his robust and commanding presence at No. 3. Relishing the big stage – and shrugging off a dash home to be present at the birth of his first child – Pietersen failed to make an impact only once, and his 47 from 31 balls in a

partnership of 111 with the opening batsman Craig Kieswetter in the final, was typical of his contributions.

However, the man who particularly rose to prominence in this tournament was Eoin Morgan, and it was his calm, calculating approach to securing run chases – often from difficult positions – that earned Morgan his chance in the Test team. Very busy at the crease, Morgan's batting is much more than simply the innovations for which he has become famous. A master at pushing singles, he also has the knack of hitting a boundary at precisely the moment it is needed.

England beat Pakistan in the first Super Eight game, by six wickets, with Pietersen's 70 not out from 52 balls, with two sixes and seven fours, sweeping them past Pakistan's 147 for 9 with three balls to spare. Then came the win over South Africa, also in Barbados, in which Pietersen's 33-ball 53, with eight fours and a six, and Kieswetter's 41 did much to set up an England total of 168 for 7 that the South Africans never looked like threatening.

Both the last Super Eight game and the semi-final were played in St Lucia, and England's superbly-judged chase to overcome New Zealand – with Michael Lumb leading an initial charge with 32 and then both Morgan, with 40 from 34 balls, and especially Tim Bresnan, who struck an unbeaten 23 from only 11 balls, sending them into the last four in confident mood.

Stuart Broad's 2 for 21 and tight bowling again from both spinners and Sidebottom restricted Sri Lanka to 128 for 6 in the semi-final, a total which England romped past with four overs in hand – a huge margin in Twenty20 cricket – with Kieswetter and Lumb posting 68 for the first wicket and Pietersen easing to 42 not out from 26 balls, with two sixes and three fours.

Australia won the other semi-final, in which Mike Hussey's quite extraordinary unbeaten 60 from a mere 24 balls – including six sixes and three fours – combined with Cameron White's 31-ball 43, featuring five sixes, to shock Pakistan. England took control right from the start of the final in Bridgetown. Australia were 8 for 3 and then 45 for 4, before David Hussey's fighting 59 and support from both White and Mike Hussey at least gave their bowlers something to defend. Kieswetter, though, demonstrated his big-match temperament with a 63 that included two sixes and seven fours – and Pietersen's powerful strokeplay was simply irresistible. Again, the margin of victory for Collingwood's team was as much as three overs.

Not so successful were England's women, the defending champions, who were surprisingly knocked

Kevin Pietersen was in majestic form throughout the ICC World Twenty20, deservedly earning himself the Player of the Tournament award.

out before the semi-finals. Their first defeat to Australia came with the scores level, but with England having hit fewer sixes. Charlotte Edwards's team was then beaten by just two runs by West Indies to confirm, at least, that the global standard of women's cricket is rising.

Group A

1 May 2010 at Beausejour Stadium, Gros Islet
Pakistan 172 for 3 (Kamran Akmal 73, Salman Butt 73)
Bangladesh 151 for 7 (Mohammad Ashraful 65, Shakib Al Hasan 47, Mohammad Sami 3 for 29)
Pakistan won by 21 runs

2 May 2010 at Beausejour Stadium, Gros Islet
Australia 191 (SR Watson 81, DJ Hussey 53, Mohammad Aamer 3 for 23, Saeed Ajmal 3 for 34)
Pakistan 157 (Misbah-ul-Haq 41, DP Nannes 3 for 41, SW Tait 3 for 20)
Australia won by 34 runs

5 May 2010 at Kensington Oval, Bridgetown
Australia 141 for 7 (MEK Hussey 47*)
Bangladesh 114 (DP Nannes 4 for 18)
Australia won by 27 runs

	P	W	L	NR	NetRR	Pts
Australia	2	2	0	0	+1.525	4
Pakistan	2	1	1	0	-0.325	2
Bangladesh	2	0	2	0	-1.200	0

Group B

30 April 2010 at Providence Stadium, Guyana
Sri Lanka 135 for 6 (DPMD Jayawardene 81)
New Zealand 139 for 8 (JD Ryder 42)
New Zealand won by 2 wickets

3 May 2010 at Providence Stadium, Guyana
Sri Lanka 173 for 7 (DPMD Jayawardene 100)
Zimbabwe 29 for 1
Sri Lanka won by 14 runs – DL Method

4 May 2010 at Providence Stadium, Guyana
Zimbabwe 84 (NL McCullum 3 for 16, SB Styris 3 for 5)
New Zealand 36 for 1
New Zealand won by 7 runs – DL Method

	P	W	L	NR	NetRR	Pts
New Zealand	2	2	0	0	+0.428	4
Sri Lanka	2	1	1	0	+0.355	2
Zimbabwe	2	0	2	0	-3.797	0

Stuart Broad stoops to field a drive from Pakistan's Abdul Razzaq off his own bowling at Bridgetown, while England wicketkeeper Craig Kieswetter looks on.

Group C

1 May 2010 at Beausejour Stadium, Gros Islet
Afghanistan 115 for 8 (Noor Ali Zadran 50, A Nehra 3 for 19)
India 116 for 3 (M Vijay 48)
India won by 7 wickets

2 May 2010 at Beausejour Stadium, Gros Islet
India 186 for 5 (SK Raina 101)
South Africa 172 for 5 (JH Kallis 73)
India won by 14 runs

5 May 2010 Day/Night at Kensington Oval, Bridgetown
South Africa 139 for 7 (Hamid Hassan 3 for 21)
Afghanistan 80 (CK Langeveldt 3 for 12,
M Morkel 4 for 20)
South Africa won by 59 runs

	P	W	L	NR	NetRR	Pts
India	2	2	0	0	+1.495	4
South Africa	2	1	1	0	+1.125	2
Afghanistan	2	0	2	0	-2.446	0

Group D

30 April 2010 Day/Night at Providence Stadium, Guyana
West Indies 138 for 9 (GH Dockrell 3 for 16)
Ireland 68 all out (R Rampaul 3 for 17,
DJG Sammy 3 for 8)
West Indies won by 70 runs

3 May 2010 at Providence Stadium, Guyana
England 191 for 5 (EJG Morgan 55, LJ Wright 45*)
West Indies 60 for 2
West Indies won by 8 wickets – DL Method

4 May 2010 at Providence Stadium, Guyana
England 120 for 8 (EJG Morgan 45)
Ireland 14 for 1
No result

	P	W	L	NR	NetRR	Pts
West Indies	2	2	0	0	+2.780	2
England	2	0	1	1	-0.452	1
Ireland	2	0	1	1	-3.500	1

Super Eight Stage

Group E

6 May 2010 at Kensington Oval, Bridgetown
Pakistan 147 for 9 (20 overs)
England 151 for 4 (19.3 overs) (KP Pietersen 73*)
England won by 6 wickets

6 May 2010 at Kensington Oval, Bridgetown
South Africa 170 for 4 (20 overs) (AB de Villiers 47*,
JA Morkel 40)
New Zealand 157 for 7 (20 overs)
South Africa won by 13 runs

8 May 2010 at Kensington Oval, Bridgetown
New Zealand 133 for 7 (20 overs)

Pakistan 132 for 7 (20 overs) (Salman Butt 67*,
IG Butler 3 for 19)
New Zealand won by 1 run

8 May 2010 at Kensington Oval, Bridgetown
England 168 for 7 (20 overs) (C Kieswetter 41,
KP Pietersen 53)
South Africa 129 all out (19 overs) (RJ Sidebottom 3 for 23,
GP Swann 3 for 24)
England won by 39 runs

10 May 2010 at Beausejour Stadium, Gros Islet
Pakistan 148 for 7 (20 overs) (Umar Akmal 51,
CK Langeveldt 4 for 19)
South Africa 137 for 7 (20 overs) (AB de Villiers 53
Saeed Ajmal 4 for 26)
Pakistan won by 11 runs

England batsman Eoin Morgan plays another of his superbly controlled reverse sweeps against New Zealand in St Lucia.

10 May 2010 at Beausejour Stadium, Gros Islet
New Zealand 149 for 6 (20 overs) (LRPL Taylor 44)
England 153 for 7 (19.1 overs) (EJG Morgan 40)
England won by 3 wickets

	P	W	L	NR	NetRR	Pts
England	3	3	0	0	+0.962	6
Pakistan	3	1	2	0	+0.041	2
New Zealand	3	1	2	0	-0.373	2
South Africa	3	1	2	0	-0.617	2

Group F

7 May 2010 at Kensington Oval, Bridgetown
Australia 184 for 5 (20 overs) (SR Watson 54, DA Warner 72)
India 135 all out (17.4 overs) (RG Sharma 79*,
DP Nannes 3 for 25, SW Tait 3 for 21)
Australia won by 49 runs

7 May 2010 at Kensington Oval, Bridgetown
Sri Lanka 195 for 3 (20 overs) (DPMD Jayawardene 98*,
KC Sangakkara 68)
West Indies 138 for 8 (20 overs) (BAW Mendis 3 for 24,
SL Malinga 3 for 28)
Sri Lanka won by 57 runs

9 May 2010 at Kensington Oval, Bridgetown
West Indies 169 for 6 (20 overs) (CH Gayle 98,
A Nehra 3 for 35)
India 155 for 9 (20 overs)
West Indies won by 14 runs

9 May 2010 at Kensington Oval, Bridgetown
Australia 168 for 5 (20 overs) (CL White 85*,
HKSR Kaluhalamulla 3 for 20)
Sri Lanka 87 all out (16.2 overs) (MG Johnson 3 for 15)
Australia won by 81 runs

11 May 2010 at Beausejour Stadium, Gros Islet
India 163 for 5 (20 overs) (G Gambhir 41, SK Raina 63)
Sri Lanka 167 for 5 (20 overs) (KC Sangakkara 46,
AD Mathews 46)
Sri Lanka won by 5 wickets

11 May 2010 Day/Night at Beausejour Stadium, Gros Islet
West Indies 105 all out (19 overs) (SPD Smith 3 for 20)
Australia 109 for 4 (16.2 overs) (BJ Haddin 42)
Australia won by 6 wickets

	P	W	L	NR	NetRR	Pts
Australia	3	3	0	0	+2.733	6
Sri Lanka	3	2	1	0	-0.333	4
West Indies	3	1	2	0	-1.281	2
India	3	0	3	0	-1.117	0

Semi-finals

13 May 2010 at Beausejour Stadium, Gros Islet
Sri Lanka 128 for 6 (20 overs) (AD Mathews 58)
England 132 for 3 (16 overs) (KP Pietersen 42*)
England won by 7 wickets

14 May 2010 at Beausejour Stadium, Gros Islet
Pakistan 191 for 6 (20 overs) (Kamran Akmal 50,
Umar Akmal 56*)
Australia 197 for 7 (19.5 overs) (CL White 43, MEK Hussey 60*,
Mohammad Aamer 3 for 35)
Australia won by 3 wickets

England become world champions in cricket for the first time, as
Paul Collingwood holds aloft the ICC World Twenty20 trophy and
his players celebrate victory in the final against Australia at the
Kensington Oval in Barbados.

FINAL – AUSTRALIA v. ENGLAND
16 May 2010 at Bridgetown

AUSTRALIA

SR Watson	c Swann b Sidebottom	2
DA Warner	run out (Lumb)	2
MJ Clarke (capt)	c Collingwood b Swann	27
*BJ Haddin	c Kieswetter b Sidebottom	1
DJ Hussey	run out (Wright/Kieswetter)	59
CL White	c Broad b Wright	30
MEK Hussey	not out	17
SPD Smith	not out	1
MG Johnson		
SW Tait		
DP Nannes		
Extras	b 1, lb 2, w 4, nb 1	8
	(6 wkts 20 overs)	**147**

	O	M	R	W
Sidebottom	4	0	26	2
Bresnan	4	0	35	0
Broad	4	0	27	0
Swann	4	0	17	1
Yardy	3	0	34	0
Wright	1	0	5	1

Fall of Wickets: 1-2, 2-7, 3-8, 4-45, 5-95, 6-142

ENGLAND

MJ Lumb	c DJ Hussey b Tait	2
*C Kieswetter	b Johnson	63
KP Pietersen	c Warner b Smith	47
PD Collingwood (capt)	not out	12
EJG Morgan	not out	15
LJ Wright		
TT Bresnan		
MH Yardy		
GP Swann		
SCJ Broad		
RJ Sidebottom		
Extras	lb 1, w 8	9
	(3 wkts 17 overs)	**148**

	O	M	R	W
Nannes	4	0	29	0
Tait	3	0	28	1
Johnson	4	0	27	1
Smith	3	0	21	1
Watson	3	0	42	0

Fall of Wickets: 1-7, 2-118, 3-121

Umpires: Aleem Dar (Pakistan) & BR Doctrove (West Indies)
Toss: England
Man of the Match: C Kieswetter
Man of the Tournament: KP Pietersen

England won by 7 wickets

TONY COZIER, the leading West Indian writer and broadcaster, reflects on the impact of the ICC World Twenty20 in May 2010…

Relief Amid Caribbean Delight After World T20

For Haroon Lorgat, the International Cricket Council's chief executive, the third ICC World Twenty20 championship turned out to be 'a truly memorable event which showcased the unique culture and passion for cricket in the Caribbean'. At the end of it, West Indies Cricket Board president Julian Hunte declared that the people of the region had 'every reason to be proud… for pulling it off in such spectacular fashion'. It was not difficult to detect a sense of relief amidst their delight.

When their predecessors, Malcolm Speed and Ken Gordon, mounted the rostrum three years earlier after the shambolic final of the 50-over World Cup, the first major ICC event held in the West Indies, they were roundly booed by spectators angered by the officious regulations that smothered 'the unique culture and passion for cricket in the Caribbean'. The primary aim of the ICC and the WICB organisers this time was to put that right. They did not need to worry too much about the cricket in a tournament involving the best 12 national teams in the newest, shortest and immediately most popular version of the game (which had come to the Caribbean only as a switch for the originally scheduled Champions Trophy).

The intense promotional campaign, under the slogan 'Bring It', had its effect. Spectators heeded the call, from even ICC president David Morgan, a dour Welshman, 'to bring your musical instruments, your songs and cheers, your flags, banners and colourful costumes'. Nor, with prices slashed by more than half, did they have to fork out an average month's wage for tickets, as in 2007. Some shrewd entrepreneur, moreover, now made a packet on his flags.

Wembley at its fullest could hardly have had so many red cross, white background standards of St George waved as there were at Kensington Oval on the day England's new-found confidence and aggression conquered Australia to finally claim an ICC limited-overs trophy. The girls in their brightly coloured – and miniscule – gear gyrated as only West Indian girls can at every six (none of the IPL's DLF Maximums here), every wicket (no Citi Moments of Success), and every catch (no Kamran Kamal to be heard anywhere).

The steelbands struck up, never more melodiously than for the national anthems in the impressive ceremonies that preceded every match. It was the only quiet time for the rest of the day as the drums beat and the horns blew – incessantly. It was, doubtless, overdone but it was done under advice. No West Indian cricket ground had ever heard such ear-splitting noise and not everyone appreciated it.

'It's not a fete in there, it's madness,' BC Pires wrote in his weekly column in *The Nation* of Barbados after one match at Kensington Oval. 'I've been in quieter sheeting iron factories. You leave cricket feeling you've been beaten inside and out.' At the Beausejour Stadium in St Lucia, reporters in the open-air press box had to seek the hush of the men's room for mobile phone contact with their offices. Such a cacophony might have kept some away but did not explain the empty seats at matches not involving West Indies, the final excepted.

Lorgat claimed that the ICC 'recognised the need to involve all the local people'. This was hardly possible when the first match of the double-headers started at 9.30 a.m. and only four were played under lights (available at each of the venues) after working, and school, hours, which is an ideal slot for three hours of all-action Twenty20. The explanation for this arrangement was to accommodate prime time viewing in the major television markets of India and the UK. Given the vast sums paid by ESPNStar for the rights, it broached no argument but it did limit local involvement.

Jonathan Agnew's assessment was that the tournament 'brought a smile back to West Indies cricket'. It did, to an extent, but there were no smiles to be found on West Indian faces following another letdown by their men's team, a

failure accentuated by the advance of their fast-improving women in reaching their semi-final.

If results on the field continue to be as dismal as they have been for a dozen years and more, West Indian passion for the game will progressively diminish. Only better results, indeed, can 'Bring It' back.

English and Caribbean flags are waved in unison after Stuart Broad takes a catch to dismiss Australian batsman Cameron White during the ICC World Twenty20 final in Barbados.

ENGLAND IN SOUTH AFRICA
by Jonathan Agnew

E ngland cricket tours to South Africa are always greatly anticipated. Few countries offer quite the variety of cricket conditions that exist within South Africa, from the altitude and swinging ball of Johannesburg and Pretoria to the sea breeze of Cape Town, via Durban's heat and humidity. Each venue is different, and both the one-day and Test series on this trip were entertaining and unpredictable.

Andrew Strauss's England led the one-day competition 2-1 before the final game in Durban was washed out. Bearing in mind the hosts were ranked number one in the world, this was an encouraging England performance and one can trace the origins of their success in the World Twenty20 and their 3-2 win against Australia the following summer from this tour.

Additional spice was added to the tour by the existence of not merely Kevin Pietersen in England's ranks, but a bevy of other former South Africans who were now lined up against their old country: Jonathan Trott, Matthew Prior and even the captain, Strauss, who was born in Johannesburg to South African parents before being schooled in England.

In the background, moreover, rumbled the likelihood that another, Craig Kieswetter, would soon qualify to play for England. South Africa's captain, Graeme Smith, tried to persuade Kieswetter who, like Trott, had represented South Africa at Under 19 level, to come home. In fact, only a few weeks after the end of the tour, Kieswetter made his England debut against Bangladesh.

Hence, the irony was not lost on the South Africans when Pietersen and Trott's partnership of 145 in the second innings denied them victory in the first Test at Centurion Park. England were left clinging on, nine wickets down with the last pair, Paul Collingwood and Graham Onions – who survived the final over to achieve hero status at home – hanging on together for the last 19 deliveries of the match. At Cape Town, in the New Year, Onions would go through the agony again. It should not have come down to that nail-biting finale, but the

Kevin Pietersen and Jonathan Trott, both South African born and raised, combined to defy the country of their youth with a second-innings, fourth-wicket stand of 145 in the opening Test at Centurion.

FIRST TEST – SOUTH AFRICA v. ENGLAND
16–20 December 2009 at Centurion

SOUTH AFRICA

	First Innings		First Innings		Second Innings		Second Innings
GC Smith (capt)	c Prior b Broad	0			(2) b Onions	12	
AG Prince	c Collingwood b Swann	45			(1) b Anderson	0	
HM Amla	c Collingwood b Onions	19			(4) b Anderson	100	
JH Kallis	c Collingwood b Anderson	120			(5) c Cook b Broad	4	
AB de Villiers	c Cook b Swann	32			(6) c Bell b Broad	64	
JP Duminy	c Collingwood b Swann	56			(7) b Anderson	11	
*MV Boucher	c Cook b Swann	49			(8) not out	63	
M Morkel	c Prior b Onions	13			(9) not out	22	
PL Harris	b Onions	38			(3) b Anderson	11	
F de Wet	lbw b Swann	20					
M Ntini	not out	4					
Extras	b 1, lb 16, w 5	22			lb 10, w 4	14	
	(all out 153.2 overs)	418			(7 wkts dec 85.5 overs)	301	

	First Innings				Second Innings			
	O	M	R	W	O	M	R	W
Anderson	37	9	104	1	20.5	1	73	4
Broad	32	8	74	1	16	5	58	2
Onions	30	5	86	3	16	3	50	1
Swann	45.2	10	110	5	27	3	91	0
Collingwood	7	1	18	0	6	1	19	0
Trott	2	0	9	0	–	–	–	–

Fall of Wickets
1-1, 2-51, 3-93, 4-159, 5-283, 6-316, 7-341, 8-377, 9-414
1-2, 2-20, 3-34, 4-46, 5-165, 6-191, 7-266

ENGLAND

	First Innings		Second Innings	
AJ Strauss (capt)	b Ntini	46	c Boucher b Morkel	1
AN Cook	c Boucher b de Wet	15	c Smith b Harris	12
IJL Trott	b Harris	28	(4) c de Villiers b de Wet	69
KP Pietersen	b Morkel	40	(5) run out (de Wet)	81
PD Collingwood	c Kallis b Harris	50	(6) not out	26
IR Bell	b Harris	5	(7) c Boucher b de Wet	2
*MJ Prior	c de Wet b Harris	4	(8) c Boucher b de Wet	0
SCJ Broad	lbw b Duminy	17	(9) c Boucher b Harris	0
GP Swann	c Smith b Harris	85	(10) lbw b Morkel	2
JM Anderson	c Morkel b Ntini	29	(3) c Boucher b de Wet	10
G Onions	not out	4	not out	1
Extras	b 8, lb 8, w 5, nb 12	33	b 10, lb 3, nb 11	24
	(all out 104 overs)	356	(9 wkts 96 overs)	228

	First Innings				Second Innings			
	O	M	R	W	O	M	R	W
Ntini	23	4	78	2	18	7	41	0
de Wet	20	3	72	1	23	8	55	4
Morkel	21	0	60	1	18	3	46	2
Harris	37	10	123	5	26	11	51	2
Duminy	3	0	7	1	8	2	17	0
Kallis	–	–	–	–	3	1	5	0

Fall of Wickets
1-25, 2-98, 3-119, 4-168, 5-189, 6-211, 7-221, 8-242, 9-348
1-5, 2-16, 3-27, 4-172, 5-205, 6-207, 7-208, 8-209, 9-218

Umpires: Aleem Dar (Pakistan) & SJ Davis (Australia)
Toss: England
Test debut: F de Wet
Man of the Match: GP Swann

Match drawn

SECOND TEST – SOUTH AFRICA v. ENGLAND
26–30 December 2009 at Durban

SOUTH AFRICA

	First Innings		Second Innings	
GC Smith (capt)	run out (Cook)	75	(2) lbw b Swann	22
AG Prince	c Swann b Anderson	2	(1) c Bell b Swann	16
HM Amla	lbw b Broad	2	b Swann	6
JH Kallis	c Collingwood b Swann	75	b Broad	3
AB de Villiers	c Prior b Broad	50	lbw b Broad	2
JP Duminy	lbw b Onions	4	b Broad	0
*MV Boucher	lbw b Swann	39	c Prior b Broad	29
M Morkel	lbw b Swann	23	lbw b Swann	15
PL Harris	lbw b Swann	2	c Broad b Anderson	36
DW Steyn	c Prior b Anderson	47	lbw b Swann	3
M Ntini	not out	6	not out	1
Extras	b 1, lb 17	18		0
	(all out 108.3 overs)	343	(all out 50 overs)	133

	First Innings				Second Innings			
	O	M	R	W	O	M	R	W
Anderson	23.3	4	75	2	8	2	24	1
Onions	23	6	62	1	4	1	12	0
Broad	20	6	44	2	17	3	43	4
Swann	35	3	110	4	21	3	54	5
Trott	4	0	19	0	–	–	–	–
Pietersen	2	0	7	0	–	–	–	–
Collingwood	1	0	8	0	–	–	–	–

Fall of Wickets
1-3, 2-10, 3-160, 4-166, 5-170, 6-233, 7-269, 8-280, 9-285
1-27, 2-37, 3-40, 4-44, 5-44, 6-50, 7-86, 8-108, 9-129

ENGLAND

	First Innings	
AJ Strauss (capt)	b Morkel	54
AN Cook	c Kallis b Morkel	118
IJL Trott	c Boucher b Morkel	18
KP Pietersen	lbw b Harris	31
PD Collingwood	c Boucher b Duminy	91
IR Bell	c Boucher b Steyn	140
*MJ Prior	b Duminy	60
SCJ Broad	c Kallis b Duminy	20
GP Swann	c Prince b Steyn	22
JM Anderson	not out	1
G Onions	not out	2
Extras	lb 10, w 6, nb 1	17
	(9 wkts dec 170 overs)	574

	First Innings			
	O	M	R	W
Steyn	34	6	94	2
Ntini	29	4	114	0
Morkel	31	6	78	3
Kallis	14	1	43	0
Harris	38	4	146	1
Duminy	24	1	89	3

Fall of Wickets
1-71, 2-104, 3-155, 4-297, 5-365, 6-477, 7-536, 8-564, 9-568

Umpires: Aleem Dar (Pakistan) & AM Saheba (India)
Toss: South Africa
Man of the Match: GP Swann

England won by an innings and 98 runs

Graeme Swann celebrates the prized wicket of South African captain Graeme Smith during the second Test at Durban.

young fast bowler Friedel de Wet, in his first Test, first ran out Pietersen for 81 and then dismissed Trott, Bell and Prior in the space of six overs.

It is not uncommon for teams to respond very positively from such a narrow escape and the tables were dramatically turned during the Christmas Test at Durban, which England won by a thumping margin of an innings and 98 runs. South Africa chose to bat first and scored 343 in helpful bowling conditions, having been 285 for 9.

England's overwhelming response of 574 for 9 declared was built on centuries by Cook and Bell – who scored 140 – Collingwood's 91 and 60 from Prior. Facing a deficit of 231 midway through the fourth day, South Africa were hurtling towards defeat at the close on 76 for 6; no fewer than three batsmen – Kallis, de Villiers and Duminy – having been dismissed by Broad playing no stroke in the space of only four overs. Swann polished them off within 18 overs on the final day for just 133, the off spinner taking 5 for 54 in the second innings and finishing with match figures of 9 for 164 and a return of 54 wickets at an average of 27.92 from 12 Tests in the calendar year.

THIRD TEST – SOUTH AFRICA v. ENGLAND
3–7 January 2010 at Cape Town

SOUTH AFRICA

	First Innings		Second Innings	
GC Smith (capt)	c Prior b Anderson	30	(2) c Collingwood b Onions	183
AG Prince	c Prior b Anderson	0	(1) lbw b Swann	15
HM Amla	lbw b Onions	14	c Cook b Swann	95
JH Kallis	c Prior b Onions	108	c Prior b Anderson	46
AB de Villiers	c Strauss b Swann	36	c Broad b Anderson	34
JP Duminy	c Prior b Swann	0	c Prior b Anderson	36
*MV Boucher	lbw b Broad	51	c Bell b Swann	15
DW Steyn	c Trott b Anderson	26	not out	1
M Morkel	c Swann b Anderson	0		
PL Harris	not out	10		
F de Wet	lbw b Anderson	0		
Extras	b 1, lb 13, w 1, nb 1	16	b 8, lb 7, nb 2, pen 5	22
	(all out 86.1 overs)	291	(7 wkts dec 111.2 overs)	447

	First Innings				Second Innings			
	O	M	R	W	O	M	R	W
Anderson	21.1	1	63	5	22.2	1	98	3
Onions	20	4	69	2	22	4	87	1
Broad	19	6	54	1	37	5	127	3
Swann	22	1	74	2	37	5	127	3
Pietersen	4	0	17	0	3	0	6	0
Trott	–	–	–	–	5	0	30	0

Fall of Wickets
1-1, 2-46, 3-51, 4-127, 5-127, 6-216, 7-280, 8-280, 9-281
1-31, 2-261, 3-346, 4-376, 5-401, 6-442, 7-447

ENGLAND

	First Innings		Second Innings	
AJ Strauss (capt)	c Boucher b Morkel	2	c Amla b Harris	45
AN Cook	c Prince b Morkel	65	c Boucher b de Wet	55
IJL Trott	b Steyn	20	b Steyn	42
KP Pietersen	c and b Steyn	0	lbw b Steyn	6
PD Collingwood	lbw b Morkel	19	(6) c Kallis b Duminy	40
IR Bell	c Duminy b Kallis	48	(7) c Smith b Morkel	78
*MJ Prior	b Steyn	76	(8) c de Villiers b Duminy	4
SCJ Broad	b Steyn	25	(9) c de Villiers b Harris	0
GP Swann	c Smith b Morkel	5	(10) not out	10
JM Anderson	c Smith b Morkel	0	(5) c Prince b Harris	9
G Onions	not out	4	not out	0
Extras	lb 6, w 2, nb 1	9	b 1, lb 4, w 1, nb 1	7
	(all out 88 overs)	273	(9 wkts 141 overs)	296

	First Innings				Second Innings			
	O	M	R	W	O	M	R	W
Morkel	22	4	75	5	28	9	51	1
de Wet	16	3	36	0	35	11	74	2
Steyn	22	5	74	4	35	11	74	2
Kallis	14	2	27	1	14	4	28	0
Harris	9	0	39	0	40	14	85	3
Duminy	5	0	16	0	12	3	30	2

Fall of Wickets
1-2, 2-36, 3-36, 4-73, 5-133, 6-174, 7-225, 8-241, 9-241
1-101, 2-107, 3-129, 4-153, 5-160, 6-272, 7-278, 8-286, 9-290

Umpires: DJ Harper (Australia) & AL Hill (New Zealand)
Toss: England
Man of the Match: GC Smith

Match drawn

At Newlands, South Africa's selectors made the decision that had been torturing them since the first Test in which the veteran Makhaya Ntini appeared to have run his course. Given the political sensitivity within the country, the matter had to be dealt with carefully and sympathetically, but the emergence of de Wet, and the team's poor performance at Durban, meant that there was no option but to drop him. In fact, de Wet pulled a hamstring during the course of the game, which was played in stifling heat in excess of 35 degrees, and was replaced for the final match.

An unchanged England bowled well, and a collapse of four wickets for 12 runs on the second morning saw South Africa dismissed for 291. Anderson took three wickets for just one run to claim 5 for 63, while Kallis's stubborn overnight hundred was ended by the first ball he faced from Onions which he edged to Prior for 108.

England's reply was laboured, with Cook making 65 and Prior 76, and they also suffered an early morning collapse, losing their last three wickets for 32 on the third day, giving South Africa a narrow advantage of 18 runs. In the broiling heat, England's bowlers struggled to prevent South Africa's captain, Smith, from

Right England spearhead James Anderson took 5 for 63 in the South African first innings at Cape Town, and eight wickets in all during the third Test.

determinedly building an unassailable position for his team. His opening partner, Prince, was reprieved by the umpires' Decision Review System when he received a dreadful decision for caught behind, but Smith's principal partner was Hashim Amla who fell just five short of his second century of the series.

Smith was eventually dismissed by what quickly was shown to have been a no-ball – which made rather a mockery of the DRS – for 183 from 273 balls; a marathon given the conditions and he declared on 447 for 7. This left England to survive for 146 overs in order to preserve their 1-0 lead and by the close, they had already lost three wickets; Cook for 55, Strauss for 45 and Pietersen for 6.

Overnight, the first drama of the series erupted in the form of a ball tampering accusation by South Africa. In particular, Broad's method of stopping the ball, in which he trapped the ball under his boot, was questioned (the theory being that the studs on the sole of his boot would damage the ball) and there was some television footage of Anderson handling the ball which

the South Africans also objected to. The match referee, Roshan Mahanama of Sri Lanka, examined the evidence and declared that England had no case to answer although, privately, it was felt that Broad should put an end to fielding the ball with his boot.

So tempers were running as high as the temperature when the final day got under way in acrimonious circumstances. By lunch, England were five wickets down, the nightwatchman Anderson having survived only 10 overs and Trott being bowled by Steyn for 42. Collingwood and Bell, however, then embarked on a determined and skilful partnership that appeared to be steering England to safety. Collingwood successfully reviewed another poor decision for a catch at slip before he had scored, and then batted for more than four and a half hours for his 40. Both were still together at tea, with England needing to survive a further 34 overs with five wickets left, and at that stage a hard-earned draw seemed to be the most likely outcome.

But Collingwood was caught by Kallis off the spinner,

Duminy, who, in his next over, also had Prior taken at short leg. With every fielder crowded around the bat, Broad was given out to a catch at silly point, which he successfully – and crucially – reviewed. He still made a duck, but batted for 33 vital minutes while doing so before presenting a catch to short leg off Harris.

Eleven overs remained with only two wickets left when Swann joined Bell, with Newlands gripped by the drama. Smith brought back Morkel and, after a stay approaching five hours, Bell presented the captain with a catch and was gone for 78. So, having saved the first Test, Onions now found himself in an identical situation. This time there were 17 balls remaining – and Onions survived the entire final over of the match to deny South Africa a second time.

The last ball of the third Test at Cape Town has been bowled and Graham Onions, England's last man and hero of the hour, is starting to celebrate another great escape.

Hashim Amla stretches to take the catch at short leg and Andrew Strauss, the England captain, falls to the left-arm spin of South Africa's Paul Harris during the Cape Town Test.

England's 1-0 lead definitely flattered them as the teams reconvened after a short interval for the final match at the Wanderers in Johannesburg. The match started in the most dramatic fashion when Strauss was brilliantly caught by Amla at short leg off the very first ball. Trott and Pietersen both looked very jittery and made just 12 between them and, when Collingwood was dismissed for 47, England were 115 for 5.

Lower order resistance raised their total to 180 all out, but South Africa already held the upper hand. This was confirmed when Smith, on 15, survived a confident appeal for caught behind off Sidebottom. So convinced were England that the moment the on-field umpire, Tony Hill, ruled not out, they immediately and confidently asked TV umpire Harper to review it.

The Sky television commentators and viewers could clearly hear a nick. Those on SABC, BBC Radio and,

crucially, Mr Harper, could hear nothing, and Smith was given not out. England's fielders were incandescent, and after Harper had been unfairly pilloried in the media, it emerged that the technician providing the sound feed to all but Sky TV had not turned the volume up!

It was a terrible blow to the integrity of the review system, and all the England could do was console themselves with the fact that the on-field umpire had not given Smith out either so, DRS or no DRS, Smith remained at the crease and, inevitably, scored a century before declaring with a huge lead of 243.

This time, England's reserves were exhausted, although Collingwood again top-scored with 71. In just 42 overs, it was all over and South Africa won by an innings and 74 runs within four days. It left the series level at one win apiece, which was a fair reflection on a series that more than lived up to expectations.

FOURTH TEST – SOUTH AFRICA v. ENGLAND
14–17 January 2010 at Johannesburg

SERIES AVERAGES
South Africa v. England

ENGLAND

	First Innings		Second Innings	
AJ Strauss (capt)	c Amla b Steyn	0	lbw b Parnell	22
AN Cook	lbw b Morkel	21	c Smith b Morkel	1
IJL Trott	lbw b Morkel	5	c de Villiers b Steyn	8
KP Pietersen	c Parnell b Morkel	7	c Boucher b Parnell	12
PD Collingwood	c Duminy b McLaren	47	c Morkel b Duminy	71
IR Bell	b Steyn	35	c Kallis b Morkel	5
*MJ Prior	c Boucher b Steyn	14	c Smith b Morkel	0
SCJ Broad	c Morkel b Kallis	13	c Boucher b Morkel	1
GP Swann	c Boucher b Steyn	27	c de Villiers b Steyn	20
RJ Sidebottom	c Boucher b Steyn	0	b Duminy	15
JM Anderson	not out	6	not out	1
Extras	lb 2, w 3	5	lb 6, w 1, nb 6	13
	(all out 47.5 overs)	180	(all out 42.5 overs)	169

	First Innings				Second Innings			
	O	M	R	W	O	M	R	W
Steyn	13.5	1	51	5	14	1	64	2
Morkel	11	1	39	3	16	5	59	4
McLaren	10	3	30	1	3	1	13	0
Parnell	3	0	18	0	8	1	17	2
Kallis	10	3	40	1	–	–	–	–
Duminy	–	–	–	–	1.5	0	10	2

Fall of Wickets
1-0, 2-7, 3-32, 4-39, 5-115, 6-133, 7-136, 8-148, 9-155
1-6, 2-21, 3-48, 4-84, 5-103, 6-103, 7-104, 8-134, 9-154

SOUTH AFRICA

	First Innings	
GC Smith (capt)	c Strauss b Sidebottom	105
AG Prince	c Swann b Broad	19
HM Amla	c Prior b Broad	75
JH Kallis	c Anderson b Sidebottom	7
AB de Villiers	c Collingwood b Broad	58
JP Duminy	c Collingwood b Swann	7
*MV Boucher	c Trott b Swann	95
R McLaren	not out	33
DW Steyn	not out	1
M Morkel		
WD Parnell		
Extras	b 7, lb 10, w 5, nb 1	23
	(7 wkts declared 119 overs)	423

	First Innings			
	O	M	R	W
Anderson	30	4	111	0
Sidebottom	31	6	98	2
Broad	29	4	83	3
Swann	23	0	93	2
Collingwood	6	1	21	0

Fall of Wickets
1-36, 2-201, 3-217, 4-217, 5-235, 6-355, 7-419

Umpires: SJ Davis (Australia) & AL Hill (New Zealand)
Toss: England
Test debuts: R McLaren & WD Parnell
Men of the Match: DW Steyn & M Morkel
Men of the Series: MV Boucher & GP Swann

South Africa won by an innings and 74 runs

Series Drawn 1–1

SOUTH AFRICA

Batting	M	Inns	NO	Runs	HS	Av	100	50	c/st
GC Smith	4	7	0	427	183	61.00	2	1	7/-
MV Boucher	4	7	1	341	95	56.83	-	3	16/-
JH Kallis	4	7	0	363	120	51.85	2	1	5/-
HM Amla	4	7	0	311	100	44.42	1	2	2/-
AB de Villiers	4	7	0	276	64	39.42	-	3	5/-
DW Steyn	3	5	2	78	47	26.00	-	-	1/-
PL Harris	3	5	1	97	38	24.25	-	-	-/-
F de Wet	2	2	0	20	20	10.00	-	-	1/-
M Morkel	4	5	1	73	23	18.25	-	-	3/-
JP Duminy	4	7	0	114	56	16.28	-	1	2/-
AG Prince	4	7	0	97	45	13.85	-	-	3/-
R McLaren	1	1	1	33	33*	-	-	-	-/-
M Ntini	2	3	3	11	6*	-	-	-	-/-
WD Parnell	1	0	0	0	0	-	-	-	1/-

Bowling	Overs	Mds	Runs	Wkts	Av	Best	5/inn	10m
WD Parnell	11	1	35	2	17.50	2-17	-	-
JP Duminy	53.5	6	169	8	21.12	3-89	-	-
M Morkel	147	28	408	19	21.47	5-75	1	-
DW Steyn	118.5	24	357	15	23.80	5-51	1	-
F de Wet	71	19	186	6	31.00	4-55	-	-
PL Harris	150	39	444	11	40.36	5-123	1	-
R McLaren	13	4	43	1	43.00	1-30	-	-
JH Kallis	55	11	143	2	71.50	1-27	-	-
M Ntini	70	15	233	2	116.50	2-78	-	-

ENGLAND

Batting	M	Inns	NO	Runs	HS	Av	100	50	c/st
PD Collingwood	4	7	1	344	91	57.33	-	3	8/-
IR Bell	4	7	0	313	140	44.71	1	1	3/-
AN Cook	4	7	0	287	118	41.00	1	2	4/-
GP Swann	4	7	1	171	85	28.50	-	1	3/-
IJL Trott	4	7	0	190	69	27.14	-	1	2/-
KP Pietersen	4	7	0	177	81	25.28	-	1	-/-
AJ Strauss	4	7	0	170	54	24.28	-	1	2/-
MJ Prior	4	7	0	158	76	22.57	-	2	12/-
JM Anderson	4	7	3	56	29	14.00	-	-	1/-
SCJ Broad	4	7	0	76	25	10.85	-	-	2/-
RJ Sidebottom	1	2	0	15	15	7.50	-	-	-/-
G Onions	3	5	5	11	4*	-	-	-	-/-

Bowling	Overs	Mds	Runs	Wkts	Av	Best	5/inn	10m
GP Swann	210	25	659	21	31.38	5-54	2	-
SCJ Broad	155	36	435	13	33.46	4-43	-	-
JM Anderson	162.5	22	548	16	34.25	5-63	1	-
G Onions	115	23	366	8	45.75	3-86	-	-
RJ Sidebottom	31	6	98	2	49.00	2-98	-	-

Also bowled: PD Collingwood 20-3-66-0, KP Pietersen 9-0-30-0, IJL Trott 11-0-58-0.

Opposite Paul Collingwood finished top of the England batting averages in the Test series against South Africa, and also scored the most runs for the side in both the Twenty20 and one-day internationals.

TWENTY20 INTERNATIONALS

Match One
13 November 2009 Day/Night at Johannesburg
England 202 for 6 (20 overs) (PD Collingwood 57, EJG Morgan 85*)
South Africa 127 for 3 (13 overs) (LL Bosman 58)
England won by 1 run

Match Two
15 November 2009 at Centurion
South Africa 241 for 6 (20 overs) (GC Smith 88, LL Bosman 94)
England 157 for 8 (20 overs) (IJL Trott 51)
South Africa won by 84 runs
Series drawn 1–1

ONE-DAY INTERNATIONALS

Match One
20 November 2009 Day/Night at Johannesburg
South Africa v. **England**
Match abandoned

Match Two
22 November 2009 at Centurion
South Africa 250 for 9 (50 overs) (HM Amla 57, AN Petersen 64)
England 252 for 3 (46 overs) (IJL Trott 87,
PD Collingwood 105*)
England won by 7 wickets

Match Three
27 November 2009 Day/Night at Cape Town
South Africa 354 for 6 (50 overs) (HM Amla 86,
GC Smith 54, AB de Villiers 121, AN Petersen 51*,
SCJ Broad 4 for 71)
England 242 all out (41.3 overs) (PD Collingwood 86,
WD Parnell 5 for 48)
South Africa won by 112 runs

Match Four
29 November 2009 at Port Elizabeth
South Africa 119 all out (36.5 overs) (AN Petersen 51,
JM Anderson 5 for 23)
England 121 for 3 (31.2 overs) (IJL Trott 52*)
England won by 7 wickets

Match Five
4 December 2009 Day/Night at Durban
South Africa v. **England**
Match abandoned
England won the series 2–1

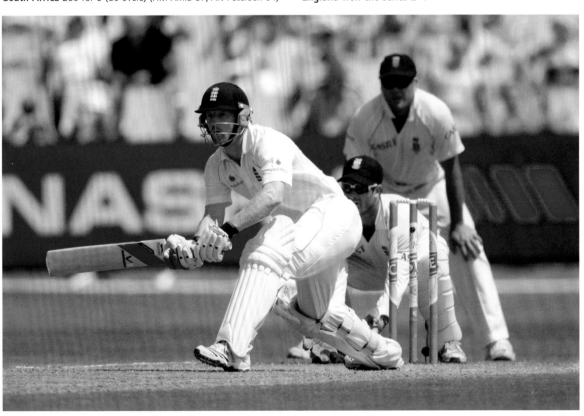

CHRISTOPHER MARTIN-JENKINS writes...

TV Reviews Should be Left to the Umpires

South Africa got the share of the series they thoroughly deserved by dint of their innings victory at Johannesburg. England's disappointed and frustrated team will feel, even if they do not say, that it might all have been different had Graeme Smith walked or been given out caught behind for 15 when his flail at a ball from Ryan Sidebottom made faint contact, but they would be fooling themselves if so. When you lose the captain to the first ball of the match and get bowled out for 180 in fewer than 50 overs there is never likely to be a means of escape.

South Africa had better fast bowlers and in this match they batted down to No. 11. Their future looks rosy with two fast bowlers of high quality in Dale Steyn and Morne Morkel and a promising one in Wayne Parnell. Had Steyn been fit from the start of the series England would probably not have achieved their honourable share of the series.

Hashim Amla's fateful catch off the first ball of the match, incisive fast bowling by Steyn and Morkel and Smith's second successive century, yet another demonstration of great skill and bottomless determination, made sure that, this time, there would be no escape for an Onionless England. They thus achieved the unlikely feat of being the first side in the last ten Johannesburg Tests to win the toss and lose the game; and only the second in ten to lose after batting first.

If AB de Villiers had not led such a charmed life after England briefly got back into the match with a brilliant start to the third day, it would not have been so easy for South Africa but it would have been a travesty had they lost the series.

The game will be remembered for its drama on a bony pitch that always offered the bowlers something and for

The captains and coaches of both England and South Africa meet with the umpires and match officials to discuss the use of the referral system ahead of the opening Test at Centurion.

underlining the need for further fine-tuning of the ICC's decision review system. Daryl Harper obviously should have paid sufficient attention to the noise picked up by the stump microphone when Smith's bat made contact with the ball. It led to the rather pathetic attempt by England, via a written submission to the ICC, to restore their lost review.

The system may only be in its infancy but already it has gone too far. Leave aside the fact that England felt that it served them so badly at the Wanderers, there is a deeper principle at stake. The preamble to the laws of the game, intended to be a part of the laws, expressly forbids the questioning of an umpire's decision 'by word, action or gesture'.

Comfortably more than 99 per cent of all cricket matches have to abide by this injunction and so, now that the ICC can see the consequences of opening Pandora's box in the first place, should Test matches and one-day internationals, whatever their duration.

As soon as possible they must leave all reviews to the three umpires, the two in the middle and the television man, working in close contact with one another by radio. If the television coverage does not include the latest gadgetry – in South Africa there was no 'hotspot' and no 'snicko' – I think that they should revert to allowing reviews only for line decisions, namely no-balls, run-outs and stumpings.

As things stand the governing body has given the elite players dangerous licence to act as if they are above the law. How can young cricketers be expected to observe the game's spirit if they see the star players regularly refusing to accept decisions?

Above Umpire Tony Hill decides to refer a decision on whether South Africa's Graeme Smith has been caught at the wicket off Ryan Sidebottom during the fourth Test at the Wanderers in Johannesburg.

Below A minute or so later, and England's players cannot believe that Smith has been reprieved by TV umpire Daryl Harper.

ENGLAND LIONS
by Mark Baldwin

The importance afforded to England Lions matches has increased since Hugh Morris, himself a former captain of what used to be called England A, became managing director of the national teams. The Lions are now an England second eleven and a development tool, all wrapped up into one.

In 2010 the Lions played a total of 13 matches, seven on foreign soil in the United Arab Emirates and six at home. There was a three-day match against the touring Bangladeshis in May, won by nine wickets, plus eight 50-over games against the A teams of Pakistan, West Indies and India, three Twenty20s against Pakistan A and even one 20-over meeting with the senior England side. That took place in February, in Abu Dhabi, and served as an extra warm-up game for the England Twenty20 team, under Paul Collingwood, which was beginning to focus on an ICC World Twenty20 some ten weeks away.

The Lions won the match by five wickets and two players central to that victory – Somerset's Craig Kieswetter and Hampshire's Michael Lumb – impressed Andy Flower and his England management so much that they went on to force their way into the World Twenty20 team itself in the West Indies.

Kieswetter struck 81 from 66 balls, including two sixes and nine fours, and Lumb finished 58 not out from only 35 balls as the Lions chased down an England total of 157 for 6. Before meeting England, moreover, Kieswetter had also starred in all three of the Twenty20 fixtures the Lions had played against Pakistan A, in Sharjah and Abu Dhabi, of which two were won. Kieswetter scored 77 not out from 52 balls in the first match, with four sixes and eight fours, and then an unbeaten 40 and a 32-ball 50, which included three more sixes.

Lumb, meanwhile, hit 110 from 128 balls to lead the Lions to victory in the second of three 50-over games at Dubai Sports City, also against Pakistan A, which followed the England match. James Taylor, the young Leicestershire batsman, contributed an excellent 61 to a 109-run fourth wicket stand with Lumb.

The Lions lost the other two 50-over contests, but the fortnight's competitive one-day cricket in the Emirates had done its prime job: it had identified the personnel to complete the team which was soon to win the Twenty20 World Cup for England, and it had also given valuable added international experience to the likes of Steven Finn, Steven Davies and James Tredwell.

Back in England, it was Davies's 81 from 88 balls and Andrew Gale's 74, plus seven wickets from Ravi Bopara's medium pacers, which highlighted the Lions' first-class victory against the Bangladeshis at Derby.

Then came, at the end of June and into early July, a triangular 50-over series in which the Lions, under Alastair Cook, were unbeaten. Cook and Jonathan Trott scored the bulk of the runs in the opening match, against West Indies A at Northampton, and a five-wicket win in the next game, in which India A were the opponents at Leicester, featured excellent unbeaten innings from Darren Stevens and Peter Trego besides a solid all-round display from Bopara.

The Lions overwhelmed West Indies A by 124 runs in their third game, with Bopara hitting a majestic 168 from 140 balls, with two sixes and 23 fours, and then taking 4 for 43 with the ball. Trego was not far behind, striking 73 from 53 balls in the Lions' total of 345 and picking up 5 for 40 when the West Indians were bowled out for 221.

A thrilling tie in the final group match, with both the Lions and India A remarkably totalling 343 for 8, was

Kent's Darren Stevens, called up to make a successful England Lions debut at the age of 34 in the triangular tournament against West Indies A and India A, hits out at Grace Road in Leicester.

also memorable for Ian Bell's 158 off 143 balls and attractive half-centuries from both Stevens and Davies.

When the two sides met again in the final, two days later and also at Worcester, it was the Lions who prevailed. India A's 278 for 7 was overhauled with eight balls to spare as Gale, with 90, Stevens, whose 53-ball 68 completed a fine first taste of international cricket, and Davies, who made 55, led the Lions to a highly-satisfying tournament success.

Other players who benefitted from Lions exposure in 2010, plus time in the Performance Programme squad which often feeds the Lions teams, included Adil Rashid, Chris Woakes, Steve Kirby, Stephen Parry and David Wainwright.

MATCHES IN UNITED ARAB EMIRATES (UAE)

Match One
12 February 2010 at Sharjah Cricket Association Stadium
Pakistan A 156 for 7 (20 overs) (Shahzaib Hasan 57)
England Lions 159 for 3 (17.4 overs) (C Kieswetter 77*)
England Lions won by 7 wickets

Match Two
14 February 2010 at Sharjah Cricket Association Stadium
Pakistan A 106 all out (19.5 overs)
England Lions 107 for 2 (16.1 overs)
England Lions won by 8 wickets

Match Three
16 February 2010 at Sheikh Zayed Stadium, Abu Dhabi
England Lions 146 for 4 (20 overs) (C Kieswetter 50)
Pakistan A 149 for 6 (19.5 overs)
Pakistan A won by 4 wickets

Match Four
17 February 2010 Day/Night at Sheikh Zayed Stadium, Abu Dhabi
England 157 for 6 (20 overs)
England Lions 158 for 5 (20 overs) (MJ Lumb 58*, C Kieswetter 81)
England Lions won by 5 wickets

Match Five
22 February 2010 Day/Night at Dubai Sports City Stadium
Pakistan A 179 all out (47.5 overs) (Mohammad Hafeez 51)
England Lions 96 all out (34.3 overs) (Abdur Rehman 4 for 25)
Pakistan A won by 83 runs

Match Six
24 February 2010 at Dubai Sports City Stadium
Pakistan A 231 for 8 (50 overs) (Umair Khan 61)
England Lions 232 for 7 (49 overs) (MJ Lumb 110, JWA Taylor 61)
England Lions won by 3 wickets

Match Seven
26 February 2010 at Dubai Sports City Stadium
Pakistan A 213 for 9 (50 overs) (Asad Shafiq 52, CR Woakes 4 for 38)
England Lions 143 all out (40.1 overs)
Pakistan A won by 70 runs

BANGLADESH TOUR MATCH

19–21 May 2010 at Derby
Bangladeshis 220 and 161 (Jahurul Islam 58*, RS Bopara 4 for 14)
England Lions 296 (AW Gale 74, SM Davies 81) and 86 for 1
England Lions won by 9 wickets

A TEAM TRI-NATIONS SERIES (England Lions matches)

Match Two
29 June 2010 at Northampton
West Indies A 279 for 6 (50 overs) (KA Edwards 147, AB Fudadin 51)
England Lions 281 for 5 (48.4 overs) (AN Cook 71, IJL Trott 118)
England Lions won by 5 wickets

Match Three
1 July 2010 at Leicester
India A 254 all out (49.3 overs) (CA Pujara 73)
England Lions 255 for 5 (45.3 overs) (DI Stevens 58*)
England Lions won by 5 wickets

Match Five
4 July 2010 at Worcester
England Lions 345 all out (49.1 overs) (RS Bopara 168, PD Trego 73, GC Tonge 4 for 69)
West Indies A 221 all out (40 overs) (DM Bravo 62, KA Stoute 64, PD Trego 5 for 40, RS Bopara 4 for 43)
England Lions won by 124 runs

Match Six
6 July 2010 at Worcester
England Lions 343 for 8 (50 overs) (SM Davies 54, IR Bell 158, DI Stevens 64)
India A 343 for 8 (50 overs) (A Mukund 114, LE Plunkett 4 for 58)
Match tied

Final
8 July 2010 at Worcester
India A 278 for 7 (50 overs) (A Mukund 62, CA Pujara 87*)
England Lions 279 for 5 (48.4 overs) (SM Davies 55, AW Gale 90, DI Stevens 68)
England Lions won by 5 wickets

LV COUNTY CHAMPIONSHIP

by Mark Baldwin

In 2010, the grand old County Championship decided it had taken enough carping and criticism from the ill informed and provided a season, and specifically a finish, which laughed in the face of its critics. Talk of reducing the Championship from 16 matches to 14 – or even 12, some said – raged like tittle-tattle at a run of summer garden parties.

There was chatter about turning it into a three-conference affair, or three divisions, and even some twaddle about inviting in some minor counties too in order that the 'perfect' number of four-day games could be played.

Well, they do say talk is cheap. But, as if to underline the Championship's continuing relevance and stature, the cricketing gods had their say too. Indeed, after the end of the season and some lengthy debate, the England and Wales Cricket Board decided to keep the same structure for 2011, with the intent to prune back some one-day cricket from 2012.

Personally, I've always felt that a properly-funded Championship (in terms of prize-money available all the way down the table) could make a one-division structure work just as well, but the evidence after ten years is also now there to support the claim that two divisions has produced highly competitive first-class cricket and – most importantly – a strong England team.

For the relevance of the County Championship, moreover, you only have to look at Graeme Swann, the current number one ranked spinner in the world, let alone in England. Nurtured by Northamptonshire, for whom he played for seven seasons before moving to Nottinghamshire, he needed NINE summers playing county cricket following his first England tour in 1999-2000 before he had developed sufficiently to make a success of it at international level.

It is also important for those who would reduce the number of first-class counties, let alone the number of games they play each season, to realise and accept that it was Northants – one of those smaller counties that some seem so keen to deem surplus to requirements – which first discovered and developed Swann. Similarly, it was Northants that produced Monty Panesar, while another smaller county, Leicestershire, produced Stuart Broad and Luke Wright. That all those four England cricketers have now moved on to represent other, 'bigger', counties is my only reservation about a two-division system which seems to be creating an ever more 'football-style' transfer market with each passing year.

For now, though, let's celebrate 2010, the year that Nottinghamshire triumphed right at the death, in which Somerset came so close in the other two domestic competitions besides almost securing the Championship for the very first time in their 128-year history, and when a predominantly young and initially unheralded Yorkshire side might have snatched the prize themselves but for an excitable batting collapse on a remarkable final day.

Nottinghamshire certainly held their nerve, after enduring three days of unbearable frustration as almost incessant rain fell on their match against Lancashire at Old Trafford. They had begun the final round of games, which took place from Monday 13 September until

The summer of 1999, and a baby-faced Graeme Swann signs autographs for young Northants supporters.

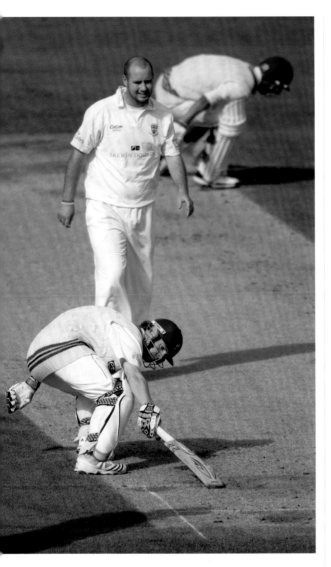

More runs for the prolific James Hildreth, who turns at bowler Chris Rushworth's end during Somerset's final County Championship game, at Durham.

Thursday 16 September, two points clear of Somerset – who were playing Durham at Chester-le-Street – and seven points in front of Yorkshire, who were hosting Kent at Headingley.

All Nottinghamshire could do by the end of day three was reach 89 for 2 from 28 overs in their first innings after Chris Read had opted to bat. At one stage, when the rain relented, the glare of the sun in batsmen's faces had even cost a number of overs. By the time the fateful final day began, moreover, the other two matches both looked to have moved towards definite conclusions.

At the unnecessarily long-winded sounding Emirates Durham International Cricket Ground, there had been a decent amount of play throughout the week with Somerset first bowling out the home side for 286 and then replying with 426, in which James Hildreth scored 105 – his seventh first-class hundred of an outstanding season.

That gave Somerset maximum bonus points, but late on day three Durham had fought hard through 47 overs to reach 171 for 2 in their second innings – an overall lead of just 31. At Headingley, meanwhile, where their title rivals knew that Yorkshire's opponents Kent also wanted a positive result in their outside bid to avoid relegation, it was the home side who seemed to hold the upper hand. Despite being dismissed for 261 in their first innings, Yorkshire had then restricted Kent to 302 even though Alex Blake, 21, hit an unbeaten maiden century, and had moved ten runs ahead at 51 for 1 in their second innings.

And so the scene was set, with 16 September also thankfully promising little chance of any further weather interruptions at the three northern venues. Indeed, the drama of the situation – with any one of three counties still in the title hunt – suddenly put Championship cricket into the forefront of the minds of a sporting media which, for most of the summer, had seemed to want to ignore it.

Sky Sports were televising the match at Old Trafford and – as both written and electronic media representatives tried to keep their readers and viewers up to date with what was happening at all three grounds – *Sky Sports News* put the following valuable information up on the screen:

- If Somerset, Notts or Yorkshire win and the other two lose, the winning team are the champions
- If Notts beat Lancashire with a total of 22 points, Somerset will not be champions
- If Somerset and Yorkshire both draw, Notts will need nine points to be champions
- If Somerset and Yorkshire win and Notts fail to win, Somerset will be champions
- If Notts and Yorkshire win, Notts will be champions
- If Somerset and Yorkshire both lose, Notts would need six points to win
- If Notts and Somerset both lose, Yorkshire would need to win to be champions

It was all very helpful, but what actually happened was none of the above! Yorkshire lost, four wickets short of the victory that would have seen them crowned in triumph, Somerset drew when they gave up an unequal struggle to chase 181 in 17 overs following Durham's tenacious second innings of 320, and Nottinghamshire got nine points – five batting points, one bowling point, and three more for the draw.

That put them level on 214 points with Somerset, but ahead of them in terms of the all-important title because they had recorded seven wins during the season compared to the West Countrymen's six.

What those bare facts do not tell, though, is the scope of the tale that unfolded throughout almost six and a half hours of brilliant sporting tension. To give but one example of how it gripped the sports audience, the *Guardian*'s excellent and popular 'County Cricket – Live' blog attracted a record level of comments, and almost as many that day as the same newspaper's 'Pope Visit – Live' blog, which was operating at the height of Pope Benedict XVI's controversial four-day tour of Britain.

To the multitude of county cricket believers around the country, keeping in touch via websites, radio, television or Internet, 16 September was a day to savour. The excitement of the finish, furthermore, was all the more appealing to them because of the slow-burn of a season stretching all the way back to 9 April that had preceded it.

There was also last-day drama in Division Two, with Worcestershire coming up on the rails to chase down 301 in 70 overs to beat second division champions Sussex at New Road, and pip Glamorgan – who could not defeat bottom club Derbyshire at Cardiff – for the second available promotion place. Moeen Ali and James Cameron both scored centuries while putting on a match-winning 215 in 209 balls for Worcestershire, while Derbyshire's sixth-wicket pair Dan Redfern and Robin Peterson batted through the final hour to deny Glamorgan.

Wonderful stuff wherever you looked, indeed, for aficionados of the county game who will also recognise that behind all the popular sympathy afforded to Somerset and their captain, Marcus Trescothick, when they came up so agonisingly short, was a harsh truth. My colleague Tim Wellock argues passionately on these pages that Nottinghamshire were fortunate to come away with the title and that Somerset, morally at least, were the best side in the competition from gun to tape. Yet, while they might well have been the best team over the best part of six months, did they *deserve* the title?

Though as a Somerset man myself it pains me to say it, I believe that Trescothick and his team only have themselves to blame for not finishing some way ahead of Notts in the final shake-up. And that has nothing to do with their failure to beat proud former champions Durham in the last game, despite gaining a 140-run first-innings lead, but everything to do with their failure to push harder for wins earlier in the summer. It was a baffling conservatism, in my view, which was to cost them dear. The two best examples of this came in Somerset's fixtures against Kent, the first at home in late July and the second during Canterbury Festival Week two weeks later.

In the game at Taunton, Trescothick needed to manufacture something after the third day's play was lost to rain. Somerset, however, in charge after dismissing Kent for just 172 in their first innings, and with Murali Kartik taking 5 for 50 on a wearing pitch, delayed their second-innings declaration until just before lunch on the final day.

Kent, missing Rob Key through illness, were struggling in the relegation zone and also struggling for any sort of collective belief and confidence after a season beset by injury and unavailability of their leading players. Surely Trescothick could have set them something a little more tempting than the eventual 335 from 71 overs? In the end, somewhat predictably with Kartik again proving the trump card with 5 for 57 from 31 overs, Kent merely managed to hang on for the draw at 191 for 7.

Another opportunity for 13 extra points, however, went begging again in the return fixture – and this time Trescothick's actions on the final day even provoked boos and slow hand-clapping from the frustrated Kent supporters! Regular attendees of Canterbury Week said they had never heard that before.

Somerset had been more than two wins behind pacesetters Nottinghamshire when they

Worcestershire's Moeen Ali sweeps against Surrey at Whitgift School.

failed to beat Kent at Taunton, but a thumping 10-wicket home victory against the leaders in their next match at least took them to Canterbury with renewed title hopes. Yet, when Somerset began the final day 146 runs ahead and with seven wickets still in hand – and Trescothick himself still at the crease – it seemed as if a declaration around lunchtime would give them a good chance of forcing a result. Yorkshire were battling to a brave draw against Notts at Headingley, reaching 406 for 8 in their second innings after being bowled out for 178 on the opening day, and Kent would have accepted any challenge to chase down a total in their own desire to move away from the first division's lower reaches.

Once again, however, Trescothick took the safe option. He himself batted all day, finishing on 188 not out in an eventual total of 387 for 7 declared, and Key showed Kent's disgust by giving himself 11.2 overs of his particular brand of off spin and using ten bowlers in all – including Geraint Jones, the wicketkeeper.

It was then galling, indeed, for Somerset when they saw Nottinghamshire collude with Lancashire and earn themselves an ultimately decisive run-chase victory at Trent Bridge in late August, but in the final analysis they too had their chances to force results. It was their choice not to take them.

But back again to 16 September. At 10.30 am, when play was due to start in every game, Nottinghamshire yet again found themselves looking to the skies and wondering if the fates were conspiring against them. Play at Old Trafford could not start for an hour and, as the minutes ticked away there, events elsewhere were moving on apace.

Yorkshire, after moving quickly to 93 for 1 – a lead of 52 – suddenly and inexplicably imploded. James Tredwell, the Kent off spinner, took 7 for 22 including a hat-trick as Yorkshire's batsmen lost their heads. Bowled out for 130, they left Kent needing only 90 to win.

Up in Durham, the home side's resistance was being led by Michael Di Venuto who made a chanceless 129 and inspired a succession of middle-order batsmen to sell their wickets dearly too. Ben Harmison, Ian Blackwell, Phil Mustard, Dale Benkenstein (batting down at No. 7 due to injury) and Scott Borthwick all played their part in denying the Somerset attack for so long that, in the end, when they were bowled out there was not enough time left on the clock. Somerset's challenge, in fact, ended between lunch and tea when Durham scored just 32 runs but lost only one wicket while advancing their overall lead to 147, with four more wickets left.

At Headingley, there was briefly some renewed hope for Yorkshire's supporters when Kent lost both their openers with only six runs on the board. Key and Martin van Jaarsveld, however, then added 62 for the third wicket and not even a tumble of wickets just before the

Andrew Gale, who impressed as Yorkshire's captain in 2010.

modest target was reached could prevent the Kent victory, by four wickets, which meant the title race had now shed Yorkshire.

Andrew Gale, Yorkshire's impressive 26-year-old captain, said after the defeat, 'For 45 minutes this morning it was dreadful really – just signs of the old Yorkshire. But that isn't the way we have played our cricket this year so I am disappointed. On reflection it's been a good year, but it will take me a week or two to get over what has just happened.

'We took the game for granted a little bit. The lads thought it was

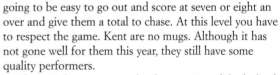

going to be easy to go out and score at seven or eight an over and give them a total to chase. At this level you have to respect the game. Kent are no mugs. Although it has not gone well for them this year, they still have some quality performers.

'There is always going to be the question of the lack of experience in our side but I think that is an easy get-out. As long as the players learn from it, then they can put it down to inexperience. But the supporters have seen how much effort we have put in. We haven't had a lot of success at Yorkshire over the past four or five years, but it feels as if we are reborn as a county. We have a lot of young players and if we can keep this squad together we are going to win trophies.'

It soon became obvious, in Chester-le-Street, that Somerset would have to settle for the draw and hope that Nottinghamshire could not gain the six bonus points they needed against Lancashire that – with three points for the draw – would clinch them the title by the narrowest of margins.

Nottinghamshire had discussed the possibility of scoring quick runs, declaring, and then doing a deal with

ROBINSON CRITICAL OF STANDARD OF PITCHES
by Bruce Talbot

Sussex coach Mark Robinson believes a lowering in the standard of county pitches could stifle the development of England's next generation of Test cricketers. Robinson had plenty to celebrate at the end of the 2010 season after his county clinched promotion as second division champions with a game to spare. They have now spent just one year outside the top flight since 2002. There were more positive results and three-day finishes in County Championship cricket this season compared to recent years because of two main factors – the early April start and the ban of the use of the heavy roller between innings.

It made for an exciting finale to the summer in both divisions but at the detriment of the overall standard, according to the experienced Robinson who has been coach at Hove since 2006 and has led his side to six trophies. He said, 'We played on some very average wickets all year and it looks as if the first division has been similar. A hobbyhorse of mine is that the standard of surfaces has to get better. There have been too many three-day matches, which isn't right for the good of the game and preparing Test cricketers. I would advocate bringing back the heavy roller between innings, which has been banned this year, but the ECB and the counties need to decide what they want to do.'

Robinson believes umpires and the ECB's pitch inspectors need to play more of a role in making sure counties do not over-step the boundaries of what is acceptable. He added, 'Making the most of home advantage and preparing a pitch which suits your team is fine but there is a balancing act and that has to be policed better by the ECB's pitch inspectors and umpires because coaches will always try to seek an advantage for their team. If it isn't going to be policed more tightly then we must bring back the heavy roller because the emphasis has gone too much towards the bowlers. People criticised high-scoring games and said it was because of bland wickets, but I believe it had more to do with a drop in standard of the bowling.'

Bruce Talbot writes on Sussex for testmatchextra.com.

Below Action from Sussex v. Middlesex at Hove in early May.

Lancashire (if it could be done) to forfeit two innings and set up a result. Yet that would mean, especially after the events at Trent Bridge three weeks earlier, that Lancashire would have to be tempted with a relatively modest target and, then, the chances of taking all ten home wickets to force a win was clearly pushing the bounds of possibility.

'We knew we had to go one way or another,' said Chris Read, the Nottinghamshire captain. 'But, over a meal on the Wednesday evening, we decided to back ourselves to get maximum batting points by reaching 400 and then leaving ourselves enough time to get three wickets.'

That plan, of course, needed both Durham and Kent to do Nottinghamshire a favour and avoid defeat against Somerset and Yorkshire. And, as the day went on, events at the other two grounds could have seen Notts declare at any stage and try to win their game too by setting Lancashire a run chase.

Long before they reached 400, though, it became obvious that the destination of the title was in Nottinghamshire's own hands and – courtesy of a well-crafted and superbly-paced fifth-wicket stand of 153 in 28 overs between Adam Voges and Samit Patel – they looked on course to gain those vital five batting points.

Then, though, both Voges (for 126) and Patel (for 96) holed out off Simon Kerrigan's slow left-arm spin and – when the youngster also removed Read, Steve Mullaney and Andre Adams, to a horrible heave across the line – Nottinghamshire faced their first crisis of the day at 390 for 9. Just the last pair of Ryan Sidebottom and Darren Pattinson remained, and if those final ten runs were not scored then Notts would need to take six Lancashire wickets and not three in what became 16 overs of bowling time at the end of the match.

Thankfully for Notts, both Sidebottom and Pattinson were equal to the task – sensibly deciding to eke out the runs in singles rather than risk any more optimistic swipes. And, with ball in hand, Sidebottom removed Karl Brown, to a catch at first slip, in his second over to give Notts the belief that they could get that crucial last bonus point.

Fittingly, as their leading wicket-taker in the campaign, it was Adams who made sure of it by dismissing Mark

Ali Brown holds the ball up having caught Hampshire's Sean Ervine off Samit Patel to help secure Nottinghamshire secure victory at the Rose Bowl. It was their third of four wins in a row and gave them the perfect platform from which to push on and secure the County Championship for the tenth time in the county's history.

Chilton and Shivnarine Chanderpaul with the first and fourth balls of his second over. Lancashire were 11 for 3, and it had taken just 4.4 overs for Nottinghamshire to crown themselves champions.

Yes, they had stuttered badly towards the end, after leading by 22 points going into the last two rounds of matches and losing at home to Yorkshire in the penultimate game, but they had performed with both bat and ball under extreme pressure on the final day.

Mick Newell, the understated but highly respected Notts coach, said, 'We've got the best seam attack in the Championship and we won five games at home and more than anyone else. We were criticised during the run-in for bottling it, but to play as well as we did on the last day was fantastic.'

'To come so close to the club's first Championship, to be within touching distance and yet to come away with nothing, is gutting,' said Trescothick. 'We will just have to learn from all this, and come back stronger next time.'

Nottinghamshire, who won £100,000 when they won the title previously in 2005, this time received £550,000 – of which £400,000 was intended as reward for the players – as a result of the ECB's upgrading of the Championship prize-money two years ago. Well done to the ECB for that, well done to Notts for getting over the line, and well done to the old competition itself. The original – and still the best.

Mark Baldwin has covered county cricket for The Times *since 1998.*

Division One – Final Table

	P	W	L	D	Bat	Bowl	Pens	Pts
Nottinghamshire	16	7	5	4	47	43	0	214
Somerset	16	6	2	8	53	41	0	214
Yorkshire	16	6	2	8	41	42	0	203
Lancashire	16	5	3	8	35	43	0	182
Durham	16	5	3	8	30	39	0	173
Warwickshire	16	6	9	1	20	47	0	166
Hampshire	16	3	6	7	47	41	0	157
Kent	16	3	7	6	42	44	-1	151
Essex	16	2	6	8	29	43	-2	126

Division Two – Final Table

	P	W	L	D	Bat	Bowl	Pens	Pts
Sussex	16	8	3	5	45	47	0	235
Worcestershire	16	7	4	5	39	42	0	208
Glamorgan	16	7	4	5	33	43	0	203
Leicestershire	16	7	5	4	31	44	0	199
Gloucestershire	16	6	9	1	28	47	-2	172
Northamptonshire	16	6	7	3	28	34	0	167
Surrey	16	4	6	6	43	36	-2	159
Middlesex	16	4	7	5	37	41	-2	155
Derbyshire	16	3	7	6	30	42	0	138

WHY SOMERSET SHOULD HAVE BEEN CHAMPIONS
by Tim Wellock

For Nottinghamshire to snatch the County Championship title by virtue of more wins was a travesty. They had lost five times, while Somerset remained unbeaten after losing the first two games of the season. Worthy champions do not implode the way Nottinghamshire did in being dismissed for 59 by Yorkshire at Trent Bridge, or for 190 in losing by ten wickets at Taunton, or for 180 when being beaten by 210 runs at Durham, or for 180 and 159 when losing to relegated Essex at Chelmsford.

Under the 2009 points system, Nottinghamshire would have been well adrift. The reduction to three points for a draw was designed to reduce the number of stalemates, but in truth it had more to do with the pitches and what can now be seen as flaws in the new system. Nottinghamshire have admitted that they requested to play as many early season matches as possible at Trent Bridge to suit their seam attack. The request, astonishingly, was granted and they won their first four games, three of them at home. They won three more, in among their five defeats.

On the final day at Chester-le-Street it was like turning back the clock two years for those Durham fans who had to wait in 2008 for Nottinghamshire's match at Trent Bridge to end before they could officially be crowned champions for the first time. But while those who made the pilgrimage to Canterbury, where Durham beat Kent, were suitably rewarded, the 300 or so travelling Somerset supporters had to endure the agony of watching Nottinghamshire take the three wickets they needed on a giant screen.

Because of a change in playing times to allow Somerset to catch a 7 pm flight from Newcastle ahead of the Clydesdale Bank 40 final against Warwickshire at Lord's, there was still an hour to play at Old Trafford. The long-time leaders had just scraped a fifth batting point with nine wickets down and they had 16 overs to grab the one bowling point that would clinch the title. It took them only 4.4 overs, with Shivnarine Chanderpaul the third victim. With most of those watching at Durham willing him to prove his usual tenacious self, he lasted only three balls before edging Andre Adams to the wicketkeeper.

Three weeks earlier the Lancashire captain, Glen Chapple, had handed Nottinghamshire victory with a generous declaration at Trent Bridge. It was a win that left them so far clear they should have cruised to the title, but after losing their next two games to Durham and Yorkshire, they limped home by the narrowest of margins. Durham had done their bit by denying Somerset victory, but were left to wonder how they themselves finished one place below that same Lancashire.

Tim Wellock writes on Durham and Yorkshire for testmatchextra.com.

COUNTY CHAMPIONSHIP FEATURES 2010

HIGHEST BATTING AVERAGES

Player	M	I	NO	HS	R	Ave	100	50
GP Smith	5	10	4	158*	509	84.83	2	3
HM Amla	4	6	1	129	377	75.40	1	4
DJ Hussey	5	7	1	251*	399	66.50	1	1
JC Hildreth	16	23	1	151	1440	65.45	7	5
RSC Martin-Jenkins	9	13	3	130	629	62.90	2	5
MR Ramprakash	16	28	2	248	1595	61.34	5	5
ME Trescothick	16	28	4	228*	1397	58.20	4	6
MJ Lumb	5	7	0	158	381	54.42	1	1
S Chanderpaul	8	14	1	120	698	53.69	2	5
CJL Rogers	15	27	3	200	1285	53.54	4	5
MW Goodwin	16	26	3	142	1201	52.21	4	5
A Lyth	16	29	0	142	1509	52.03	3	9
JA Rudolph	16	29	2	228*	1375	50.92	4	6
AC Voges	3	5	0	126	254	50.80	1	1
MJ Cosgrove	15	26	2	142	1187	49.45	5	4
SM Davies	12	20	2	137	887	49.27	1	4
MM Ali	15	28	2	126	1260	48.46	3	9
GC Wilson	5	7	0	125	339	48.42	1	1
JHK Adams	16	29	1	196	1351	48.25	3	8
SD Peters	15	29	2	199	1296	48.00	3	7

BEST BOWLING AVERAGES

Player	M	O	Mdns	R	W	Ave	BB	5/inn	10m
SCJ Broad	2	66	7	299	19	15.73	8-52	2	1
JKH Naik	7	186	32	586	31	18.90	7-96	1	0
TS Roland-Jones	7	206.2	27	688	36	19.11	5-41	2	0
M Kartik	11	383.2	107	882	45	19.60	6-42	5	2
G Chapple	14	372.4	89	1027	52	19.75	5-27	2	0
M Ntini	5	164	44	474	24	19.75	6-51	2	1
RSC Martin-Jenkins	9	201.1	35	593	30	19.76	5-45	1	0
CD Collymore	14	414	115	1133	57	19.87	6-48	2	0
CT Tremlett	12	361.5	88	969	48	20.18	4-29	0	0
JAR Harris	13	443.4	115	1293	63	20.52	5-56	2	0
CW Henderson	16	489.3	136	1179	56	21.05	6-21	3	0
RJ Sidebottom	8	218	58	582	27	21.55	5-35	1	0
JM Anderson	4	130.5	39	345	16	21.56	6-44	1	0
CR Woakes	13	396.2	100	1165	54	21.57	6-52	3	1
J Allenby	16	330.1	82	885	41	21.58	5-59	1	0
AJ Ireland	8	222.5	33	784	36	21.77	5-25	2	0
DA Cosker	16	432	101	1128	51	22.11	5-93	1	0
NM Carter	11	356.2	70	1129	51	22.13	5-60	4	0
AR Adams	14	455.5	101	1508	68	22.17	6-79	4	0
G Keedy	7	246.5	43	688	31	22.19	7-68	2	1

For full scorecards and day-to-day match reports and details of every game played in the 2010 County Championship, and for full listings of averages and other statistical details, please go to **www.cricketarchive.com**

BEST INDIVIDUAL SCORES

Player	Score	For	Against	Venue
RWT Key	261	Kent	Durham	Canterbury
DJ Hussey	251*	Nottinghamshire	Yorkshire	Leeds
MR Ramprakash	248	Surrey	Northamptonshire	The Oval
SM Ervine	237*	Hampshire	Somerset	Southampton
JA Rudolph	228*	Yorkshire	Durham	Leeds
ME Trescothick	228*	Somerset	Essex	Colchester
MR Ramprakash	223	Surrey	Middlesex	The Oval
JWA Taylor	206*	Leicestershire	Middlesex	Leicester
CJL Rogers	200	Derbyshire	Surrey	The Oval
SD Peters	199	Northamptonshire	Middlesex	Lord's
DI Stevens	197	Kent	Nottinghamshire	Tunbridge Wells
JHK Adams	196	Hampshire	Yorkshire	Scarborough
JHK Adams	194	Hampshire	Lancashire	Liverpool
ME Trescothick	188*	Somerset	Kent	Canterbury
CD Nash	184	Sussex	Leicestershire	Leicester
SD Peters	183*	Northamptonshire	Middlesex	Northampton
JM Vince	180	Hampshire	Yorkshire	Scarborough
WL Madsen	179	Derbyshire	Northamptonshire	Northampton
MR Ramprakash	179	Surrey	Leicestershire	Leicester
GO Jones	178	Kent	Somerset	Canterbury

MOST RUNS

Player	County	Matches	Runs
MR Ramprakash	Surrey	16	1595
A Lyth	Yorkshire	16	1509
JC Hildreth	Somerset	16	1440
ME Trescothick	Somerset	16	1397
MA Carberry	Hampshire	16	1385
JA Rudolph	Yorkshire	16	1375
JHK Adams	Hampshire	16	1351
SD Peters	Northamptonshire	16	1320
CJL Rogers	Derbyshire	15	1285
MM Ali	Worcestershire/England Lions	16	1270
A McGrath	Yorkshire	16	1219
MW Goodwin	Sussex	16	1201
AN Kervezee	Worcestershire	16	1190
M van Jaarsveld	Kent	17	1188
MJ Cosgrove	Glamorgan	15	1187
DKH Mitchell	Worcestershire	16	1180
JWA Taylor	Leicestershire/England Lions	18	1095
MJ Di Venuto	Durham	16	1092
SM Davies	Surrey/England Lions	14	1090
IJL Trott	Warwickshire/England	12	1084

BEST INNINGS BOWLING (6 wickets or more)

Player	Analysis	For	Against	Venue
ST Finn	9-37	Middlesex	Worcestershire	Worcester
SCJ Broad	8-52	Nottinghamshire	Warwickshire	Birmingham
Imran Tahir	8-114	Warwickshire	Durham	Birmingham
JEC Franklin	7-14	Gloucestershire	Derbyshire	Bristol
JC Tredwell	7-22	Kent	Yorkshire	Leeds
SJ Harmison	7-29	Durham	Warwickshire	Chester-le-Street
Shakib Al Hasan	7-32	Worcestershire	Middlesex	Lord's
DS Harrison	7-45	Glamorgan	Worcestershire	Worcester
IE O'Brien	7-48	Middlesex	Gloucestershire	Lord's
G Keedy	7-68	Lancashire	Durham	Manchester
JA Tomlinson	7-85	Hampshire	Somerset	Taunton
JKH Naik	7-96	Leicestershire	Surrey	The Oval
RA Jones	7-115	Worcestershire	Sussex	Hove
CW Henderson	6-21	Leicestershire	Northamptonshire	Leicester
RA Jones	6-37	Worcestershire	Middlesex	Worcester
M Kartik	6-42	Somerset	Warwickshire	Birmingham
Shakib Al Hasan	6-42	Worcestershire	Surrey	Worcester
JM Anderson	6-44	Lancashire	Essex	Chelmsford
CD Collymore	6-48	Sussex	Leicestershire	Leicester
M Ntini	6-51	Kent	Durham	Chester-le-Street

MOST WICKETS

Player	County	Matches	Wickets
AR Adams	Nottinghamshire	14	68
GM Hussain	Gloucestershire	15	67
ST Finn	Middlesex/England	13	64
JAR Harris	Glamorgan/England Lions	14	63
CM Willoughby	Somerset	16	58
CR Woakes	Warwickshire/England Lions	14	58
CD Collymore	Sussex	14	57
AU Rashid	Yorkshire	16	57
Imran Tahir	Warwickshire	16	56
CW Henderson	Leicestershire	16	56
A Richardson	Worcestershire	14	55
J Lewis	Gloucestershire	16	54
DD Masters	Essex	14	53
G Chapple	Lancashire	14	52
MS Panesar	Sussex/England Lions	16	52
JW Dernbach	Surrey	15	51
DA Cosker	Glamorgan	16	51
RJ Peterson	Derbyshire	15	51
NM Carter	Warwickshire	11	51
MJ Hoggard	Leicestershire	15	50

MOST CATCHES (excluding wicketkeepers)

Player	County	Matches	Catches
M van Jaarsveld	Kent	16	35
DKH Mitchell	Worcestershire	16	32
MJ Di Venuto	Durham	16	29
ME Trescothick	Somerset	16	26
CDJ Dent	Gloucestershire	16	24
R Clarke	Warwickshire	15	23
AJ Hall	Northamptonshire	15	21
ND McKenzie	Hampshire	14	20
JA Rudolph	Yorkshire	16	20
DJG Sales	Northamptonshire	15	20
JC Tredwell	Kent	11	20
MAG Boyce	Leicestershire	14	19
JWM Dalrymple	Glamorgan	15	19
PJ Horton	Lancashire	16	19
DJ Malan	Middlesex	16	19
CJL Rogers	Derbyshire	15	19
VS Solanki	Worcestershire	15	18
JHK Adams	Hampshire	16	17
J Allenby	Glamorgan	16	16
APR Gidman	Gloucestershire	16	16

MOST DISMISSALS (wicketkeepers)

Player	County	Matches	Catches	Stumpings	Dismissals
CMW Read	Nottinghamshire	16	59	4	63
JN Batty	Gloucestershire	15	53	3	56
JS Foster	Essex	16	48	5	53
GO Jones	Kent	16	48	5	53
MA Wallace	Glamorgan	16	43	4	47
JA Simpson	Middlesex	16	42	2	44
TJ New	Leicestershire	16	42	1	43
P Mustard	Durham	16	40	2	42
LD Sutton	Lancashire	13	37	5	42
TR Ambrose	Warwickshire	11	33	3	36
N Pothas	Hampshire	9	33	0	33
BJM Scott	Worcestershire	7	30	1	31
SM Davies	Surrey	12	29	0	29
C Kieswetter	Somerset	12	29	0	29
AJ Hodd	Sussex	10	26	1	27
D Murphy	Northamptonshire	9	26	0	26
LJ Goddard	Derbyshire	8	24	0	24
JM Bairstow	Yorkshire	16	18	5	23
AM Bates	Hampshire	7	23	0	23
OB Cox	Worcestershire	9	18	1	19

CHRISTOPHER MARTIN-JENKINS, the *Test Match Special* commentator, outlines why he is passionate in his support of the county cricket festival week…

Why Cricket Festival Weeks Matter

Throughout this past year there has been much talk in official cricket circles of cutting down the amount of County Championship cricket from 2011. To my mind it has been foolish talk, for a number of reasons that include the uncertainty of the weather and the danger that festival cricket, the very essence of the county game, will become even rarer than it already is.

There was a time, and still is in the more enlightened counties, when the county coming to town was a big event, anticipated long in advance, relished while the cricket was in progress and reviewed with pleasure months later. Sometimes games are never forgotten, such as the one started and finished after a thunderstorm on the extraordinary opening day of the Tunbridge Wells week in 1960. Kent and Worcestershire began battle at 11.30 am, Kent reaching 80 for 4 by lunch before being bowled out for 187 at 3.40 pm. The left-handed Peter Jones made 73, very nearly as many as Worcestershire managed in their two innings of 25 and 61. Witnesses reported small craters appearing when the ball pitched, much to the liking of Kent's Dave Halfyard and Alan Brown, who took nine cheap wickets each. By 7.15 it was all over.

Every now and then freak events occur and pitches are not what they should be for top-class cricketers. They are the exceptions to the general rule that county cricket is better tuned to small, intimate grounds than it is to echoing

Watching county cricket at Arundel is always a pleasurable experience, especially when the sun is out and the clouds are white and fluffy.

caverns like The Oval or Edgbaston, places that come alive on the big international occasion but that too often seem glum and empty when they play host to the homespun atmosphere of the County Championship game.

County cricket flourishes, absorbs and excites in places such as Arundel and Abergavenny, Bath and Burton-on-Trent, Colchester and Colwyn Bay, Dover and Dudley, Eastbourne and Ebbw Vale. I shall not try to get to the end of the alphabet but there would not be many letters missing if I did. Many of the places that no longer get the chance to stage county cricket have quite beautiful grounds, and those that remain generally do so still.

The cricket is characterised by a strong local spirit, while players and spectators are brought close together to the

Top right Arundel's historic pavilion looks down on its beautiful surroundings from on top of a grassy bank.

All Saints Church stands guard over May's Bounty, the home of Basingstoke and North Hants Cricket Club and Hampshire's northern-most venue.

benefit of both. The surroundings, seldom far from a church or pub or both, are invariably adorned by old and beautiful trees that help the ball to swing, not to mention shortish boundaries that encourage bats to do the same. Good weather usually guarantees good-sized crowds and a precious amalgam of tension and relaxation.

We all know the reasons for the decrease in the number of festival games. All counties have more or less developed their main grounds, at an accelerated rate in recent years. Some have got into serious financial difficulties as a result. Once there has been investment at a county's headquarters it makes sense to use that ground as often as the number of pitches will sensibly allow. Overheads are less expensive that way.

The strong counter-arguments are that festival matches spread the gospel around the county, encourage local cricketers and cricket-watchers, make everyone feel part of the family of the game and give a focal point to the season for those clubs on whose grounds the county team comes to play. I know from the experience of my own local club, Horsham, how much that means to the members, many of

whom get involved year after year in the nitty-gritty of preparing the pitches, making the teas, watering the flower-baskets, erecting the tents that go up round the ground and organising the arrangements for dealing with an invasion of cars and spectators.

More than this, matches on out-grounds can still be great events for the town in question. I suppose I have been to one of these games without seeing the local mayor in attendance on one or other of the days but if so I cannot remember it. There always seems to be a large black car with a pennant billowing out from the bonnet parked in a position of prominence with a driver at the ready (albeit with an eye and a half on the cricket) to whisk the VIP back to the town hall after a good lunch.

At one match in Wales, in the glorious parkland setting of Pontypridd one wet day after play had been called off for the day and everyone had gone home, I promise you that the mayor went ahead with his prepared lunchtime speech from the balcony, like Hitler at the Nuremberg rally, even though the field in front of him was empty and the handful of people who could actually hear him were all standing behind him, most of them invited journalists anxious not to waste the chance of a drink and some free sandwiches. By the same token the mayor was not going to miss the opportunity to make a speech. 'I've prepared it, boy, so I'm damned well going to give it.'

It was, of course, at another mining town, Ebbw Vale, that Emrys Davies called his partner Gilbert Parkhouse across at the end of the over to tell him that he had just tapped down the pitch with his bat on a length and had a nasty surprise. 'I could have sworn I heard someone answering back from below,' he said.

The fact is that if towns, cricket clubs and county executives all co-operate and appreciate the possibilities of festival games, they will benefit everyone concerned. The local economy gets a boost from an influx of visitors, helping shops, pubs, hotels and garages amongst others; the county gets a guaranteed profit if its officials have negotiated sensibly; and the home club itself gets plenty back in bar takings and prestige.

For me the likes of Aigburth and Basingstoke, not to mention more established favourites such as Cheltenham and Scarborough and Tunbridge Wells, are quintessential settings for the county game. Like the Championship itself, the county festival weeks are a small but precious part of the English way of life.

GOOD NEWS FOR SCARBOROUGH

The future of Scarborough Cricket Club's festival week at their historic North Marine Road ground was secured in late August when they signed a ten-year staging agreement with Yorkshire to host ten days of county matches there annually until at least 2020.

Bill Mustoe, the Scarborough club chairman, said, 'The contract is for two County Championship games and two days of one-day cricket and that's wonderful news for everyone associated with cricket here at Scarborough – and for Yorkshire supporters too because they love coming here to watch their team play.

'Indeed, everyone loves coming to Scarborough – players, umpires and spectators alike. Scarborough is something special in English cricket, and people come back to watch the first-class game being played here year after year. We get excellent attendances for all matches, and many of the people who come back every year are bringing their children and their grandchildren with them.

'There is a unique atmosphere for cricket here, and a great illustration of why Scarborough is so popular was provided by this year's Clydesdale Bank 40 match against Middlesex. There were 6,500 people at the ground, they saw 500 runs scored on a superb cricket wicket – and Yorkshire won in the last over!'

Scarborough Cricket Club, with help from Yorkshire, the local tourist board and from the ECB through its NatWest Cricket Force initiative, have also done much in 2010 to smarten up the ground and improve the facilities.

'We had 350 people here working on NatWest Cricket Force day at the start of the season, painting and decorating and doing all sorts of jobs,' added Mustoe. 'And Mike Gatting, who is now the ECB's managing director of cricket partnerships, was among those who were here all day. Gatt was wielding his paint brush with the best of them!'

The College Ground at Cheltenham is one of England's best-attended annual county cricket festival week venues.

North Marine Road in Scarborough is a historic venue for Yorkshire's most popular cricket festival.

FRIENDS PROVIDENT t20

by Mark Baldwin

Twenty20 cricket, the cash cow of the English domestic game, was milked for all its worth in 2010. There were a total of 151 matches – 144 of them at the group stage – and gate receipts topped the £5 million mark, unsurprisingly the highest in the competition's nine-year history. Yet, despite 54 more matches being played than in 2009 (and in the previous two seasons, for that matter) the gate revenue collected by the 18 first-class counties did not rise in direct pro rata terms. And that, in essence, is the rub.

True, the destination of the trophy itself went down to the final ball of the very last game; with a youthful Hampshire side pipping favourites Somerset amid dramatic scenes on their home turf at the Rose Bowl. Finals Day itself, albeit with the advantage of Hampshire being involved, also attracted a capacity audience of 23,000 at what has become an excellent arena.

But, for players and spectators alike, the competition went on for far too long and the fixtures themselves were too tightly packed together. The players, straining to give of their very best, complained that tiredness and too many games diluted their ability to do so. As for the fans, they simply voted with their feet and with their wallets.

Some counties reported significant increases in attendance income. Middlesex, for instance, boosted by the imaginative recruitment of Adam Gilchrist, took £684,698 at the gate from a combined audience of 68,378 for their eight home matches – five of which were at Lord's. With their average ticket price down a pound from 2009 at £10, that still represented an increase of £173,321 on the previous year. Essex and Somerset, two counties who were able to sell to their public a successful team on the field, both did extremely well with total gate receipts of £549,000 and £327,000 respectively. That translated into a rise of £166,602 from 2009 for Essex, and £147,000 for Somerset.

Other clubs who will not be complaining at their levels of ticket sales income are Glamorgan and Sussex but too many counties saw either a miniscule rise in revenue (and, therefore, when taking into account the three extra home matches staged, a net reduction) or – in four cases – none at all. Yorkshire, Kent, Derbyshire and Hampshire actually took less on the gate than they had from three fewer home games in 2009. The biggest irony of the whole event, indeed, was that winners Hampshire saw overall ticket income from their home matches fall by a staggering £60,874 from the £291,468 they had banked from just five group games the previous summer.

In percentage terms, too, when the average amount of ticket revenue per game is compared with 2009, only two counties – Somerset and Glamorgan – managed an increase on 2009. Across the board, moreover, average gate receipts per game fell to £33,000 in 2010 compared to £42,600 in 2009 and £48,000 in 2008.

Adam Gilchrist hits out for Middlesex in the Friends Provident t20.

The statistics showing average gates per Twenty20 group game are also revealing: around 4,400 in 2010 but just over 5,000 in 2009 and almost 6,100 in 2008. Back in 2005, just under 6,350 people on average watched domestic Twenty20 before the knockout stage.

But perhaps the most damning evidence of the comparative fall in popularity of county Twenty20 matches over the past couple of years is the fact that no fewer than eight counties actually took less money at the gate in 2010 than in 2008 – despite having those three extra home fixtures. Remarkably, Surrey took £150,000 more in overall ticket sales in 2008 than they did last season.

Somerset, the only county to see both gate and ticket income rise year on year from 2008, even threatened to sue the England and Wales Cricket Board for compensation on the basis that they would suffer future loss of revenue if the number of Twenty20 group matches were reduced in 2011. Essex and Sussex both announced before the season's end that they also wanted to keep their eight home games, with Essex chairman Nigel Hilliard even coming up with a radical proposal aimed at meeting the differing views of all the county clubs on the issue (see page 78).

On the field, the clear front-runners throughout the bloated group stage, which began on 1 June and continued until 18 July – with, bizarrely, two County Championship rounds also being played during that period while a number of Twenty20 matches continued for the benefit of Sky Sports – were Warwickshire and Nottinghamshire in the North Division and Somerset and Essex in the South.

Sussex had started like a bullet from a gun in the southern section, but were going backwards at a rate of knots when they actually

---

Adam Gilchrist, Middlesex's star signing for their Friends Provident t20 campaign, earned £5,000 – to be donated to charity – after winning the Walter Lawrence Trophy for the fastest hundred of the summer.

Gilchrist, the fifth Australian in eleven seasons to win the award, hit a blistering 47-ball century, which included seven sixes and nine fours, in Middlesex's victory against Kent at Canterbury on 11 June.

It was Gilchrist's typically flamboyant reaction to taking over Middlesex's Twenty20 captaincy that day following Shaun Udal's resignation as club captain. He retired from international cricket in 2008, having played 96 Tests and 287 one-day internationals for Australia.

---

confirmed their qualification for the quarter-finals, while Hampshire just squeezed into the last eight, ahead on net run-rate of both Surrey and Middlesex, by beating Sussex at the Rose Bowl in their final group match. Neil McKenzie, with an unbeaten 67 in a challenging total of 195 for 5, led the way.

Both Warwickshire and Notts only lost four of their 16 group games in the northern division – a statistic bettering even southern winners Somerset – and Lancashire also qualified comfortably for the quarter-finals. Northamptonshire were the last team to earn their place in the 'elite' of eight, beating Durham by seven wickets on the final day of group matches while Derbyshire, their nearest challengers, went down at home to Yorkshire by six wickets in a game watched by little more than a thousand people despite ancillary attractions which included a falconry display, a craft fair and a children's water wheel.

By then the word overkill was being used even more regularly in relation to the competition than the various marketing slogans attempting to sell the t20 product, although in fairness there were decent crowds at three

Somerset captain Marcus Trescothick employs a reverse paddle sweep to keep the scoreboard ticking over.

Jimmy Adams reverse sweeps in Hampshire's semi-final victory against Essex at the Rose Bowl.

of the four quarter-final venues which saw Hampshire, Nottinghamshire, Somerset and Essex make it through to Finals Day.

The one poor attendance was at Edgbaston, where just 4,020 turned out to watch as Warwickshire were beaten by five wickets with just one ball remaining by Hampshire, for whom James Vince, 19, scored a mature and at times elegant 66 not out from 52 balls with two sixes and five fours.

At Trent Bridge, 8,558 witnessed the Nottinghamshire attack strangle the challenge of Sussex, the home side skilfully defending their moderate 20-over total of 141 for 9 to win by 13 runs.

The smaller and more intimate county grounds at Taunton and Chelmsford were full to see, respectively, Somerset's straightforward seven-wicket victory against Northants and Essex's thrilling run-chase to beat Lancashire. Mark Pettini, with 81 from 56 balls, and Matt Walker, with an unbeaten 74 from just 49, added 147 for the second wicket from only 93 balls to hunt down Lancashire's 183 for 6. Then, when Pettini was bowled by Sajid Mahmood, James Foster marched in to hit his first three balls for four.

On 14 August, a Finals Day which was often threatened by bad weather but which resulted in just the second semi-final being decided by Duckworth-Lewis, there was ultimate triumph for a Hampshire team which had opted to do without Kevin Pietersen – soon to leave the club – even though both Essex (with

Alastair Cook) and Nottinghamshire (with Stuart Broad and Graeme Swann) had included their England stars.

Hampshire overhauled Essex's 156 for 7 with four balls to spare in the first semi-final, Abdul Razzaq bludgeoning 44 to put into even sharper relief the failure of Dwayne Bravo to justify his one-off stint as Essex's overseas player – reportedly at a cost of £10,000 – with either bat or ball. Bravo had been called in because Scott Styris, one of the stars of Essex's qualification, was unavailable due to New Zealand commitments.

The second semi-final went, probably justly, to Somerset by the narrow margin of three runs on the Duckworth-Lewis calculations after rain had interrupted Nottinghamshire's chase at 117 for 4 from 13 overs of Somerset's 182 for 5. Kieron Pollard's spectacular leap at long-on to dismiss Samit Patel for 39, moments before the weather drove the players off, ended up as the key moment in a contest earlier dominated by the power of Marcus Trescothick, who hit 60 from 28 balls, and the precocious talent of 19-year-old Jos Buttler, whose unbeaten 55 from 23 balls included a last-over assault on Broad.

In the final itself, the 18-year-old slow left-arm spinner Danny Briggs again impressed for Hampshire – underlining the eye-catching contributions that a new generation of young English talent made to county cricket generally in 2010. Yet it was the oldest man on show, 39-year-old former England all-rounder Dominic Cork, who produced perhaps the turning point of the whole match as well as captaining Hampshire with verve and tenacity in the injury absence of Dimitri Mascarenhas.

Somerset, boosted initially by Craig Kieswetter's 71 and sustained further by a cameo 33 from Peter Trego, began the last over of their innings on 170 for 4 and, crucially, with the big-hitting West Indian giant Pollard at the crease and already warmed up with 22 to his name from a mere six balls faced. Cork, striving for extra effort, then sent down a superbly directed bouncer that clearly surprised Pollard for pace and slammed into the grille of his helmet as he missed a desperate hook at the ball. Sadly, it squeezed through the grille and felled Pollard, raising an ugly bruise around his left eye, which also rapidly began to close.

After receiving attention, with Cork the first to call for aid, Pollard was able to walk dazed from the field and thankfully an immediate check-up at a local hospital confirmed no lasting eye damage.

The blow, however, also stalled Somerset's planned big finish – especially with Pollard now out of action and later also unable to bowl his highly-effective medium-pacers – and only three runs in total were garnered from Cork's final over.

If Somerset had managed to get up above 180 for the second time in the day – which would surely have been possible had Pollard not been injured – then Hampshire's brave chase may well have come up short. As it was, with Razzaq hitting 33 and Jimmy Adams – the tournament's leading run-scorer – contributing another useful 34, the Hampshire bid for glory was then led at the death by McKenzie, with 52, and Sean Ervine, who finished on 44 not out.

But no one could have predicted the whole drama of the finish, shortly before 11 pm, with Dan Christian scrambling a leg bye to level the scores and give Hampshire their first Twenty20 Cup trophy by virtue of losing fewer wickets. Christian had called for a runner before the final delivery was bowled by Zander de Bruyn, after pulling a hamstring, but in the frenzied excitement of the situation Christian had also sprinted down the pitch for the leg bye as well as Adams, his runner.

If Somerset's players had realised it, they could have run out Christian by removing the bails at the striker's end. As he had a runner, Christian should not have left his crease. But, as the umpires waited to see what happened, and as the other Hampshire players ran on to the field in jubilation but then stopped short as they wondered what Somerset would do, Trescothick and his team did nothing.

The umpires then removed the stumps and the Hampshire celebrations really could begin. As Trescothick said later, 'We had the game if we'd known it, but we clearly just did not think at the end there.'

Neither Hampshire nor Somerset, meanwhile, as the two qualifying finalists, were permitted by the ECB to take part in the Champions League, held in South Africa in September 2010, due to a clash with the end of the English domestic season that should have been avoided by all parties. Like the overcrowded and confused scheduling of the 2010 Twenty20 Cup itself, that is something that must never be allowed to happen again.

North Division Final Table

	P	W	T	L	NR	A	AT	Adj	Pts	NetRR
Warwickshire	16	11	0	4	1	0	0	0	23	0.403
Nottinghamshire	16	10	2	4	0	0	0	0	22	0.640
Lancashire	16	9	0	6	1	0	0	0	19	0.479
Northamptonshire	16	7	3	6	0	0	0	0	17	-0.160
Derbyshire	16	6	0	8	2	0	0	0	14	-0.151
Yorkshire	16	6	1	9	0	0	0	0	13	-0.121
Leicestershire	16	6	0	9	0	1	0	0	13	-0.234
Durham	16	4	0	8	2	1	1	0	12	-0.296
Worcestershire	16	5	0	10	0	0	1	0	11	-0.653

South Division Final Table

	P	W	T	L	NR	A	AT	Adj	Pts	NetRR
Somerset	16	11	0	5	0	0	0	0	22	0.418
Essex	16	10	0	6	0	0	0	0	20	0.395
Sussex	16	9	0	7	0	0	0	0	18	0.606
Hampshire	16	8	0	8	0	0	0	0	16	0.385
Surrey	16	8	0	8	0	0	0	0	16	0.183
Middlesex	16	8	0	8	0	0	0	0	16	0.018
Kent	16	7	0	9	0	0	0	0	14	-0.163
Glamorgan	16	6	0	10	0	0	0	0	12	-0.979
Gloucestershire	16	5	0	11	0	0	0	0	10	-0.943

Quarter-finals

26 July
Day/Night at Trent Bridge
Nottinghamshire 141 for 9 (20 overs) (Yasir Arafat 4 for 34)
Sussex 128 for 7 (20 overs) (DJ Pattinson 3 for 17)
Nottinghamshire won by 13 runs

at Edgbaston
Warwickshire 153 for 5 (20 overs) (DL Maddy 44, DR Briggs 3 for 29)
Hampshire 154 for 5 (19.5 overs) (JM Vince 66*)
Hampshire won by 5 wickets

Kieron Pollard, Somerset's West Indian all-rounder, is felled by a Dominic Cork bouncer in the FP t20 final.

27 July
Day/Night at Chelmsford
Lancashire 183 for 6 (20 overs) (PJ Horton 44,
CJC Wright 4 for 25)
Essex 184 for 2 (19.1 overs) (ML Pettini 81, MJ Walker 74*)
Essex won by 8 wickets

at Taunton
Northamptonshire 112 for 6 (20 overs) (SD Peters 40*)
Somerset 115 for 3 (17 overs)
Somerset won by 7 wickets

Semi-finals

14 August
at the Rose Bowl
Essex 156 for 7 (20 overs) (ML Pettini 55, DR Briggs 3 for 29)
Hampshire 157 for 4 (19.2 overs) (Abdul Razzaq 44)
Hampshire won by 6 wickets

at the Rose Bowl
Somerset 182 for 5 (20 overs) (ME Trescothick 60,
JC Buttler 55*)
Nottinghamshire 117 for 4 (13 overs)
Somerset won by 3 runs – DL Method: target 121 from 13 overs

FRIENDS PROVIDENT WINNERS 2010

FINAL – HAMPSHIRE v. SOMERSET
14 August 2010 at the Rose Bowl

SOMERSET

ME Trescothick (capt)	c Christian b Abdul Razzaq	19
*C Kieswetter	c Carberry b Christian	71
PD Trego	c Ervine b Briggs	33
JC Hildreth	c Christian b Abdul Razzaq	12
JC Buttler	c Vince b Cork	5
KA Pollard	retired hurt	22
Z de Bruyn	not out	0
AV Suppiah	c Bates b Cork	0
BJ Phillips	not out	0
AC Thomas		
M Kartik		
Extras	lb 1, w 8, nb 2	11
	(6 wkts 20 overs)	**173**

	O	M	R	W
Cork	4	0	24	2
Wood	4	0	51	0
Abdul Razzaq	4	0	37	2
Christian	4	0	30	1
Briggs	4	0	30	1

Fall of Wickets

1-41, 2-97, 3-145, 4-149, 5-173, 6-173

HAMPSHIRE

JHK Adams	b Suppiah	34
Abdul Razzaq	c Kieswetter b Trego	33
JM Vince	run out (Hildreth/Kieswetter)	0
ND McKenzie	c Trescothick b Phillips	52
SM Ervine	not out	44
MA Carberry	c Kieswetter b Phillips	0
DT Christian	not out	3
DG Cork (capt)		
CP Wood		
*AM Bates		
DR Briggs		
Extras	b 2, lb 4, w 1	7
	(5 wkts 20 overs)	**173**

	O	M	R	W
Thomas	4	0	23	0
Phillips	4	0	44	2
de Bruyn	3	0	29	0
Trego	4	0	38	1
Kartik	4	0	27	0
Suppiah	1	0	6	1

Fall of Wickets

1-60, 2-62, 3-84, 4-163, 5-164

Umpires: RJ Bailey & RK Illingworth
Toss: Somerset
Man of the Match: ND McKenzie

Hampshire won – having lost fewer wickets

Hampshire, a potent mix of spirited youth and gnarled experience, joyously lift the Friends Provident t20 trophy.

Average Gates per Game – Twenty20 Cup, 2008-2010

County	2008	2009	2010
Derbyshire	3,049	2,183	1,757
Durham	3,460	3,257	3,906
Essex	5,282	5,550	4,552
Glamorgan	4,447	2,740	3,955
Gloucestershire	3,012	3,701	2,483
Hampshire	8,115	5,526	4,204
Kent	4,197	3,917	3,091
Lancashire	7,675	4,412	4,346
Leicestershire	2,931	3,256	2,157
Middlesex	10,539	9,233	8,547
Northamptonshire	3,541	3,760	2,740
Nottinghamshire	8,773	6,744	6,204
Somerset	4,131	5,536	6,160
Surrey	15,791	10,787	8,415
Sussex	5,599	4,423	5,257
Warwickshire	7,959	5,962	3,899
Worcestershire	3,936	3,263	2,282
Yorkshire	6,123	5,216	4,896

Average Gate Receipts per Game – Twenty20 Cup, 2008-2010 (in £)

County	2008	2009	2010
Derbyshire	21,234	20,034	8,769
Durham	27,576	27,119	18,215
Essex	77,840	76,479	68,625
Glamorgan	17,021	14,297	21,276
Gloucestershire	32,379	24,685	15,980
Hampshire	51,063	58,293	28,824
Kent	38,482	48,806	28,271
Lancashire	56,001	52,422	33,607
Leicestershire	12,642	13,258	8,431
Middlesex	132,471	102,275	85,587
Northamptonshire	26,893	23,067	15,544
Nottinghamshire	47,084	31,021	24,533
Somerset	25,000	36,000	40,875
Surrey	166,880	114,423	85,139
Sussex	54,020	40,020	35,012
Warwickshire	51,387	33,630	23,239
Worcestershire	21,190	34,054	22,811
Yorkshire	38,463	42,847	25,766

TWENTY20 CUP – THE DEBATE

Before the decision on its long-term future was deferred following the end of the 2010 season, the arguments both for and against maintaining a bigger and longer group stage were neatly summed up by the following two articles published on the countycricketextra.com website last summer:

In Favour of an Expanded t20

Gloucestershire chief executive Tom Richardson has joined his Somerset counterpart Richard Gould in coming out against any plan to reduce the number of Twenty20 matches next season.

Gould has slammed suggestions that it might be timely to reduce the number of group matches from 16 to ten, stressing the massive effect that would have on his club's finances. And, while Gloucestershire do not attract the 5,000-plus crowds who regularly watch 20-over cricket at Taunton, Richardson is equally convinced that it would be a mistake to radically change the current format. Instead, he believes the 16 group matches should be spread over a longer period and played on either Friday evenings or Sunday afternoons.

'There were a number of factors affecting attendances this summer,' said Richardson. "The football World Cup hampered us to an extent and reduced the size of our crowds on a number of occasions. It was hopeless trying to compete with it.

'Secondly, it was attempted to play too many fixtures in too short a period of time. At one point we had three game in four days, a floodlit match away to Essex, which meant the team getting back at 2.30 in the morning, followed by Somerset at home the next day.

'That was on a Friday and we also played on the Sunday against Surrey, which was manifestly ridiculous. The players couldn't perform to the best of their ability because they were tired and for a club like us with a relatively small squad it was very difficult.

'There is a lot of talk about reducing the number of games. But before we go down that route we should go back to the original concept, which was fixtures on a Friday evening or a Sunday, once a week and the tournament played over six to eight weeks.

'I would like to see that tested before we have yet another change. It may be that we are playing too much, but logically let's see how the programme works if we extend the amount of time allocated to it.' (continues overleaf)

The Best Twenty20 XI of the Season

Cricket Year commissioned a selection panel of its writers on English domestic cricket – Paul Bolton, Tim Wellock, Richard Latham, Richard Thomas and Mark Baldwin – to come up with their best Twenty20 XI, chosen from those who played in the Friends Provident t20 in 2010.

Marcus Trescothick was the only player chosen by all five writers and, with honourable mentions for Danny Briggs of Hampshire and Samit Patel of Nottinghamshire, the following XI (containing two overseas players as per t20 rules) was selected:

1 Marcus Trescothick (Somerset)
2 Jimmy Adams (Hampshire)
3 Matt Prior (Sussex, wkt)
4 Ravi Bopara (Essex)
5 David Hussey (Nottinghamshire, capt)
6 Kieron Pollard (Somerset)
7 Ryan ten Doeschate (Essex)
8 Adil Rashid (Yorkshire)
9 Alfonso Thomas (Somerset)
10 Robert Croft (Glamorgan)
11 Chris Tremlett (Surrey)

HILLIARD'S RADICAL TWENTY20 CUP PLAN
by Paul Hiscock

Fierce debate took place between all 18 first-class counties before a decision on the future of the Twenty20 competition was deferred until 2011. There was a clear divide between those who wanted to retain the increased number of matches played in the 2010 competition and others who were against such a heavy schedule and correspondingly wanted the number of matches reduced.

Those in favour of retaining the increased schedule cited the extra income that it has brought in while others took the opposite view and argued that they only generated the same revenue for eight home matches last summer as from the five matches in previous seasons.

On 17 August, and then again in both September and October, the England and Wales Cricket Board deferred a decision on whether to cut the number of matches in the Friends Provident t20 for 2011, following hard lobbying from three of the so-called smaller counties. Essex, Somerset and Sussex wanted to retain the increased number of group games and, during the ensuing debate, Essex chairman Nigel Hilliard came up with a suggested formula to satisfy all parties.

'We proposed one league of eight teams that would play 14 group matches and two leagues of five teams playing eight matches in the initial stage,' he explained at the time.

'That would give seven home games and seven away games for the likes of Essex, Somerset and Sussex, while the Test match grounds would have fewer games, which is what they appear to want... The top four in the league of eight and the top two in the leagues of five would play in the quarter-finals, and I think that would create the level of competition that is required.

'There is certainly support from Somerset and Sussex but we have to ascertain whether there is support beyond that. Clearly, having put the proposals forward, we are interested to see how many counties would be interested in playing in the group of eight.'

Essex attracted capacity crowds to many of their fixtures in 2010 and the potential loss of income from a reduced number of Twenty20 home matches was a great concern to Hilliard. 'There is no other revenue stream for us that brings in anything like the numbers that Twenty20 does,' he said. 'We felt as though we have done really well but that we were going to be penalised for it... We take a total of £90,000 net of VAT from one night of Twenty20 cricket, adding other income to gate receipts, and we don't take that in three years of County Championship cricket at Chelmsford. That's quite a startling statistic.

'At Essex, we were fortunate in 2010 because we had ten Twenty20 home matches. We had eight in the group stage

of the Friends Provident t20, plus a home quarter-final tie and an additional Twenty20 match against Pakistan.

'We are basically looking at a reduction of as much as £450,000 in gate and other revenue net of VAT if we go back to just five home Twenty20 fixtures in a season and you simply can't replace that sort of income in any other way in this current economic environment.'

Furthermore, Hilliard pulled no punches regarding the consequences of any significantly reduced income, were that to happen. 'Clearly we would have to look at our budgets because we would have that much less money,' he added. 'If we went down to five matches we would have to make people redundant. There would be no other way of dealing with it. What we were talking about was reducing the one element of our cricket that gets people in the ground.'

TWENTY20 CUP – THE DEBATE (continued)

Against an Expanded t20

Paul Sheldon, Surrey's long-serving chief executive, has called on English cricket to grasp 'the opportunity' for success that he believes domestic Twenty20 still possesses despite a general fall in attendances in 2010. Sheldon was speaking ahead of Surrey's Friends Provident t20 London derby clash against Middlesex at the Brit Oval on 8 July, for which 16,000 advance tickets had been sold. That meant that the biggest crowd for this year's competition was expected, when 'walk-up' sales were added.

'Our crowds for this year's Friends Provident t20 have been generally disappointing with total numbers for the eight home games being the same as to those for five home games in 2009', said Sheldon.

'The crowd for the Middlesex match, though, shows that the appetite for Twenty20 cricket is very much alive and well. However, it only attracts this level of interest if it is put on against local opposition, at the right time of day and on a Thursday or Friday night. Good weather is a great bonus, and the football World Cup has not helped.

'We have evidence that the number of matches in this year's competition has not increased interest. We are strongly in favour of creating an enhanced competition, in a concentrated period of three to four weeks, involving both England and overseas players.

'As finances come under further pressure, this is an opportunity we have to grasp. We simply have to find solutions to the problems which are preventing it happening.'

Sheldon also expressed his dissatisfaction with the punishing schedule imposed on Surrey Lions players throughout the tournament, adding, 'The competition has been very frenetic with players dashing around the country in very, very short order.

'At one stage, we played a four-day match against Derbyshire and then had to start an FPt20 match back at the Brit Oval less than 24 hours later. The time for preparation has really been foreshortened.'

Sheldon added, during an interview on Surrey TV, 'We are looking for a shorter, punchier competition. The quality needs to be stronger and the quantity fewer.'

FRIENDS PROVIDENT t20 FEATURES 2010

MOST RUNS

Player	M	I	NO	HS	R	Ave	100	50	SR
JHK Adams	19	19	2	101*	668	39.29	2	2	132.27
ME Trescothick	19	19	1	83	572	31.77	0	6	157.14
MJ Cosgrove	16	16	0	89	562	35.12	0	4	132.23
TC Smith	17	17	2	92*	543	36.20	0	3	119.60
DJ Hussey	17	17	5	81*	524	43.66	0	3	142.00
RS Bopara	16	16	2	105*	473	33.78	1	2	128.88
JEC Franklin	15	15	3	90	470	39.16	0	2	130.19
SM Ervine	19	19	6	74*	470	36.15	0	3	146.41
AD Hales	18	18	2	83	466	29.12	0	4	135.86
JC Hildreth	19	19	5	77*	459	32.78	0	2	110.60
SR Patel	18	18	2	63	459	28.68	0	3	133.04
DL Maddy	17	17	3	88	456	32.57	0	1	132.55
WJ Durston	16	15	3	111	445	37.08	1	2	129.36
HH Gibbs	15	15	3	101*	443	36.91	1	2	148.16
MJ Prior	14	14	1	117	443	34.07	1	2	169.08
ND McKenzie	17	17	6	73	440	40.00	0	5	123.94
BJ Hodge	15	15	0	103	431	28.73	1	2	124.20

BEST BATTING STRIKE RATE

Player	County	Matches	Strike Rate
SI Mahmood	Lancashire	15	190.90
RN ten Doeschate	Essex	6	177.24
KA Pollard	Somerset	17	175.24
LRPL Taylor	Durham	11	173.07
GK Berg	Middlesex	14	170.21
MJ Prior	Sussex	14	169.08
SM Davies	Surrey	13	162.08
SB Styris	Essex	15	161.98
JC Buttler	Somerset	19	160.00
ST Jayasuriya	Worcestershire	10	158.92
ME Trescothick	Somerset	19	157.14
A Lyth	Yorkshire	10	156.55
AC Gilchrist	Middlesex	7	153.62
SC Moore	Lancashire	17	152.53
A Symonds	Surrey	15	152.02
WTS Porterfield	Gloucestershire	13	151.83
TL Maynard	Glamorgan	16	150.19

MOST BOUNDARIES

Player	County	Matches	Fours	Sixes	Boundaries
JHK Adams	Hampshire	19	78	17	95
ME Trescothick	Somerset	19	72	22	94
MJ Cosgrove	Glamorgan	16	65	14	79
MJ Prior	Sussex	14	53	18	71
AD Hales	Nottinghamshire	18	58	12	70
DL Maddy	Warwickshire	17	46	18	64
SR Patel	Nottinghamshire	18	47	16	63
TC Smith	Lancashire	17	53	10	63
RS Bopara	Essex	16	46	16	62
SM Ervine	Hampshire	19	49	12	61
SM Davies	Surrey	13	47	13	60
LL Bosman	Derbyshire	15	46	13	59
HH Gibbs	Yorkshire	15	43	16	59
BJ Hodge	Leicestershire	15	50	7	57
WPUJC Vaas	Northamptonshire	17	45	11	56
WTS Porterfield	Gloucestershire	13	42	13	55
WJ Durston	Derbyshire	16	42	13	55

MOST SIXES

Player	County	Matches	Sixes
KA Pollard	Somerset	17	29
SB Styris	Essex	15	24
LRPL Taylor	Durham	11	23
ME Trescothick	Somerset	19	22
TL Maynard	Glamorgan	16	20
RN ten Doeschate	Essex	6	19
DJ Hussey	Nottinghamshire	17	19
MJ Prior	Sussex	14	18
DL Maddy	Warwickshire	17	18
JHK Adams	Hampshire	19	17
ST Jayasuriya	Worcestershire	10	16
HH Gibbs	Yorkshire	15	16
SR Patel	Nottinghamshire	18	16
RS Bopara	Essex	16	16
A Symonds	Surrey	15	15
WI Jefferson	Leicestershire	13	15
DJ Malan	Middlesex	16	15

MOST WICKETS

Player	M	O	Mdns	R	W	Ave	BB	4wI
AC Thomas	19	72.5	3	460	33	13.93	3-11	0
DR Briggs	19	67	0	445	31	14.35	3-5	0
KA Pollard	17	58.2	0	438	29	15.10	4-15	1
SD Parry	17	60	0	427	26	16.42	4-28	1
AU Rashid	16	61	0	428	26	16.46	4-20	1
CT Tremlett	16	60	1	411	24	17.12	3-17	0
WPUJC Vaas	17	57.3	0	364	23	15.82	3-16	0
SI Mahmood	15	53	0	430	23	18.69	4-21	1
RDB Croft	16	57.5	0	343	22	15.59	3-19	0
KHD Barker	14	48.3	0	350	21	16.66	4-19	1
RM Pyrah	16	58	0	408	21	19.42	3-12	0
SJ Cook	16	57	1	413	21	19.66	3-13	0
CJC Wright	18	66	0	609	21	29.00	4-25	1
DJ Pattinson	15	50	1	353	20	17.65	4-19	1
Imran Tahir	17	61	1	401	20	20.05	3-14	0
CP Wood	19	65.1	1	551	20	27.55	3-27	0
BJ Phillips	18	60	1	466	19	24.52	3-33	0

BEST BOWLING ECONOMY RATE

Player	County	Matches	Economy Rate
MH Yardy	Sussex	8	5.48
RDB Croft	Glamorgan	16	5.93
JA Brooks	Northamptonshire	14	6.25
AC Thomas	Somerset	19	6.31
WPUJC Vaas	Northamptonshire	17	6.33
SA Piolet	Warwickshire	7	6.33
JD Middlebrook	Northamptonshire	17	6.35
NM Carter	Warwickshire	17	6.38
SR Patel	Nottinghamshire	18	6.50
NL McCullum	Lancashire	13	6.50
Imran Tahir	Warwickshire	17	6.57
M Kartik	Somerset	17	6.59
SC Kerrigan	Lancashire	12	6.60
DG Cork	Hampshire	19	6.61
DR Briggs	Hampshire	19	6.64
GR Breese	Durham	15	6.75
AG Botha	Warwickshire	17	6.83

VIKRAM SOLANKI, the Worcestershire and England batsman and chairman of the Professional Cricketers' Association, gives his verdict on the Friends Provident t20…

Domestic Twenty20 needs Quality not Quantity

Domestic Twenty20 cricket last summer was still at its knockout stage when the England and Wales Cricket Board began canvassing opinion on whether the new format in 2010 was a success or not. As part of the review process, at the request of the ECB, the Professional Cricketers' Association conducted a survey of all players who played in last season's t20 and the general consensus seemed to be that the emphasis should be on quality rather than quantity.

The view of the players, speaking purely from a cricketing perspective, was that it has been a tough season. County cricket has always placed demands on players but this year the schedule was particularly arduous. The increase in the number of t20 matches did not allow players to prepare as well as they might, or to get the necessary rest and recovery to be in prime condition for games.

From a commercial perspective, counties also apparently experienced mixed fortunes as a result of the increased number of matches – all of which perhaps suggests that the product may not be as vibrant and as appealing to the public as it could be. That said, it must also be noted that some counties bucked the trend and made significant gains by staging a greater number of home matches.

There are obvious arguments for the schedule to be arranged in a way that allows players adequate time to prepare according to the format of the next match. But preparation time was difficult for most teams with a number of County Championship

Above Mark Pettini, of Essex, looks shattered after being dismissed in the t20 semi-final against Hampshire.

Below and opposite Thrills, spills and flying bails, but more t20 matches did not mean more revenue for many county clubs in 2010.

The player dugouts are now an integral feature of domestic Twenty20 cricket in England.

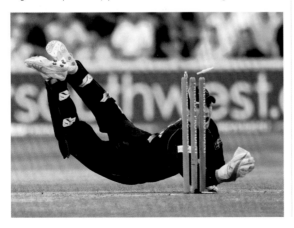

matches played during the period allocated for the t20. As a result, teams were in a situation where they played a t20 match one day, travelled to the next location (sometimes arriving late), and commenced a Championship match the following morning.

It is difficult adapting between different formats with such a quick turnaround between matches and no time to prepare appropriately. To some extent that is the nature of county cricket, but last season was a particularly difficult one in this regard. The previously planned involvement of English teams in the Champions League, which shortened the season and created a situation compounded by the increased number of matches, also contributed to the inevitable consequence of a tougher schedule.

It is not part of the PCA's remit to propose a structure for future seasons. However, we have a responsibility to ensure players' views are represented and fed into any mechanism making decisions on such matters, and therefore we have carried out extensive research of their opinions. There is no doubt the general consensus among players is that there is too much t20 being played and that the schedule needs to be smarter. On a positive note, meanwhile, it seems likely that the Champions League will be rescheduled to suit all parties, which should give the fixture planners more flexibility.

Fewer games and a longer season ought to provide for a more balanced schedule. Like many cricket discussions of recent times, the topic of our domestic structure is a complex one. It is one where cricketing imperatives are sometimes viewed as being in conflict with commercial viability and vice versa. Resolution of the debate lies in establishing that these are not mutually exclusive concepts but vital ingredients to ensure the longevity and future success of our game.

A version of this article first appeared on testmatchextra.com.

CLYDESDALE BANK 40

by Mark Baldwin

Warwickshire, a team who have lost just three games of 40-over cricket in the last two seasons, overcame a shattered Somerset at Lord's to win a cup final that became a showpiece for the batting mastery of Ian Bell and the leg-spin variations of Imran Tahir.

Those two players beat Somerset virtually by themselves in the first domestic final of its kind to be played in a day-night format, leaving Marcus Trescothick's band of West Countrymen – local and naturalised – to reflect on a summer that had seen them become the most unfortunate of bridesmaids in all three competitions.

It was sunny and bright despite the 18 September dateline, though distinctly chilly later on as the floodlights illuminated a ground less than half-full. A combination of the late date in the calendar, the scheduled finishing time of around 9 pm (and thus accompanying travel problems getting home for both sets of supporters) and the ridiculously short gap (five working days) between the semi-finals and the final meant it was actually something of a miracle that 13,000 turned up.

Imran Tahir has just trapped Somerset's Nick Compton lbw and runs away in celebration, chased by his Warwickshire teammates Ian Bell (right) and Jonathan Trott. Leg spinner Tahir and batsman Bell, also captain of his county for the match, were the heroes of Warwickshire's Clydesdale Bank 40 final triumph at Lord's.

More runs for Ian Bell, who guided his Warwickshire team to their three-wicket victory with a brilliant 107.

At the end of a season when the congested and almost unintelligible fixture list brought the England and Wales Cricket Board so much well-deserved criticism, it would also be interesting to hear what Clydesdale Bank, as new sponsors of the domestic game, thought of having their big day so devalued.

Bell's exquisite batting, however, and the skill and *joie de vivre* of Tahir's contribution – after his first wicketless four-over spell had gone for 27 runs – at least brought a true world-class sheen to proceedings out in the middle. Somerset, having been 176 for 3 with nine overs of their innings still to be bowled, will feel they threw the game away, and yet they still had their chances in the field and can be proud of the determination they showed to make Warwickshire, and Bell, fight hard for victory.

It was a mystery to most Somerset supporters why Charl Willoughby, their redoubtable new ball bowler in County Championship cricket, was not asked to send down just eight more overs at the season's end. The 35-year-old left-armer might have been tired after a long season – hey, they were all tired – but were not Somerset just desperate to win something after being denied both the county title and the Twenty20 crown by a hair's breadth?

With all-rounder Zander de Bruyn already absent after being allowed back to South Africa to play for the Lions in the Champions League – again, with so much at stake, why? – Somerset's bowling line-up was worryingly thin and short of depth. Mark Turner, at best, is only an impact bowler in one-day cricket and should not be depended upon to bowl his full quota of overs. Yet, in this Somerset line-up, only the rarely used slow left-arm spinners of Arul Suppiah provided a sixth bowler option.

Warwickshire, moreover, had not just Bell in their side as he continued his impressive comeback from the foot injury suffered on England duty in mid-summer, but also Jonathan Trott – given special permission by England's management to take time out between matches in the one-day series against Pakistan to play in the game.

Ashley Giles, Warwickshire's director of cricket, said afterwards that his side – led by Bell after Ian Westwood had lost his one-day place – had arrived at Lord's in a confident frame of mind after a successful month in which they had hauled themselves up out of the Championship's Division One relegation places with a run of wins.

On the previous Saturday they had also made a fine job of chasing down Yorkshire's 257 for 5 in the semi-final at Scarborough, reaching a slightly-adjusted Duckworth-Lewis target of 257 from 37 overs following a short rain shower with something to spare. Varun Chopra had stroked 76, an innings not enough to save his place for the final when Trott returned, and Bell a composed 57, which provided mid-innings acceleration at just the right time.

Somerset, before their Championship heartbreak up at Durham, had battered Essex in the other semi-final at Taunton. Trescothick had opened up with 79 from 62 balls and Nick Compton had made 55 in a formidable 40-over total of 312 for 6. In reply, despite 58 from James Foster, Essex had crumbled to 217 all out.

And, for the first three-quarters of their innings at Lord's, it looked as if Somerset's batting strength would bring them another challenging total. But then came Tahir's remarkable spell of 5 for 14 in four overs as Somerset imploded from 176 for 3 to 199 all out. In the end, they did not even use up their allocation of overs.

James Hildreth had joined Compton in a third wicket stand of 95 that had been notable for its running between the wickets. Then, however, Compton pushed Tahir into the off side and called Hildreth for an unrealistic single. Trott picked up smartly and threw to the keeper's end and Hildreth was run out for 44. Little did Somerset realise how significant that misjudgement would prove to be.

Two balls later, Jos Buttler propped forward and played across a straight ball from Tahir and was palpably leg-before. In the leg spinner's next over, Suppiah yorked himself as he danced down the pitch to drive and Compton was struck on the pad playing back to a top-spinner, having made 60 from 65 balls.

With stunning suddenness, the guts had been torn out of a Somerset innings that had looked on course for at least 230 – if not 240 – and Tahir celebrated each wicket of his game-turning spell with increasing exuberance. Ben Phillips was caught at cover and Murali Kartik smartly stumped after overbalancing as he tried to flick at a ball spinning outside the left-hander's pads.

A total of 199 was seriously sub-par but, to their credit, Somerset came out fighting. Phillips delivered a magnificent eight-over, new-ball spell, in which he

removed Neil Carter to a flail to third man and Trott to the ball of the match, a perfectly pitched leg-cutter that only a top-class batsman would have touched on its way through to the keeper. With Alfonso Thomas dismissing Keith Barker, Warwickshire slid to 39 for 3 and Somerset had their major opportunity. At the very least they had to heap the pressure on Bell, still new to the crease, and Jim Troughton.

But Trescothick naively opted to keep Turner in the attack and his second over went for 12 runs – relieving the pressure far too easily. Too late, the Somerset skipper called up Kartik, his chief spin weapon, but Bell and Troughton were now more than content merely to keep the Indian left-arm spinner at bay and take no risks against him. Kartik was then kept on too long, and Suppiah's spin option was given just one exploratory over.

Despite the manful efforts of Thomas, who removed Troughton for 30 to keep Somerset hopes alive, and Kartik in a tight short second spell, Somerset predictably ran out of quality bowling resources as Bell ignored the wickets still falling around him and guided his team towards their target. Rikki Clarke made a run-a-ball 19, before brainlessly swinging high to long on at the start of the four-over batting power play, but Ant Botha hung around with Bell. With three overs remaining, Warwickshire still needed 22, but Bell seized the moment, mercilessly attacking the pacy but erratic

Warwickshire's players and coaching staff celebrate winning the 2010 Clydesdale Bank 40 trophy.

Turner to take 20 from the 38th over and put the outcome beyond doubt. When he hit a full-pitched ball from Thomas straight to mid-off with the scores level, Bell had made 107 from 95 balls, and he had led his side to victory with immense composure and control. Two balls later, Chris Woakes sliced Thomas over cover and Warwickshire had won by three wickets with an over to spare.

Warwickshire had qualified by heading Group C, one of three groups of seven – the 18 first-class counties were augmented by Holland, Scotland and the Unicorns,

Group A Final Table

	P	W	T	L	NR	A	AT	Adj	Pts	NetRR
Somerset	12	10	0	2	0	0	0	0	20	1.491
Sussex	12	7	1	3	0	1	0	0	16	0.903
Surrey	12	6	1	4	0	1	0	0	14	-0.006
Lancashire	12	6	0	6	0	0	0	0	12	-0.315
Worcestershire	12	4	0	8	0	0	0	0	8	-0.196
Unicorns	12	3	0	7	0	1	1	0	8	-0.470
Glamorgan	12	2	0	8	0	1	1	-1	5	-1.585

Group B Final Table

	P	W	T	L	NR	A	AT	Adj	Pts	NetRR
Yorkshire	12	10	0	2	0	0	0	0	20	0.384
Essex*	12	9	0	2	0	1	0	0	19	0.314
Gloucestershire	12	9	0	3	0	0	0	0	18	0.659
Derbyshire	12	4	0	8	0	0	0	0	8	-0.037
Northamptonshire	12	4	0	8	0	0	0	0	8	-0.038
Middlesex	12	3	0	7	1	1	0	0	8	-0.445
Netherlands	12	1	0	10	1	0	0	0	3	-0.999

Group C Final Table

	P	W	T	L	NR	A	AT	Adj	Pts	NetRR
Warwickshire	12	9	0	3	0	0	0	0	18	0.314
Kent	12	7	0	3	1	1	0	0	16	0.773
Nottinghamshire	12	7	0	4	1	0	0	0	15	0.348
Hampshire	12	6	0	6	0	0	0	0	12	0.006
Durham	12	5	0	6	0	1	0	0	11	0.262
Leicestershire	12	4	0	8	0	0	0	0	8	-0.220
Scotland	12	2	0	10	0	0	0	0	4	-1.225

* Essex qualified for the semi-finals as the best second-placed team

Semi-finals

11 September
at Taunton
Somerset 312 for 6 (40 overs) (ME Trescothick 79, NRD Compton 55)
Essex 217 all out (29.3 overs) (JS Foster 58)
Somerset won by 95 runs

at Scarborough
Yorkshire 257 for 5 (37 overs) (JA Rudolph 106, GL Brophy 64)
Warwickshire 260 for 6 (35.5 overs) (V Chopra 76, IR Bell 57)
Warwickshire won by 4 wickets

FINAL – SOMERSET v. WARWICKSHIRE
18 September 2010 Day/Night at Lord's

SOMERSET

ME Trescothick (capt)	c Woakes b Barker	21
*C Kieswetter	c Barker b Carter	37
PD Trego	c Clarke b Barker	11
NRD Compton	lbw b Imran Tahir	60
JC Hildreth	run out	44
JC Buttler	lbw b Imran Tahir	0
AV Suppiah	b Imran Tahir	1
BJ Phillips	c Bell b Imran Tahir	1
AC Thomas	not out	6
M Kartik	st Johnson b Imran Tahir	3
ML Turner	c Clarke b Carter	8
Extras	w 5, nb 2	7
	(all out 39 overs)	199

	O	M	R	W
Carter	6	0	40	2
Woakes	8	1	31	0
Barker	7	0	33	2
Botha	8	0	39	0
Imran Tahir	8	0	41	5
Maddy	2	0	15	0

Fall of Wickets
1-41, 2-62, 3-81, 4-176, 5-176, 6-178, 7-179, 8-180, 9-187

WARWICKSHIRE

IJL Trott	c Kieswetter b Phillips	17
NM Carter	c Trego b Phillips	5
KHD Barker	c Turner b Thomas	3
IR Bell (capt)	c Buttler b Thomas	107
JO Troughton	c Kieswetter b Thomas	30
DL Maddy	c Kartik b Turner	9
R Clarke	c Hildreth b Trego	19
AG Botha	not out	4
CR Woakes	not out	1
*RM Johnson		
Imran Tahir		
Extras	b 1, lb 2, nb 2	5
	(7 wkts 39 overs)	200

	O	M	R	W
Thomas	8	1	33	3
Phillips	8	0	24	2
Turner	7	0	71	1
Kartik	8	0	27	0
Trego	7	0	36	1
Suppiah	1	0	6	0

Fall of Wickets
1-12, 2-20, 3-39, 4-118, 5-135, 6-164, 7-199

Umpires: PJ Hartley & RA Kettleborough
Toss: Warwickshire
Man of the Match: IR Bell

Warwickshire won by 3 wickets

an ECB-raised collection of young hopefuls and the odd older former professional raised from the ranks of recreational cricket. To their credit, the Unicorns won three of their twelve games, and former Somerset all-rounder Wes Durston impressed so much during the first phase of the league – 54 matches were played between 25 April and 31 May before a resumption on 19 July following the Twenty20 Cup group stage – that he was snapped up by Derbyshire.

But the very presence of the three other teams meant that the task of winning a mini-league of seven (only the winners were guaranteed a semi-final berth) became that much more difficult. The fact that the three groups had been decided by an open draw meant, too,

that travelling was a far bigger issue (as also in the Twenty20 Cup of just two initial groups) than it would have been if a more tightly regionalised structure had been imposed.

In the end, it was Essex who earned themselves the last semi-final spot by finishing as the best of the three group runners-up, with 19 points, courtesy of a seven-wicket win against Yorkshire at Headingley on 4 September, a day which featured all nine of the last group games. Alastair Cook led Essex home with an unbeaten 101 after he and Mark Pettini (82) had put on 161 for the first wicket in reply to Yorkshire's 209.

You had to feel sorry for Gloucestershire, though, who won nine of their own twelve group games but still finished third in Group B with a points tally – and net run rate – that would have won them Group C. Somerset dominated Group A and, like Yorkshire at the head of Group B, won ten of their twelve games.

At the end of it all, though, it was a competition structure that again seemed to make little sense. How much better, and easier to follow, it would have been with four regional groups of five (with just two of Holland, Scotland and the Unicorns included), followed by quarter-finals for the top two in each group. Yet, in this particular season, perhaps that would have been just too simple.

Jos Buttler, the highly talented 20-year-old Somerset batsman, topped the 2010 Clydesdale Bank 40 charts for both strike rate of scoring and number of sixes hit.

CLYDESDALE BANK 40 FEATURES 2010

MOST RUNS

Player	M	I	NO	HS	R	Ave	100	50	SR
JA Rudolph	13	13	4	124*	861	95.66	4	5	91.79
JC Hildreth	14	14	5	100*	627	69.66	1	5	110.19
IR Bell	9	9	0	107	554	61.55	1	6	106.53
GW Flower	12	11	3	116	527	65.87	2	2	95.64
JEC Franklin	12	12	5	133*	511	73.00	2	2	91.74
JHK Adams	11	11	1	131	496	49.60	1	4	95.56
SM Davies	9	9	1	101	485	60.62	1	4	128.98
J du Toit	12	12	0	141	485	40.41	1	3	89.64
RJ Hamilton-Brown	11	11	0	115	478	43.45	1	4	150.78
SR Patel	12	11	1	108*	467	46.70	1	3	95.50
JL Denly	11	11	1	102*	467	46.70	1	2	79.42
IJL Trott	8	8	2	103	460	76.66	1	4	83.18
AW Gale	13	13	1	125*	458	38.16	1	1	93.27
CD Nash	11	11	0	85	457	41.54	0	5	105.29
APR Gidman	12	12	1	104*	452	41.09	1	2	87.42
JC Buttler	14	13	5	90*	440	55.00	0	4	153.84
VS Solanki	12	12	0	129	436	36.33	1	2	92.76

MOST SIXES

Player	County	Matches	Sixes
JC Buttler	Somerset	14	19
RJ Hamilton-Brown	Surrey	11	17
C Kieswetter	Somerset	9	15
GM Andrew	Worcestershire	11	13
RN ten Doeschate	Essex	10	11
GJ Bailey	Scotland	12	11
SM Davies	Surrey	9	11
JHK Adams	Hampshire	11	11
MP O'Shea	Unicorns	8	10
WJ Durston	Derbyshire/Unicorns	12	10
PD Trego	Somerset	14	10
SJ Croft	Lancashire	12	10
JEC Franklin	Gloucestershire	12	10
IR Bell	Warwickshire	9	10
RA White	Northamptonshire	7	9
TL Maynard	Glamorgan	11	9
SR Patel	Nottinghamshire	12	9

BEST BATTING STRIKE RATE

Player	County	Matches	Strike Rate
JC Buttler	Somerset	14	153.84
GM Andrew	Worcestershire	11	151.82
RJ Hamilton-Brown	Surrey	11	150.78
RN ten Doeschate	Essex	10	134.65
JM Bairstow	Yorkshire	9	130.76
SM Davies	Surrey	9	128.98
CT Tremlett	Surrey	7	127.02
DG Cork	Hampshire	11	124.69
NM Carter	Warwickshire	13	124.11
ME Trescothick	Somerset	14	122.00
R Clarke	Warwickshire	12	121.58
SJ Mullaney	Nottinghamshire	11	120.56
MJ Cosgrove	Glamorgan	10	120.30
PD Trego	Somerset	14	119.63
Shakib Al Hasan	Worcestershire	5	119.10
SD Snell	Gloucestershire	12	118.66
JG Thompson	Unicorns	11	118.13

MOST WICKETS

Player	M	O	Mdns	R	W	Ave	BB	4wI
AC Thomas	14	81.1	2	430	27	15.92	4-34	2
RJ Kirtley	11	72.4	2	476	24	19.83	4-30	3
Imran Tahir	13	81	1	431	22	19.59	5-41	2
SA Patterson	13	92	4	470	21	22.38	6-32	1
M Kartik	10	69.3	1	321	20	16.05	4-30	1
LM Daggett	10	71	7	330	20	16.50	4-17	1
RM Pyrah	13	81	1	484	20	24.20	4-24	2
BJ Phillips	13	83.5	4	466	19	24.52	4-31	1
CP Wood	10	71.1	4	368	18	20.44	4-33	1
JD Shantry	12	81.4	3	487	18	27.05	3-33	0
SP Kirby	11	73	5	400	17	23.52	3-41	0
G Goudie	12	79.2	2	541	17	31.82	4-51	1
DA Payne	6	36.5	2	179	16	11.18	7-29	2
J Lewis	10	67	4	350	16	21.87	3-3	0
C Rushworth	9	52	7	226	15	15.06	3-6	0
WB Rankin	8	41.4	0	244	15	16.26	4-34	1
Z de Bruyn	12	47.2	0	291	15	19.40	3-27	0

MOST BOUNDARIES

Player	County	Matches	Fours	Sixes	Boundaries
JA Rudolph	Yorkshire	13	82	4	86
RJ Hamilton-Brown	Surrey	11	60	17	77
NM Carter	Warwickshire	13	69	7	76
SM Davies	Surrey	9	59	11	70
JC Hildreth	Somerset	14	58	7	65
AW Gale	Yorkshire	13	55	8	63
IR Bell	Warwickshire	9	52	10	62
JC Buttler	Somerset	14	40	19	59
MJ Cosgrove	Glamorgan	10	50	8	58
ME Trescothick	Somerset	14	49	7	56
MM Ali	Worcestershire	12	50	6	56
SR Patel	Nottinghamshire	12	47	9	56
PD Trego	Somerset	14	44	10	54
VS Solanki	Worcestershire	12	48	6	54
CD Nash	Sussex	11	47	7	54
CF Hughes	Derbyshire	12	48	5	53
JL Denly	Kent	11	48	5	53

BEST BOWLING ECONOMY RATE

Player	County	Matches	Economy Rate
JC Tredwell	Kent	8	3.76
N Boje	Northamptonshire	6	3.92
HMCM Bandara	Kent	5	4.33
C Rushworth	Durham	9	4.34
HF Gurney	Leicestershire	6	4.46
J Needham	Derbyshire	7	4.59
M Kartik	Somerset	10	4.61
DD Masters	Essex	11	4.61
LM Daggett	Northamptonshire	10	4.64
RT Lyons	Scotland	8	4.78
AU Rashid	Yorkshire	13	4.82
PW Borren	Netherlands	12	4.84
DR Briggs	Hampshire	7	4.85
DA Payne	Gloucestershire	6	4.85
ID Blackwell	Durham	10	4.88
RJ Peterson	Derbyshire	8	4.92
SJ Cook	Kent	9	4.92

JOHN EMBUREY, the former England captain, explains why careful thought needs to be given to the future structure of the domestic game…

Championship Cuts Would Harm Player Development

The 2010 county season was played out against a backdrop of yet another debate about the future structure of our domestic game. And I'd like to add my voice to this debate by saying, 'Hang on, let's be very careful about what we are doing'.

As someone who played the first-class game for many years, played for England and captained my country, and as someone who is still very involved in coaching and mentoring, I think I know what I am talking about when I say that players only ever improve as cricketers by playing. Indeed, I would want to make it very clear that I would not have become as good a player as I did if I had played less cricket.

I enjoyed playing, and both as a spinner and a lower middle-order batsman I learned to improve my skills through the constant demands of being out in the middle. One hour's batting, or bowling, in a competitive game did far more for me than four hours spent in the nets.

The problem with the current theory about players needing to play less so that they can practice, or rest, is that you often don't improve that much simply by practising. In fact, I would say that short, sharp net practices are better for every type of cricketer. And match practice is far better than that.

Spinners, in particular, are often asked to bowl too much in the nets simply because they are slow bowlers with short run-ups and therefore don't get as physically tired as fast bowlers, even when they bowl for longer periods. But their fingers get tired, and if you start putting the ball there rather than actively bowling it, or if your arm drops a little and you undercut the ball rather than spin it, then you quickly get yourself into bad habits that can have a hugely detrimental effect on your game.

During the 2009–10 winter, for instance, Adil Rashid spent a ridiculous amount of time bowling in the nets with England when he would have been far better served playing matches. It is only out in the middle that you are properly tested, only there can you get the intensity that simply cannot be replicated in practice. Yes, players need quality practice, but they also need to play in matches to do full justice to the development of their skills.

A lot of people keep banging on about the fact that Australia and South Africa have domestic systems with only about ten first-class games, but they forget that young Australians and South

Yet more net practice for Adil Rashid (right) and James Tredwell, the reserve England spinners, during England's winter tour to South Africa in 2009-10.

Rope-a-dope: England's players engage in an unusual training drill ahead of the third Test against Pakistan at The Oval. Does more time for practice and training produce better cricketers?

Africans supplement that by playing a lot in the northern hemisphere. English county and club cricket has been used for years in this regard, and it is now happening too in the IPL where a lot of young Australians in particular are going to hone their skills.

There has been discussion this year about the claimed merits of a three-conference County Championship, in which every team plays the 12 counties in the other two conferences, followed by semi-finals and final and possibly other final 'placement' matches all the way down to 17th and 18th. That would mean every county playing a maximum of 14 matches, rather than 16 as at present in the two-division system.

All this has come about because coaches and players in particular think we play too much cricket, but that has only happened because the amount of one-day cricket had been increased from 2009 – despite the axing of one of the previous three different one-day competitions!

But what if the weather is bad during our summer and every county loses the best part of either two or three Championship games from their allocation of 14? That would not be unusual in an average English summer, but it would suddenly leave some players – and especially younger players – facing a significantly reduced amount of cricket-playing time compared to the present structure.

My belief is that we need to safeguard the amount of first-class cricket we play every summer – which is about right at the moment – because our players need that if they are to develop fully. I don't think we should go back to three-day Championship cricket, as was the case when I was coming up through the system in the 1970s, and I regard four-day cricket as the better training ground for Test cricket.

But we need to think very carefully indeed about the impact of reducing the amount of four-day first-class cricket that our best young players get to play. Because, in my view, we could be seriously harming the rate of their development if we do cut it down.

A version of this article first appeared on the testmatchextra.com website.

John Emburey, the former Middlesex off-spinner, played 64 Tests for England between 1978 and 1995.

DERBYSHIRE

by Mark Eklid

The bare figures say that Derbyshire won more matches in the County Championship in 2010 than they did in the previous season and that they also took more wins from the two one-day competitions than they did from three competitions in 2009. But this only proves that bare facts do not tell the whole story.

No one could reasonably argue that the season was anything other than a miserable one, especially in light of a heartening first three weeks that affirmed the feeling of progress made under John Morris' tenure.

Derbyshire laid a sound foundation in the first two years under Morris, becoming a doughty side that was difficult to beat but whose main failing was that it could not convert enough promising positions into winning ones. Two Championship victories out of the first three suggested an outfit ready to take the next step forward but optimism crumbled after rain and stern rearguard resistance denied them a third win at Northampton.

Opposite Chris Rogers gets in a tangle against the bowling of Northamptonshire off spinner James Middlebrook at Wantage Road, in the game that Derbyshire's bright start to the 2010 campaign began to falter. Rogers did not see the season out as Derbyshire captain, and left the club at the end of it.

Right Greg Smith, now confirmed as Derbyshire's new captain after initially deputising for Rogers.

Six defeats out of their next nine Championship fixtures, with the other three drawn, sent Derbyshire from top in April to bottom in August and there they stayed, collecting a fourth wooden spoon in the last 10 seasons.

It was a descent to sap the spirit and it claimed casualties along the way, with Chris Rogers the most significant of them. The prolific Australian batsman, in his third season as the county's overseas player and his second full term as captain, began with 340 runs for once out, in a resounding defeat of Surrey in the opening round of matches, but took his team's failures greatly to heart and gave up the captaincy in mid-August when it became clear he was ready to listen to what other counties had to offer.

Greg Smith stepped in, with view to a long-term succession, and Rogers agreed to leave for Middlesex. He did so after leading the Derbyshire batting again and 4,118 first-class runs over the last three seasons at an average of 60.56 will take some replacing.

Another end-of-season departure was Graham Wagg, the sparky all-rounder who spent four months of the summer on the sidelines with a torn calf muscle. His absence was a key contributing factor in Derbyshire's struggles but they were faced with the problem of being without Wagg for good when the county's best offer of a new contract did not measure up to that made by Glamorgan, who won his signature for 2011.

Robin Peterson's farewell was not a voluntary one. The South African left-arm spinner was signed under the Kolpak ruling to add international experience and guile and though he clearly felt the strain of having to bowl many more overs than he had been used to, a final first-class haul of 51 wickets and just short of 500 runs was a good one. Visa regulations mean Peterson will not be eligible to return to the club.

Smith Pledges to Renew 'Derbyshire Grit'
by Andy Wilson

South African Greg Smith said he will preach good old-fashioned Derbyshire values after being appointed as the county's new captain. The 27-year-old all-rounder Smith has had his eye on captaincy for a long time – through age group cricket, school and as vice-captain under Hashim Amla in the 2001-02 Under-19 World Cup, when South Africa reached the final. Smith says he would like to bring back the days when the cold wind blowing in from the racecourse was not the only reason opponents hated to take on Derbyshire. The reputation for defiant bloody-mindedness has long been a cornerstone of Derbyshire's successes, most recently in the Kim Barnett and Eddie Barlow eras. 'I'm from South Africa and the first captain I played under was Daryll Cullinan,' Smith said. 'He was a very aggressive sort of character – get stuck in and don't be scared and the intent was very clear. People didn't like playing against us. I want to try to get that attitude back into our dressing room. There have never been super-stars around at Derbyshire but they have always played as a team, so we need to get back to that mentality and keep fighting together.'

44 All Out – And Still Won!
by Andy Wilson

Speaking after a match that will go down in Derbyshire folklore – the amazing County Championship fixture against Gloucestershire at Bristol – the county's director of cricket, John Morris, said he was anxious that the quality of the match-winning innings played by Chesney Hughes is never forgotten.

Derbyshire's fight back to claim victory by 54 runs after being tumbled out for a mere 44 at the start of the game provided one of the stories of the 2010 summer. But, amid all the drama, teenager Hughes continued an impressive debut season in first-class cricket with an unbeaten 96 from 156 balls in Derbyshire's second-innings total of 236, ensuring almost single-handed that the county's seamers had something to defend.

Hughes was left agonisingly short of a third century of the summer when Steffan Jones's resistance in a last-wicket stand of 25 was ended by a low second slip catch, the umpires taking the word of Gloucestershire's Alex Gidman that the ball had carried. But Morris said, 'If ever an innings deserved a century, it was Chesney's. That could get overlooked with everything else that happened in the match, but it shouldn't be. It was a phenomenal innings for a 19-year-old, to dominate a game on that wicket.'

Hughes, the big Anguillan who was recommended to Derbyshire by his compatriot Cardigan Connor after coming to England to play league cricket for Fleetwood in 2009, finished second in the county's Championship averages with 784 runs from twelve matches at 41.26.

Derbyshire's remarkable win at Bristol was sealed by the performance of their seamers, with Tim Groenewald doing the early damage to set Gloucestershire's nerves jangling and Graham Wagg, Jon Clare and Jones all chipping in with wickets as the hosts were themselves bowled out for 70 in their second innings.

'In all the games of cricket I've played in and watched – and somewhere along the line that includes Botham's Ashes – I've never seen anything like it,' added Morris. 'To win a game when you've been bowled out for 44 – I'm not sure any of our lads have still quite got their heads around it.'

Morris also thought Gloucestershire had been hoisted by their own petard in suffering a defeat that was a hammer blow to their own promotion hopes, saying, 'It just goes to show that if you mess about with this game, it bites you back.

'Gloucestershire decided to have a result pitch. I thought it was under-prepared and it came back to bite them on the second day because the ball left little indentations and it was hard to bat on. The pressure went back into the Gloucestershire dressing room and, with respect, they didn't bat very well.'

As Morris came to terms with the depth of change needed, John Sadler, Lee Goddard and Tom Lungley, the county's longest-serving player in his 11th season, were released before the end of the campaign.

Derbyshire will not start again with a completely blank sheet. Wayne Madsen, the right-handed opening batsman in his first full season of county cricket, scored four centuries, though inconsistency left him 60 runs short of 1,000 in the end, and he also performed well in a mid-order role in the 40-over game.

Promising all-rounder Jon Clare showed signs of a welcome return to old sharpness following extensive winter shoulder surgery and Wes Durston's second county career began with outstanding batting in the Friends Provident t20 as Derbyshire earned the chance

Wes Durston won himself a Derbyshire contract, and a second chance in county cricket, after impressing with the Unicorns in the Clydesdale Bank 40.

Above Yes, Chesney Hughes can do defensive too – an uncharacteristic stroke from Derbyshire's exciting Hughes, a teenage giant who can hit the ball uncommonly hard.

Right Wayne Madsen, the Derbyshire batsman, hits out against Essex.

to qualify for the quarter-finals only to make a hash of a home game they needed to win against the county that qualified in their place, Northamptonshire.

Among the bowlers, Smith, Steffan Jones and Tim Groenewald can only be applauded for the burden they shared in the extended absences of Wagg, Clare, Lungley and Ian Hunter. It is reasonable to suggest that had Derbyshire been able to throw more fit bowlers into the mix of options, they would not have struggled as badly as they did.

The injuries also meant Mark Footitt was given more opportunities than he might have expected following his move from Trent Bridge. He remains erratic but bowls at good pace and showed enough signs to merit hope that a more consistently dangerous bowler can be coaxed out by the coaching staff.

Injury–Jinxed Lungley Released
by Andy Wilson

It may have been a coincidence but there was a sad irony in the fact that Tom Lungley was released by Derbyshire on the day his close friend Graham Wagg began to look forward to a bright new future after agreeing to sign for Glamorgan on a three-year contract. Derby-born right-arm seamer Lungley's time with his home county ended after 11 seasons when Derbyshire decided not to offer him a new contract. He was by some way the longest-serving player in the squad, having made his first-class debut in 2000, but the story of Lungley's career with Derbyshire has been too much about injuries and not enough about taking wickets.

The final chapter in that story came at Chesterfield at the beginning of July, with his club trying to pull off a record run chase on the final day against Surrey. Lungley, at the non-striker's end, was batting well but could not get out of the way of a firm drive from Steffan Jones and his right arm was broken. Bravely, he returned as last man to face 21 more balls before being bowled by Chris Tremlett and that was to be his last appearance for Derbyshire. Ill fortune has dogged Lungley's career. Any injury he picked up always seemed to be a different one to the last and would always prove hard to shake off and that is why he was able to play only 53 first-class matches for Derbyshire, taking 144 wickets at 32.25. His one injury-free golden summer came in 2007, when he took 59 first-class wickets at 26.35 and was named player of the year.

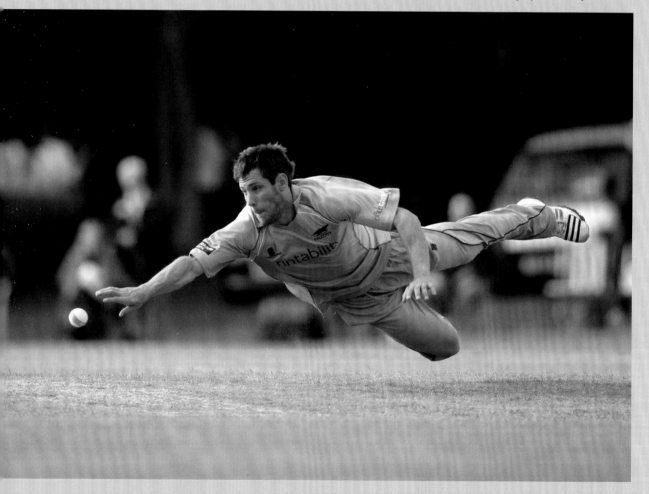

A typically wholehearted effort in the field from Tom Lungley, in the Clydesdale Bank 40 match against Essex in early May which also saw Derbyshire return to the Staffordshire town of Leek. Sadly, due to continuing injury problems, 2010 was to prove to be Lungley's final season with his native county.

Robin Peterson proved to be a very useful addition to the Derbyshire staff in 2010 with his steady left-arm spin and valuable late middle-order batting.

By far the brightest source of hope for the future, however, was the arrival of Chesney Hughes, a 19-year-old from the small island of Anguilla in the West Indies who came to Derbyshire the previous year on the recommendation of his coach, Cardigan Connor, and has set his sights on qualifying to play international cricket for England.

He showed exceptional poise through a poor team performance on his first-class debut, scoring 41 and 59 not out against Middlesex at Lord's in May, and became the county's youngest centurion with 118 against Gloucestershire two weeks later.

There were learning failures along the way, too, but the potential was plain to see in a dynamic 156 against Northants at Chesterfield and during his most memorable innings. That was played on a Bristol green-top after Derbyshire had been bowled out for 44 in their first innings yet recovered to win before tea on the second day. Without Hughes' battling 96 not out, such a remarkable turnaround would not have been possible.

That was one of too few joyous days for Derbyshire and Hughes was one of too few players to emerge with credit. The rebuilding has begun, with wicketkeeper-batsman Luke Sutton returning after five years with Lancashire and Mark Turner recruited from Somerset to add more pace to the bowling attack, but the main source of improvement has to come from within the current squad.

PLAYER OF THE SEASON

Chesney Hughes had a hugely impressive debut campaign for a 19-year-old, even more so in the context of such a tough season for the county. His first Championship hundred made him the youngest ever Derbyshire centurion, his second was sublime, but his match-winning unbeaten 96 at Bristol was better still.

YOUNG PLAYER OF THE SEASON

Chesney Hughes for all the reasons listed above. A powerful driver of the ball, well balanced and patient at the crease, he is physically and mentally mature well beyond his years.

A YEAR TO REMEMBER

- Chris Rogers signed off his three years for the county with 1,285 first-class runs
- Robin Peterson took 51 wickets and scored just short of 500 runs on his debut season
- Steffan Jones took valuable wickets and made precious runs from the bottom of the order

A YEAR TO FORGET

- Garry Park struggled to match the consistency of his first year with the bat
- Lee Goddard was patchy as wicketkeeper and even patchier as batsman
- Tom Lungley – another unfortunate injury was the last act of 11 seasons with the club

DERBYSHIRE CCC

FIRST–CLASS MATCHES
BATTING

Match	WL Madsen	GM Smith	RJ Peterson	CJL Rogers	TD Groenewald	PS Jones	CF Hughes	GT Park	MHA Footitt	DJ Redfern	LJ Goddard	PM Borrington	T Lungley	WJ Durston	GG Wagg	T Poynton	SJ Adshead	JL Clare	JL Sadler	A Sheikh	Extras	Total	Wickets	Result	Points
v. Surrey	5	66	23	200	5			10	30	1	33*	21			37						20	451	10		
(The Oval) 9-12 April	15	20	-	140*	-			19	-	44	-	12			16						8	274	6	W	23
v. Leicestershire	26	54	54	3	2	20*	8	12	6	5	0										17	207	10		
(Derby) 15-18 April	109	28	1	0	12	0	5	2*	0	0	25										17	199	10	L	4
v. Glamorgan	3	165*	19	28	33			61			0	27	1		0				10		16	363	10		
(Derby) 21-24 April	17	-		51*				43*			8		-		-				2		2	121	2	W	22
v. Northamptonshire	179	8	22*	141	-			0		-	-	79*	-					14			37	480	5		
(Northampton) 27-30 April																								D	10
Middlesex	29	1		9	4		41	1	7		15	46	20*					16			7	196	10		
(Lord's) 10-12 May	2	8		10	27		59*	19	0		1	0	4					5			8	143	10	L	3
v. Worcestershire	8	3	46	50	35*	86	18	14				0	8		13						14	295	10		
(Worcester) 17-20 May	34	64	25	32	14	21	20	124*				25	14		2						14	389	10	L	3
v. Gloucestershire	0	4	8	115	34*		118	4		12			1		22					6	21	345	10		
(Derby) 24-27 May	4	0	3	7	4*		75	0		27			11		12					0	23	166	10	L	6
v. Sussex	0	2	31	79			38*	62	24	0	44	5				14					38	337	10		
(Derby) 5-8 June																								D	8
v. Surrey	109	2	5	14	4*	4	2	6			67		0	8							16	237	10		
(Chesterfield) 28 June-1 July	105	34	40	33	3	20*		54			0		21	16							39	365	10	L	4
v. Worcestershire	75	91	26	22	3*	40	44	1	2	19	38										44	405	10		
(Derby) 21-24 July																								D	9
v. Leicestershire	14	4	6	8	21	14	0	9	2*	85	0										19	182	10		
(Leicester) 3-6 August	66	27	1	47	11	1	32	29	0*	17	6										25	262	10	L	3
v. Northamptonshire	0	4	58	9	13*	6	156			21			3			13	9				27	319	10		
(Chesterfield) 9-12 August	25*	-	42*	-									-			-	-				9	76	10	D	9
v. Sussex	2	9	20		35*	22		6	0		2			69			49	0			28	242	10		
(Horsham) 18-20 August	23	49	6		17	4		4	19		1			33			31*	12			26	225	10	L	1
v. Middlesex	10	5	15	75	9*		30	0					17	3	7						7	182	10		
(Derby) 25-28 August	41	15	9*	96	-		0	-					1	4	11*						12	189	6	D	6
v. Gloucestershire	0	0	15	1	2*	7	5						2	6		4	0				2	44	10		
(Bristol) 31 August-1 September	39	4	12	31	0	10	96*						7	16		10	0				11	236	10	W	19
v. Glamorgan	0	42	5	33	13*	45	29			7				46		25		24			7	276	10		
(Cardiff) 13-16 September	0	12	34*	9	-	-	1			29*				38		-		-			0	123	5	D	8
Matches	16	16	15	15	13	12	12	11	9	9	8	7	7	6	4	4	4	4	3	1					
Innings	29	27	24	27	19	18	21	19	12	15	11	13	10	11	7	6	7	6	4	2					
Not Out	1	1	3	3	9	4	2	2	3	1	1	1	1	0	0	0	2	0	0	0					
Highest Score	179	165*	58	200	35*	86	156	124*	30	85	67	79*	21	69	37	25	49	24	16	6					
Runs	940	721	484	1285	216	427	784	431	69	331	165	246	85	240	82	88	125	45	45	6					
Average	33.57	27.73	23.04	53.54	21.60	30.50	41.26	25.35	7.66	23.64	16.50	20.50	9.44	21.81	11.71	14.66	25.00	7.50	11.25	3.00					
100s	4	1	0	4	0	0	2	1	0	0	0	0	0	0	0	0	0	0	0	0					
50s	2	4	2	5	0	1	4	2	0	1	1	1	0	1	0	0	0	0	0	0					
Catches/Stumpings	11/0	4/0	9/0	19/0	3/0	4/0	12/0	6/0	3/0	3/0	24/0	4/0	6/0	9/0	1/0	5/0	13/0	4/0	3/0	1/0					

Home Ground: Derby
Address: County Ground, Nottingham Road, Derby, DE21 6DA
Tel: 01332 388101
Fax: 0844 586 0368
Email: info@derbyshireccc.com
Directions: *By road:* From the South & East, exit M1 junction 25, follow the A52 into Derby, take the fourth exit off the Pentagon Island. From the North, exit M1 junction 28, join the A38 into Derby, follow directional signs, the cricket ground is seen on the left approaching the city. From the West, on A50 follow signs for A52 Nottingham and on leaving the city centre inner ring road take the second exit off the Pentagon Island into the ground.

Capacity: 9,500
Other grounds used: Chesterfield
Year Formed: 1870
Chief Executive: Keith Loring
Head of Cricket: John Morris
Academy Director: Karl Krikken
Captains: Chris Rogers, Greg Smith
County colours: Light and royal blue

Honours
County Championship
1936
Sunday League/NCL/Pro40
1990
Benson & Hedges Cup
1993
Gillette Cup/NatWest/C&G Trophy
1981

Website:
www.derbyshireccc.com

FIRST-CLASS MATCHES
BOWLING

Match	RJ Peterson	GM Smith	TD Groenewald	PS Jones	MHA Footitt	T Lungley	JL Clare	GG Wagg	GT Park	A Sheikh	T Poynton	WL Madsen	WJ Durston	CF Hughes	CJL Rogers	DJ Redfern	Overs	Total	Byes/Leg-byes	Wickets	Run outs
v. Surrey	30.2-8-87-3	20-5-58-4	26-6-90-1		20-6-62-1			13-1-47-0									109.2	352	8	10	1
(The Oval) 9-12 April	20.1-10-32-3	13-5-35-2	20-6-47-2		13-5-25-2			5-2-13-1									71.1	165	13	10	
v. Leicestershire	10-2-24-2	15.2-2-45-2		16-5-44-3		17-3-64-1	13-0-51-0		6-0-25-1								77.2	279	26	10	1
(Derby) 15-18 April	42-11-91-4	27-4-76-0		20-8-46-1		17-4-38-1	19-4-43-1		3-1-6-1							1-0-5-0	129	330	25	8	
v. Glamorgan	25-7-77-3	10-1-39-1		17.4-2-60-4			15-5-30-1	12-1-25-0	10-0-31-1								89.4	272	10	10	
(Derby) 21-24 April	22-4-51-2	20-1-66-4		11-3-36-1			9-1-31-1		7.3-2-20-2								69.3	211	7	10	
v. Northamptonshire	24.2-8-33-3	8-2-20-0	12-5-32-0			17-1-78-4	13-2-39-3		4-0-12-0								78.2	220	6	10	
(Northampton) 27-30 April	40-14-82-2	27-9-47-4	11-3-26-0			12-1-42-1	13-3-42-0		4-1-14-1								107	237	4	9	1
v. Middlesex		18-5-91-0	22.1-6-62-4		15-0-54-2		21-4-67-2		10-0-36-1					7-0-56-0			93.1	374	8	10	1
(Lord's) 10-12 May																	-	-	-	-	-
v. Worcestershire	47-7-170-4	21-2-93-0	24-2-96-0	28-6-79-1		21-1-90-2			1-0-7-0								142	559	24	8	1
(Worcester) 17-20 May	5.5-0-46-1		2-0-21-0	3-2-5-0		3-0-29-1			2-0-24-0								15.5	126	1	2	
v. Gloucestershire	16-5-19-2	13-4-28-2		16-5-45-1		11-1-45-2			4-2-2-0	12-1-78-3			2-0-16-0				72	242	25	10	
(Derby) 24-27 May	28-3-124-1	12.3-1-54-3		12-3-53-2		15-3-59-2			4-0-14-0	13-0-74-2							86.3	403	9	10	
v. Sussex	37-7-94-2	16-2-70-0		24-6-62-2	17.5-3-48-2	15-1-71-3			7-0-46-0								116.5	429	38	10	1
(Derby) 5-8 June	11-5-10-4	9-3-24-2		6-2-17-0	7-1-15-1												33	71	5	7	
v. Surrey	20-5-65-1	11-0-52-0		27-8-86-5	22-4-65-4	14-2-67-0			4-0-25-0					2-0-14-0			100	391	17	10	
(Chesterfield) 28 June-1 July	18.2-3-46-3	13-2-36-2		19-1-63-3	13-3-37-0	15-2-60-2											78.2	253	11	10	
v. Worcestershire	12.2-1-66-2	18-4-33-2		13-5-65-3	16-3-57-1	17-6-39-0			4-1-13-1					2-0-9-1	1-0-5-0	2-0-8-0	82.2	279	6	10	
(Derby) 21-24 July	22-4-81-1	20-4-80-0		20-6-49-0	9-2-22-1	19-6-39-2			9-2-42-1								104	328	12	6	
v. Leicestershire	11-4-22-0	23-4-40-3		22-6-65-1	27-7-67-3	18.1-6-67-2			1-0-2-0								103.1	276	13	10	
(Leicester) 3-6 August	5-0-17-0	9.4-2-30-0		10-1-34-0	5-1-13-0	8-2-41-0			3-0-8-0								40.4	170	27	0	
v. Northamptonshire	1-0-4-0	19-6-54-5	18-4-57-1		15-4-42-0	11-3-42-4											64	201	2	10	1
(Chesterfield) 9-12 August	34.1-5-91-2	20-2-81-1	37-3-136-1		29-7-96-4	16-3-54-1											136.1	469	11	10	
v. Sussex	27.4-2-130-1	21-2-108-2		23-4-82-0	20-1-104-0		12-0-107-0						8-0-33-0				111.4	576	12	3	
(Horsham) 18-20 August																	-	-	-	-	-
v. Middlesex	19-7-48-2	5-0-33-0	16.4-8-30-2	10-1-45-1	13-4-50-3			14-3-35-1					2-0-9-1				79.4	263	13	10	
(Derby) 25-28 August	15-2-45-1	7-2-25-0	11-3-36-1	5-2-18-1	9.2-2-28-2			10-1-41-2					4-0-20-0				61.2	221	8	7	
v. Gloucestershire		6-0-28-1	4-0-16-1	7.1-1-26-4			5-0-23-1	13-2-54-3									35.1	156	9	10	
(Bristol) 31 August-1 September			10-5-22-4	2-0-9-1			2.3-0-7-2	10-3-31-3									24.3	70	1	10	
v. Glamorgan	5.2-5-0-2	7-3-19-2	19-7-43-2	7-1-19-1			19-2-75-3				8-0-96-2						57.2	166	10	10	
(Cardiff) 13-16 September	4-0-31-0	5-0-23-0	4-1-31-0				4-0-16-0					8.2-0-68-1					33.2	269	4	3	

	RJ Peterson	GM Smith	TD Groenewald	PS Jones	MHA Footitt	T Lungley	JL Clare	GG Wagg	GT Park	A Sheikh	T Poynton	WL Madsen	WJ Durston	CF Hughes	CJL Rogers	DJ Redfern
Overs	553.3	414.3	413.5	313.5	239.2	165	69.3	77	83.3	25	8	8.2	16	11	1	3
Maidens	129	77	105	68	48	25	8	13	9	1	0	0	0	0	0	0
Runs	1566	1368	1295	959	786	630	324	246	327	152	96	68	76	81	5	14
Wickets	51	42	38	31	23	19	11	10	9	5	2	1	1	1	0	0
Average	30.71	32.57	34.08	30.94	34.17	33.16	29.45	24.60	36.33	30.40	48.00	68.00	76.00	81.00	-	-

FIELDING

24	LJ Goddard (24 ct)
19	CJL Rogers
13	SJ Adshead (13 ct)
12	CF Hughes
11	WL Madsen
9	WJ Durston
9	RJ Peterson
6	T Lungley
6	GT Park
5	T Poynton (5 ct)
4	PM Borrington
4	JL Clare
4	PS Jones
4	GM Smith
3	MHA Footitt
3	TD Groenewald
3	DJ Redfern
3	JL Sadler
1	A Sheikh
1	GG Wagg

Division Two – Final Table

	P	W	L	D	Bat	Bowl	Pens	Pts
Sussex	16	8	3	5	45	47	0	235
Worcestershire	16	7	4	5	39	42	0	208
Glamorgan	16	7	4	5	33	43	0	203
Leicestershire	16	7	5	4	31	44	0	199
Gloucestershire	16	6	9	1	28	47	-2	172
Northamptonshire	16	6	7	3	28	34	0	167
Surrey	16	4	6	6	43	36	-2	159
Middlesex	16	4	7	5	37	41	-2	155
Derbyshire	16	3	7	6	30	42	0	138

CB40 & FPt20

Limited overs nickname:
DERBYSHIRE FALCONS

Derbyshire FALCONS

DURHAM

by Tim Wellock

During their two title-winning seasons in 2008 and 2009 Durham dropped a total of one bowling point, but in their forlorn attempt to become the first team since Yorkshire in 1968 to complete a hat-trick they dropped nine. Graham Onions missed the entire season with a back injury, Steve Harmison played in half the games, Mark Davies and Callum Thorp managed five each, while Liam Plunkett never found his best form with bat or ball.

In total, 15 members of the full-time staff were incapacitated at some stage, but 13 injuries in the first month triggered an astonishing decline from the pre-season thrashing of MCC in Abu Dhabi to a situation that necessitated a change of captaincy a month later.

In 2009, his first year as captain, Will Smith had been unable to recapture his form from the previous year but it had scarcely mattered as Durham won the title by 47 points. This time the bowling problems were compounded by advancing years beginning to catch up with the leading batsmen, Dale Benkenstein and Michael Di Venuto.

When Smith stood down, Phil 'the Colonel' Mustard surprisingly took the reins, but after an initial rise in fortunes the inconsistency continued. Durham finished fifth in Division One of the County Championship, fifth in their group in the Clydesdale Bank 40 and next to the bottom in the northern group of the Friends Provident t20.

Onions took 40 wickets in his first five games in 2009; this time the leading seamers were Plunkett and Mitch Claydon with 35 apiece.

With a pink ball, and under the Abu Dhabi floodlights, Durham leg spinner Scott Borthwick bowls against MCC in the 2010 season's curtain raiser.

The combative wicketkeeper-batsman Phil Mustard was installed as Durham captain following the resignation of Will Smith.

Both frequently lacked control and Claydon was left out for the final game to give West Indian triallist Ruel Brathwaite a chance. A product of Dulwich College, Loughborough and Cambridge, the 25-year-old paceman impressed sufficiently to be offered a contract. Given the depth of their seam attack, Durham might have seemed the least likely county for Brathwaite to join, especially after they had taken on Sunderland swing bowler Chris Rushworth during the winter. Initially seventh or eighth in the queue, Rushworth featured in nine games.

Of the other back-up seamers, Will Gidman and Luke Evans were rarely fit and Neil Killeen appeared only in three one-day games. After a 15-year career he announced his retirement, while Gidman decided to join Gloucestershire. Di Venuto's average was well down on previous years, but he reached 1,000 Championship runs for the season in the final match, while no other batsman topped 800. Ben Stokes would have done so had he not missed the last three games through a broken foot. He topped the averages with 760 runs at 46.25, with his two centuries in May, while still only 18, providing the season's highlights and confirming him as an England player in the making.

Durham rightly cite the success of Stokes and Scott Borthwick, who became a regular in the side, as evidence of progress. But what of the rest? Gordon Muchall cemented his place after scoring two centuries once he had taken over Smith's No. 3 slot, while Mark Stoneman showed some encouraging signs but still failed to average 30 after regaining the opening spot

RIVERSIDE NAME IS NOW IN DURHAM'S PAST

Durham's ground, previously known succinctly as Riverside, was renamed the Emirates Durham International Cricket Ground in June. It is, of course, located inf Chester-le-Street, which means the full address would take up most of the characters in a Tweet. Emirates became Durham's major sponsors in 2010, improving a previous one-day arrangement in a deal which will be in place for a minimum of six years. As well as stadium naming rights it also includes branding on the team's Twenty20 shirts. A competition to find the new name attracted hundreds of entries and the winner was Robin Harker, of Northallerton in North Yorkshire. It was stressed that he is no relation to Durham's chief executive, David Harker. A ceremony to unveil the name, involving a giant pitch banner, was held before the club's Friends Provident t20 match against Lancashire Lightning. Durham have agreed that the title of their ground can be abbreviated to Emirates Durham ICG.

My Reason for Resigning the Captaincy
by Will Smith

It is very hard to take in the fact that I am no longer Durham captain, but on the other hand I am greatly looking forward to another new stage of my career: a relaxed, determined and fresh stage that will hopefully see me become the kind of prolific, reliable batsman I have always aspired to be.

I wasn't really thinking about resigning the captaincy; at the time I wanted to fight through a tough period. But when the suggestion was put to me I couldn't really see any way round it. Big decisions are not easily taken and if the club saw that as the best way forward I had to respect that and go about what I do as best I can to help Durham. I hope the decision will turn out to be to the benefit of both parties. Right now I see it as a chance to be a bit more relaxed. I was enjoying my cricket two years ago and if I can get back to that I will be very

happy. I'm a proud man and I need to look after my own game and my own situation.

It was very flattering when Dale Benkenstein nominated me to take over from him after the 2008 season, and apart from my own form falling away results went really well in my first season. In 2009, when I was honoured to lead Durham to the club's second County Championship title, I would pop up every now and again in tough situations and score important runs, but I now need to get back to the level of consistent run-scoring I had two years ago.

Finally, I would like to say how pleased I am for 'the Colonel' (Durham's new captain, Phil Mustard). He has worked incredibly hard at his game over the course of his career and has a really sharp cricket brain, allied to his effervescent personality. I am sure he is just the man to take Durham CCC to new levels. Hopefully the club now have a local lad to remain at the helm for as long as possible, and I hope he receives all the backing he deserves.

Lack of runs was the main reason given by Will Smith, who led Durham to the County Championship title in 2009, for resigning the captaincy midway through the 2010 campaign.

One of a number of young players to make a splash in 2010 was Ben Stokes of Durham. Powerfully built, he hits the ball hard enough for comparisons already to be made with Andrew Flintoff (he also bowls medium-fast), and his 161 against Kent at Canterbury came two weeks before his 19th birthday.

from Kyle Coetzer. It seemed tough on Coetzer to be dropped after being exposed by some brilliant bowling from Makhaya Ntini in the South African fast bowler's last two appearances for Kent.

The Scot followed his century against Nottinghamshire at the end of 2009 season with an innings of 170 against the MCC in Abu Dhabi, but taking the annual curtain-raiser away from Lord's

Ian Blackwell, Durham's most consistent player in a season to forget, bowls here against Kent at Canterbury.

Immediately after the first Championship defeat for 23 games the captain told the media he was determined to fight on, yet less than 24 hours later it was announced that he had stood down by mutual consent. This wasn't strictly true. Smith spent the rest of the season trying to find form in the second team and making the odd one-day appearance, in which he batted down the order and was usually required to slog. He deserved much sympathy.

The captaincy brought the best out of Mustard's batting as he scored two Championship centuries four years after his first two. But his one-day form declined and without his runs at the top of the order Durham

PLAYER OF THE SEASON

Phil Mustard – ever present and never buckled under the extra burden of captaincy, which was unexpectedly thrust upon him. Averaged 39.05 in the Championship with the help of two centuries.

YOUNG PLAYER OF THE SEASON

Ben Stokes, a 15-stone athlete, he mixed exceptionally powerful striking with surprising finesse to score two Championship centuries in May before his 19th birthday. He's also a brilliant fielder and useful seam bowler. Comparisons with Andrew Flintoff are not far-fetched.

A YEAR TO REMEMBER

- Chris Rushworth became a semi-regular in the side four years after being released from the academy

A YEAR TO FORGET

- Will Smith lost the captaincy and his place in the team
- Graham Onions didn't play and had to wait until late in the season for medics to decide he needed back surgery
- Mark Davies played in the first three games without taking a wicket and two more after recovering from injury, only to break down again

appeared to do Durham no favours. Coetzer failed to maintain his form and against a depleted attack on dry, flat early season pitches, opponents began putting together much bigger stands than in 2009. Questions were raised about whether the previous year's celebrations had gone on too long, with Harmison and Ian Blackwell looking a few pounds heavier.

After stressing how hard he had worked to get fit for his first season with Durham, Blackwell looked less than nimble in the field. His one-day form declined, but his natural talent allowed him to be the most valuable member of the four-day side in terms of both runs and wickets – scoring eight half centuries and taking 47 wickets at 24.47. He was twice a match-winner, at home to Hampshire and away to Lancashire. Blackwell was carrying an ankle injury during the innings defeat at Trent Bridge, further reducing Smith's options.

rarely played to their potential. They decided to do without an overseas player for the Championship, but signed New Zealander Ross Taylor and South African Albie Morkel for the Twenty20.

Taylor lived up to his big-hitting reputation, but after building momentum by twice breaking their own batting records, first at Edgbaston then at home to Leicestershire, followed by an easy home win against Yorkshire, Durham fell away. Taylor was available for only the first 11 of the 16 games, but by the time he left they were out of contention.

Ben Harmison put in some notable performances when Stokes' broken foot allowed him to play in the last three Championship games. Steve Harmison believes his brother should be involved more often and having to accept that his England career was over may also have lowered his incentive. But he has three years left on his county contract and still has a huge amount to offer. Onions will hopefully be fit by June following his back operation and if Davies could finally have an injury-free run Durham might again have the strongest attack in the country.

Killeen, Last of the Originals, Retires
by Tim Wellock

The last playing link with Durham's original first-class squad in 1992 has been severed by the retirement of Neil Killeen. At 34 the seam bowler from Annfield Plain, in the north west of the county, bade an emotional farewell when he bowed out with figures of 3 for 24 in the Clydesdale Bank 40 League match at home to Kent.

The Durham members gave him a standing ovation as he led the team off and coach Geoff Cook led the tributes, saying, 'I've enjoyed watching Neil play cricket throughout his career. For him to retire as the leading wicket-taker for Durham in one-day cricket is certainly an accolade that is much deserved. He has worked extremely hard to give his best to the team and the club.'

Killeen was 16 when he was taken out of school to go on Durham's tour to Zimbabwe as a late replacement for the injured John Wood in February 1992. That was Durham's final preparation for first-class cricket and Killeen made his first-class debut in 1995, going on to play in 101 games, taking 262 wickets at 30.99. Only Simon Brown and Steve Harmison have taken more first-class wickets for Durham and Killeen leads the way in limited-overs cricket. In the one-day league he finished with 209 wickets. He was part of the team that secured Durham's first silverware, the Friends Provident Trophy, in 2007 when they beat Hampshire Hawks in the final at Lord's.

Killeen said, 'I've enjoyed every minute of my time with Durham and that Lord's final was the absolute highlight of my career. It was great seeing the hard work of so many people coming to fruition. It was a massive achievement for the team and that weekend is something I will always remember.'

Neil Killeen has been a valuable member of Durham's one-day attack in recent years, and a loyal servant.

DURHAM CCC

FIRST-CLASS MATCHES
BATTING

Match	DM Benkenstein	MJ Di Venuto	P Mustard	ID Blackwell	BA Stokes	LE Plunkett	ME Claydon	SG Borthwick	MD Stoneman	SJ Harmison	GJ Muchall	C Rushworth	KJ Coetzer	WR Smith	CD Thorp	AM Davies	BW Harmison	GR Breese	L Evans	MJ Richardson	PD Collingwood	RMR Brathwaite	Extras	Total	Wickets	Result	Points
v. MCC (Abu Dhabi) 29 March-1 April	41	131	23*	13	51		0	0	-				172	13	0								15	459	9		
	0	-	50	26	7		-	-					52*	11	79*								3	228	6	W	
v. Essex (Chester-le-Street) 15-18 April	18	21	2	17	7	14	4						55	44	0	0*							16	198	10		
	98	99	60*	52	4	0							0	0	10*								29	352	7	D	4
v. Hampshire (Chester-le-Street) 21-24 April	10	71	0	83	41	41	6*						47	28	11	27							19	384	10		
	10	18	32*	62	27*	-							72	20	-	-							21	262	5	W	23
v. Yorkshire (Headingley) 27-30 April	64	108*	0	21	28	51		20*			5		8	8		0							17	330	9		
	-	-	-	-	-	-		21*			-		23*	-		-							2	46	0	D	6
v. Durham UCCE (Durham) 5-7 May								46	118	7	12		22	57		0	21	14	4*	2			21	324	10		
																										D	
v. Nottinghamshire (Trent Bridge) 10-13 May	36	15	31	43	32	3		4*		9	3	10					14						18	218	10		
	8	29	23	15	106	3		4*		6	45	4					18						18	279	10	L	3
v. Kent (Canterbury) 17-20 May	114	67	10	17	161*		3	1	0		18	12					8						7	418	10		
	49	10	-	53*	42*		14		-		-	1					-						3	172	4	W	23
v. Kent (Chester-le-Street) 24-25 May	1	9	2	27	9	22*		0		4		16	10				8						13	121	10		
	7	86	16	53	0	11*	1	0		0		4					5						12	195	10	L	3
v. Warwickshire (Edgbaston) 29 May-1 June	26	4	100	0	16	41	14	0	77		60		3*										38	379	10		
																										D	10
v. Warwickshire (Chester-le-Street) 28 June-1 July	14	6	35	86	16		18		12	0*	27	26					29						19	288	10		
	1	92	25	36	4		20		60	1*	18	0					6						26	289	10	W	21
v. Lancashire (Chester-le-Street) 20-23 July	21	12	71*	3	37	5	5		11	0							8			12			31	216	10		
																										D	
v. Hampshire (Basingstoke) 3-6 August	5	4	0	1	99	-		54	9	-	140*				-								8	320	7		
																										D	7
v. Lancashire (Old Trafford) 9-12 August	32	13	0	65	32	28	2	30	7	1*	14												13	237	10		
	41*	63	-	20*	-	8		14	-	3													24	173	4	W	20
v. Yorkshire (Chester-le-Street) 16-19 August	0	117*	53	6	0	0	4	1	4	12	0												16	213	10		
	74	18	2	13	8	30	29	78	11*	31	28												18	340	10	L	4
v. Somerset (Taunton) 24-27 August	-	10*	-	-	-	-	-	22*	-					-									5	37	0		
																										D	5
v. Nottinghamshire (Chester-le-Street) 31 Aug-3 Sept	13	0	120	59	0	1	68	67		13				5*	2								24	372	10		
	58	15	51*	50	-	-	43*	13		111					11								9	361	6	W	23
v. Essex (Chelmsford) 7-10 September	0	0	31	24	0	38*	3	0	3	0							66						12	177	10		
	2	58	24*	22	-	-		5	6	-							96						21	234	6	D	6
v. Somerset (Chester-le-Street) 13-16 September	72	18	42	23	11		9	15	37	0*					35							2	22	286	10		
	25	129	12	23	2		5	16	33	16					15							0*	44	320	10	D	8

	DM Benkenstein	MJ Di Venuto	P Mustard	ID Blackwell	BA Stokes	LE Plunkett	ME Claydon	SG Borthwick	MD Stoneman	SJ Harmison	GJ Muchall	C Rushworth	KJ Coetzer	WR Smith	CD Thorp	AM Davies	BW Harmison	GR Breese	L Evans	MJ Richardson	PD Collingwood	RMR Brathwaite
Matches	17	17	17	16	14	14	13	12	11	10	10	9	8	6	6	6	6	2	1	1	1	1
Innings	28	28	26	26	21	17	16	17	17	12	15	14	15	10	8	5	10	3	1	1	1	2
Not Out	1	3	6	2	2	4	1	3	1	6	1	2	2	0	2	2	0	0	1	0	0	1
Highest Score	114	131	120	86	161*	51	38*	68	118	11*	140*	28	172	57	79*	27	96	14	4*	2	12	2
Runs	840	1223	815	833	798	238	185	315	525	36	520	127	526	195	143	32	286	27	4	2	12	2
Average	31.11	48.92	40.75	34.70	44.33	14.00	15.41	22.50	32.81	6.00	37.14	10.58	40.46	19.50	23.83	10.66	28.60	9.00	-	2.00	12.00	2.00
100s	1	4	2	0	2	0	0	0	1	0	2	0	1	0	0	0	0	0	0	0	0	0
50s	5	7	5	8	3	1	0	2	4	0	1	0	3	1	1	0	2	0	0	0	0	0
Catches/Stumpings	14/0	30/0	43/2	2/0	8/0	8/0	2/0	9/0	5/0	2/0	3/0	1/0	3/0	3/0	3/0	0/0	1/0	0/0	0/0	0/0	0/0	0/0

Home Ground: Chester-le-Street
Address: Emirates Durham International Cricket Ground, Chester-le-Street, County Durham, DH3 3QR
Tel: 0191 3871717
Fax: 01913 874698
Email: reception@durhamccc.co.uk
Directions: *By rail:* Chester-le-Street station (approx 5 minutes by taxi or a 10-minute walk). *By road:* Easily accessible from junction 63 of the A1(M).

Capacity: 15,000
Year formed: 1882

Chief Executive: David Harker
Head Coach: Geoff Cook
Captain: Will Smith, Phil Mustard
County colours: Yellow, blue and burgundy

Honours
County Championship
2008, 2009
Friends Provident Trophy
2007

Website:
www.durhamccc.co.uk

FIRST-CLASS MATCHES
BOWLING

Match	ID Blackwell	ME Claydon	LE Plunkett	SJ Harmison	SG Borthwick	C Rushworth	CD Thorp	BW Harmison	BA Stokes	RMR Brathwaite	DM Benkenstein	AM Davies	PD Collingwood	GJ Muchall	GR Breese	L Evans	WR Smith	KJ Coetzer	Overs	Total	Byes/Leg-byes	Wickets	Run outs
v. MCC (Abu Dhabi) 29 March-1 April	8-2-16-0	10-3-31-0		9-2-37-2	4.5-0-27-4		10-7-25-3	4-0-14-1											45.5	162	12	10	
	25-8-70-4	6-1-22-0		11-2-39-2	12-1-57-4			5-1-23-0											59	214	3	10	
v. Essex (Chester-le-Street) 15-18 April	25-4-85-1	27-6-83-1		31.3-3-112-4			36-12-79-4	10-0-34-0				29-9-54-0						4-0-15-0	162.3	484	22	10	
v. Hampshire (Chester-le-Street) 21-24 April	15-5-33-2	23-3-84-3		28.2-3-107-4			14-3-54-0	5-0-15-1			19-5-49-0								104.2	345	3	10	
	30-7-78-3	3.4-0-8-1		32.2-7-86-2			14.1-1-71-1	8.3-1-32-2			10-5-15-0								98.3	298	8	10	1
v. Yorkshire (Headingley) 27-30 April	43-15-105-2		23-3-110-0		27-0-122-2	27-7-86-0			9-0-52-1		12-6-21-0	28-10-60-0					4-0-27-0	3-0-18-0	176	610	9	6	1
v. Durham UCCE (Durham) 5-7 May				5-1-18-0	3-1-3-0						3-2-9-0				3-1-5-0	2-0-11-0			16	46	0	0	
v. Nottinghamshire (Trent Bridge) 10-13 May	16-5-39-0		21-1-115-3	28-4-123-1			28-4-113-3	19-1-86-1	6-0-59-0										118	559	24	8	
v. Kent (Canterbury) 17-20 May	13-2-62-0	21-1-106-0		18-5-52-4	4-0-20-0	15-2-66-2		15.4-2-87-3	1-0-11-0		6-3-13-1								93.4	424	7	10	
	11-4-35-3	8-3-23-1		11.5-2-39-2	9-1-22-2	10-1-36-2													49.5	162	7	10	
v. Kent (Chester-le-Street) 24-25 May		15-2-50-3		18-1-94-3	11-0-83-2	3-0-8-0	16-3-72-2												63	320	13	10	
v. Warwickshire (Edgbaston) 29 May-1 June	8-0-25-2	9-3-17-3	9-3-16-3						9-1-38-2										35	100	4	10	
	24-11-26-1	9-1-52-1	14-4-50-0				17-1-69-2												72	229	17	4	
v. Warwickshire (Chester-le-Street) 28 June-1 July	4-1-12-0	13-1-42-1			19-6-45-2		16.5-3-46-3	20-4-54-4	2-0-12-0										74.5	224	13	10	
	5-1-10-0	14-2-47-3			15.2-6-29-7		4-1-19-0	8-3-23-0	2-1-4-0										48.2	134	2	10	
v. Lancashire (Chester-le-Street) 20-23 July	9-1-28-0	15.3-3-65-3	17-1-75-2		25-3-93-2			28-7-60-2					7-3-11-1						101.3	344	12	10	
	9-6-5-1	6-1-25-1	8-0-22-1					7-2-14-0	1-0-10-0										40	91	1	4	1
v. Hampshire (Basingstoke) 3-6 August	17-2-61-1		14-0-72-0	28-4-106-1	8-0-52-0		19-6-66-2	9-2-41-0			14-6-19-1								109	421	4	5	
	25-7-79-5		4.2-0-14-0	6.3-0-34-0	8-1-41-0		2.3-1-6-0	3-1-8-0			13-11-5-0								62.2	203	16	5	
v. Lancashire (Old Trafford) 9-12 August	23.2-6-78-5	9-3-29-2		16-5-29-0	18-8-27-3	3-0-6-0													69.2	181	12	10	
	33-8-102-4	11-4-28-1		18.5-6-41-1	10-2-19-1	11-4-32-2					1-1-0-0								84.5	226	4	10	1
v. Yorkshire (Chester-le-Street) 16-19 August	13-5-17-1	8-0-37-2	17-4-56-3	23-3-81-3			11-4-50-1												72	255	14	10	
	5-0-24-0	18-5-74-3	11-1-57-0	18-3-56-2			13.5-2-51-0	7-0-26-1											72.5	299	11	6	
v. Somerset (Taunton) 24-27 August	28-7-79-1	20-3-86-1	16-2-64-1	7.4-0-38-1					3-1-24-0		3-0-17-2	27-5-85-0							104.4	400	7	6	
v. Nottinghamshire (Chester-le-Street) 31 Aug-3 Sept	21-8-33-0	21-2-78-2	25-5-66-3		20-2-78-1			4-0-28-2			7-2-31-0	15-11-10-2							113	343	19	10	
	19-13-23-3	15-4-61-2	2-0-8-0		3.1-0-11-1			15-2-70-4											54.1	180	7	10	
v. Essex (Chelmsford) 7-10 September	16-3-30-2	12-1-60-1		14.2-4-33-3	14-5-41-2	22-8-69-1		8-2-20-0				7-4-11-0							93.2	268	4	10	1
	23.1-4-70-4	9-1-32-0		15-1-54-0	19.4-7-52-0	20-4-90-4		7-2-17-0				18-10-26-0							111.1	367	3	10	
v. Somerset (Chester-le-Street) 13-16 September	14-3-47-0		29-3-105-2			14-1-70-1		18-1-94-4		24.1-2-93-3				1-0-2-0					100.1	426	15	10	
	6-1-19-2									6-0-25-1									12	48	4	3	
Overs	488.3	303.1	384.4	265.4	173.4	214.4	158.3	86.4	75.3	30.1	81	131	7	1	3	2	4	7					
Maidens	139	53	57	55	20	43	46	10	7	2	43	47	3	0	1	0	0	0					
Runs	1291	1140	1386	895	702	821	452	402	365	118	143	282	11	2	5	11	27	33					
Wickets	47	35	35	34	23	21	16	14	6	4	4	2	1	0	0	0	0	0					
Average	27.47	32.57	39.60	26.32	30.52	39.10	28.25	28.71	60.83	29.50	35.75	141.00	11.00	-	-	-	-	-					

FIELDING

45	P Mustard (43 ct, 2 st)
30	MJ Di Venuto
14	DM Benkenstein
9	SG Borthwick
8	LE Plunkett
8	BA Stokes
5	MD Stoneman
5	KJ Coetzer
3	GJ Muchall
3	WR Smith
3	CD Thorp
2	ID Blackwell
2	ME Claydon
2	SJ Harmison
1	GR Breese
1	C Rushworth

Division One – Final Table

	P	W	L	D	Bat	Bowl	Pens	Pts
Nottinghamshire	16	7	5	4	47	43	0	214
Somerset	16	6	2	8	53	41	0	214
Yorkshire	16	6	2	8	41	42	0	203
Lancashire	16	5	3	8	35	43	0	182
Durham	16	5	3	8	30	39	0	173
Warwickshire	16	6	9	1	20	47	0	166
Hampshire	16	3	6	7	47	41	0	157
Kent	16	3	7	6	42	44	-1	151
Essex	16	2	6	8	29	43	-2	126

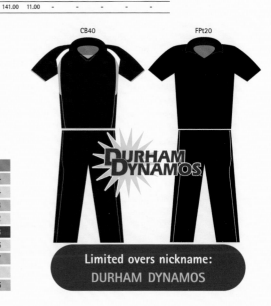

CB40

FPt20

Limited overs nickname:
DURHAM DYNAMOS

ESSEX

by Paul Hiscock

While Essex retained their reputation as a competitive one-day outfit, reaching two semi-finals, the loss of their County Championship first division status was a real body blow to the county. It had taken them six years to reclaim their place in the top flight and just one season to lose it after a campaign in which they managed a mere two victories.

Ironically, one of those two wins came inside three days against title winners Nottinghamshire, but after a constant struggle for runs in Championship cricket their fate was sealed during a wretched run in the closing weeks with four successive defeats including three matches without a single batting point.

Fellow relegation candidates Warwickshire orchestrated two of those with a remarkable sequence of scores. The Midlanders, bottom of the table at the time, scored 155 and 155 for 3 at Southend followed by identical totals in the return game three weeks later at Edgbaston and recorded crucial seven-wicket victories in both games.

A paucity of runs remained the chief reason for the county's demise, with no batsman managing to reach 1,000 Championship runs. Only on one occasion did

A brilliant legside take by James Foster off Danish Kaneria, who struggled to make much of an impact in the County Championship in 2010.

the side score 400. There was also a change in captaincy halfway through the season when Mark Pettini decided to stand down after three successful years in the role. After a two-week week break, he returned to a side now under the stewardship of the steadfast James Foster.

The season had started promisingly for Essex, who beat Hampshire in their opening four-day match after their opponents lost all ten second-innings wickets in the final scheduled session of the match at Chelmsford. Rain then probably denied them the opportunity of a follow-up win at Durham. Two heavy losses soon followed, against Yorkshire and Lancashire, and the cracks began to show as the lack of substantial runs and associated problems became all too evident.

Even the availability of England opener Alastair Cook for seven matches did not offer the weight of runs required. Cook managed only one century in 12 visits to the crease although Ravi Bopara did show snatches of brilliance. He scored centuries in both innings of the drawn match with Yorkshire at Chelmsford but then amassed just 56 runs in his next seven innings.

There was, however, a silver lining amid the batting gloom with the emergence of 21-year-old Jaik Mickleburgh who showed sound temperament and a well-organised approach. Foster also proved a useful middle-order batsman with 839 runs to add to his exemplary wicketkeeping and the responsibilities of captaincy.

Tireless workhorse David Masters was the most effective bowler of the county's attack, whose potency suffered badly due to a torrid year for Danish Kaneria. At the start of the season, the Pakistan leg spinner was charged with spot-fixing during a Pro40 match at Durham in 2009 – he denied the charge but was only cleared at the end of the season – and found himself axed from the Pakistan tour party because of poor form during their Test schedule. All that badly affected Kaneria, who was seldom the force of past years.

Mervyn Westfield was also named in the spot-fixing allegations and was subsequently charged and ordered to appear in court after the end of the season. But, by that time, he learned he was not to be re-engaged by Essex with the club stating that the decision did not relate to the fraud investigations.

With no effective spin back up, the county lacked incisive support for Masters. The absence of Graham Napier, who only played four matches because of a stress

Top Maurice Chambers made giant strides as a fast bowler in 2010, and his ultimate reward was selection for the England Performance Programme squad.

Right Jaik Mickleburgh was another young Essex cricketer who impressed. Here he pulls against Kent at Chelmsford.

Scott Styris, the New Zealand all-rounder, was a huge hit as an Essex overseas player during the Friends Provident t20, but he was sadly unavailable for the knockout stage of the competition due to international commitments.

fracture of the back, did not help the cause while Ryan ten Doeschate missed two months of the season with a torn calf. That led to lanky Nottinghamshire pace bowler Andy Carter joining the team although he only played three Championship matches before he too broke down.

Five overseas players were used. New Zealand paceman Chris Martin was drafted in at the start of the season as a replacement for Kaneria who was involved in a Pentangular Tournament in Pakistan but his intended month's stay lasted little over a week due to a combination of visa problems and the Icelandic volcanic ash cloud and he played just three matches in all competitions, taking just two wickets.

Australian leg spinner Bryce McGain proved a better recruit. Arriving in late July to replace Kaneria, now on Test duty, the 38-year-old claimed a five-wicket haul in his first Championship match at Kent, took five wickets in the defeat by Warwickshire at Southend and also made an

'WE WERE NAIVE', SAYS GRAYSON

Essex's relegation from Division One of the County Championship provoked little sympathy from first-team coach Paul Grayson, who identified in particular the failures against Kent, Warwickshire and Somerset. 'We had opportunities to win all three games and if you don't take them, you can't have any complaints when you get punished,' he said. 'You can go around feeling sorry for yourselves, and we could blame the weather at Trent Bridge, Old Trafford and the Riverside earlier in the season that possibly denied us victories there. But over the course of a season you get what you deserve and we didn't deserve anything.

'We brought relegation upon ourselves. Some of our cricket was pretty good but you have to take the defining moments in a game that come your way and we didn't do that. Our cricket has been soft; it's been naive. The players don't need telling but they know they let themselves down, both with bat and ball, and we just didn't play well enough.'

appearance in a 40-over match before Kaneria's fall from favour with the Pakistan tourists and subsequent return to county cricket forced McGain to bid an early farewell.

Scott Styris was the most successful of the overseas quintet. Recruited for the Friends Provident t20 campaign, he proved a shrewd choice with all-round contributions and at least three match-winning innings – including a magnificent unbeaten 106 from 50 balls against Surrey to steal the game.

He was unable to play in the knockout stages, though, having been called up by New Zealand for a tour but, even without him, the county overcame the odds and Lancashire to reach the semi-finals. The decision to recruit Dwayne Bravo just for t20 Finals Day, at a reputed cost of £10,000 and to the consternation of many members, proved a spectacular failure. The West Indian proved a costly flop scoring just five runs and returning 1 for 46 from his four overs before jumping on a plane back to the Caribbean.

Evergreen Walker Signs for 2011
by Paul Hiscock

Matt Walker signed in September a contract extension with Essex that will commit him to the county until the end of the 2011 season, and the popular left-hander then marked the occasion with a century in the County Championship match against Durham at Chelmsford.

The 36-year-old had spent his entire career with Kent until he was surprisingly released at the end of the 2008 season. Essex swooped for his services and he admits that his switch of allegiance has been a move to savour. 'It has re-launched my career really and I couldn't be happier,' said Walker. 'The two years I've had so far with Essex have given me a new lease of life. The guys in the dressing room are brilliant and I've enjoyed working with them and everyone else involved in the club.

'For me, it's a nice stage in my career where I am aware of youngsters coming through and if I can help them in any way, then I'm delighted. I also feel my game has improved under the guidance of Paul Grayson (the Essex first-team head coach) and I hope to achieve more success across all formats of the game in the years to come. I've certainly no thoughts of retirement yet. I feel that I still have a lot to offer and I want to play as long as I can because I love the game, but I wouldn't want to compromise either myself or the team if I felt I wasn't performing well enough.

'At the moment, I think that I'm playing as well as I have done for a number of years and, when you get to the stage in your career that I'm at now, you always want to prove things to yourself. As long as you think you can do it, that your eyes are still fine and it's not too painful to get out of bed and you're contributing, then it's the right decision to carry on playing.'

Matt Walker hits out in a Friends Provident t20 match against his former county Kent, at Chelmsford.

Flower's Fine Farewell
by Paul Hiscock

Grant Flower marked his final home appearance for Essex with a typical fighting innings of 81 not out that took his side one step closer to their Clydesdale Bank 40 semi-final place. It helped Essex to beat Middlesex by seven wickets and Flower received a standing ovation from the Chelmsford faithful. The 39-year-old was offered the position of Second XI captain at the end of the season but decided to return to his native Zimbabwe where he has been given the role of batting coach for the national team. He was then persuaded to play international cricket again. 'I've decided to return to Zimbabwe as things have improved out there although there are still a number of things that aren't good. But I think the country is definitely on the up,' he said.

Flower will be chiefly remembered at the county for his ice-cool temperament, which was particularly in evidence when his 70 not out guided Essex to victory in the 2008 Friends Provident Trophy final against Kent at Lord's. 'That match is an outstanding memory,' said Flower, 'but just being at Essex for six years has been terrific. I was lucky that Essex gave me an opportunity and I've tried to make the most of it. It's been a great time.'

Flower made 67 Test appearances for Zimbabwe before his initial international retirement in 2004, scoring 3,457 runs including six centuries. Before coming out of retirement in October 2010, he had also played in 219 ODIs, amassing 6,536 runs, again with six centuries. Additionally, he had taken 25 Test wickets and 104 ODI victims with his slow left-armers, besides being renowned for his brilliant fielding, usually in the gully.

Grant Flower strikes a ball into the offside field during his century for Essex in their Clydesdale Bank 40 league match against Gloucestershire at Chelmsford.

The Clydesdale Bank 40 competition saw the county enjoy a splendid run of nine wins in 10 matches to clinch their place in the semi-finals before Somerset ended hopes of a Lord's final.

PLAYER OF THE SEASON

David Masters. The 32-year-old evergreen paceman and model professional carried the attack with 53 Championship wickets at 23.07 from 487 overs, which was 250 overs more than any of his colleagues. He also proved an economical and wicket-taking strike bowler in the shorter form of the game.

YOUNG PLAYER OF THE SEASON

Jaik Mickleburgh enjoyed his first full season of county cricket, and the 21-year-old showed a cool head and well-organised approach to finish joint top of the list of the county's Championship run-scorers with James Foster, amassing 839 runs.

A YEAR TO REMEMBER

- James Foster added the role of captaincy from mid-June with no ill effects on his own game, and continued to show the highest standard of wicketkeeping skills
- Maurice Chambers turned potential into performance, and won himself a place on the winter Performance Programme squad
- Ryan ten Doeschate enjoyed a productive all-round season despite missing two months through injury

A YEAR TO FORGET

- Danish Kaneria often bowled poorly and was clearly affected by issues on and off the field
- Graham Napier was ruled out for the season after incurring a stress fracture in the lower back in the first week of June
- Mervyn Westfield was named in the spot-fixing charge, he failed to play a game was not re-engaged at the end of the season

David Masters was again a model of consistency, in all forms of the game, during the 2010 season.

Friday night Twenty20 cricket continued to attract capacity crowds to Chelmsford but finances remain tight although first-team coach Paul Grayson is anxious to freshen up the squad for 2011 with at least two new faces. Promotion in the Championship heads his wish list while he is also expecting his side to maintain their prowess in the limited-overs game.

ESSEX CCC

FIRST-CLASS MATCHES

BATTING

	JS Foster	JC Mickleburgh	ML Pettini	DD Masters	BA Godleman	MJ Walker	MA Chambers	RN ten Doeschate	CJC Wright	TJ Phillips	T Westley	RS Bopara	JK Maunders	AN Cook	Danish Kaneria	AP Palladino	GR Napier	GW Flower	A Carter	MA Comber	M Osborne	BE McCain	CS Martin	AJ Wheater	Extras	Total	Wickets	Result	Points
v. Hampshire	88		10	4	92	57	0*	23	9		1			33			13								15	345	10		
(Chelmsford) 9-12 April	27		23	0	4	25	2	66*	9		69			1			7								23	256	10	W	21
v. Durham	169	174	4	9	0			3	5*		22		11	44			0								43	484	10		
(Chester-le-Street) 15-18 April																												D	9
v. Lancashire	27	9	28	2	4		0	55*	21	5			0	3											22	176	10		
(Chelmsford) 21-23 April	14	27	22	17	7	11*	0	15	0				1	50											9	173	10	L	3
v. Somerset	35	23	14	50	106		1	21	9*		22	22		41											9	353	10		
(Taunton) 27-30 April																												D	10
v. Yorkshire	35	33	44	11	15			24	4		19		6	7									0*		8	206	10		
(Scarborough) 4-6 May	5	33	47	9	1			35	4		19*		33	10									11		7	214	10	L	2
v. Kent	21	2	13	36*	45			66	6		0	132		0	1										19	341	10		
(Chelmsford) 10-13 May		25	40*	-				13	-		58*			72											15	254	10	D	8
v. Bangladeshis		2		17	45	0		11					126			0		46		19	0*			22	25	313	10		
(Chelmsford) 14-16 May		11		20	11	-		21					2			-		34*		-	-			19*	12	130	5	W	
v. Lancashire	6	39	12	33	39	42	1	85	1			-			0	36*									13	307	10		
(Old Trafford) 24-27 May	-	64	14*		6	53*		56	8			5													6	212	5	D	8
v. Nottinghamshire	59	10	96	32		6	1*	26	0			17	22				12								48	329	10		
(Trent Bridge) 29 May-1 June		25				46*						23	57*			-									1	152	2	D	9
v. Hampshire	14	21	0	15	99	0*		6				36	39			8	35								11	284	10		
(Rose Bowl) 4-7 June	18	2	12*			3	-	0				1	61			-	0*								2	99	6	D	8
v. Nottinghamshire	122	2	10	20	15	13	14				46*	4	2		2										4	154	10		
(Chelmsford) 5-7 July	8	91	11	0	3	70	8				12*	32	70		9										14	328	10	W	19
v. Yorkshire	61	38			26	0	13*	30	6			142	44				5	8							26	399	10		
(Chelmsford) 20-23 July	22*	0			38		-	-	-		7	102	102				2	-							20	293	10	D	10
v. Kent	41	20	88	42	10	6			11		0	2							16*			14			29	279	10		
(Canterbury) 29 July-1 August	12	24	4	1	35	0			12		25	31							11			8*			14	177	10	L	4
v. Warwickshire	3	10	1	5	29				9		12	1				32*			2			24			22	150	10		
(Southend-on-Sea) 4-6 August	12	30	16	34	39				1		1	6				0			8			0*			12	159	10	L	3
v. Somerset	16	2	34	4	32	3		40	10			1			0*	6									3	151	10		
(Colchester) 18-20 August	10	15	6	14	53	13		41	7*			15			0	16									22	212	10	L	3
v. Warwickshire	0	14	3	0	22	0	7					53*		0		0									15	114	10		
(Edgbaston) 25-28 August	8	0	35	18	39	38	9*	10				13		8		0									15	193	10	L	3
v. Durham	42	72	10	9		32			28*		16			33		10				0	5				11	268	10		
(Chelmsford) 7-10 September	64	34	2	9		105			12		0			68		66				0	0*				7	367	10	D	8
Matches	16	16	15	14	12	12	11	11	11	10	9	8	7	7	6	5	4	3	3	2	2	2	1	1					
Innings	27	30	27	22	22	24	16	19	17	16	18	15	12	12	9	9	6	5	5	3	3	4	2	2					
Not Out	1	0	3	1	0	2	5	2	5	3	1	2	0	0	1	1	1	2	1	0	2	2	1	1					
Highest Score	169	174	96	50	106	105	14	85	28*	46*	132	142	126	102	9	66	35	46	16*	19	5	24	11	22					
Runs	839	852	599	356	569	838	53	577	161	240	440	550	307	474	28	130	67	123	45	19	5	46	11	41					
Average	32.26	28.40	24.95	16.95	25.86	38.09	4.81	33.94	13.41	18.46	25.88	42.30	25.58	39.50	3.50	16.25	13.40	41.00	11.25	6.33	5.00	23.00	11.00	41.00					
100s	1	1	0	0	1	1	0	0	0	0	1	2	1	0	0	1	0	0	0	0	0	0	0	0					
50s	4	3	2	1	2	4	0	5	0	0	2	3	3	1	0	1	0	0	0	0	0	0	0	0					
Catches/Stumpings	48/5	11/0	7/0	8/0	12/0	8/0	5/0	9/0	2/0	8/0	1/0	4/0	6/0	6/0	1/0	1/0	1/0	3/0	2/0	1/0	0/0	0/0	0/0	7/0					

Home Ground: Chelmsford
Address: Ford County Ground, New Writtle Street, Chelmsford, Essex, CM2 0PG
Tel: 01245 252420
Fax: 01245 254030
Email: administration.essex@ecb.co.uk
Directions: *By rail:* Chelmsford station (8 minutes' walk away). *By road:* M25 then A12 to Chelmsford. Exit Chelmsford and follow AA signs to Essex Cricket Club.
Capacity: 6,500
Other grounds used: Colchester, Southend-on-Sea
Year formed: 1876

Chief Executive: David East
First Team Coach: Paul Grayson
Captain: Mark Pettini, James Foster
County colours: Royal and navy blue

Website:
www.essexcricket.org.uk

Honours
County Championship
1979, 1983, 1984, 1986, 1991, 1992
Sunday League/NCL/Pro40
1981, 1984, 1985, 2005, 2006
Refuge Assurance Cup
1989
Benson & Hedges Cup
1979, 1998
Gillette Cup/NatWest/C&G Trophy/
Friends Provident Trophy
1985, 1997, 2008

FIRST-CLASS MATCHES
BOWLING

	DD Masters	MA Chambers	CJC Wright	RN ten Doeschate	Danish Kaneria	TJ Phillips	AP Palladino	A Carter	BE McGain	M Osborne	T Westley	MA Comber	RS Bopara	MJ Walker	GR Napier	GW Flower	AN Cook	CS Martin	JC Mickleburgh	Overs	Total	Byes/Leg-byes	Wickets	Run outs
v. Hampshire (Chelmsford) 9-12 April	36.4-9-67-4	19-2-76-2	25-6-66-0	10-1-46-1							4-0-7-1				30-7-68-1					124.4	354	24	10	1
	13-4-24-2	5-0-21-1	11-0-55-1	5.5-2-13-5							1-0-6-0				12-1-61-1					47.5	185	5	10	
v. Durham (Chester-le-Street) 15-18 April	20-9-48-1		19-8-42-3	17.2-3-53-3	5-0-8-3										18-4-37-0				1-0-6-0	79.2	198	10	10	
	21-4-57-2		18-2-76-0	17-1-44-1	36-5-113-4										12-2-32-0					105	352	24	7	
v. Lancashire (Chelmsford) 21-23 April	29-6-81-4	23-4-58-2	16.2-3-76-3	15-1-62-1		14-6-24-0														97.2	312	11	10	
	3-1-13-1	6.3-1-16-0				3-1-4-1														12.3	38	5	2	
v. Somerset (Taunton) 27-30 April	27-5-83-4	8-1-30-1	23-8-84-1	20-1-69-1		29.4-6-107-1											1-0-3-0			108.4	387	11	10	2
	3-0-13-0	9.3-0-47-0	7-1-29-0																	24.3	100	1	0	
v. Yorkshire (Scarborough) 4-6 May	29-9-89-1		25.1-4-97-3	31-1-117-3		34-3-112-2												25-10-84-1		144.1	516	17	10	
v. Kent (Chelmsford) 10-13 May	29-10-67-1		24-3-118-1	17.2-1-77-4	33-3-124-2	14-1-57-1				2-0-9-1										119.2	474	22	10	
	16-5-41-2		11-1-37-2	10-0-51-1	24-5-68-4	4-1-6-0														63	204	1	10	1
v. Bangladeshis (Chelmsford) 14-16 May		15.4-3-32-4				1-1-0-0	23-3-91-3			14-2-60-2		7-0-44-1								60.4	231	4	10	
		17-5-51-2					15-2-75-3			6-1-35-3		7.2-1-34-2								45.2	211	16	10	
v. Lancashire (Old Trafford) 24-27 May	13-7-15-1	15.4-4-52-2	8-1-23-1	6-0-30-2	13.1-3-42-3								3-0-16-0							58.1	184	6	10	1
	11.4-4-25-1	15.5-5-36-0	13-4-30-2	10-2-26-1	33-16-49-1								1-0-1-0							83.4	177	10	5	
v. Nottinghamshire (Trent Bridge) 29 May-1 June	16.4-6-48-4	15-3-63-3	12-1-44-1	1-0-5-1											14-3-47-1					58.4	217		10	
																				—				
v. Hampshire (Rose Bowl) 4-7 June	19-6-46-1	19-5-49-5	14-1-63-0		27-7-71-2								10-2-33-2		9-1-35-0					98	300	3	10	
	16.5-3-61-1	19-5-50-2	11-2-33-1		30-7-100-1								11-0-49-2							87.5	311	18	7	
v. Nottinghamshire (Chelmsford) 5-7 July	16-4-47-0	15-2-68-6			10-1-42-2	6-0-17-2														47	180	6	10	
	13-2-48-2	13-2-55-4			15.3-2-51-4	3-1-4-0														44.3	159	11	10	
v. Yorkshire (Chelmsford) 20-23 July		17-6-39-0	15-3-64-1		44-15-94-4	24.1-3-77-3				10-2-25-1						2-0-13-0				112.1	324	12	10	1
		13-1-59-0	7-1-42-2		28.4-3-116-2	15-1-55-1				12-1-30-1						7-0-19-1				82.4	333	12	7	
v. Kent (Canterbury) 29 July-1 August	29-7-82-2	8-1-24-1				16-1-65-0		26-4-81-2	33.3-1-151-5		3-0-19-0				8-1-35-3					115.3	420	18	10	
	16-6-34-2							17.4-5-40-5	6-0-19-0											39.4	135		7	
v. Warwickshire (Southend-on-Sea) 4-6 August	19.4-8-51-3								17-8-30-1	12.2-1-41-2	10-2-33-4									59	155		10	
	16.2-3-36-2					3-0-15-0			9-4-18-0	5.4-1-17-0	15-1-57-1								0.1-0-5-0	49.1	155		7	3
v. Somerset (Colchester) 18-20 August	21.1-6-43-5		13-1-56-2		11-0-51-1	13-2-61-2									9-0-36-0					58.1	215		10	
	18-4-53-3		11-1-83-2		20-1-120-1	12-1-67-2														74	367	8	8	
v. Warwickshire (Edgbaston) 25-28 August	19-5-39-3	14.3-1-55-2		6-0-27-2		2-0-7-1				10-4-17-2										51.3	155		10	
	18-6-45-2	5.5-0-31-0				8-0-28-1				7-1-42-0										38.5	155		9	3
v. Durham (Chelmsford) 7-10 September			17.5-2-70-5			21-3-57-4			7-1-31-0	7-2-10-0	2-0-4-1				1-1-0-0					55.5	177	5	10	
			17-4-48-1			15-2-41-1			9-1-26-1	29-5-68-2	6-1-12-0						7-1-33-1			83	234	7	6	

	DD Masters	MA Chambers	CJC Wright	RN ten Doeschate	Danish Kaneria	TJ Phillips	AP Palladino	A Carter	BE McGain	M Osborne	T Westley	MA Comber	RS Bopara	MJ Walker	GR Napier	GW Flower	AN Cook	CS Martin	JC Mickleburgh	Byes/Leg-byes	Wickets	Run outs
Overs	487	269.3	301.5	191.3	226.4	246.2	142	100.5	64.3	36	68	22.2	25	18	95	9	8	25	1.1			
Maidens	138	51	55	16	45	45	30	15	4	5	10	2	2	2	18	0	1	10	0			
Runs	1223	909	1156	716	753	752	499	311	260	151	174	94	99	71	280	32	36	84	11			
Wickets	53	38	31	27	23	20	18	13	10	6	6	4	4	3	3	1	1	1	0			
Average	23.08	23.92	37.29	26.52	32.74	37.60	27.72	23.92	26.00	25.17	29.00	23.50	24.75	23.67	93.33	32.00	36.00	84.00	–			

FIELDING

53	JS Foster (48 ct, 5 st)
12	BA Godleman
11	JC Mickleburgh
9	RN ten Doeschate
8	DD Masters
8	TJ Phillips
8	MJ Walker
7	ML Pettini
7	AJ Wheater (7 ct)
6	AN Cook
6	JK Maunders
5	MA Chambers
4	RS Bopara
3	GW Flower
2	A Carter
2	CJC Wright
1	MA Comber
1	Danish Kaneria
1	GR Napier
1	AP Palladino
1	T Westley

Division One – Final Table

	P	W	L	D	Bat	Bowl	Pens	Pts
Nottinghamshire	16	7	5	4	47	43	0	214
Somerset	16	6	2	8	53	41	0	214
Yorkshire	16	6	2	8	41	42	0	203
Lancashire	16	5	3	8	35	43	0	182
Durham	16	5	3	8	30	39	0	173
Warwickshire	16	6	9	1	20	47	0	166
Hampshire	16	3	6	7	47	41	0	157
Kent	16	3	7	6	42	44	-1	151
Essex	16	2	6	8	29	43	-2	126

CB40 FPt20

Limited overs nickname:
ESSEX EAGLES

GLAMORGAN

by Richard Thomas

Glamorgan went into the season with a clear view of what was expected of them – success in one-day cricket. That demand had come from the suits on high who were intent on considerable commercial return from the shorter game and especially the Friends Provident t20.

But when that failed to materialise – the county only won eight of their 28 one-day matches – the default position became promotion from the Division Two of the County Championship. With two rounds of the Championship remaining it looked almost certain Glamorgan would go up in second place with Sussex. They were, after all, 22 points ahead of Worcestershire.

Their fate came down to the final day of the season with the final round of matches all rain-affected. Glamorgan were hoping a draw against Derbyshire at Cardiff would have been enough, but when Worcestershire struck a controversial deal with Sussex – they were left 301 to win in 71 overs – Jamie Dalrymple, the captain, knew he had to contrive his own result. In the end Derbyshire held on in the final couple of hours and Glamorgan were left demoralised and

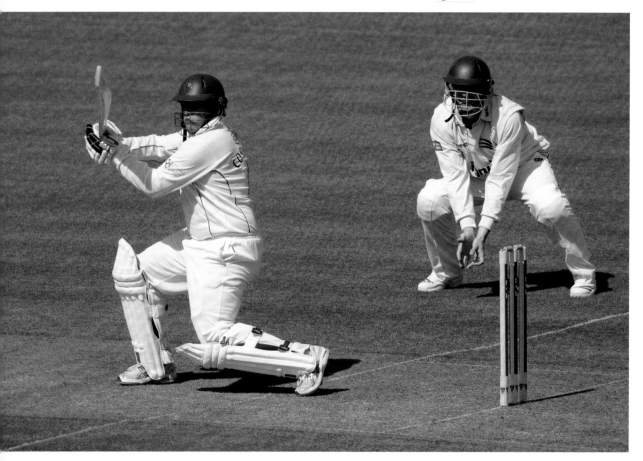

Mark Cosgrove square drives for Glamorgan in their County Championship match against Middlesex at Lord's. The Australian left-hander had a prolific season for the Welsh county.

frustrated, and not a little angry about the way Sussex had capitulated at New Road.

The failure to secure promotion left Dalrymple visibly upset and he and Matthew Maynard, the director of cricket, were also ignored by a committeeman as they traipsed off the field on that final day as everyone contemplated a sixth straight season in the bottom flight.

It also left Glamorgan's players – particularly Mark Cosgrove – questioning Sussex's generous tactics. 'To beat Worcestershire twice and for them to go up above us was gutting,' complained Cosgrove. 'I am disappointed with the way Sussex played their cricket. Four an over for 70 overs – you would take that any week. The way they bowled looks like they threw the ball back to them.

'If they can wake up and look themselves in the mirror and say they played that game to the best of their ability, then fair credit to them. But I think there are a couple of blokes in that Sussex side we will be staying away from at public dinners.'

Tribute to Croft from 'The Don' of Wales
by Richard Thomas

Glamorgan great, Don Shepherd, believes Robert Croft's achievement of doing the 1,000-wicket/ 10,000-run double in first-class county cricket is truly special. Shepherd, Glamorgan's leading wicket-taker with 2,174 victims, brought champagne onto the field at St Helen's in Swansea with club president Peter Walker to toast Croft's landmark after Leicestershire's Wayne White became his 1,000th scalp. 'I think it's a terrific achievement – unique in the history of Glamorgan cricket, and arguably one of the great events of Welsh sport as a whole,' said Shepherd. 'Robert has done everything in cricket having played in Tests and one-day internationals, but I know this landmark means a great deal to him. Apart from skill you have to have good heart, good body and the will to bowl, and Robert has bowled some phenomenally long spells in his life.

'Above all, he has listened to people and taken on board a lot of advice, and he is shrewd enough and wise enough to work out what he has needed to do. I think he really deserves to reach such a milestone, a milestone that I doubt will be repeated in the history of county cricket. To think that only eight other players have done it since the war, and to think they were playing 30 first-class games a season and it hasn't been done since 1972.' The other players to achieve the feat are Trevor Bailey, Tony Brown, Tom Cartwright, Ray Illingworth, Derek Morgan, John Mortimore, Fred Titmus and Peter Sainsbury, who was the last to do it 38 years ago.

Shepherd believes that 40-year-old Croft's achievement is even more special considering the changes in county cricket over the last two decades. 'The emphasis has been more and more on one-day cricket, and let's not forget the part Robert has played in Glamorgan's one-day successes. Furthermore, I believe Robert has it in him to carry on for at least two more years and there is no reason why he can't play for another three or four seasons.'

Robert Croft reached a landmark unique in the annals of Glamorgan cricket during 2010.

Maynard Gives Backing to Swansea Festival

Jamie Dalrymple, pictured above in action in Twenty20 cricket, impressed as Glamorgan captain during the 2010 campaign.

The survival of the annual Swansea Cricket Festival has been continually in doubt over the last few years, but Glamorgan director of cricket Matthew Maynard is hoping St Helen's will continue to host county cricket for the foreseeable future. This year's event was well supported with good crowds for both the four-day clash with Leicestershire, during which Robert Croft took his 1,000th first-class wicket for Glamorgan, and the Clydesdale Bank 40 match against Sussex. But the development of the Swalec Stadium into a Test venue has threatened the existence of Swansea's annual five-day festival. Maynard, however, is confident a deal can be reached between the Welsh county, Swansea Council, and the St Helen's Balconiers – the band of supporters which has fought hard to preserve the festival – to keep hosting matches at St Helen's. 'I am hopeful we'll carry on playing at Swansea for the next few years,' insisted Maynard. 'From my point of view, it would be nice to sign a staging agreement with the council. The players love playing at the ground. I know the club would need a few guarantees and the decision is nothing to do with me. But from a playing point of view we do enjoy going to Swansea. Both Swansea and Colwyn Bay are musts in the Glamorgan calendar.

Although Glamorgan can complain about last-day contrivances, the blame for failure lies substantially at their own door. Though they won seven games in Division Two (their best haul of wins since they won the Championship in 1997) their form tailed off in the final four games.

Despite the team's failure to secure promotion, there were some good individual contributions throughout the season, and in fact five players had their best summers yet – Cosgrove, who was relied on too heavily in the batting department, James Harris, Dean Cosker, Tom Maynard and Ben Wright. Most notably there were 2,146 runs provided by Cosgrove in one-day and first-class cricket, 63 Championship wickets from James Harris and a good all-round display from James Allenby in his first full season with the county.

Maynard is hoping that Dalrymple is given a third season as captain even though the Middlesex man had a poor season with the bat by his own high standards. 'If Jamie is not captain next year I won't be director of cricket,' insisted Maynard. 'For me there are no questions. He is an outstanding leader and next year his form will return and he will be bigger and better again. I look forward to working with him once more. We are different characters but we get on well and think similarly about the game.

'County cricket is captain-led, not coach-led, because it's about what happens on the pitch. If you look at anyone who is captain, the first year you grab the bull by the horns and then you develop your management side and learn how to get the best out of the players.'

And Maynard was sure Glamorgan developed as a squad during 2010 despite the ultimate failures in both forms of the game. He believed the club had come a long way since he took over the reins three years ago. 'I am a positive bloke and see the development of Ben Wright, Tom Maynard and James Harris, who are exciting young players coming through. We can build on this and we will put it right next season when we will look to go out and win the division convincingly.'

But he had to put his hands up where one-day cricket was concerned. Eighteen defeats, including one to the Unicorns, in 28 matches is a statistic that tells its own sorry tale. 'One-day cricket is more of a concern and a dramatic

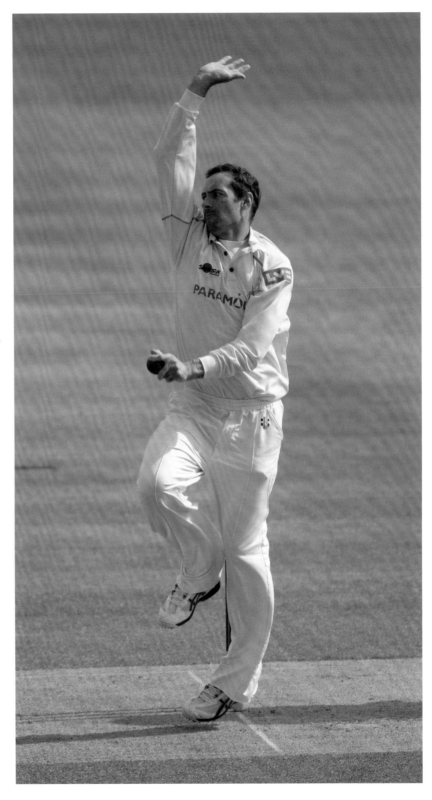

Left-armer Dean Cosker emerged as Glamorgan's number one spinner after spending a long time in the shadow of his slow-bowling partner Robert Croft.

improvement is required,' he added. 'Some players are not up to it at the moment and there is a lot of work needed to be done this winter to get up to standard.

"We need to get a better method and a clarity in people's roles because we still don't have a successful system in place. We don't have a solid batting order that is guaranteed and the bowling line-up has been disappointing... You look at the good one-day sides around the country, like Somerset and Nottinghamshire,

and they have experienced players who are over 30. We have got young kids and it will take them time to develop, but the likes of Chris Ashling and Will Owen have got potential.'

As this book went to press, Glamorgan were undergoing an internal review of the season and until it was completed they were delaying any announcement of the re-signing of Cosgrove. 'We are going to sit down with Matthew [Maynard] and reflect on 2010 and

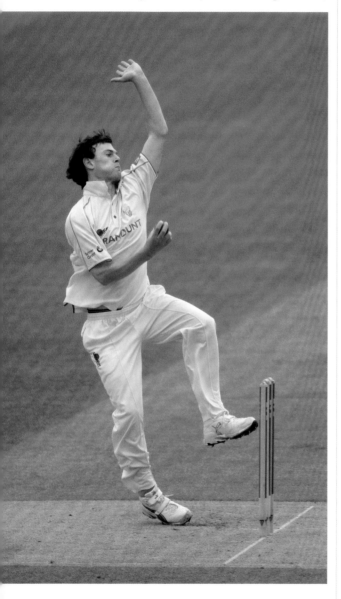

James Harris, who turned 20 in May, bowled quickly and effectively with the new ball and delighted Glamorgan supporters by signing a new contract at the end of the season.

PLAYER OF THE SEASON

Mark Cosgrove led the batting in Championship and in one-day cricket with a total of 2,146 runs in all forms of cricket for the county (1,187 at 49.45 in the County Championship). It's all the more baffling that Glamorgan did not immediately tie Cosgrove up with a contract for next season.

YOUNG PLAYER OF THE SEASON

James Harris is only 20, but 63 first-class wickets proved what an asset the England Lion is. He shouldered the Welsh county's new-ball attack with maturity beyond his years and the ability to move the ball both ways, and his pace is getting better too.

A YEAR TO REMEMBER

- Robert Croft took his 1,000th first-class wicket for Glamorgan and the first hat-trick of his career
- James Allenby had a good all-round season, especially in four-day cricket – 900 runs and 40 wickets
- Dean Cosker took 50 wickets in a first-class season for the first time in his career

A YEAR TO FORGET

- Michael Powell was awarded a benefit for 2011 but did not play first-team cricket after May
- Jamie Dalrymple scored only 554 Championship runs at 25.18
- David Brown – CB40 & t20 averages: batting – 17.37 & 11.00, bowling – 141.50 & 71.50

identify where we were good and where we were poor with a view to trying to prepare for 2011,' said Glamorgan chief executive Alan Hamer.

'We always want to win things and, like any other county who has not won something this season, will be looking for improvement next year. We need to look to see what we can do to improve our fortunes, especially in one-day cricket. Everyone at the club wants us to be competitive in all formats so we will see what is required.'

Wagg Confident it's the Right Move

Graham Wagg has joined Glamorgan looking to fulfil a twin goal of playing Division One cricket and representing his country at the highest level. The 27-year-old all-rounder has signed a three-year deal with the Welsh county after a five-season spell with Derbyshire and is relishing his move to the Swalec Stadium. 'Matt Maynard has tried to snap me up for the last few years so I have had a few conversations with him in the past, and I know Jamie Dalrymple quite well from playing with him in the Hong Kong Sixes,' said Wagg. 'The Swalec Stadium is a great place to play now and, of course, the club is ambitious, which is fantastic. I also still want to play for my country. That's an ambition I've had since I was child. I'm now 27 and still young enough. I've represented England Lions and there is only one step to go whether that's playing Test cricket, one-day internationals or Twenty20.' Maynard said, 'Graham is a quality player and a superb addition to the squad, and I'm sure he will help bring some silverware to the club in future years.'

Mark Wallace stumps Neil Dexter off the bowling of David Brown during Glamorgan's Friends Provident t20 fixture against Middlesex at Richmond.

GLAMORGAN CCC

GlamorganCricket
CricedMorgannwg

FIRST-CLASS MATCHES
BATTING

	GP Rees	BJ Wright	J Allenby	DA Cosker	MA Wallace	JWM Dalrymple	MJ Cosgrove	JAR Harris	DS Harrison	HT Waters	TL Maynard	ROB Croft	MJ Powell	CP Ashling	WD Bragg	WT Owen	DO Brown	NA James	AJ Shantry	Extras	Total	Wickets	Result	Points
v. Sussex	9	10	0	11	21	31		19			9*		48	2	6					25	191	10		
(Cardiff) 9-12 April	15	57	62	12	0	4		7			7*		24	0	1					14	203	10	L	3
v. Middlesex	38	11	57	10	79*	24	0	7	9	5			55							20	315	10		
(Lord's) 15-18 April	20	4	15	49*	37	0	17	2	24	1			47							3	219	10	W	22
v. Derbyshire	15	60	57	11	58	21	4		5	5			10	7*						19	272	10		
(Derby) 21-24 April	102	13	12	7	11	3	11		2	13*			4	20						13	211	10	L	5
v. Worcestershire	42	79	55	2*	14	25	26	6	1	0			5							12	267	10		
(Worcester) 27-28 April	21*	-	-	-	-	-	10	-	-	-			10*							0	41	1	W	21
v. Northamptonshire	64	25	72	3	27	105	85	2	27	0*			10							30	450	10		
(Cardiff) 10-13 May																							W	23
v. Gloucestershire	48	172	105	11*	0	58	34		10	-		63	37							45	583	9		
(Cardiff) 17-20 May																							W	23
v. Leicestershire	14	1	8	8	36	17	25	23	17		2					0*				15	166	10		
(Leicester) 24-26 May	73*	-	-	-	-	-	113*	-	-		-					-				12	198	0	W	19
v. Surrey	86	23	15	6*	58	11	82	49	1	2	3									36	372	10		
(Cardiff) 29 May-1 June	2*	-	-	-	-	-	5*	-	-	-	-									0	7	0	D	10
v. West Indies A	55	17									0	4	25	8*	0	0	99	15	22	16	261	10		
(Cardiff) 5-7 June	0	9									21	56*	0	-	0	-	15	60*	-	15	176	6	D	
v. Northamptonshire	29	5	59*	0	21	8	0	8	18		6					38				15	207	10		
(Northampton) 5-7 July	14	33	0	7*	20	0	115	39	15		64					0				18	325	10	L	2
v. Leicestershire	15	3	30	0	9	48	117	15*	19		19	6								9	290	10		
(Swansea) 21-24 July																							D	7
v. Gloucestershire	9	17	3	1	72	11	41	0	0*	0	44									18	216	10		
(Cheltenham) 30 July-1 August	2	16	15	10	113	36	123	11	8*	6	17									14	371	10	W	20
v. Worcestershire	25	72	14	41*	0	56	84		11	10	21	9								26	369	10		
(Colwyn Bay) 9-12 August	65	121*	62	14*	12	6	0		3	-	98	4								12	397	8	W	22
v. Middlesex	6	0	20	28*	0	37	0	7	35		37	12								6	198	10		
(Cardiff) 16-19 August	0	17	91*	1	1	27	11	3	26		40	0								15	232	10	L	3
v. Sussex	12	16	13	9*	8		142	0	25	-	12				44					19	300	9		
(Hove) 27-30 August	20	25	8	2	16		9	14*	5	4	76				5					26	210	10	D	9
v. Surrey	4	17	68*	21	0	25	26	9		16	61	8								21	276	10		
(The Oval) 7-10 September																							D	8
v. Derbyshire	7	0	57	4*	3	1	32	36		3	4	5								14	166	10		
(Cardiff) 13-16 September	106*	24	35*	-	-		75	-		-	-	25								4	269	3	D	6

	GP Rees	BJ Wright	J Allenby	DA Cosker	MA Wallace	JWM Dalrymple	MJ Cosgrove	JAR Harris	DS Harrison	HT Waters	TL Maynard	ROB Croft	MJ Powell	CP Ashling	WD Bragg	WT Owen	DO Brown	NA James	AJ Shantry					
Matches	17	17	16	16	16	15	15	13	12	11	11	9	7	3	3	3	1	1	1					
Innings	30	27	25	24	24	22	26	19	18	13	18	14	12	5	6	4	2	2	1					
Not Out	4	1	4	10	1	0	2	2	0	4	0	3	1	2	0	1	0	1	0					
Highest Score	106*	172	105	49*	113	105	142	49	35	16	98	63	55	20	44	38	99	60*	22					
Runs	918	847	933	268	626	554	1187	257	253	67	495	244	275	37	56	38	114	75	22					
Average	35.30	32.57	44.42	19.14	27.21	25.18	49.45	15.11	14.05	7.44	27.50	22.18	25.00	12.33	9.33	12.66	57.00	75.00	22.00					
100s	2	2	1	0	1	1	5	0	0	0	0	0	0	0	0	0	0	0	0					
50s	5	4	10	0	4	2	4	0	0	0	4	2	1	0	0	0	0	1	1	0				
Catches/Stumpings	6/0	7/0	16/0	7/0	43/4	19/0	10/0	2/0	2/0	1/0	11/0	0/0	1/0	0/0	3/1	0/0	1/0	0/0	0/0					

Home Ground: Cardiff
Address: The SWALEC Stadium, Cardiff, CF11 9XR
Tel: 029 2040 9380
Fax: 029 2040 9390
Email: info@glamorgancricket.co.uk
Directions: *By rail:* Cardiff Central station.
By road: From the North, A470 and follow signs to Cardiff until junction with Cardiff bypass then A48 Port Talbot and City Centre. Cathedral Road is situated off A48 for Sophia Gardens.

Capacity: 16,000
Other grounds used: Swansea, Colwyn Bay, Abergavenny
Year formed: 1888

Executive Chairman: Paul Russell
Cricket Director: Matthew Maynard
First XI Coach: Adrian Shaw
Captain: Jamie Dalrymple
County colours: Navy blue and yellow/gold

Honours
County Championship
1948, 1969, 1997
Sunday League/NCL/Pro40
1993, 2002, 2004

Website:
www.glamorgancricket.com

FIRST-CLASS MATCHES
BOWLING

	JAR Harris	DA Cosker	J Allenby	DS Harrison	T Waters	RDB Croft	JWM Dalrymple	P Ashling	J Cosgrove	WT Owen	J Shantry	A James	A Wallace	P Rees	BJ Wright	TL Maynard	Overs	Total	Byes/Leg-byes	Wickets	Run outs
v. Sussex	23-6-68-4	20.3-4-43-3	18-4-53-2		14-0-33-0		6-2-11-0	15-2-61-1									96.3	284	15	10	
(Cardiff) 9–12 April	16-2-46-4	32-4-90-2	11-2-33-0		20-2-75-2		4-0-16-0	9-0-35-1									92	311	16	9	
v. Middlesex	7-1-21-0	3-1-8-1	13.2-3-29-4	18-2-62-5		10-1-28-0											51.2	160	12	10	
(Lord's) 15–18 April	27-10-66-1	10-2-37-2	7-0-31-0	14-2-64-1		21.1-7-39-4	14-1-31-2		2-0-14-0								95.1	296	14	10	
v. Derbyshire		30-7-76-1	6-1-17-1	20.5-4-53-4		22-5-71-2	14-2-35-0	17-1-74-1	4-1-17-1					2-0-7-0			115.5	363	13	10	
(Derby) 21–24 April		17-3-53-2		2-0-16-0			13.5-1-42-0	3-0-8-0									35.5	121	2	2	
v. Worcestershire	15-5-50-2		9-2-20-1	16.5-5-45-7		7-2-14-0											47.5	134	5	10	
(Worcester) 27–28 April	17.2-7-56-5	2-0-7-0	13-6-23-4	13-3-44-1		7-0-33-0											52.2	171	8	10	
v. Northamptonshire	20.1-4-77-3	3-2-1-1	20-10-29-2	19-3-74-0		25-8-55-3	1-0-1-0		6-1-13-1								94.1	253	3	10	
(Cardiff) 10–13 May	22.5-3-62-5	3-2-3-1	10.5-1-23-2	12-2-54-1		19-7-54-0											66.5	193	8	10	
v. Gloucestershire		29-8-66-2	21-6-71-3	29-1-105-1	15.1-3-45-2	27.3-6-92-2	3.3-1-18-0		4-1-9-0								129.1	417	11	10	
(Cardiff) 17–20 May		25-13-32-3	6-3-8-1	6-0-22-0	28.1-7-51-2	8-1-29-1	5-2-14-1										78.1	162	6	10	2
v. Leicestershire	27-7-74-3	18-4-44-2	19-6-29-1	18-0-71-4			1-0-1-0			20-5-65-0							103	291	7	10	
(Leicester) 24–26 May	14.4-7-34-4		6-2-10-1	12-4-17-4						4-1-8-0							36.4	71	2	10	1
v. Surrey	20-2-82-4	15-4-40-2	15-2-44-1	17-1-73-0		16-4-43-1	1-0-5-1										84	303	16	9	
(Cardiff) 29 May–1 June																	–	–	–	–	
v. West Indies A				10.3-2-39-4			10-2-18-3		14-2-65-3	10-3-20-0	1-0-1-0						45.3	151	8	10	
(Cardiff) 5–7 June				1-1-0-0			1.1-0-4-0		4-0-28-0	4-1-21-1							10.1	58	5	1	
v. Northamptonshire	27-7-75-2	33-3-96-2	21-3-54-0	28-4-96-2			18.4-1-71-4		3-0-24-0	12-0-66-0							142.4	494	12	10	
(Northampton) 5–7 July	4-1-10-0	3-1-6-0		6.1-2-24-0													13.1	40	0	0	
v. Leicestershire	29-11-45-2	19.2-7-35-3	14-1-45-1	15-2-39-1	33-11-54-3		3-0-12-0		3-1-10-0								116.2	247	7	10	
(Swansea) 21–24 July	18-6-40-3	26-13-33-1		2-0-8-0	40-8-77-1		20-3-56-1				1-0-3-0						107	221	4	6	
v. Gloucestershire	5.4-0-30-0	10-1-42-2	23-6-59-5		12.2-1-42-1	19-6-64-2											70	243	6	10	
(Cheltenham) 30 July–1 August	17-1-73-3	6-1-16-0	5-2-11-0		6.3-0-20-4	17.9-29-3	4-0-16-0										55.3	168	3	10	
v. Worcestershire		15-3-51-1	15-0-71-1	13-0-64-2	23.1-4-63-2	20-3-82-0			1-0-3-0								92.1	350	6	8	
(Colwyn Bay) 9–12 August		10.5-5-27-4	11-2-36-2	14-1-48-3	7-5-11-0	14-4-31-0			3-0-20-0								59.5	175	2	10	1
v. Middlesex	19-4-83-3	0.3-0-0-2	18-6-43-3	18-1-60-0	5-3-4-1												60.3	181	11	10	1
(Cardiff) 16–19 August	16-3-53-0	17-2-61-1	7-3-15-0	12.4-2-56-1	29-5-66-2												81.4	253	2	4	
v. Sussex	16-6-37-3	10.3-0-38-2	8-0-33-2	12-2-61-0		20-7-71-3			1-0-1-0						3-0-20-0		67.3	250	9	10	
(Hove) 27–30 August	9-4-14-0	5-1-21-0	1-0-2-0			9-1-35-2											27	93	1	2	
v. Surrey	27-6-120-3	17-4-48-4	17.5-1-70-2		10-2-41-0	17-2-74-0	3-0-12-0		4-1-12-1					1-0-3-0			95.5	380	3	10	
(The Oval) 7–10 September	14-5-36-4	9-1-27-0	0-4-14-0		21-4-54-1	9-3-16-1	7-0-25-1		4-0-17-0								75	206	14	7	
v. Derbyshire	22-5-46-3	30.2-4-83-5		38-8-100-1	8-3-16-0	5-0-16-1											103.2	276	5	10	
(Cardiff) 13–16 September	10-2-15-2	12-1-34-2	5-1-23-1	9.5-1-30-0	2-0-12-0	3-0-9-0											41.5	123	0	5	

	JAR Harris	DA Cosker	J Allenby	DS Harrison	T Waters	RDB Croft	JWM Dalrymple	P Ashling	J Cosgrove	WT Owen	J Shantry	A James	A Wallace	P Rees	BJ Wright	TL Maynard
Overs	443.4	432	330.1	323.3	323.4	297.4	127	55.1	35	54	14	1	1	1	2	3
Maidens	115	101	81	44	67	79	13	5	5	8	4	0	0	0	0	0
Runs	1293	1128	885	1156	805	898	391	200	140	232	41	1	3	3	7	20
Wickets	63	51	41	37	26	26	11	6	3	3	1	0	0	0	0	0
Average	20.52	22.12	21.59	31.24	30.96	34.54	35.55	33.33	46.67	77.33	41.00	–	–	–	–	––

FIELDING

47	MA Wallace (43 ct, 4 st)
19	JWM Dalrymple
16	J Allenby
11	TL Maynard
10	MJ Cosgrove
7	DA Cosker
7	BJ Wright
6	GP Rees
4	WD Bragg (3 ct, 1 st)
2	JAR Harris
2	DS Harrison
1	DO Brown
1	MJ Powell
1	HT Waters

Division Two – Final Table

	P	W	L	D	Bat	Bowl	Pens	Pts
Sussex	16	8	3	5	45	47	0	235
Worcestershire	16	7	4	5	39	42	0	208
Glamorgan	16	7	4	5	33	43	0	203
Leicestershire	16	7	5	4	31	44	0	199
Gloucestershire	16	6	9	1	28	47	-2	172
Northamptonshire	16	6	7	3	28	34	0	167
Surrey	16	4	6	6	43	36	-2	159
Middlesex	16	4	7	5	37	41	-2	155
Derbyshire	16	3	7	6	30	42	0	138

CB40 FPt20

GLAMORGAN DRAGONS

Limited overs nickname:
GLAMORGAN DRAGONS

GLOUCESTERSHIRE

by Richard Latham

It was a year of missed opportunity for Gloucestershire, who by common consent started the season with the most potent seam attack in the LV County Championship second division. Promotion chances were blown by a series of weak batting displays, which ensured a once promising campaign ended in total frustration.

In the experienced Jon Lewis, Steve Kirby, Anthony Ireland and all-rounder James Franklin, Gloucestershire had a proven quartet of wicket-takers to take into the 2010 season. The dramatic rise of Gemaal Hussain from little known rookie to a lofty place in the national bowling averages was an unexpected bonus that should have reaped more reward,

Hussain, 26, discovered playing club cricket by Jack Russell and given a two-year contract in 2009, had been employed sparingly in his first season at Bristol, his first-team experience coming mainly in Twenty20 cricket. Now he emerged fitter and stronger from his winter training schedule and was soon using his height and exemplary action to make a big impression on the Championship. Consistent throughout the summer, he claimed 67 victims in the competition, a figure bettered only by Nottinghamshire's Andre Adams.

From the outset, Gloucestershire sought to cash in on their riches in seam bowling by producing what director of cricket John Bracewell described as 'sporting' pitches at Nevil Road. On three occasions more than 20 wickets fell on the opening day of Championship games at the County Ground, but each time the ECB pitch inspectors decided that swing, more than excessive seam movement, had undone the groping batsmen.

In any event, leaving more grass on the pitches proved a controversial policy. Some supporters felt it led to a lack of confidence in the batting department and allowed less talented visiting attacks to prosper. Whether that was true or not, there was no

Gemaal Hussain, one of the bowlers of the season, celebrates the wicket of Middlesex's Tim Murtagh in the County Championship match at Lord's.

Payne Re-lives Bowling Glory
by Richard Latham

David Payne revealed he was 'in a bit of a daze' when he returned the best one-day bowling figures in Gloucestershire's history. The England Under-19 left-arm seamer took 7 for 29 in his side's Clydesdale Bank 40 defeat by Essex at Chelmsford, including four wickets with successive balls in the final over of the home side's innings.

Having dismissed Mark Pettini in his first spell and Ryan ten Doeschate and Graham Napier in the 38th over, Payne then accounted for James Foster, Grant Flower, Tim Phillips and Jaik Mickleburgh with the first four deliveries of the 40th. That made it six wickets in the space of eight balls, and seven scalps in all. When Chris Martin was run out off the final delivery of the innings, Essex had lost their last five wickets in a single over without adding a run.

Of his amazing achievement, Payne, who hails from Poole in Dorset, admitted, 'I was in such a daze it didn't even register at the time that I had taken a hat-trick. I just concentrated on bowling my slower ball in the final over and the batsmen kept hitting it down the throats of our fielders. It was unbelievable. Only later did someone tell me that my figures were the best by a Gloucestershire bowler in one-day cricket. That's amazing, but I won't be getting carried away.

'There was a suggestion that Martin's dismissal might have been a stumping because he didn't get far out of his crease. But the umpires ruled it a run out and I wasn't going to be greedy!'

The previous best one-day bowling figures for Gloucestershire were 6 for 13 by Mike Procter in a Benson & Hedges Cup match against Hampshire at Southampton in 1977. That performance also featured a hat-trick.

It didn't take cricket long to bring Payne back down to earth following his dream exploits at Chelmsford, however. Playing in a second XI game against Kent at Beckenham he was struck on the thigh by a fierce drive from an opposition batsman and had to return to Bristol for treatment on an injury that ruled him out of Gloucestershire's next Clydesdale Bank clash with Middlesex at Lord's.

Above David Payne, the young Gloucestershire left-arm fast bowler, enjoyed a day of remarkable success in the Clydesdale Bank 40 game against Essex.

disputing the fact that no Gloucestershire batsman reached even 900 first-class runs. By the closing stages of the season collapses had become commonplace and at times embarrassing.

The club were still in with a chance of promotion when bowling out bottom-placed Derbyshire for 44 at Bristol at the end of August, Franklin returning career-best figures of 7 for 14, having taken his first five wickets without conceding a run. From there Gloucestershire couldn't lose – but they did. A victory target of 125 in the final innings of the match proved far too big as the home side were skittled for 70. Skipper Alex Gidman admitted afterwards to being in a state of shock before conducting the most difficult of post-match interviews with his usual courtesy and honesty.

The final home Championship fixture against Surrey again saw Gloucestershire snatch defeat from the jaws of victory, going down by ten runs having reached 216 for 4 chasing 261, and they eventually finished fifth, having drawn only one of their 16 games. Six victories was only one less than promoted Worcestershire had achieved, but nine defeats was the highest number inflicted on any team.

Chris Taylor is one of the experienced players who Gloucestershire will be depending on in 2011 after the loss of a number of senior personnel to other counties.

Kirby: Hussain is Fast Bowling Gem

Steve Kirby believes Gemaal Hussain has all the attributes to go a long way in the game.

'Gemaal has a fantastic work ethic and, while he still has a lot to learn, the necessary attributes are there to make him a top bowler,' said the England Lions paceman. 'He hits the wicket hard being 6 foot 5 inches, and shapes the ball away from right-handers. He also makes it swing late and gets a lot of kick off a length.

'Personally, I don't think Gemaal should aim to become a swing bowler because he has the ability to generate real pace. He is still growing into his physique and will get a lot stronger. I see a massive future for him, as he is a naturally aggressive bowler and a real gem.'

Through all the batting disasters in four-day cricket, Chris Dent emerged as a young player of potential and maturity for his years. A pre-season century against Cardiff MCCU earned him an early opportunity and, while he went on to average no more than 25.89 in playing every Championship game, that figure did not do justice to the number of times the 19-year-old left-hander walked to the wicket in tough situations with his team in trouble. Three times he got within touching distance of a maiden first-class century only to fall short. It didn't stop Bracewell praising him as having 'as much talent and potential as any batsman of his age in the country'.

Gloucestershire arrived at their annual Cheltenham Festival in early August with no batsman having made a Championship century. Then, like buses, two came along at once as Will Porterfield hammered a brilliant 175 and Franklin a more measured 108 in the first innings of the opening game against Worcestershire. That Gidman's men also contrived to lose that match after gaining a first-innings lead of 202 summed up their season and led to close self-examination by the conscientious skipper, who had decided not to enforce the follow-on.

There was an improvement in Gloucestershire's one-day cricket, even though they failed to reach the final stages of either competition. In the Clydesdale Bank 40 the team missed out on a semi-final place having won nine of their 12 Group B matches – as many as eventual winners Warwickshire won in Group C – only to finish third behind Yorkshire and Essex on 18 points. Sussex qualified for the semi-finals in Group A with 16 points.

Strangely, the batting department which failed so abysmally in four-day cricket found a decent level of consistency in the shorter formats, led by Franklin, who averaged 73 in 40-over games and nearly 40 in Twenty20. Chris Taylor and Gidman also prospered in the Clydesdale Bank competition, which also saw Steve Snell make some enterprising contributions with the bat.

But the most spectacular one-day performance of the season came from a bowler. In the CB40 match with Essex at Chelmsford, England Under-19 left-arm seamer David Payne claimed 7 for 29, the best figures ever by a Gloucestershire player in limited-overs cricket. An extraordinary final over saw him dismiss James Foster, centurion Grant Flower, Tim Phillips and Jaik Mickleburgh with successive deliveries before

PLAYER OF THE SEASON

Gemaal Hussain claimed 67 wickets at an average of 22.34 in his first full season of County Championship cricket, having made just one previous appearance in the competition. The 26-year-old pace bowler proved he could both swing the ball and nip it about off the seam.

YOUNG PLAYER OF THE SEASON

Chris Dent. The England Under-19 batsman was expected to be given limited opportunities when the season started, but became a first-team regular in all competitions, often being asked to bat in tough situations and bolster a fragile top order.

A YEAR TO REMEMBER

- James Franklin – 862 Championship runs and 46 wickets, while heading the batting averages in both one-day competitions
- Jon Lewis took 54 Championship wickets
- Jack Taylor made his Championship debut at the age of 18

A YEAR TO FORGET

- Jonathan Batty averaged only 16 as regular opener in the Championship
- Abdul Kadeer Ali scored just 270 Championship runs at an average of under 22
- Steve Kirby took 29 Championship wickets, less than half his 2009 tally

Wicketkeeper Jon Batty and captain Alex Gidman are overjoyed at claiming the prized scalp of Surrey's Mark Ramprakash, caught by Batty off the bowling of James Franklin at The Oval.

claiming a stumping off his final ball, which the umpires ruled as a run-out by wicketkeeper Jonathan Batty.

The improvement in one-day performances was not as marked in the Friends Provident t20, which saw Gloucestershire finish bottom of the South Division, despite some encouraging displays. A shortage of power hitters proved their undoing as only five of the 16 games brought victories. That was three more wins than the club had achieved in the previous year's competition (from ten fixtures), but with several experienced players leaving at the end of an ultimately disappointing 2010, there are challenging times ahead at Nevil Road.

GLOUCESTERSHIRE CCC

FIRST-CLASS MATCHES
BATTING

Match	CDJ Dent	JEC Franklin	APR Gidman	J Lewis	JN Batty	GM Hussain	HJH Marshall	CG Taylor	SP Kirby	SD Snell	AJ Ireland	V Banerjee	WTS Porterfield	K Ali	EGC Young	JMR Taylor	Extras	Total	Wickets	Result	Points
v. Northamptonshire (Bristol) 15-17 April	1	0	9	16	14	1	28*	4	0	0			8				5	86	10		
	23	1	21	4	6	4	27	31	22*	52			29				29	249	10	L	3
v. Sussex (Bristol) 21-23 April	0	2	11	23	1	10	14	37	0*	9				13			8	128	10		
	10	29	13	3	4	11	7	3	0*	25				6			8	119	10	L	3
v. Middlesex (Lord's) 27-30 April	19	44*	16	11	49	1	72	32	0	0			7				17	268	10		
	42	11	43	43	22	3*	9	61	1	0			1				7	223	10	W	21
v. Surrey (The Oval) 4-6 May	32	35	1	17	8	5	1	13	20*	48	35						14	229	10		
	17	92*	24	1	31	22	4	10	0	0	16						31	248	10	W	20
v. Leicestershire (Bristol) 10-13 May	34	15	99	0	6	28	86	62		28	0*		0				18	376	10		
	5*	-	-	-	7*	-	-	-	-	-	-		1				2	15	1	W	23
v. Glamorgan (Cardiff) 17-20 May	6	95	97	50	6	5*	1	65		71	2	8					11	417	10		
	3	28	34	37*	11	7	22	10		4	0	0					6	162	10	L	6
v. Derbyshire (Derby) 24-27 May	0	29	37	14	61	3	5		0	9		3*		5			76	242	10		
	98	37	42	34	18	2*	40		13	21		2		74			22	403	10	W	20
v. Worcestershire (Worcester) 29 May-1 June	5	32	10	14	38		37	71	15*	6	6	0					11	245	10		
	21	23	18	16*	43		50	30		-	7	17*					18	243	7	D	7
v. Middlesex (Bristol) 28-30 June	53	99	61	30	20	28*	68	1	9		0		13				38	420	10		
	-	-	-	-	18*	-	-	-	-		-		26*				1	45	0	W	23
v. Sussex (Arundel) 7-9 July	35	0	20	32	4	13*	9	89	14			12		58			21	307	10		
	0*	4	18	0	3	0	89*	1	0			2		0			14	131	10	L	6
v. Glamorgan (Cheltenham) 30 July-1 August	45*	59	17	8	18	1	34	8	5			1	41				6	243	10		
	12	2	4	24	10	0	1	63*	0			8	41				3	168	10	L	7
v. Worcestershire (Cheltenham) 4-7 August	38	108	40	19	1	6*	14	39			2	4	175				34	480	10		
	6	9	1	10	3	0	20	45			0	0*	33				9	136	10	L	7
v. Northamptonshire (Northampton) 16-18 August	92	7	1	11	2	0		21*	1	0			150		1		16	302	10		
	28*	-	9	-	5	-		-	-	10*			23		-		1	76	3	W	22
v. Derbyshire (Bristol) 31 August-1 September	4	5	13	0		0	45	37		31	0*		0			6	15	156	10		
	2	1	0	2		1*	44	0		1	11		0			3	5	70	10	L	3
v. Leicestershire (Leicester) 7-10 September	0	23	8	0	29	0*	61	5			0		5	19			9	159	10		
	0	31	29	0	1	1*	45	4			0		1	38			8	158	10	L	3
v. Surrey (Bristol) 13-16 September	0	1*	-	-	10	-		33			-		54			0	8	106	5		
	94	40	3	0	1	1*	51	28			0		7			2	23	250	10	L	3

	CDJ Dent	JEC Franklin	APR Gidman	J Lewis	JN Batty	GM Hussain	HJH Marshall	CG Taylor	SP Kirby	SD Snell	AJ Ireland	V Banerjee	WTS Porterfield	K Ali	EGC Young	JMR Taylor
Matches	16	16	16	16	15	15	15	15	10	10	8	7	7	6	2	2
Innings	31	29	29	28	30	26	27	27	17	19	12	14	14	12	3	4
Not Out	3	3	0	2	2	10	2	2	5	1	2	3	0	1	0	0
Highest Score	98	108	99	50	61	28*	89*	89	22*	71	11	35	175	74	38	6
Runs	725	862	679	419	450	153	884	803	100	322	21	108	531	240	58	11
Average	25.89	33.15	23.41	16.11	16.07	9.56	35.36	32.12	8.33	17.88	2.10	9.81	37.92	21.81	19.33	2.75
100s	0	1	0	0	0	0	0	0	0	0	0	0	2	0	0	0
50s	4	4	3	1	1	0	7	6	0	2	0	0	1	2	0	0
Catches/Stumpings	24/0	7/0	16/0	7/0	53/3	1/0	15/0	11/0	2/0	18/0	0/0	1/0	6/0	5/0	3/0	2/0

Home Ground: Bristol
Address: County Ground, Nevil Road, Bristol, BS7 9EJ
Tel: 0117 9108000
Fax: 0117 9241193
Email: reception@glosccc.co.uk
Directions: *By road:* M5, M4, M32 into Bristol, exit at second exit (Fishponds/Horfield), then third exit – Muller Road. Almost at end of Muller Road (bus station on right), turn left at Ralph Road. Go to the top, turn left and then right almost immediately into Kennington Avenue. Follow the signs for County Cricket.

Capacity: 8,000
Other grounds used: Gloucester, Cheltenham College
Year formed: 1870

Chief Executive: Tom Richardson
Director of Cricket: John Bracewell
Captain: Alex Gidman
County colours: Navy blue, light blue and yellow

Honours
Sunday League/NCL/Pro40
2000
Benson & Hedges Cup
1977, 1999, 2000
Gillette Cup/NatWest/C&G Trophy
1973, 1999, 2000, 2003, 2004

Website:
www.gloscricket.co.uk

FIRST-CLASS MATCHES
BOWLING

	GM Hussain	J Lewis	JEC Franklin	AJ Ireland	SP Kirby	V Banerjee	APR Gidman	CG Taylor	JMR Taylor	EGC Young	CDJ Dent	WJS Porterfield	HJH Marshall	Overs	Total	Byes/Leg-byes	Wickets	Run outs
v. Northamptonshire	11.5-3-36-5	15-3-58-1	12-4-36-1		10-2-37-1		6-2-10-2							54.5	186	9	10	
(Bristol) 15-17 April	17.2-4-62-4	15-3-56-3	16-4-35-2		17-4-41-0		7-0-34-1	3-0-4-0						75.2	243	11	10	
v. Sussex	10-1-42-2	9-1-32-1	15-2-27-4		9.3-3-25-2		3-0-14-1							46.3	152	12	10	
(Bristol) 21-23 April	18-5-66-3	14.1-1-55-1	19-4-56-2		18-3-54-3		3-0-14-1	2-0-7-0					14-4-28-0	88.1	302	22	10	
v. Middlesex	13.5-2-50-3	16-4-47-1	15-5-42-2		14-2-50-4								6-3-8-0	64.5	203	6	10	
(Lord's) 27-30 April	15-0-46-5	14-6-31-1	7-0-34-0		11.4-1-36-3		4-0-24-1	1-0-2-0					2-0-9-0	54.4	185	3	10	
v. Surrey	13-2-53-2	12-2-46-3	9-1-32-1		10.4-0-42-3	2-1-2-0								46.4	178	3	10	1
(The Oval) 4-6 May	12-2-74-2	8-4-32-1	5-1-9-1		13-4-30-1	19.2-4-74-5								57.2	222	3	10	
v. Leicestershire	11-4-26-3	9-2-33-1	7.3-1-21-3		7-1-21-3			8-2-13-1						34.3	102	1	10	
(Bristol) 10-13 May	26-8-57-1	26-9-44-2	25-9-44-2		30-6-85-4			3-0-8-0					9-4-17-0	127	285	17	10	
v. Glamorgan	24-3-107-0	25-4-85-1	15-2-63-1	29.5-2-114-5		38-5-132-2							14-2-44-0	145.5	583	38	9	
(Cardiff) 17-20 May																		
v. Derbyshire	18-2-65-3	20.4-3-73-2	5-1-24-0		25-11-54-0		27-6-62-4	3-0-24-0					7-2-25-0	105.4	345	18	10	1
(Derby) 24-27 May	11-1-46-1	12.5-3-25-4	5-2-20-1		13-5-22-2		16-2-38-2							57.5	166	15	10	
v. Worcestershire		20.3-4-55-4		8-1-61-0	20-2-92-3	9.4-1-56-0	13-0-79-2	11-2-34-1						82.1	388	11	10	
(Worcester) 29 May-1 June														-	-	-	-	
v. Middlesex	15-2-70-2	13-4-29-2	9-1-37-1	11-2-25-5	13-3-43-0								6-3-17-0	67	236	15	10	
(Bristol) 28-30 June	15-3-61-3	14.2-5-45-4	5-1-22-1	12-2-38-1	14-3-29-0			7-1-19-1						67.2	228	14	10	
v. Sussex	19-1-78-3	17-1-63-0	21-5-57-1		20.1-4-75-1	30-5-94-5	2-0-7-0	2-0-7-0						111.1	389	8	10	
(Arundel) 7-9 July	2-0-15-0				4-1-11-1	5-0-23-1								11	52	3	2	
v. Glamorgan	13.3-3-57-4	13-5-19-2	8-1-26-2		12-0-68-2	5-1-34-0								51.3	216	12	10	
(Cheltenham) 30 July-1 August	13.3-1-60-3	22-5-72-3	18-2-79-2		17-3-68-2	18-1-80-0					1-1-0-0			89.3	371	12	10	
v. Worcestershire	15.4-6-30-4	15-5-45-0	14-3-43-2	22-5-76-3		21-2-51-1		3-0-14-0			2-0-5-0			92.4	278	14	10	
(Cheltenham) 4-7 August	16-4-53-1	9-2-27-1	16-3-49-1	13-1-53-0		27.4-1-124-1		6-0-24-0						87.4	339	9	4	
v. Northamptonshire	12-5-39-3	10-1-25-1			9-2-32-3									36.5	124	6	10	
(Northampton) 16-18 August	17-6-46-4	19.2-5-45-3	16-2-54-2		21-7-62-1		2-1-3-0			9-1-29-0				84.2	252	13	10	
v. Derbyshire	4-0-15-0	4.1-0-13-2	6-3-14-7	2-1-2-1										16.1	44	0	10	
(Bristol) 31 August-1 September	21-7-53-3	15-1-50-1	17-2-67-1	20-2-59-4										73	236	7	10	1
v. Leicestershire	16-4-54-1	16.1-9-42-4	11-5-17-1		13-0-71-2		4-0-26-1			18-0-75-1	11-0-50-0			78.1	295	10	10	
(Leicester) 7-10 September	16-3-58-0	13-4-28-1	10-2-38-1		18-3-73-1			21-4-49-1		11-0-50-0	11-0-43-0			100	351	12	4	
v. Surrey	11-2-48-2	15.2-6-25-3	11-0-49-1	16-4-50-3					4-2-8-1					57.2	186	6	10	
(Bristol) 13-16 September	10-2-30-0	6-1-12-1	3-1-5-0	9-2-25-1				4.2-0-38-1	1-0-5-0			5-0-49-0		38.2	180	6	3	

	GM Hussain	J Lewis	JEC Franklin	AJ Ireland	SP Kirby	V Banerjee	APR Gidman	CG Taylor	JMR Taylor	EGC Young	CDJ Dent	WJS Porterfield	HJH Marshall
Overs	417.4	419.3	334.2	222.5	261.4	222	53	52.2	5	38	11	5	61
Maidens	86	103	69	33	59	28	7	5	2	1	0	0	19
Runs	1497	1222	1083	784	835	793	203	172	13	154	43	49	153
Wickets	67	54	46	36	29	23	9	3	1	1	0	0	0
Average	22.34	22.63	23.54	21.78	28.79	34.48	22.56	57.33	13.00	154.00	-	-	-

FIELDING

56	JN Batty (53 ct, 3 st)
24	CDJ Dent
18	SD Snell
16	APR Gidman
15	HJH Marshall
11	CG Taylor
7	JEC Franklin
7	J Lewis
6	WTS Porterfield
5	K Ali
3	EGC Young
2	SP Kirby
2	JMR Taylor
1	V Banerjee
1	GM Hussain

Division Two – Final Table

	P	W	L	D	Bat	Bowl	Pens	Pts
Sussex	16	8	3	5	45	47	0	235
Worcestershire	16	7	4	5	39	42	0	208
Glamorgan	16	7	4	5	33	43	0	203
Leicestershire	16	7	5	4	31	44	0	199
Gloucestershire	**16**	**6**	**9**	**1**	**28**	**47**	**-2**	**172**
Northamptonshire	16	6	7	3	28	34	0	167
Surrey	16	4	6	6	43	36	-2	159
Middlesex	16	4	7	5	37	41	-2	155
Derbyshire	16	3	7	6	30	42	0	138

CB40   FPt20

GLADIATORS

Limited overs nickname:
GLOUCESTERSHIRE GLADIATORS

SUPPORTING THE DISABILITY SCHOOLS CRICKET PROGRAMME

Children from four local disability schools enjoyed free cricket coaching at the County Ground in Bristol when Gloucestershire County Cricket Club, Gloucestershire Cricket Board and John Lewis Cribbs Causeway arranged a special joint event to celebrate the start of the 2010-11 disability schools programme.

The event was held in mid-September and allowed 30 children to meet four professional players and receive free coaching from GCB coaches. These were the first of hundreds of children who will benefit from the arrangement. The John Lewis sponsorship of Gloucestershire Cricket's disability cricket programme has allowed free coaching sessions to be offered to all 15 special schools in South Gloucestershire and Bristol.

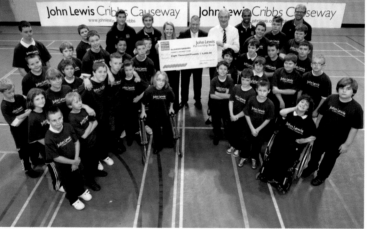

The four schools taking part were Culverhill School and Brimsham Green School, in Yate, Shrubberies School in Stroud and Belmont School from Cheltenham. The event is just one of the many disability coaching initiatives that the John Lewis sponsorship helps to cover, enabling young people with disabilities to be introduced into cricket and allowing greater involvement with the sport.

Alan Andrews, Community Liaison Co-ordinator of John Lewis Cribbs Causeway, said, 'At John Lewis Cribbs Causeway we are proud to support disability cricket. This is the second year we've help Gloucestershire County Cricket Club continue its fantastic work to offer young disabled people the chance to play cricket and receive professional coaching. John Lewis Cribbs Causeway has a strong history of supporting sports events in the local community, from football and cricket to athletics. Sport is an incredibly powerful way to engage with young people, and disability cricket proves how well cricket can do this.'

Chris Munden, Gloucestershire Cricket Board Community Coach, said, 'This is a great initiative as it is really important to offer even more children with disabilities the opportunity to improve their cricketing skills in a safe and enjoyable environment. I would like to thank John Lewis for their support of disability cricket as their sponsorship allows us to run a whole host of events within our disability programme that otherwise would not be possible.'

GCCC Commercial Manager, Kevin Ashley, added, 'We are really pleased that the schools disabilities programme will be in place for another year. It is fantastic to be able to continue offering these coaching sessions to special schools in South Gloucestershire and Bristol. Coaching sessions like those at this event are only possible due to the generous sponsorship and continued support from John Lewis.'

HAMPSHIRE

by Simon Walter

When Hampshire suffered their worst start to a season since 1906, a second trophy in as many years seemed fanciful. But despite several injuries to key players – club captain Dimitri Mascarenhas and winter signing Kabir Ali were both long-term absentees – Hampshire became the first county to win Twenty20 Finals Day on their own ground before retaining their first division status in the LV County Championship.

With vice-captain Nic Pothas also injured, Dominic Cork's leadership inspired the county's colts to the Friends Provident t20 Cup at the Rose Bowl in August. Having squeezed into the quarter-finals by beating defending champions Sussex in their final group game, Hampshire booked a place at Finals Day for the first time when 19-year-old James Vince held his nerve with an unbeaten 66 against Warwickshire at Edgbaston.

So impressive were Hampshire's youngsters that, despite Michael Lumb's broken foot, Kevin Pietersen was surplus to requirements when made available by England for the season's showpiece. It was left to home-grown rookies Vince, Danny Briggs, Michael Bates and Chris Wood to help Hampshire achieve what Rod Bransgrove described as the highlight of his ten seasons as chairman. 'We targeted this and wanted it so badly,' he said. Briggs, a slow left-armer from the Isle of Wight, was Man-of-the-Match for his three wickets in the semi-final against Essex before Cork's experience – and Somerset's failure to take the bails off in a dramatic finish – helped ensure a thrilling last-ball win in the final.

Cork took two wickets and hospitalised dangerman Keiron Pollard with a wicked short ball in the last, decisive over of the Somerset innings. But with the trophy there for the taking, Hampshire threatened a repeat of their capitulation against the same opponents in a televised group match two months earlier. Hampshire will begin next season's Twenty20

James Vince, the young Hampshire batsman, won a stream of rave reviews in 2010 for the quality of his batting. Some observers remarked on the similarity of his style at the crease to Michael Vaughan, the former England captain.

Above Dominic Cork proudly holds the Friends Provident t20 trophy after Hampshire's triumph at the Rose Bowl.

Right Opening batsman Jimmy Adams had a season to remember, with more than 2,500 runs in all competitions. Only James Hildreth, of Somerset, was more prolific in 2010 than the left-handed Adams.

competition with minus two points after being punished for the pitch on which they collapsed from 93 for 4 to 97 all out, needing 105 to win, during the first of two brutal group defeats against Somerset (they were also on the receiving end of Marcus Trescothick's 13-ball 50 at Taunton).

Those scars reappeared when, with only 11 runs needed, Neil McKenzie and Michael Carberry fell in the penultimate over of the final. An incredible night culminated with Dan Christian needing one run off the final ball from Zander de Bruyn, who had given the Australian his black eye with a bouncer in the Championship match between the sides at Taunton two days earlier. Batting with Jimmy Adams as his runner after pulling a thigh muscle while sprinting two off the penultimate delivery, Christian nearly cost Hampshire the silverware when he ran a leg bye instead of remaining in his crease. But Somerset failed to realise Christian was at the wrong end, and so with the scores tied it was left to the PA announcer to confirm Hampshire had won, having lost fewer wickets.

Hampshire maintained their t20 momentum to keep alive their hopes of qualifying for the Clydesdale Bank 40 semi-finals. In their first season as Hampshire Royals – following the formation of the global Royals franchise with IPL giants Rajasthan, among others – they equalled a club record by winning eight successive limited-overs matches for the first time since 1990. It is to the credit of Hampshire's academy director Tony

Neil McKenzie, the former South Africa batsman, played a number of important innings in both four-day and one-day cricket.

Middleton and his coaching team that eight home-grown players were fielded in the Clydesdale Bank 40 win against Leicestershire at the Rose Bowl, seven of whom were 21 or under.

Losing the first four CB40 games proved insurmountable as Hampshire failed to reach another semi-final, but with minds focused on the LV County Championship they avoided relegation with a game to spare. Hampshire were bottom of the first division after beginning the season with four successive first-class defeats for the first time in 104 years. With Cork away commentating on the Indian Premier League, where Mascarenhas sustained the Achilles injury that kept him out all year, Hampshire suffered a rudderless start, losing all ten second-innings wickets in the final session of their opening game against newly promoted Essex at Chelmsford.

But McKenzie's maiden County Championship century, a perfectly judged 115 not out against Nottinghamshire at Trent Bridge in May, ensured a dramatic two-wicket win that restored confidence. Jimmy Adams, Hampshire's Player of the Year for a second successive season, was the county's best batsman. Only Somerset's James Hildreth scored more than his 2,515 runs in all competitions, which included two t20 centuries and a pair of elongated hundreds in successive Championship matches either side of the Pennines.

During his 196 against Yorkshire at Scarborough, Adams helped Vince set a new record for the county's fourth wicket (278), while the teenager raced to 180, the biggest maiden century by a Hampshire batsman for 41 years. Adams' 194 against Lancashire at Liverpool in September, from 508 balls over more than ten-and-a-half hours, is the longest recorded innings by a Hampshire batsman. But he finished on the losing side when Lancashire chased down the 168 they needed to win, by three wickets off the penultimate ball of an absorbing match. So it was fitting that, a week later, Adams took the winning catch at Canterbury to complete the double against Kent, securing first division cricket at the Rose Bowl for 2011.

Ashes Hero Jones Ready for 'New' Career
by Mark Pennell

Former England pace bowler Simon Jones put his injury nightmare behind him by making a successful return to County Championship cricket for his third county, Hampshire. The 31-year-old made a shock comeback to the game for Hampshire's Friends Provident t20 clash with Surrey at The Oval. And, at the end of the season, he enjoyed taking 4 for 60 against Warwickshire in the County Championship.

Overall, England's Ashes hero from 2005 hopes to use the short-form game as a springboard back into first-class cricket. 'I feel stronger every time I bowl and play and hope that regular four-day cricket will soon be an option for me,' said Jones. 'It's the traditional form of the game and a format I love playing.'

'Staying in Division One with kids in the side is as satisfying as winning the Twenty20 Cup,' said Hampshire's manager, Giles White. Adams and Briggs, who took 69 wickets in all cricket, were rewarded with a place in England's winter Performance Programme squad, alongside Carberry.

Simon Jones's successful comeback from a serious knee injury in the last match of the season against Warwickshire provided more hope for the future. Having spent most of the season scaring second XI batsmen; the former England fast bowler took 4 for 60 in his first Championship outing for more than two years. Next year he hopes to ease the burden on Cork, who can reach the first-class milestones of 10,000 runs and 1,000 wickets in 2011, while Imran Tahir returns, from Warwickshire, as Hampshire's overseas player.

PLAYER OF THE SEASON

Jimmy Adams. Hampshire's leading run-scorer in all competitions showed he is a man for all formats. Made more Twenty20 runs (668) than anyone has managed in a county season and his ten-and-a-half hour 194 against Lancashire at Liverpool was the marathon knock of the summer.

YOUNG PLAYER OF THE SEASON

Danny Briggs. Only two players took more than his 31 Twenty20 wickets, and the 19-year-old's haul of 37 in the LV County Championship also included several additions to his collection of big-name scalps. One of two teenagers on this winter's England Performance Programme.

A YEAR TO REMEMBER

- Simon Jones proved critics wrong with a successful comeback
- James Vince reached 1,000 first-class runs for Hampshire in fewer innings than the legendary Phil Mead
- Dominic Cork took 73 wickets in all cricket – his biggest haul since 2003

A YEAR TO FORGET

- Dimitri Mascarenhas was injured all summer and fined £1,000 for one Tweet
- Kevin Pietersen was shunned by Hampshire and dropped by England
- Kabir Ali missed most of debut season with serious knee injury
- Michael Lumb suffered IPL and World Twenty20 burnout then Craig Kieswetter broke his foot

Danny Briggs, the 19-year-old slow left-arm spinner from the Isle of Wight, capped an impressive season by winning a place on England's winter Performance Programme.

HAMPSHIRE CCC

FIRST-CLASS MATCHES
BATTING

Match	SM Ervine	JHK Adams	MA Carberry	JM Vince	ND McKenzie	JA Tomlinson	DR Briggs	DG Cork	N Pothas	LA Dawson	DJ Balcombe	AM Bates	CC Benham	DA Griffiths	MJ Lumb	K Ali	HMRKB Herath	CP Wood	PJ Hughes	H Riazuddin	DT Christian	SP Jones	Extras	Total	Wickets	Result	Points
v. Essex	8	169	3		39	7	21		9	9			21	9*	10								49	354	10		
(Chelmsford) 9-12 April	3	45	47		8	4*	1		39	7			24	0	0								7	185	10	L	6
v. Oxford UCCE	-		164	46*	141*		-		32	-	-		5						-	-			16	404	3		
(Oxford) 15-17 April	32		-	50*	-		-		86		0*		5						-	-			3	176	3	D	
v. Durham	3	68	113	13	30	0	28		14				30	7*	18								21	345	10		
(Chester-le-Street) 21-24 April	46	25	18	46	5	9	0		76				43	1*	9								20	298	10	L	5
v. Warwickshire	70	4	74	6	13	29	0		47				8	0*	16								16	283	10		
(Edgbaston) 27-30 April	59	0	14	52	8	1	2		23				6	4*	1								6	176	10	L	5
v. Nottinghamshire	25	15	132	39	2		21		6				9	3	10	16*							22	300	10		
(Rose Bowl) 4-7 May	45	60	14	46	12		28		30				18	5*	0	0							15	273	10	L	6
v. Somerset	237*	1	8	26	48	42	0		87	28			5			15							15	512	10		
(Rose Bowl) 10-13 May	-	0	2	20*			-		-	13*			-			-							2	37	2	D	7
v. Nottinghamshire	31*	96	19	0	55	5	11		22	4	4		38			1							38	305	10		
(Trent Bridge) 17-20 May	26	21	8	115*	-		1		17	21	6		45			10*							11	281	8	W	22
v. Yorkshire	20	82	19	24	91	0*	26		23	-	30				0	17*							19	351	9		
(Rose Bowl) 24-27 May	-	6*	6*	-	-		-		-		-				-								0	12	0	D	9
v. Essex	15	3	50	44	83	1*	0		55	1	6				31								11	300	10		
(Rose Bowl) 4-7 June	19	56	35	16	8				41*	10*					38								29	311	7	D	8
v. Kent	56*	0	158	57	113	11			15*	78	6		-										59	553	7	W	24
(Rose Bowl) 5-7 July																											
v. Lancashire	56	72	0	33	33	19	1		54*		0	7			48								46	369	10	D	10
(Rose Bowl) 29 July-1 August																											
v. Durham	8	18	162	27*	1	31*	-		-		-				158								16	421	5		
(Basingstoke) 3-6 August	3*	5	107	0	3*	2	-		-		-				64								19	203	5	D	10
v. Somerset	48	34	71	4	23	0	0*		12				2		42						28		20	284	10		
(Taunton) 9-12 August	-	19	22	43	60*	-	-		-				16*		-						36		28	224	4	D	8
v. Yorkshire	30	196	40	180	0	-	-		-		1*	26											25	498	6	D	11
(Scarborough) 23-26 August																											
v. Lancashire	0	5	30	21	0	12	2*		24		0							35	20				11	160	10		
(Liverpool) 31 August-3 September	48	194	17	0	31	3	15*		8		31							1	11				46	405	10	L	2
v. Kent	11	84	15	36		2*	8		20	9	1							8	1				9	204	10		
(Canterbury) 7-10 September	0	52	56	68*	12	-	14		50		26							24	38				15	355	9	W	20
v. Warwickshire	15	13	7	0	1	27	41		74	2								11				0*	27	218	10		
(Rose Bowl) 13-16 September	62	8	1	6	7	11	9		9	6								4				0*	9	132	10	L	4
Matches	17	16	16	16	15	15	13	13	9	8	8	8	7	5	5	4	4	3	3	1	1	1					
Innings	27	29	28	27	25	21	14	17	15	13	6	11	13	9	7	8	6	4	6	0	2	2					
Not Out	4	1	1	4	5	5	3	3	0	1	0	3	0	6	0	0	3	0	0	0	0	2					
Highest Score	237*	196	164	180	141*	42	28	55	87	86	30	31	45	9*	158	18	17*	35	38	0	36	0*					
Runs	976	1351	1385	891	942	198	116	380	531	348	56	92	278	34	381	64	59	68	85	0	64	0					
Average	42.43	48.25	51.29	38.73	47.10	12.37	10.54	27.14	35.40	29.00	11.20	11.50	21.38	11.33	54.42	8.00	19.66	17.00	14.16	-	32.00	-					
100s	1	3	6	1	3	0	0	0	0	0	0	0	0	0	1	0	0	0	0	0	0	0					
50s	5	8	4	4	4	0	0	2	4	3	0	0	0	0	1	0	1	0	0	0	0	0					
Catches/Stumpings	7/0	17/0	9/0	11/0	20/0	3/0	2/0	8/0	33/0	4/0	2/0	28/0	11/0	1/0	4/0	2/0	1/0	0/0	0/0	0/0	0/0	0/0					

Home Ground: The Rose Bowl
Address: The Rose Bowl, Botley Road, West End, Southampton, SO30 3XH
Tel: 02380 472002
Fax: 02380 472122
Email: enquiries@rosebowlplc.com
Directions: From the North: M3 Southbound to junction 14, follow signs for M27 Eastbound (Fareham and Portsmouth). At junction 7 of M27, filter left onto Charles Watts Way (A334) and from there follow the brown road signs to the Rose Bowl. From the South: M27 to junction 7 and follow the brown road signs to the Rose Bowl.

Capacity: 22,000
Year formed: 1863

Chairman and Chief Executive: Rod Bransgrove
Director of Cricket: Tim Tremlett
First Team Manager: Giles White
Captains: Dimitri Mascarenhas, Dominic Cork
County colours: Navy blue, old gold

Website:
www.rosebowlplc.com

Honours
County Championship
1961, 1973
Sunday League/NCL/Pro40
1975, 1978, 1986
Benson & Hedges Cup
1988, 1992
Gillette Cup/NatWest/C&G Trophy/
Friends Provident Trophy
1991, 2005, 2009
Twenty20 Cup
2010

FIRST-CLASS MATCHES
BOWLING

	DG Cork	JA Tomlinson	DR Briggs	DJ Balcombe	SM Ervine	K Ali	DA Griffiths	CP Wood	HMRKB Herath	MA Carberry	H Riazuddin	D McKenzie	DT Christian	LA Dawson	JHK Adams	SP Jones	JM Vince	Overs	Total	Byes/Leg-byes	Wickets	Run outs
v. Essex (Chelmsford) 9-12 April	24-7-75-0		21-7-61-3		15-5-44-0	24.5-4-71-1	22-5-85-5											107.4	345	9	10	1
	25-8-72-2		9-2-22-0		22.4-9-33-5		18-3-75-2				3-3-0-1		5-1-8-0					96.4	256	13	10	
v. Oxford UCCE (Oxford) 15-17 April			12-3-20-1	23-9-54-2	10-2-26-1			20.1-7-54-5			4-2-9-0	11-4-29-1		12-2-42-0			1-1-0-0	93.1	242	8	10	
			7-3-12-1	9-1-37-1	7-1-24-1			10-1-30-2			1-0-1-0	2-2-0-1		3-2-4-0				39	111	3	6	
v. Durham (Chester-le-Street) 21-24 April	24-7-55-0		29-5-89-2		18-2-39-1	24-4-98-5	19-2-79-1			2-0-5-1			1-0-6-0					117	384	13	10	
	10-4-20-2		14.1-1-75-3			11-0-67-0	10-0-54-0											53.1	262	12	5	
v. Warwickshire (Edgbaston) 27-30 April	24-3-87-1		12-4-41-0		14.1-4-38-1	24-7-89-4	20-1-96-4						1-0-2-0					95.1	382	19	10	
	6-1-42-1		0.2-0-4-0			4-0-27-1	2-0-7-0											12.2	80	0	2	
v. Nottinghamshire (Rose Bowl) 4-7 May		16.3-7-34-4			13-0-48-1	24-2-92-3	14-1-70-0	34-7-68-2		1-1-0-0								102.3	328	16	10	
		7-2-16-0			8-1-41-0	20-2-11-0	16-4-59-3	23-2-111-2										56	246	8	5	
v. Somerset (Rose Bowl) 10-13 May	35-6-107-0	20-7-50-0			15-5-33-0		31-2-121-4	38.3-10-98-4			3-0-19-0		1-0-1-0		18-1-61-1	2-1-5-0	1-0-9-0	164.3	524	20	10	1
v. Nottinghamshire (Trent Bridge) 17-20 May	25-7-66-5	13-2-43-2		17-1-92-2	15-4-47-1				15-5-19-0									85	270	3	10	
	23-6-90-1	23-2-85-4		18-1-80-1	15-2-31-4				13-3-38-0									92	315	11	10	
v. Yorkshire (Rose Bowl) 24-27 May	33-2-115-3	34-11-78-3		24.1-6-69-3	24-1-88-0				21-5-51-1								2-0-9-0	136.1	415	14	10	
	18-5-53-0	14-4-30-1			17-2-48-2				31-10-78-1	9-3-16-1			5-1-24-0					100	292	19	5	
v. Essex (Rose Bowl) 4-7 June	28-4-66-3	30-8-60-2	15-4-42-2	21.4-9-47-2	22-5-62-1													116.4	284	7	10	
	12.2-5-37-1	12-4-12-1	7-3-18-1	8-3-14-2	12-5-16-1													51.2	99	2	6	
v. Kent (Rose Bowl) 5-7 July	20-5-47-0	22.2-6-50-5	11-3-26-2	12-1-67-2	5-4-43-1													80.2	251	18	10	
	12-4-28-2	12-3-16-2	12-0-56-1	13.2-2-48-2	11-1-36-2													60.2	191	7	9	
v. Lancashire (Rose Bowl) 29 July-1 August	21-5-51-1	24-5-57-4	18-4-54-2	22-3-75-2	14-5-33-1						2-0-11-0							101	283	2	10	
	17-7-40-1	17-4-45-0	47-6-142-3	21-6-41-1	17-4-43-0						8-1-31-1							127	351	9	6	
v. Durham (Basingstoke) 3-6 August	16-4-43-2	19.4-2-73-2	21-1-68-1	15-2-67-2	11-0-65-0													82.4	320	4	7	
																		-	-	-	-	
v. Somerset (Taunton) 9-12 August	32-6-108-5	10.1-2-22-0	27.5-0-139-1		6-1-21-0								1-0-1-0	10-1-24-0	22.1-1-115-2			109.1	412	5	10	
																		-	-	-	-	
v. Yorkshire (Scarborough) 23-26 August	22-6-96-1	23-6-64-5		16-2-46-0	16-4-58-2	14-5-41-1												91	322	17	9	
	10-2-46-0	9-1-48-1		15-2-60-2	9-2-35-1	8-2-20-0					1-0-4-0							52	225	12	4	
v. Lancashire (Liverpool) 31 August-3 September	30-13-60-1	33-13-77-1		8-0-36-1	28-5-89-1			26-8-85-3					9-0-30-2					134	398	21	10	1
	9-2-27-3	11.4-0-55-1		7-0-49-0				5-0-32-3										32.4	171	8	7	
v. Kent (Canterbury) 7-10 September	21-4-59-4	22-8-44-3		8-2-23-1	12.4-4-35-2			5-1-11-0										68.4	182	10	10	
	23-9-41-2	18-4-43-4		28-3-93-4	5-1-13-0			5-0-28-0			7-1-13-0							86	247	16	10	
v. Warwickshire (Rose Bowl) 13-16 September	31.5-12-83-3	16-1-40-0		24-2-100-3	7-1-15-0					22-5-60-4								100.5	303	5	10	
	7-1-23-0			8-2-18-0													1.2-0-6-0	16.2	51	4	0	

	DG Cork	JA Tomlinson	DR Briggs	DJ Balcombe	SM Ervine	K Ali	DA Griffiths	CP Wood	HMRKB Herath	MA Carberry	H Riazuddin	D McKenzie	DT Christian	LA Dawson	JHK Adams	SP Jones	JM Vince
Overs	559.1	407.2	377.2	246.1	362.5	137.2	152	71.1	175.3	22	42	13	32	22.1	33	2	5.2
Maidens	149	102	59	52	77	27	18	17	42	5	11	6	3	1	5	1	1
Runs	1624	1042	1294	812	1073	488	646	240	463	60	110	29	95	115	107	5	24
Wickets	46	45	34	27	20	19	19	13	10	4	4	2	2	2	1	0	0
Average	35.30	23.16	38.06	30.07	53.65	25.68	34.00	18.46	46.30	15.00	27.50	14.50	47.50	57.50	107.00	-	-

FIELDING

33	N Pothas (33 ct)
28	AM Bates (28 ct)
20	ND McKenzie
17	JHK Adams
11	CC Benham
11	JM Vince
9	MA Carberry
8	DG Cork
7	SM Ervine
4	LA Dawson
4	MJ Lumb
3	JA Tomlinson
2	K Ali
2	DJ Balcombe
2	DR Briggs
1	DA Griffiths
1	HMRKB Herath

Division One – Final Table

	P	W	L	D	Bat	Bowl	Pens	Pts
Nottinghamshire	16	7	5	4	47	43	0	214
Somerset	16	6	2	8	53	41	0	214
Yorkshire	16	6	2	8	41	42	0	203
Lancashire	16	5	3	8	35	43	0	182
Durham	16	5	3	8	30	39	0	173
Warwickshire	16	4	6	9	20	47	0	166
Hampshire	16	3	6	7	47	41	0	157
Kent	16	3	7	6	42	44	-1	151
Essex	16	2	6	8	29	43	-2	126

CB40 & FPt20

Limited overs nickname:
HAMPSHIRE ROYALS

KENT

by Mark Pennell

Kent supporters were unsure whether to laugh or cry into their beer come the end of the LV County Championship campaign. With their beloved club in dire financial straits and with rumours of senior players wanting away spreading quicker than head lice in a primary school playground, circumstances – on the surface at least – could not have seemed much gloomier.

Yet, with a 'glass half-full mentality', a good number of the county's 4,000 members began to feel by the end of September that a couple of seasons in the lower tier would at least reduce the pressure on their depleted squad and allow time to blood young, local talent.

With only one home win and two on the road to show for their efforts in four-day cricket during 2010, it came as no surprise when Rob Key's side made an immediate return to Division Two of the County Championship despite an admirable last round win over title-chasing Yorkshire in Leeds.

Sadly, there is little to offer by way of mitigation for their underachievement. Seamers Robbie Joseph and Dewald Nel picked up injuries that left both sidelined for much of the campaign. Then, joint leading wicket-

Rob Key, the Kent captain, comes down the pitch to hit Durham's Ian Blackwell for four during the County Championship match at Canterbury.

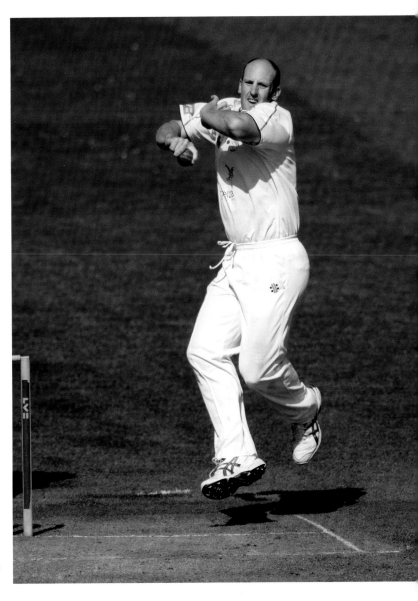

James Tredwell won his first Test cap for England in Bangladesh in March 2010, and was also a member of England's victorious ICC World Twenty20 squad in the West Indies in May.

taker Amjad Khan, with 38 scalps from 12 appearances, sat out the final weeks with a knee problem before being released to join Sussex.

With no cutting edge to their pace attack and with overseas wrist-spinner Malinga Bandara finding wickets hard to come by, the reality was Kent were always unlikely to bowl sides out twice – a prerequisite for winning Championship matches. The county's senior batsmen also seriously under-achieved, as only the dogged yet reliable Martin van Jaarsveld and the flamboyant Geraint Jones edged past the 1000-run milestone for the first-class campaign. Captain Key suffered his worst summer since becoming a first-team regular, with his tally of 814 runs massaged somewhat by his season's best knock of 261 against Durham in May.

The expectation surrounding young thrusters Joe Denly and Sam Northeast also fell flat as they struggled to muster 1,300 Championship runs between them. Denly, with only one century, too often edged drives to the slip cordon, while Northeast, with a modest top-score of 71, endured a season's long propensity for playing around his front pad to often fall leg before.

Disappointingly, the team's one-day performances were no better and with a Friends Provident t20 South Group playing record of seven wins from 16 starts the Kent Spitfires finished seventh, failing to reach finals day for the first time in four seasons. Player-of-the-season Darren Stevens at times carried the side and topped the t20 averages with 369 runs at 41.00, yet was inexplicably under-utilized when batting at No. 5. By the time he arrived at the crease the game was often already lost. Crucially, both he and James Tredwell also missed several games through international duty.

Simon Cook, Matt Coles and Bandara enjoyed better performances with the ball, but Azhar Mahmood, left wearied by Kent's necessity to play him in four-day games, sadly underachieved with the bat.

Kent also misfired badly at times during their Clydesdale Bank 40 divisional campaign, chalking up seven wins from their dozen matches as they finished runners-up in Group C to eventual winners Warwickshire. Denly was the sole batsman to top 400 runs in this competition, and only he and van Jaarsveld hit hundreds while just four bowlers returned 10 wickets or more in a one-day season to forget.

Though their Championship success at Headingley Carnegie in September failed to ward off relegation, it at least helped marginally when lifting the spirits of a membership craving for crumbs of Kentish comfort. Despite suffering a broken finger, rookie all-rounder Coles put in another gutsy performance at Leeds where Alex Blake hit a maiden century. A revitalised Nel took nine wickets in the match and James Tredwell eight,

Key Kicks off Kent Ground Development
by Mark Pennell

Kent captain Rob Key was dubbed 'Bob the Builder' after taking to an excavator to cut the all-important first sod of Kent's ground re-development programme in Canterbury on 27 September. New retractable floodlights, a two-storey dressing room block, pristine members' facilities in a refurbished pavilion and a new club shop and office complex are the three initial stages of this winter's multi-million pound St Lawrence refurbishment scheme. Club skipper Key said he and the squad will enjoy their more spacious dressing rooms and new floodlights in 2011 but, in the bigger picture, the fact that the county will be seen to be moving forward is more vital.

Key said, 'I don't think new floodlights will help my cover drive, but the landscape of cricket is changing massively and the thing I love about Kent is that the club doesn't merely want to exist, it wants to evolve and move forward. Things like this redevelopment plan are crucial to that. Cricket is changing and we have to make sure we are right at the forefront, so this scheme will really help us move forward.

'After a really tough year on the field, it's really encouraging to me to see how quickly things have gone in the last week. At last we're starting to see light at the end of the tunnel and I can now see Kent as a thriving club in years to come.'

After watching his captain break the topsoil to commemorate the start of their plans, Kent's chief executive officer, Jamie Clifford, said, 'I'm tremendously excited. It's been a long haul getting to this point, but it's tremendous to know now that this project is going to happen. We've been in existence as a club since 1870, the Ames Stand was built in 1890 and the pavilion in 1900, so other than the Colin Cowdrey Stand not much has happened here building-wise since the Second World War. There is now the opportunity to really invest in our infrastructure and make sure the asset we have here is really as good as it can be. That gives us a tremendous amount of hope and a real sense of vision of where we want to get to, which is a standard of facility that the 21st century sports fan expects.'

Below The historic St Lawrence Ground at Canterbury is set to undergo significant changes during a redevelopment phase that is vital to the future health and growth of the county club.

Matt Coles, an all-rounder from Maidstone who turned 20 in late May, was a rare good news story for Kent in a difficult season.

including his first hat-trick, to move the off-spinner level with Khan as joint leading wicket-taker.

After a horrendous first term in charge, head coach Paul Farbrace is doing his best to remain phlegmatic. Unable to flash the cheque book by signing a clutch of Kolpaks, as his predecessor Graham Ford had done, Farbrace is already resigned to not having an overseas star in 2011 and working with a skeleton staff of 16, at least five of whom will remain in full-time education. 'Our numbers will be limited and what we can realistically aim for in terms of competing for things will be limited as well,' conceded former Kent and Middlesex wicketkeeper.

'It will take time for the ground redevelopment and improvements to kick in and for new money to be generated, and so until then, and for the next couple of years for certain, we won't be able to add to our squad because we won't have the finances to do so.'

Not surprisingly then, Farbrace is bitterly disappointed that Kent will be plying their trade in the second tier next summer. 'I don't buy into the theory that we could be better off in Division Two for a little while,' added

Blake Aims to Improve All-round Game

Kent youngster Alex Blake has set out a winter programme to fine-tune his bowling action in the hope of featuring in 2011 as an all-rounder. Though the 21-year-old from Farnborough won England Under-19 caps and made his List A debut for the Spitfires as a pace bowler, his bowling, through injury and a slump in confidence, has barely featured over the past two seasons.

The left-hander revealed his prowess with the bat by scoring a maiden LV County Championship century against Yorkshire in the final game of the season at Headingley, but his close season programme will involve getting his right-arm seamers back on track. Having resumed the final year of his Leisure and Culture degree course at Leeds Metropolitan University, Blake is intent on finding time for some work in the gymnasium and some winter nets.

He said, 'My bowling has been a bit inconsistent over the past couple of years and that, together with an ankle injury, knocked my confidence. I went on tour with England Under-19s, didn't do that well with the ball and haven't bowled much since. So it's my main winter project to get my bowling on track and get stronger physically.

'I'm hoping to do some work up here with Yorkshire's Academy bowling coach, Steve Oldham, and hope that will improve my confidence. It's something I really want to carry on doing because it gives me more strings to my bow and, as an all-rounder, a greater opportunity of getting into the side. I've got to go through a similar learning process to Matt Coles, I guess. He played a few games at the start of last season where he hardly bowled a ball, but gradually he bowled a few overs here and there, earned Rob Key's confidence and trust and, by the end of the summer, he was one of our leading bowlers. I thought he did especially well in Twenty20, so that can be one of my targets for next year.'

by Mark Pennell

Geraint Jones, Kent's former England wicketkeeper, enjoyed another good season with the bat, reaching 1,000 first-class runs in Division One for the first time.

Farbrace. 'I want to be involved with a team that's competing at the top end and pushing for trophies, but we are where we are because of the way we performed throughout the year.

'You have to say we didn't score enough runs, we dropped vital catches and didn't have enough bowling depth. They are the three basic reasons we went down.'

Farbrace has pledged to work hard during the close season in a bid to iron out the errors, but with limited resources to hand he will do well to keep everyone happy. Other counties are rumoured to have courted van Jaarsveld, Stevens and Tredwell, all of whom remain on contract for the time being, so the re-appointment of Key as captain could prove crucial in helping to retain the backbone of the side.

Key also had the unenviable task of releasing six players as James Hockley, Rob Ferley, Warren Lee, Phil Edwards and Paul Dixey all joined Khan on the departure list.

Perhaps the first tender shoots of recovery started to emerge toward the season's end, however, with those encouraging displays by Blake, Coles and Nel. Kent also handed a three-year contract to their academy's teenage player-of-the-year, batsman Daniel Bell-Drummond, and gave a Chester-le-Street CB40 debut to left-arm bowler Adam Ball, who at 17 years and 184 days, became the youngest player ever to appear in a limited-overs game for Kent.

Clifford Hails Oval Experiment a Success

Kent chief executive Jamie Clifford has hailed the county's decision to stage their Friends Provident t20 clash against Essex on 9 July at the Brit Oval as a financial and commercial success story. Although Kent lost the match by four wickets in a thrilling last over finish, the game attracted a crowd of 7,620 – the Spitfires' largest of the season – which according to Clifford vindicated the decision to play the fixture in south-east London.

Many of the corporate boxes in the OCS Stand at the Test venue were also in use, representing new commercial business, and Clifford said, 'There were corporate clients at the game who wouldn't come to Canterbury because we're too far away. So it has many benefits for us. It's repositioned our brand and said to people that we're willing to try different things. Kent has been a fairly traditional county in its approach to life and in one move we were saying that we are now willing to look at things slightly differently.'

Clifford also believes the club's fans responded positively to the bold move to switch venues, adding, 'Going around the ground talking to the members and supporters, I think they liked the change of scenery. Quite a few in the pavilion, who maybe work in the City, have said to me "this is great, you must do more of this. It gives me a chance to see some Twenty20 cricket." The crowd figure we needed to cover costs was low. After that there were agreements in place on how to share the proceeds but let's be clear, it made us money. If we'd had a full house of 17,000 or so it would have changed the complete picture for us because a full house would have been worth £150,000 more than we might expect to take from a normal fixture in Canterbury. That's why we wanted to test the water.'

by Mark Pennell

PLAYER OF THE SEASON

Darren Stevens pushed his body to its limits in an effort to try to stave off relegation. Fully deserved his England Lions call and should have won World t20 recognition.

YOUNG PLAYER OF THE SEASON

Matthew Coles. After a poor start that left captain Key distinctly underwhelmed, Coles showed great character to fight back with a maiden Championship 50 and by taking wickets in all formats.

A YEAR TO REMEMBER

- Martin van Jaarsveld went past 1,000 first-class runs for the sixth successive season since joining Kent
- Geraint Jones proved his stamina and ability by keeping adequately and reaching 1,000 runs for the first time in Division One

A YEAR TO FORGET

- Rob Key suffered relegation for the second time as skipper and misfired with the bat
- Amjad Khan failed to win a contract despite being Kent's leading pace bowler of the season
- Rob Ferley and James Hockley were both released by the county for a second time after failing to shine

At the age of 34 Darren Stevens blossomed in 2010 into an all-round cricketer of real stature and also made his England Lions debut during the summer.

KENT CCC

FIRST-CLASS MATCHES
BATTING

	JL Denly	GO Jones	SA Northeast	M van Jaarsveld	RWT Key	SJ Cook	DI Stevens	MT Coles	JC Tredwell	A Khan	AJ Blake	Azhar Mahmood	JB Hockley	HMCM Bandara	M Ntini	JD Nel	PD Edwards	RH Joseph	RS Ferley	PG Dixey	JE Goodman	MAK Lawson	CD Piesley	Extras	Total	Wickets	Result	Points
v. Loughborough UCCE	0	112	10	106	140	25*	25	40*	11							-	-							35	504	7		
(Canterbury) 10-12 April	106	26	21	-	-	19	19	4*	6							-	1							10	212	7	D	
v. Nottinghamshire	0	28	38	7	4		7	6	19	24		52					6*							9	200	10		
(Trent Bridge) 15-17 April	37	11	18	1	15		42*	28	20	9		19					13							11	224	10	L	4
v. Yorkshire	32	28	27	20	5		92	6*	32	1		21	14											39	317	10		
(Canterbury) 21-24 April	2	53	1	78	9		5	-	72*			18	82											37	357	8	D	9
v. Lancashire	14	25	13	1	5	0	101*	33		0		9		0										12	213	10		
(Old Trafford) 27-30 April	10	1	-	-	19*	-	-	10*		-		-		-										5	45	2	D	7
v. Warwickshire	95	10	40	47	18	1	57	41		0		20		3*										45	377	10		
(Canterbury) 4-7 May	0	12	26	59	22	7	18	1		4*		1		0										6	156	10	L	7
v. Essex	1	135	65	51	7	19	100	0				64	2	0*										30	474	10		
(Chelmsford) 10-13 May	17	36	71	7	25	19*	9	6				6	3	0										5	204	10	D	11
v. Durham	0	9	4	30	261	0			10	31	43				2*				19					15	424	10		
(Canterbury) 17-20 May	14	17	9	44	20	5			12*	7	11				13				1					9	162	10	L	7
v. Durham	24	21	8	36	40	0	102	34	-	16*	2				7									30	320	10	W	22
(Chester-le-Street) 24-25 May																												
v. Nottinghamshire	0	37	12	44	56	26*	197	22	115	5				29										27	570	10	D	10
(Tunbridge Wells) 4-7 June																												
v. Pakistanis	63						12			0	28	0				4		18*		22	59	31	0	22	259	10		
(Canterbury) 28-30 June	69						-			28	-	2*				-		-		-	0*	-	43	8	150	3	D	
v. Hampshire	67	11	50	17	17	2			21	31	0	0			7*									28	251	10		
(Rose Bowl) 5-7 July	9	1	32	82*	4*	16			0	13	8	12			5									9	191	9	L	3
v. Somerset	34	16	24	4	7*	22	23	14	0	15					5									8	172	10		
(Taunton) 20-23 July	36	47	40	6	-	9	1*	15	-	10					4*									23	191	7	D	6
v. Essex	40	99	25	106	13	7	34		19	1		28		19*										29	420	10		
(Canterbury) 29 July-1 August	6	4	7	18	0	7*	0		40	0		19		23										11	135	10	W	24
v. Somerset	8	178	18	71	17	0*	33		7	11		0		0										29	372	10	D	10
(Canterbury) 3-6 August																												
v. Lancashire	69	10	0	34	8	8	28	24	20	1*	28													19	249	10		
(Canterbury) 18-21 August	12	0	18	30	30	10	3	51	36	0*	10													17	217	10	L	4
v. Warwickshire	0	0	32	0	0	9	0	13*	12	33	8													4	111	10		
(Edgbaston) 31 August-2 September	4	41	14	110*	7	0	14	13	7	0	0													18	228	10	L	3
v. Hampshire	42	8	0	41	19	11*	13	9	18	0					4									17	182	10		
(Canterbury) 7-10 September	10	21	71	5	1	2	45	1	14	46					9*									22	247	10	L	3
v. Yorkshire	26	6	20	89	25	5	0	0	8		105*					2								16	302	10	W	22
(Headingley) 13-16 September	1	0	5	44	27	-	4*	-	4*	0						-								5	90	6		
Matches	18	17	17	17	16	15	14	14	12	12	9	8	6	6	5	3	2	2	1	1	1	1	1					
Innings	33	31	30	29	28	24	26	23	20	18	17	14	11	10	8	2	3	3	2	1	2	1	2					
Not Out	0	0	0	2	2	7	3	6	2	5	1	0	1	3	3	0	1	2	0	0	1	0	0					
Highest Score	106	178	71	110*	261	26*	197	51	115	24	105*	64	82	29	13	4	13	18*	19	22	59	31	43					
Runs	848	1003	719	1188	814	205	979	378	489	115	359	317	141	105	25	6	20	30	20	22	59	31	43					
Average	25.69	32.35	23.96	44.00	31.30	12.05	42.56	22.23	27.16	8.84	22.43	22.64	14.10	15.00	5.00	3.00	10.00	30.00	10.00	22.00	59.00	31.00	21.50					
100s	1	3	0	3	2	0	4	0	1	0	1	0	0	0	0	0	0	0	0	0	0	0	0					
50s	5	2	4	6	1	0	2	1	1	0	0	2	1	0	0	0	0	0	0	0	1	0	0					
Catches/Stumpings	10/0	49/6	6/0	36/0	1/0	2/0	6/0	4/0	21/0	5/0	5/0	1/0	6/0	5/0	0/0	2/0	0/0	0/0	0/0	0/3	0/0	0/0	0/0					

Home Ground: Canterbury
Address: St Lawrence Ground, Old Dover Road, Canterbury, CT1 3NZ
Tel: 01227 456886
Fax: 01227 762168
Email: jon.fordham.kent@ecb.co.uk
Directions: From the North, from M20 junction 7 turn left onto A249. At M2 junction 5 (Sittingbourne) bear right onto M2. At junction 7 (Boughton Street) turn right on to A2. Follow this to junction with A2050, turn left. Follow yellow signs to cricket ground. From the South, from M20 junction 13 bear right onto A20. Follow this road to junction with A260. Bear left and continue to junction with A2 (north). Continue to junction with A2050 and then proceed as north.

Capacity: 15,000
Other grounds used: Beckenham, Tunbridge Wells
Year formed: 1859

Chief Executive: Jamie Clifford
Director of Cricket: Paul Farbrace
Coaching Coordinator: Simon Willis
Captain: Robert Key
County colours: Navy blue, silver and yellow

Honours
County Championship
1906, 1909, 1910, 1913, 1970, 1978
Joint Champions 1977
Sunday League/NCL/Pro40
1972, 1973, 1976, 1995, 2001
Benson & Hedges Cup
1973, 1978
Gillette Cup/NatWest/C&G Trophy
1967, 1974
Twenty20 Cup
2007

Website:
ww.kentccc.com

FIRST–CLASS MATCHES
BOWLING

	JC Tredwell	A Khan	SJ Cook	Azhar Mahmood	DI Stevens	MT Coles	M Ntini	HMCM Bandara	JD Nel	MAK Lawson	M van Jaarsveld	AJ Blake	PD Edwards	JL Denly	RWT Key	RS Ferley	JB Hockley	RH Joseph	JE Goodman	SA Northeast	GO Jones	Overs	Total	Byes/Leg-byes	Wickets	Run outs
v. Loughborough UCCE (Canterbury) 10-12 April	24.5-8-50-1		21-10-24-3	7-1-29-1	22-8-50-2						10-1-29-1		18-6-60-2		1-0-7-0							103.5	259	10	10	1
	4-2-3-0										3-2-4-1		2-1-8-0	5-0-8-1	3-0-7-0					3-2-6-0		28	60	2	3	
v. Nottinghamshire (Trent Bridge) 15-17 April	18-2-68-1		25-5-108-3		26-5-75-1	12-1-41-1	15.4-2-65-2							14-3-77-1	1-0-4-0							111.4	456	16	10	1
																						–				
v. Yorkshire (Canterbury) 21-24 April	18-3-53-2		25-9-60-3		21.3-5-58-4		11-0-40-0				5-0-12-0					5-1-13-1						97.3	283	17	10	
	29-15-69-3		19-1-95-0		3-0-11-0									6-1-29-0								84	300	8	5	1
v. Lancashire (Old Trafford) 27-30 April		17-2-67-1	13-5-44-0		20-4-44-4	10-0-49-0	23-5-46-3				12-1-38-1					4-0-14-0						97.3	320	18	10	1
		11-2-67-1	6-0-23-0		7-3-23-0	2-1-10-0	13-6-31-2				2-0-3-0					2-0-16-0						43	177	4	3	
v. Warwickshire (Canterbury) 4-7 May			20-6-68-2		14.4-0-66-4	21-6-34-0	14-0-55-4				2-1-6-0							2-0-10-0				80.4	250	11	10	
			20-6-63-3		25.5-4-75-3	6-1-30-1	19.5-4-7-1		26-2-47-0		30-6-50-2							2-0-10-0				118.5	327	5	10	
v. Essex (Chelmsford) 10-13 May			22-5-60-2		25.2-4-63-5	2-1-3-0	19-4-72-0		23-7-89-3		8-0-22-0			9-0-38-0		5-1-8-1						108.2	341	15	10	
			3-0-9-0			16-4-56-1	5.4-3-5-0				19-3-48-0			27-1-100-2								81.4	254	10	4	
v. Durham (Canterbury) 17-20 May			28-7-81-3		14-2-64-0	24.4-3-66-1			29-8-84-5		5-0-27-0			1-0-3-0			18-2-88-1					119.4	418	5	10	
			3-1-6-1			9-0-35-1			12-3-44-1		1-0-6-0			1-0-26-0			8-0-54-1					34	172	1	4	
v. Durham (Chester-le-Street) 24-25 May			11.5-1-43-5			9-0-43-2			6-1-20-1		17-6-53-4											34.5	121	5	10	
	5-1-20-0		13-3-29-2			3-0-13-0			6-2-20-0		17.3-3-51-6											54.3	195	8	10	
v. Nottinghamshire (Tunbridge Wells) 4-7 June	36-4-120-2		19.5-3-77-0		22-2-85-4		6-0-37-1	40.1-5-125														124	462	18	10	
	22-1-88-1				7-4-9-0		8-1-35-1	25-7-63-1														62	210	15	3	
v. Pakistanis (Canterbury) 28-30 June					11-2-33-1	13-1-61-1			12-1-54-1	16-0-93-4				5-1-9-2		7-1-27-0	16-2-51-0	6-0-16-1				87	360	14	10	
					11-2-40-1	9-1-40-0			6-1-17-0	18-2-71-2				1-0-2-0		12-1-60-0	9-3-22-0					65	264	14	4*	
v. Hampshire (Rose Bowl) 5-7 July		8-0-33-0			29-6-95-2			47-10-167-1			14-2-47-0	14-1-60-1					6-1-27-0	27-3-112-2				145	553	17	7	
																						–				
v. Somerset (Taunton) 20-23 July	0.4-0-1-1	18-4-63-3			14-1-65-2		13-4-38-4	4-0-28-0														49.4	205	10	10	
	11-1-64-1	13-4-60-1			7-0-23-0		13-1-73-3	10-1-67-2														54	301	14	7	
v. Essex (Canterbury) 29 July-1 August	20-5-63-1	22-7-47-3			16-7-35-1	22-6-54-2	10-5-13-0	12.2-4-44-3														102.2	279	23	10	
	17.5-3-40-2	10-2-33-1			8-2-26-1	21-5-62-5		2-0-6-0														59.5	177	10	10	1
v. Somerset (Canterbury) 3-6 August	12-3-56-2	26.4-4-89-3			8.5-3-25-1	22-7-65-3	18.1-5-64-0	16-2-72-0			4-0-25-0			2-0-5-0	11.2-3-31-2							103.4	380	9	10	1
	42-9-95-5	23-5-74-0			21-2-60-0	7-2-16-0	13-0-60-0									3-1-2-0	1-0-8-0					127.2	387	6	7	
v. Lancashire (Canterbury) 18-21 August	16-2-56-1	19-6-61-2			15-2-65-2	14-5-33-3	12-1-35-2				2-1-1-0											76	266	16	10	
	25.2-2-99-2	20-4-59-0			20-5-62-4	20-6-55-2	11-1-35-2															98.2	321	10	10	
v. Warwickshire (Edgbaston) 31 August-2 September	14-1-51-1				16-4-65-2	15-5-56-1	21-4-63-3	17.4-3-49-3						1-0-4-0								84.4	294	6	10	
	3.1-0-21-1				13-3-51-4	13-3-51-4	4-0-21-1															33.1	140	9	10	
v. Hampshire (Canterbury) 7-10 September		24-8-49-2			13-3-46-2	19-8-31-1	9-1-28-1	16.5-3-42-4														81.5	204	8	10	
		30-10-84-2			6-1-20-0	15-3-51-3	19-3-78-0	28.2-2-99-4						5-0-10-0								103.2	355	13	9	
v. Yorkshire (Headingley) 13-16 September	0.3-0-0-1				15-2-67-1	17-4-51-0	19-3-68-2	25-9-62-6														76.3	261	13	10	
	6.5-1-22-7				3-0-15-0	8-1-28-0	1-1-0-0	11-1-57-3														29.5	130	8	10	

	JC Tredwell	A Khan	SJ Cook	Azhar Mahmood	DI Stevens	MT Coles	M Ntini	HMCM Bandara	JD Nel	MAK Lawson	M van Jaarsveld	AJ Blake	PD Edwards	JL Denly	RWT Key	RS Ferley	JB Hockley	RH Joseph	JE Goodman	SA Northeast	GO Jones
Overs	377	372.2	331.3	279.3	280.1	280	164	210.4	54	34	123	19	34	53	15.2	26	43	52	6	6	1
Maidens	71	82	68	55	74	42	44	32	12	2	17	2	10	2	3	2	5	8	0	3	0
Runs	1151	1258	1132	847	768	1040	474	745	190	164	332	69	145	215	45	142	175	185	16	8	8
Wickets	38	38	37	30	28	27	24	18	10	6	5	3	3	3	2	2	2	2	1	0	0
Average	30.29	33.11	30.59	28.23	27.43	38.52	19.75	41.39	19.00	27.33	66.40	23.00	48.33	71.67	22.50	71.00	87.50	92.50	16.00	–	–

Key:
* Fawad Alam retired out for 68

FIELDING

55	GO Jones (49 ct, 6 st)
36	M van Jaarsveld
21	JC Tredwell
10	JL Denly
6	JB Hockley
6	SA Northeast
6	DI Stevens
5	HMCM Bandara
5	AJ Blake
5	A Khan
4	MT Coles
3	PG Dixey (0 ct, 3 st)
2	SJ Cook
2	JD Nel
1	Azhar Mahmood
1	RWT Key

Division One – Final Table

	P	W	L	D	Bat	Bowl	Pens	Pts
Nottinghamshire	16	7	5	4	47	43	0	214
Somerset	16	6	2	8	53	41	0	214
Yorkshire	16	6	2	8	41	42	0	203
Lancashire	16	5	3	8	35	43	0	182
Durham	16	5	3	8	30	39	0	173
Warwickshire	16	6	9	1	20	47	0	166
Hampshire	16	3	6	7	47	41	0	157
Kent	16	3	7	6	42	44	-1	151
Essex	16	2	6	8	29	43	-2	126

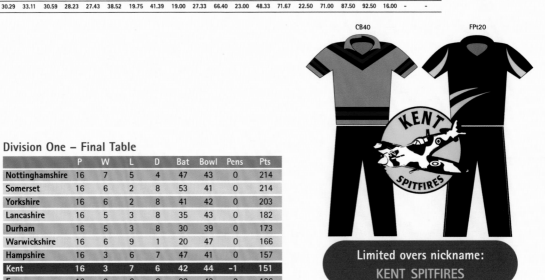

CB40   FPt20

Limited overs nickname:
KENT SPITFIRES

LANCASHIRE

by Andy Wilson

I t was the sight that so many Lancashire followers have dreamed of witnessing for so long – jubilant celebrations on the Old Trafford outfield for the newly crowned county champions. Unfortunately, it was the Nottinghamshire players who were spraying champagne on a sunny September afternoon after a dramatic climax to the season, leaving the home team to watch from the balcony of their dressing room and wonder what might have been.

Fourth place did represent a solid achievement, with one more win and seven more points than in 2009, especially considering the disruption caused by the loss of Kumar Sangakkara before the start of the season and serious injuries to Gary Keedy and Stephen Moore, plus confirmation of the end of Andrew Flintoff's career. But there were the usual cluster of if-onlys that convinced Lancashire's coach Peter Moores and captain Glen Chapple they could have been in contention with Notts going into that last fixture.

Lancashire could plausibly argue that rain denied them good opportunities to press for three more wins – against Kent at Old Trafford, Yorkshire at Headingley and Durham at the Riverside. The last two of those games was arguably the most authoritative performances of the season, when the side was at its strongest, featuring quality centuries from the middle order by Tom Smith and Luke Sutton, and penetrative seam bowling from an attack skilfully led by Glen Chapple and boosted at Durham by James Anderson's bonus appearance.

In addition, two of the three defeats – the most Lancashire had suffered in a Championship season since they were relegated in 2004 – were in tight games that hung in the balance for long periods. But Moores and Chapple were honest enough to concede that at home to Durham on a dusty Old Trafford turner, and against Notts at Trent Bridge when a combination of rain and the title situation forced Lancashire to dangle a tasty carrot; the limitations of a youthful team were exposed.

As so often in recent years, the problems began with the top-order batting. Paul Horton played in all 16 games but only managed 634 runs from 30 innings. Moore was faring no better, with an average of 25 and only two half centuries in his first nine appearances after a winter move from Worcestershire, until he suffered a serious shoulder dislocation diving in the outfield in the draining Friends Provident t20 quarter-final defeat against Essex at Chelmsford.

More runs for Tom Smith, this time against Essex at Chelmsford. Chris Wright is the bowler.

Cross is First-Choice Keeper
by Andy Wilson

Gareth Cross will definitely start the 2011 season as Lancashire's first-choice wicketkeeper. The county were linked with a number of other 'keepers since Luke Sutton's return to Derbyshire was confirmed including Warwickshire's Tim Ambrose and Andrew Hodd of Sussex, both of whom are well-known to the Red Rose coach Peter Moores.

But Moores confirmed during the dramatic County Championship climax against Nottinghamshire at Old Trafford that Cross would be given a longer chance to establish himself as Sutton's successor. 'He's a good 'keeper, and he's waited a long time for it,' the former England coach said of the 26-year-old from Leigh who made his senior debut way back in 2005. 'The big test for him next year is going to be doing the job day in day out for a long period of time. He had a bit of a run at the back end of last season, but doing it for a whole summer is very different.'

Cross played in six of Lancashire's 16 Championship games, but only kept wicket in the last three after Sutton had confirmed his move. Moores has also challenged him to refine his batting style over the winter, and believes that the experience gained this season – especially in a partnership with Shivnarine Chanderpaul in the victory against Kent at Canterbury – will stand him in good stead. 'You could see the benefit of batting with Shiv, as Crossy picked up his rhythm and took that into the next game when Shiv wasn't at the other end,' added Moores. 'Finding the right tempo for batting in first-class cricket is another challenge for him.'

Lancashire will have another wicketkeeping option available next year as Andrea Agathageou, a 20-year-old South African who was a second-team regular in 2010, has plenty of experience behind the stumps, even though he played as a batsman who bowls a bit of leg spin last summer. Agathageou, who captained the Lancashire team beaten by Essex in the final of the Second XI Trophy, qualifies as a non-overseas player because he holds a Cypriot passport.

Mark Chilton grafted hard for a few handy half-centuries but was unable to go on to three figures, and although Smith continued to put his hand up to open when required, his lack of experience was exposed during a torrid early-season run – when, to be fair, batsmen up and down the country were struggling – and he looked much happier scoring that unbeaten century at Headingley from No. 6.

Sutton was also thrust up the order against Somerset at Old Trafford in May, and responded with an excellent century. But he too had returned to more familiar territory in the lower middle-order when he batted so well at the Emirates Durham ICG, and at the end of the season he returned to Derbyshire to give

Chapple Enters Exclusive 700 Wickets Club
by Andy Wilson

Glen Chapple became a very modest member of an exclusive Lancashire club when he moved past 700 first-class wickets during the 2010 season. The 36-year-old Lancashire captain is only the 21st bowler to reach that milestone in the county's history. If he can maintain form and fitness, Chapple could climb significantly up the higher echelons of Lancashire's list of all-time bowling greats.

'Actually, I'm the same as everyone at the club in that my main priority is winning games, and I'm really happy that I'm still playing and involved. I suppose it's good to get to 700, but it's only one more than 699, and I hope there are a few milestones left yet. I've got a couple more years in me, hopefully more. I'd love it if I could get to 1,000 but that's highly improbable, so as it goes I'll just get as many as I can. It is crazy when you think that I'm still 1,500 or so wickets behind Brian Statham's overall tally.'

The great Statham took 1,816 first-class wickets for Lancashire and 2,260 in all. But he doesn't figure in the subset of only four Lancastrian cricketers to have scored 7,000 first-class runs in addition to taking 700 wickets – Mike Watkinson, Jack Simmons, RG Barlow and Johnny Briggs.

Chapple, of course, has a third string to his bow these days, having taken over the captaincy in 2009. His initial appointment came as something of a surprise, as Chapple's apparently uncomplicated approach to cricket and life had never really marked him out as captaincy material – and he admits that he hadn't given the prospect much thought himself. But he has taken to the job naturally, forming an effective partnership with the Lancashire coach Peter Moores, and to listen to him chatting about a range of cricketing topics – declaration options, the new Championship points system, or the pitches at Old Trafford – is to realise that here is a deep thinker about the game with a wealth of experience to add weight to his views.

Glen Chapple has not only grown impressively into the role of Lancashire captain in the past two years but has also added significantly to his record of individual achievement.

Gareth Cross an opportunity to stake a claim to be his permanent successor.

The other comings and goings were largely confined to the overseas positions. Lancashire had hoped to build their team around Sangakkara for most of the season but when Sri Lanka accepted additional commitments, they were forced into a hasty rethink. Ashwell Prince extended his early-season stay until June, and again gave good value. But Simon Katich struggled for the bulk of the Twenty20 qualifying campaign, and Lancashire were relieved when the predictably excellent Shivnarine Chanderpaul arrived to replace him. Nathan McCullum made useful contributions in t20 without doing anything spectacular, and Daren Powell, the Jamaican seamer who was signed as a Kolpak to add more depth and experience, was a disaster. He took seven wickets in four Championship appearances, but it was an embarrassingly bad fielding performance in a floodlit Clydesdale Bank 40 game against Sussex that left no alternative but to cut short his Old Trafford stay.

Powell's appearance in that game was an anomaly as by that stage, Lancashire were already using the 40-over competition to give more experience to their younger players, their chances of qualification having disappeared with four defeats from their first six matches. That made the four wins they secured from their last six all the more satisfying – even if two of them were against the Unicorns – with Luke Procter, Karl Brown and the debutant Jordan Clark all making an impression, and Smith, Steven Croft, Kyle Hogg and Horton, as captain, responding to the extra responsibility.

Croft made good progress in all forms of the game, Hogg finally earned his county cap nine seasons after making his debut, and there was also a significant transformation in Sajid Mahmood from gifted but erratic youngster to a senior pro who could be relied on to lead the attack with Chapple and, increasingly, to score handy runs. He put the latter contribution down to a simple change in approach. 'I've started to watch the ball,' he said.

But if Lancashire could reflect on a small step forward in the Championship, then they undeniably deteriorated in the one-day competitions, with the Friends Provident t20 defeat at Essex following a far less convincing qualification than in 2009.

Bizarrely, Lancashire chose to go into that quarter-final with three left-arm spinners, a decision that backfired on the night but reflected one of the club's real strengths. Stephen Parry's consistent one-day excellence was recognised by his selection for the England Lions, and Simon Kerrigan seized the chance presented when Keedy suffered a dislocated shoulder in pre-season to take 30 wickets from 13 Championship appearances – including three five-fers or better – a highly encouraging debut campaign.

Perhaps inspired by the extra competition, Keedy then bowled as well as ever when he returned for the last seven matches. But his 31 wickets at 22 were eclipsed by Chapple's 52 at less than 20, another outstanding season for the apparently ageless captain who became only the 21st man to take 700 first-class wickets for Lancashire. He will start the 2011 season having climbed to 17th with 743, and is only 55 first-class runs short of 7,000 and a double previously achieved by only four Lancashire all-rounders.

Simon Kerrigan, a slow left-arm spinner from Preston, turned 21 in 2010 and also came of age on the cricket field with a series of excellent performances.

Moores Sees Signs of Real Progress
by Andy Wilson

Peter Moores believes that a hat-trick of breathless victories towards the end of the 2010 campaign represented significant progress for his increasingly young Lancashire team. The County Championship win against Hampshire was the most memorable, significant, and hard earned, with Mark Chilton creaming the penultimate ball of the match from Dominic Cork to the backward point boundary. Moores conceded that Lancashire made heavy weather of getting over the finishing line, while giving a large part of the credit for that to Hampshire's opener Jimmy Adams for his marathon knock.

But the silver lining to that cloud was the fact that Chilton and Kyle Hogg kept their cool at the death, just as Hogg had in clinching victory off the last ball against the Unicorns in Colwyn Bay a few days earlier, and as Luke Procter did again to secure another Clydesdale Bank 40 win with five balls to spare against Worcestershire at Aigburth. 'We've had some tight games in my time at the club, but we've missed out on a few,' said Moores, with the heartbreaking defeat at Essex in the Twenty20 quarter-final at Chelmsford the most obvious example. 'What was nice was that we then won three close games on the bounce.'

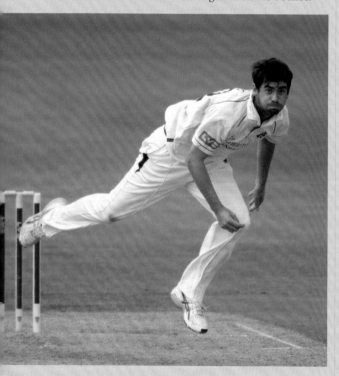

Nine years after making his Lancashire debut, in 2001, Kyle Hogg was finally awarded his county cap during the 2010 season.

PLAYER OF THE SEASON

Glen Chapple – even at 36, the captain showed that he remains one of the most effective purveyors of swing and seam in county cricket, taking 52 Championship wickets at less than 20 each to take his first-class tally for Lancashire to 743.

YOUNG PLAYER OF THE SEASON

Simon Kerrigan was handed a surprise debut, aged 20, in the Championship opener against Warwickshire following Gary Keedy's pre-season injury, and the left-arm spinner from Preston bowled so well that he retained his place for most of the year.

A YEAR TO REMEMBER

- Stephen Parry is another young slow left-armer who showed that his one-day success in 2009 was no fluke, earning the 24-year-old Mancunian an England Lions call-up
- Kyle Hogg – son of Willie and grandson of Sonny Ramadhin – was finally awarded his county cap nine years after making his debut before anyone had heard of James Anderson
- Sajid Mahmood did nothing spectacular with the ball, but relished his development as a genuine all-rounder, climbing to fifth in Lancashire's first-class batting averages with 564 runs at 31 including five half centuries, two more than he had managed in the previous eight summers combined

A YEAR TO FORGET

- Stephen Moore struggled for the consistent runs Lancashire wanted when they signed him from Worcestershire until his season was ended in late July by a nasty shoulder injury
- Daren Powell – signing the veteran Jamaican seamer as a Kolpak was never a popular move with the members, who therefore chortled knowingly when he was released less than halfway through his contract
- Andrew Flintoff – the proud Prestonian finally conceded defeat in his battle to recover from major knee surgery after the 2009 Ashes triumph, denying him the Old Trafford swansong that he and Lancashire had wanted

LANCASHIRE CCC

FIRST-CLASS MATCHES
BATTING

	MJ Chilton	SJ Croft	PJ Horton	SI Mahmood	G Chapple	TC Smith	SC Kerrigan	LD Sutton	SC Moore	KW Hogg	S Chanderpaul	AG Prince	GD Cross	G Keedy	JM Anderson	DBL Powell	LA Procter	KR Brown	SM Katich	Extras	Total	Wickets	Result	Points
v. Warwickshire	3	64	2	0	54*	0	3	33	6		82		0							6	253	10		
(Old Trafford) 15-18 April	0	56	26	52	53*	7	2	33	43		0		10							37	319	10	W	21
v. Essex	1	56	123	14	1	7	0*	11	61		16		0							22	312	10		
(Chelmsford) 21-23 April	-	-	12*	-	-	1	-	-	17		1*		-							7	38	2	W	22
v. Kent	11	93	15	4	27	7	3*	14	0		115				5					26	320	10		
(Old Trafford) 27-30 April	52*	-	10	-	-	2	-		38		71*				-					4	177	3	D	9
v. Somerset	41	18	2	64	10		0*	118	4	4	2				6					23	292	10		
(Old Trafford) 4-7 May	16	66*	25	-	30*		-	38	31	6	3				-					6	221	6	D	8
v. Warwickshire	39	89*	24	9	29	7	6	3	61		51			-		13				23	354	10		
(Edgbaston) 17-20 May	43	0	5	72	22	0	2	0	13		0			25*						17	199	10	W	23
v. Essex	49	4	19	58	10		4	4	3	7	2				16*					8	184	10		
(Old Trafford) 24-27 May	12*	0	64	-	21*		-	26	5	-	29				-					20	177	5	D	6
v. Yorkshire	42	15	24	3	29	108*	-	20	43	37	78									17	416	9		
(Headingley) 29 May-1 June																							D	8
v. Yorkshire	7	16	63		21	16	0	47*	40	88					2				32	26	358	10		
(Old Trafford) 28 June-1 July	23	85*	19		23	11	-	0	8	4*					-				8	11	192	7	D	8
v. Durham	1	4	29	42	4	23	1	101*	27		92			0						20	344	10		
(Riverside) 20-23 July	25	1	9	-	-	2*	-	-	26		23*			-						5	91	4	D	9
v. Hampshire	17	41	21	21*	9	2	4	29			118	4	8							9	283	10		
(Rose Bowl) 29 July-1 August	47	23	5	-	11*	128	-	2			11	100*	-							24	351	6	D	7
v. Durham	69	17	9	20	5	0	4	12			10	17	2*							16	181	10		
(Old Trafford) 9-12 August	50	28	8	0	19	2	0*	6			67	13	24							9	226	10	L	3
v. Kent	0	65	16	60	1	32		13		20*	0		30	5						24	266	10		
(Canterbury) 18-21 August	7	43	29	41*	5	5		9			120		50	0						12	321	10	W	21
v. Nottinghamshire	67	9	51	4	0*	61		11		0	92		0	4						20	319	10		
(Trent Bridge) 24-27 August	49*	-	4	-	-	76*		-			-		-	-						14	143	1	L	4
v. Hampshire	48	3	0	47	19	31				81	38	44	12*				21			54	398	10		
(Liverpool) 31 August-3 September	18*	10	5	24	-	9				17*	51	26	-				0			11	171	7	W	22
v. Somerset	12	31	7	29		23	16*			0	56	6	34				19			26	259	10		
(Taunton) 7-9 September	0	46	2	0		16	0			37*	20	0	0				32			17	170	10	L	5
v. Nottinghamshire	1	-	6*	-	-	-	-				0		-					4		0	11	3		
(Old Trafford) 13-16 September																							D	6
Matches	16	16	16	15	14	14	13	13	9	9	8	7	7	7	4	4	2	2	1					
Innings	29	26	30	20	22	25	15	21	17	13	14	13	11	9	5	4	3	3	2					
Not Out	4	3	2	2	6	3	5	2	0	4	1	2	1	2	1	1	0	0	0					
Highest Score	69	93	123	72	54*	128	16*	118	61	88	120	115	100*	34	25*	16*	32	21	32					
Runs	750	883	634	564	403	576	45	530	426	301	698	450	290	89	35	29	64	25	40					
Average	30.00	38.39	22.64	31.33	25.18	26.18	4.50	27.89	25.05	33.44	53.69	40.90	29.00	12.71	8.75	9.66	21.33	8.33	20.00					
100s	0	0	1	0	0	2	0	2	0	0	2	1	1	0	0	0	0	0	0					
50s	4	8	3	5	2	2	0	2	2	2	5	4	1	0	0	0	0	0	0					
Catches/Stumpings	6/0	13/0	19/0	2/0	4/0	14/0	3/0	37/5	6/0	3/0	2/0	7/0	12/0	0/0	0/0	0/0	0/0	0/0	1/0					

Home Ground: Old Trafford
Address: Old Trafford Cricket Ground, Talbot Road, Manchester, M16 0PX
Tel: 0161 282 4000
Fax: 0161 282 4100
Email: enquiries@lccc.co.uk
Directions: *By rail:* Manchester Piccadilly or Victoria then Metro link to Old Trafford. *By road:* M60, Stretford slip-road (junction 7) on to A56; follow signs.
Capacity: 21,500
Other grounds used: Blackpool, Liverpool, Southport

Year formed: 1864
Chief Executive: Jim Cumbes
Director of Cricket: Mike Watkinson
Head Coach: Peter Moores
Captain: Glen Chapple
County colours: Red, navy blue and green

Website:
www.lccc.co.uk

Honours
County Championship
1881, 1897, 1904, 1926, 1927, 1928, 1930, 1934. Joint Champions 1879, 1882, 1889, 1950
Sunday League/NCL/Pro40
1970, 1989, 1998, 1999
Benson & Hedges Cup
1984, 1990, 1995, 1996
Gillette Cup/NatWest/C&GTrophy
1970, 1971, 1972, 1975, 1990, 1996, 1998

FIRST-CLASS MATCHES
BOWLING

	G Chapple	TC Smith	SI Mahmood	G Keedy	SC Kerrigan	KW Hogg	JM Anderson	DBL Powel	LA Procter	SJ Croft	Overs	Total	Byes/Leg-byes	Wickets	Run outs
v. Warwickshire	15-1-50-2	16-2-48-1	8-1-24-2		18-4-44-2		20-5-62-2				77	254	26	10	1
(Old Trafford) 15-18 April	3-1-7-1	18.5-3-65-2	14-6-27-2		17-2-43-5		15-7-27-0			2-0-16-0	69.5	197	12	10	
v. Essex	16-6-30-3	16-1-38-1	13-0-40-0		5-2-4-0		20.5-5-44-6				70.5	176	20	10	
(Chelmsford) 21-23 April	20-6-60-2	11-3-18-3	8-2-20-1		4.4-1-13-1		22-7-53-3				65.4	173	9	10	
v. Kent	16-4-45-3	18.5-4-55-5	13-2-49-2		1-0-1-0			12-3-51-0			60.5	213	12	10	
(Old Trafford) 27-30 April	6-0-19-0	5.5-1-21-2									11.5	45	2	2	2
v. Somerset	33-5-146-3				12-5-41-1	30.2-11-96-4		24-5-81-2		3-0-9-0	102.2	383	10	10	
(Old Trafford) 4-7 May											–	–	–	–	
v. Warwickshire	12-4-27-5	13-5-44-3	8-2-29-2						1-0-8-0		34	113	5	10	
(Edgbaston) 17-20 May	21-3-69-4	21.5-3-83-2	16-2-55-1		28-7-66-1		26-7-85-2				112.5	375	17	10	
v. Essex	22-7-47-2	23-3-89-1			38.3-10-74-6	21-6-51-1		11-2-40-0			115.3	307	6	10	
(Old Trafford) 24-27 May	10-5-20-0	17-5-37-0			15-1-66-1	16-4-45-2		14-5-38-1			72	212	6	5	1
v. Yorkshire	6-3-6-2	12-2-53-0	15-5-46-4		19-3-58-2	11-3-36-0					63	199	0	8	
(Headingley) 29 May-1 June											–	–	–	–	
v. Yorkshire	31-7-75-4		28-7-80-2		27-4-101-0	21.3-4-78-1		20-0-88-2			127.3	447	25	10	1
(Old Trafford) 28 June-1 July	10-3-24-0		5-0-14-0		24-8-77-4	11-0-47-1		18-1-45-2	1-0-2-0		69	215	6	7	
v. Durham	23.2-4-65-5	5-0-25-0	9-1-29-1				27-8-74-3				64.2	216	13	10	1
(Riverside) 20-23 July											–	–	–	–	
v. Hampshire	25-5-68-4	18-0-69-1	10-3-38-0	25.2-3-56-4	31-6-90-0					3-0-17-1	112.2	369	31	10	
(Rose Bowl) 29 July-1 August											–	–	–	–	
v. Durham	14-0-45-1	3-0-24-1	7-2-33-0	21.2-2-68-7	16-3-60-1						61.2	237	7	10	
(Old Trafford) 9-12 August	9-3-16-0		2-0-11-0	32-8-80-3	25.5-5-64-1						68.5	173	22	4	
v. Kent	23-6-45-4	22-3-90-1	8-2-22-0	19.5-9-49-4		9-2-32-1					81.5	249	11	10	
(Canterbury) 18-21 August	17-5-39-3	12-2-48-0	12-2-44-3	10.3-3-53-4		5-1-15-0				1-0-5-0	57.3	217	13	10	
v. Nottinghamshire	13-3-41-1	15-4-43-2	13-1-49-0	5.1-1-19-0		12-2-47-2					58.1	203	4	5	
(Trent Bridge) 24-27 August	17.2-4-67-1	16-1-77-2	5-0-31-0	14-0-57-2		3-0-20-2					55.2	261	9	7	
v. Hampshire	10-4-16-2	11.4-1-40-1		12-1-40-3		14-2-53-4					47.4	160	11	10	
(Liverpool) 31 August-3 September		31-4-129-1		41-10-94-6	58-13-105-1	31.3-12-50-2				4-2-2-0	165.3	405	26	10	
v. Somerset		26-7-77-1	16.5-5-67-2	26-1-81-5	16-2-82-0	7-1-33-0			5-0-26-1		96.5	382	16	10	1
(Taunton) 7-9 September		3-0-21-1	3-1-11-0		1-0-3-0				1.3-0-13-0		8.3	48	0	1	
v. Nottinghamshire		12-0-69-2	13-3-50-1	34.4-3-140-1	20-3-80-5	10-0-47-0					89.4	400	14	9	
(Old Trafford) 13-16 September											–	–	–	–	

	G Chapple	TC Smith	SI Mahmood	G Keedy	SC Kerrigan	KW Hogg	JM Anderson	DBL Powel	LA Procter	SJ Croft
Overs	372.4	348	279.5	246.5	319	202.2	130.5	99	7.3	14
Maidens	89	54	58	43	66	48	39	16	0	2
Runs	1027	1263	913	688	967	650	345	343	47	51
Wickets	52	33	32	31	30	20	16	7	1	1
Average	19.75	38.27	28.53	22.19	32.23	32.50	21.56	49.00	47.00	51.00

FIELDING

42	LD Sutton (37 ct, 5 st)
19	PJ Horton
14	TC Smith
13	SJ Croft
12	GD Cross (12 ct)
7	AG Prince
6	MJ Chilton
6	SC Moore
4	G Chapple
3	KW Hogg
3	SC Kerrigan
2	S Chanderpaul
2	SI Mahmood
1	SM Katich

Division One – Final Table

	P	W	L	D	Bat	Bowl	Pens	Pts
Nottinghamshire	16	7	5	4	47	43	0	214
Somerset	16	6	2	8	53	41	0	214
Yorkshire	16	6	2	8	41	42	0	203
Lancashire	16	5	3	8	35	43	0	182
Durham	16	5	3	8	30	39	0	173
Warwickshire	16	6	9	1	20	47	0	166
Hampshire	16	3	6	7	47	41	0	157
Kent	16	3	7	6	42	44	-1	151
Essex	16	2	6	8	29	43	-2	126

CB40   FPt20

Limited overs nickname:
LANCASHIRE LIGHTNING

LEICESTERSHIRE

by Paul Bolton

Leicestershire's encouraging rise from wooden spoonists in 2009 to fourth in the County Championship second division was largely overshadowed by a summer of in-fighting and blood-letting at Grace Road.

The sudden resignation of chief executive David Smith in late June began several months of claim and counter-claim in an unpleasant civil war which brought further casualties in former county batsman Paul Haywood, who resigned from the board, and Tim Boon, who stepped down as senior coach to return to an old job as England Under-19 coach.

Smith, a former Warwickshire batsman, cited alleged interference in team selection by chairman Neil Davidson and his co-directors. Davidson responded by

Despite a turbulent season off the field, on it Leicestershire had a season of real progress with a team that blended experienced campaigners and talented youngsters and only just missed out on promotion to Division One.

Leicester-born off-spinner Jigar Naik had a superb season, taking 35 Championship wickets at 17.69. His best performance came against Surrey at The Oval where his 7 for 96 in the second innings secured a valuable win.

saying that he was concerned that Leicestershire's 'dreadful' performances in Friends Provident t20 and other one-day cricket were having a damaging impact on the club's finances and he was only acting to protect members' interests.

The dispute escalated when Boon and captain Matthew Hoggard sent a letter to the board claiming to represent the players, coaching, administrative and groundstaff calling for a vote of no confidence in the board. The board, minus Haywood, supported Davidson and Boon, whose position had been described as 'unsustainable' by his chairman, then tendered his resignation during the final match of the season at Northampton. But Davidson also resigned at the end of the season saying that his position had become untenable after Hoggard had refused his request to retract his letter to the board. Davidson's resignation came shortly after a date had been fixed for a special general meeting which was due to include a vote of no confidence in the chairman and his co-directors.

This special general meeting was then, in turn, cancelled after the board – now with Haywood reinstated as the new chairman – agreed to resign en masse early in 2011 so that re-elections of all board positions (thus creating, in theory, a clean sheet) could be held. Davidson, meanwhile, revealed that he had loaned the club more than £100,000 interest-free so that the Leicestershire players' wages could be paid during the final two months of the season, and began proceedings to take his money back.

All of which detracted from a Championship season of real progress in which a side that had a nice blend of seasoned campaigners and talented youngsters almost clinched promotion. Leicestershire were close to victory when rain denied them against Middlesex at Lord's and fell just short in a thrilling last-day run-chase against Surrey. A win in either of those draws would have been enough to clinch the second promotion place.

They lost only one of their last eight matches – against champions Sussex – after Smith announced his resignation on the opening day of the match against Worcestershire at New Road.

'We faced some very demanding situations but the players coped with them admirably,' Boon said. 'The off-field events probably helped to bring the squad closer together.'

James Taylor showed no signs of second season syndrome as he followed up his magnificent season in 2009 with one of solid progress. The England Lions batsman again topped 1,000 first-class runs, including a double-century against Middlesex, and expanded his game in the t20 in which he made his maiden half-century in the competition.

Durham University student Greg Smith suggested that he has the technique and temperament to play at a

Henderson Scoops Clutch of Awards
by Paul Bolton

Former South Africa left-arm spinner Claude Henderson picked up three awards at Leicestershire's end-of-season presentation night. Henderson, who took 56 Championship wickets, was named Cricketer of the Year, Players' Player of the Year and took the Frank S. Smith bowling prize.

Leicestershire have also awarded Henderson, 38, a Testimonial in 2011. He made history in 2004 when he became the first ever Kolpak registration in county cricket, but his registration status has changed this year after he was granted British citizenship after serving a residential qualification period in England.

Batsman James Taylor shared the John Josephs Award for best individual performance with off-spinner Jigar Naik. Taylor was recognised for his double-century against Middlesex and Naik for his match-winning bowling against Surrey at The Oval.

Taylor also won the Livingston Cup for batting in the first team and the Roger Goadby fielding award. Batsman Jacques du Toit was voted Supporters' Player of the Year, with seamer Nathan Buck taking the Livingston Award for the best uncapped player after taking 49 wickets in his first full season in the county game.

Left-armer Claude Henderson celebrated getting his British citizenship by signing a new two-year deal with Leicestershire at the start of the summer. He struck up a superb spin partnership with Jigar Naik, which realised 91 Championship wickets, of which Henderson's contribution was 56.

James Taylor's form in 2009 earned him a place in the MCC side for the traditional curtain raiser against champions Durham. He played well again in 2010, scoring over 1,000 Championship runs, which included 203 not out against Middlesex in May.

higher level with consecutive Championship centuries at the end of the season against Gloucestershire and Northamptonshire. Smith deputised for the injured Will Jefferson, who appeared to have rediscovered his appetite for the game after three tough years with Nottinghamshire as he topped 700 runs before a persistent Achilles tendon problem ended his season.

Jacques du Toit and Paul Nixon, two out-of-contract players at the end of the season, scored consistently and seamer Nadeem Malik returned to form after missing the entire 2009 campaign through injury.

Hoggard had more to cope with than he might have expected when he accepted the challenge of captaincy for the first time following his surprise release by Yorkshire. The increased responsibilities did not appear to affect Hoggard's swing bowling as he topped 50 wickets for the third time in his career, but he looked less comfortable as team spokesman in an increasingly tangled political web.

Nathan Buck, a big-hearted teenage seamer from Ashby-de-la-Zouch, took 49 wickets in an excellent first full season but it was spinners Claude Henderson and

Jigar Naik, with 91 Championship wickets between them, who were the unsung and hard-working heroes.

Australian Andrew McDonald was a popular addition to the squad, although his appearances were limited by unexpected Australia A commitments and then a shoulder injury which ended his season early. McDonald made two Championship centuries and has been re-engaged for 2011. He impressed in the t20 making his maiden half-century in that format and recording the best figures in the country in the competition – 5 for 13 against Nottinghamshire – but those performances came either side of a lengthy absence on international duty.

Had McDonald been available for the full t20 campaign, as Leicestershire envisaged when they signed him, they would surely have improved on a dismal record of seven defeats and a washout at Grace Road. Their six away wins included four at Test match grounds – Old Trafford, Edgbaston, Headingley and Trent Bridge.

The Clydesdale Bank 40 campaign was a disappointment as only Scotland, who completed the

LEICESTERSHIRE CCC

FIRST-CLASS MATCHES
BATTING

	TJ New	JWA Taylor	CW Henderson	PA Nixon	MAG Boyce	NL Buck	MJ Hoggard	J du Toit	WI Jefferson	WA White	MN Malik	JKH Naik	AB McDonald	JJ Cobb	HF Gurney	GP Smith	AJ Harris	SJ Cliff	JOE Benning	Extras	Total	Wickets	Result	Points
v. Northamptonshire	82	88	6	5	47	0	2		7	89				27			20*			22	395	10		
(Leicester) 9-12 April	14*	1	-	8	3	-	-		10	-				20*			-			9	65	4	W	22
v. Derbyshire	61	6	25	37	0	0	0		94	4				13			5*			34	279	10		
(Derby) 15-18 April	20	25	1	12	90	14	-		6	101*				25			1*			35	330	8	W	21
v. Cambridge UCCE	12	56		11				154	23	48	35*	48*	1	-				-		23	411	7		
(Cambridge) 21-23 April	44*	-		-				0	101*	-	-	72	55*	-				-		13	285	2	D	
v. Sussex	18	6	3	0	18	1			27	11			4	2			0*			24	114	10		
(Hove) 27-29 April	4	24	1	93	28	8*			44	47			47	5			1			36	338	10	L	3
v. Worcestershire	22	5	23	74	19	1	0*	0	9	7			15							6	181	10		
(Leicester) 4-7 May	42	3	0	45	4	4*	3	52	60	-			0							18	231	9	L	3
v. Gloucestershire	0	4	28	0	6	1	0*	5	51				0			0				7	102	10		
(Bristol) 10-13 May	9	39	29	63	62	0	33*	9					12			0				23	285	10	L	3
v. Glamorgan	1	0	0	90	45	10	3*				15		113	3	0					11	291	10		
(Leicester) 24-26 May	5	34*	6	9	1	0	0				6		2	2	4					2	71	10	L	5
v. Middlesex	-	206*	-	4	42	-	-	-	0				176*	-						36	464	3		
(Leicester) 29 May-1 June																							D	9
v. Surrey	91	63	9	41	0	0	1*	81	135			34		2						22	479	10	W	23
(The Oval) 4-6 June																								
v. Worcestershire	58	27	8	11		4	6	57	64	13*	10								29	22	309	10		
(Worcester) 28-30 June	-	43*	-	55		-	11	32	-	-	-								26*	15	182	3	W	22
v. Glamorgan	7	70	1	0	38		0	75	27	8	0	12*								9	247	10		
(Swansea) 21-24 July	18	43	-	57*	0		-	26	10	24*	0	35								8	221	6	D	
v. Sussex	9	19	11	22		4*	2	18	7	21	0		63							28	204	10		
(Leicester) 29-31 July	2	5	0	0		8*	1	81	6	23	6		10							14	156	10	L	4
v. Derbyshire	54	18	24	18	60	5	1*	44		4	0					21				27	276	10		
(Leicester) 3-6 August	-	-	-	-	86*	-	-	-								52*				32	170	0	W	21
v. Middlesex	14	106*	31	10	5	1	4	0		0	36					65				10	282	10		
(Lord's) 9-12 August	41*	0	-	24	52	-	-	10		-	6*					0				6	139	5	D	8
v. Surrey	-	-	-	-	57*	-	-	-		-						58*				8	123	0		
(Leicester) 24-27 August	2	0	3	106	44	4*	-	122		7	0*					23				27	338	8	D	4
v. Gloucestershire	63	0	33	43	1	26	2*	46			34	0				28				19	295	10		
(Leicester) 7-10 September	10*	36	-	23	36	-	-	70			-	-				158*				18	351	4	W	21
v. Northamptonshire	43	156	23*	65	2	2	0	14					27			104	0*			12	448	9		
(Northampton) 13-16 September	-	-	-	-	4*	-	-	-					-			0*				0	4	0	W	23
Matches	17	17	16	16	15	15	15	13	11	9	8	8	6	5	5	5	5	1	1					
Innings	27	28	21	27	27	20	17	20	20	13	9	12	11	10	4	10	7	0	2					
Not Out	4	4	1	1	3	5	6	1	1	2	3	3	1	2	1	4	4	0	1					
Highest Score	91	206*	33	106	90	26	6	154	135	101*	35*	72	176*	55*	4	158*	20*	0	29					
Runs	746	1083	265	915	761	93	31	899	722	394	88	301	442	153	6	509	27	0	55					
Average	32.43	45.12	13.25	35.19	31.70	6.20	2.81	47.31	38.00	35.81	14.66	33.44	44.20	19.12	2.00	84.83	9.00	-	55.00					
100s	0	3	0	1	0	0	0	2	1	2	0	0	2	0	0	2	0	0	0					
50s	6	4	0	7	6	0	0	6	4	1	0	1	1	1	0	3	0	0	0					
Catches/Stumpings	46/1	15/0	6/0	4/0	19/0	4/0	5/0	16/0	14/0	4/0	0/0	5/0	2/0	3/0	0/0	6/0	2/0	0/0	1/0					

Home Ground: Grace Road, Leicester
Address: County Ground, Grace Road, Leicester, LE2 8AD
Tel: 0871 2821879
Fax: 0871 2821873
Email: enquiries@leicestershireccc.co.uk
Directions: *By road:* Follow signs from city centre, or from southern ring road from M1 or A6.
Capacity: 12,000
Other ground used: Oakham School
Year formed: 1879

Chief Executive: David Smith, Mike Siddall
Senior Coach: Tim Boon
Club Captain: Matthew Hoggard
County colours: Dark green and yellow

Website:
www.leicestershireccc.co.uk

Honours
County Championship
1975, 1996, 1998
Sunday League/NCL/Pro40
1974, 1977
Benson & Hedges Cup
1972, 1975, 1985
Twenty20 Cup
2004, 2006

FIRST-CLASS MATCHES
BOWLING

	CW Henderson	MJ Hoggard	NL Buck	JKH Naik	MN Malik	AB McDonald	AJ Harris	HF Gurney	WA White	JGE Benning	PA Nixon	SJ Cliff	MAG Boyce	JWA Taylor	J du Toit	JJ Cobb	Overs	Total	Byes/Leg-byes	Wickets	Run outs
v. Northamptonshire	20-9-21-6	14.4-3-35-2	13-5-32-0					15-5-55-2	8-0-35-0								70.4	190	12	10	
(Leicester) 9-12 April	25-9-47-2	13-2-67-0	12.4-4-36-3					14-3-46-1	16-3-58-4							1-1-0-0	81.4	269	15	10	
v. Derbyshire	18-6-30-3	18-4-43-3	15-4-44-4					11-1-49-0	6-1-27-0								68	207	14	10	
(Derby) 15-18 April	28-17-32-2	21-8-45-2	20-9-35-3					12.4-4-43-3	8-3-26-0						2-0-3-0		91.4	199	15	10	
v. Cambridge UCCE				11-4-24-4	16.2-3-50-2		12-5-32-1		10-0-53-2			12-4-29-1					61.2	199	11	10	
(Cambridge) 21-23 April				8-4-9-0	10-1-28-0		8-2-24-1		8-2-14-0			9-2-25-0				2-1-7-0	45	116	9	1	
v. Sussex	18-2-89-2		22-6-70-3				21-4-79-3	19-5-77-1	10.5-1-38-1								93.5	392	11	10	
(Hove) 27-29 April	3-1-4-0		4-1-19-0					5-0-25-0	1.3-0-9-0							3-0-28-0	13.3	64	7		
v. Worcestershire	14-3-60-1		26-7-69-3	19-2-64-3		20-3-54-2			13-5-31-1								92	308	30	10	
(Leicester) 4-7 May	4-0-17-0		22-4-70-1	20-2-72-3		17-4-40-5			12-1-63-0								75	277	15	9	
v. Gloucestershire	25.2-6-50-2		25-6-67-4	24-5-91-2		17-1-60-0	20-5-90-2				2.1-1-7-1		1-0-2-0		1-0-4-0		111.2	376	18	10	
(Bristol) 10-13 May																	4.1	15	2	1	
v. Glamorgan	6-5-8-2	14.1-2-32-4	8-1-31-0	9-0-33-1		7-4-14-1	12-6-33-2										56.1	166	15	10	
(Leicester) 24-26 May	7-1-45-0	8-1-48-0	5.5-0-34-0	4-0-16-0		5-1-21-0	4-0-24-0										33.5	198	10	0	
v. Middlesex	20-2-78-0	24-9-46-1	18-4-71-0			16-4-52-1	24-3-82-3								1-0-16-0		103	356	11	5	
(Leicester) 29 May-1 June																					
v. Surrey	30.5-8-84-6	5-1-27-0	11-5-36-1	15-3-37-1			15-3-42-1										76.5	236	10	10	1
(The Oval) 4-6 June	28-10-45-2	7-6-1-0	6-4-3-1	23-3-96-7			5-1-21-0										69	183	17	10	
v. Worcestershire	8.1-1-21-2	5-3-34-1		12-3-29-2		5-2-15-2	12-4-50-2			9-2-21-1							59.1	175	5	10	
(Worcester) 28-30 June	17-5-33-1	14-1-62-0		17-1-65-3		7.1-1-41-1	25-6-73-3			10-0-38-2							90.1	315	3	10	
v. Glamorgan	24.5-3-72-5		13-1-50-0	31-3-110-4	11-2-44-1			2-0-9-0									81.5	290	5	10	
(Swansea) 21-24 July																					
v. Sussex	19.5-3-75-2	25-4-81-5	20-0-110-3			20-4-53-0			14-2-48-0								98.5	379	12	10	
(Leicester) 29-31 July																					
v. Derbyshire	2.2-0-12-1	24-6-77-4	14-4-38-1			14-6-32-4			2-0-8-0								56.2	182	15	10	
(Leicester) 3-6 August	25-7-46-3	14-1-59-2	20-6-60-4			18.5-3-77-1			12-1-37-0								86	262	23	10	
v. Middlesex	18-6-40-1	20-5-63-6	7-1-23-0			2.4-0-7-1			15-8-57-2					1-0-2-0			65.4	219	9	10	
(Lord's) 9-12 August	28-5-49-3	12.5-3-54-1	9-2-37-3			27-4-78-2			11-3-26-1								88.5	255	9	10	
v. Surrey	33.1-3-119-4	27-5-68-3	23-5-105-0			24-4-83-3			11-1-75-0						3-0-13-0		121.1	483	20	10	
(Leicester) 24-27 August																					
v. Gloucestershire	18-9-17-2	15-4-47-1	12-2-47-3	3.5-0-9-2		11-2-32-2											59.5	159	7	10	
(Leicester) 7-10 September	34-12-62-3	12-6-15-1	10.2-5-25-3	25-13-35-3		6-2-14-0											87.2	158	7		
v. Northamptonshire	9-0-18-1	21-7-48-5	19-5-74-1			18.4-2-51-3	10-0-50-0										77.4	250	9	10	
(Northampton) 13-16 September	5-3-5-0	8-4-14-1	20-2-89-3			14.4-1-58-4	6-2-24-2										53.4	198	8	10	
Overs	489.3	416.4	381.5	205	193.2	103	96	96.4	134.2	19	2.1	21	1	4	2	8					
Maidens	136	105	88	40	45	21	22	23	20	2	1	6	0	0	0	2					
Runs	1179	1222	1340	619	599	320	332	385	531	59	7	54	2	15	20	38					
Wickets	56	50	49	35	21	12	10	9	8	3	1	1	0	0	0	0					
Average	21.05	24.44	27.35	17.69	28.52	26.67	33.20	42.78	66.38	19.67	7.00	54.00	-	-	-	-					

FIELDING

47	TJ New (46 ct, 1 st)
19	MAG Boyce
16	J du Toit
15	JWA Taylor
14	WI Jefferson
6	CW Henderson
6	GP Smith
5	MJ Hoggard
5	JKH Naik
4	NL Buck
4	PA Nixon
4	WA White
3	JJ Cobb
2	AJ Harris
2	AB McDonald
1	JGE Benning

Division Two – Final Table

	P	W	L	D	Bat	Bowl	Pens	Pts
Sussex	16	8	3	5	45	47	0	235
Worcestershire	16	7	4	5	39	42	0	208
Glamorgan	16	7	4	5	33	43	0	203
Leicestershire	16	7	5	4	31	44	0	199
Gloucestershire	16	6	9	1	28	47	-2	172
Northamptonshire	16	6	7	3	28	34	0	167
Surrey	16	4	6	6	43	36	-2	159
Middlesex	16	4	7	5	37	41	-2	155
Derbyshire	16	3	7	6	30	42	0	138

CB40   FPt20

Limited overs nickname:
LEICESTERSHIRE FOXES

Youngster Greg Smith impressed everyone at Grace Road with back-to-back centuries in the last two games of the season.

double over Leicestershire, finished below them. Once it became clear that they were not going to progress beyond the group stage, Leicestershire used the competition to give first-team exposure to youngsters such as Alex Wyatt and Josh Cobb, sacrificing short-term competitiveness for long-term development.

PLAYER OF THE SEASON

Claude Henderson, the first Kolpak player in county cricket, celebrated his first season as a newly qualified British citizen with a heavy workload – 489.3 overs – but 56 Championship wickets.

YOUNG PLAYER OF THE SEASON

James Taylor passed 1,000 first-class runs for the second successive season, and expanded his skills in one-day and t20 cricket. He remains an outstanding prospect.

A YEAR TO REMEMBER

- Greg Smith started the season with a century for Durham MCCU against Nottinghamshire and ended it with successive Championship centuries against Gloucestershire and Northamptonshire
- Matthew Hoggard reached 50 first-class wickets in his first season at Grace Road and had unexpected political issues to grapple with as the new captain
- Nathan Buck is a young man with a fast bowler's build who stayed fit all season and finished with an impressive 49 wickets

A YEAR TO FORGET

- Brad Hodge arrived with high expectations and as the leading run-scorer in the history of Twenty20 cricket but failed to spark
- Josh Cobb struggled to establish himself in the Championship side and was overshadowed by the success of James Taylor and Greg Smith
- James Benning, the former Surrey all-rounder, was initially troubled by a back injury and then released just as he had showed signs of finding form

Injury Forces Paceman Cliff to Quit
by Paul Bolton

Leicestershire's highly rated young seamer Sam Cliff has been forced to retire from first-class cricket because of injury.

Cliff was famously up a ladder in Preston doing his day job as a painter and decorator when he received the call to make his County Championship debut against Northamptonshire in 2007.

Leicestershire had high hopes for the 22-year-old local product but injuries restricted Cliff to just two first-class appearances in the last two seasons, the last of them against Cambridge UCCE at Fenner's in April 2010. He also played in three Clydesdale Bank 40 games and one Friends Provident t20 match last season.

The county have also released seamer Dan Masters and reserve wicketkeeper Joel Pope. Masters, the younger brother of Essex seamer David, made his debut in a side comprised entirely of uncapped players in a Pro-40 League match against Warwickshire at Edgbaston in 2009. His only first team appearances in 2010 were restricted to two CB40 matches, the last of them against his native Kent in August.

Pope, the nephew of Middlesex wicketkeeper Ben Scott, joined Leicestershire from the MCC Young Cricketers three years ago. He made only three one-day appearances during his three seasons at the club, two of them last season in the CB40 against Warwickshire at Grace Road and Kent at Canterbury.

Insurance Broking

You and us -
a great result

Oval Insurance Broking is the proud sponsor of LCCC

www.theovalgroup.com

5 Western Boulevard
Leicester
LE2 7EX

Switchboard: 0116 254 6221

We have offices throughout the UK.
Please visit our website for full contact details.

MIDDLESEX

by Mark Pennell

Taking over the captaincy of a stuttering second division county midway through an already trouble-some season does not sound the most inviting introduction to leadership you could ever wish for. To do so when your two immediate predecessors were legends of the game in their own right, moreover, transforms the appointment into something of a baptism of fire.

Yet that was the exact scenario facing Neil Dexter when, in late June and aged only 25, he took over the Middlesex helm and followed in the footsteps of Shaun Udal and Adam Gilchrist. With less than 50 first-class appearances under his belt, South African-born Dexter bravely accepted the invitation from his club's director of cricket, Angus Fraser, to take up the baton as skipper.

After Udal decided he had given the role his all and once Gilchrist's brief and marginally successful sojourn into English Twenty20 cricket had come to an end, Dexter was ushered in to lead quietly and effectively from the front. Having taken over midway through the Panthers' Friends Provident t20 campaign, Dexter made a decent impact with the bat as Middlesex, despite the presence of Tyron Henderson, David Warner, Pedro Collins and Gilchrist, finished sixth with a disappointing 50 per cent win ratio.

Having missed the start of the season with two fractured vertebrae, the legacy of slipping down the

Dawid Malan, the Middlesex left-hander, was the only batsman from the county to top 1,000 first-class runs in 2010 – a collective run-scoring failure which was at the root of the team's mediocre season.

Udal Proud of His Long Innings
by Mark Pennell

Middlesex and former Hampshire off-spinner Shaun Udal brought an end to an illustrious career that spanned 22 seasons when he announced his retirement from first-class cricket in mid-October. The decision also concluded Udal's three-year association with Middlesex, whom he captained for just over a year until June 2010.

Udal, 41, a wily bowler and lusty late-order batsman, and known universally in cricket as 'Shaggy' after his alleged resemblance to the Scooby Doo cartoon character, won four England Test caps and played in 11 one-day internationals.

Picking up the wicket of 'the Little Master', Sachin Tendulkar, during his spell of 4 for 14 in the Mumbai Test on England's 2005-06 tour of India proved his finest hour and helped the tourists to square that series 1-1.

Commenting on his decision to call time on his playing days, Udal said, 'I am extremely lucky to have played the game I love for such a long period. Cricket has been extremely good to me and I have enjoyed every moment I have spent in the game. I have played with and against some great cricketers and characters, and treasure the moments I spent playing with and competing against these men.

'I have many good friends in cricket and hope to continue to enjoy their company. It is obviously a sad day – waving goodbye to something very special is always difficult – but I look forward to getting stuck in to the next chapter of my life.'

Having initially retired in 2007 after winning four trophies in 19 seasons with Hampshire, Udal was lured back into the game by Middlesex's then head coach, John Emburey. The decision brought immediate reward as Middlesex won the 2008 Twenty20 Cup, beating Kent in a tense finish at the Rose Bowl.

In 301 first-class games Udal took 822 wickets at an average of 32.47 and claimed 1,330 wickets in all forms of the game. Added to that, he scored more than 11,000 runs in all formats at an average of just over 20.

Shaun Udal, seen here throwing the ball to Tim Murtagh, resigned as Middlesex captain during 2010 and retired from first-class cricket at the end of the summer.

steps outside his London flat, Dexter's Middlesex team then enjoyed an innings triumph at Lord's over neighbours Surrey in July. A satisfying six-wicket win on a turning pitch in Cardiff against a Glamorgan side that included Robert Croft and Dean Cosker was also vital, helping to stave off the ignominy of a first County Championship wooden spoon in club history.

Under Dexter, Middlesex won only three of their 12 Clydesdale Bank 40 games, however, but these are difficult times in St John's Wood and, overall, his leadership reign has seen signs of hope for the future. With Eoin Morgan, Andrew Strauss and Steven Finn absent for much of the season on England duty, Dexter's overall resources with bat and ball were thin on the ground and selection policy appeared unsure.

In one-day cricket, uncertainty surrounded Ben Scott and John Simpson as to which of them was better behind the stumps, and then, in the extended game, there seemed few options in terms of seam-bowling support for leading wicket-taker Tim Murtagh (38 wickets at 36.97). Collins (36 at 27.75) and promising all-rounder Gareth Berg (24 at 36.54) did their bit, but neither managed a five-wicket haul.

It made matters worse that even by mid-season Udal, Dawid Malan and new recruit Scott Newman were still

Sussex's loss is Middlesex's gain. After a poor season, Middlesex director of cricket, Angus Fraser, moved quickly to sign a number of good new players. One of the best is Corey Collymore, whose guile and economy will add a new edge to the London club's attack.

Emotional Collymore Puts Family First
by Bruce Talbot

Corey Collymore says he has put his family first after leaving Sussex to sign for Middlesex. The 32-year-old from Barbados has left Hove after three seasons and has signed a two-year contract at Lord's. Sussex also offered him a two-year extension after he took 57 County Championship wickets this season to help the club seal an immediate return to Division One.

After an emotional dressing-room address to his team-mates at New Road, where Sussex played their final game of the season against Worcestershire, Collymore said, 'No one is more disappointed than me to be leaving but it is based on my family's needs. My wife is studying in London and I want my two children to go to school there so from that point of view it could not have come at a better time. It would be too much to commute to Hove. It took a lot of time to make this decision and we didn't really want to leave because we and the children love Brighton and the seaside but it was a family decision.'

At least Collymore bowed out from Sussex on a high, having won his first domestic trophy in a career that began in 1998. He added, 'I was never really involved in the one-day team so to be part of a Sussex team which won a trophy when we beat Northamptonshire to become second division champions was a very special moment. I was treated very well by Sussex and have had three of the most enjoyable years of my career there, but now I am looking forward to a new challenge with Middlesex.'

not entirely hitting their best form, or that overseas seamer, Ian O'Brien, was sidelined through injury. When Owais Shah learned of his release after 15 years with the county in a local newspaper article, the county's new captain might have been forgiven for falling on his sword. But that would be to underestimate Dexter and his quietly determined nature.

Recalling his tough introduction to the post Dexter said, 'I'd been given a prior warning about taking over the captaincy by Angus, who'd approached me earlier on to say that if "Shaggy" [Shaun Udal] was to get injured, or maybe retired, I would be the one to take over. Although I knew that, it still came as a huge shock when it did happen. It wasn't an easy time after the way we'd performed in the t20s, but part of me felt that, actually, things couldn't get much worse.

'I was completely new to captaincy and I'll admit I found it hard at first. There were a lot more aspects to it than I expected but, looking back on it now, I think I coped with things quite well. As time went on I think I became a lot more natural and relaxed into the role, but I've still got a lot to learn.

'Decision-making on the field was the easy part. It's the off-the-field things that I found harder. It's not easy to tell some people they're being left out and having the time to communicate things as you'd want to. Keeping players in the loop can be quite difficult.

'I was fortunate that Shaggy was very supportive and I had other experienced players like Owais around who I could turn to. I know Owais had his critics here, but I can only compliment him. He was excellent with me.'

Other than Morgan, who made only one Championship appearance, Dexter was the only Middlesex batsman to average in excess of 40 as he accumulated 907 runs from 12 starts, averaging 47.73. He was only out-scored by left-handers Malan and former Surrey opener Newman, who both recovered from patchy starts to score 1,001 and 945 Championship runs respectively.

In praise of Newman's resolve, Dexter added, 'There's no point being a hero for the first month and then fading away, it's how you finish the season that matters most. Scott was on the verge of being left out the team but, by September, he couldn't help but score runs. He kept working and kept believing.

'We're still a long way from where we want to be as a side but, in my opinion, we're in better shape now than we were last year. If we can take it one game at a time I'm confident that we can look to build toward promotion. There's a process to everything and we

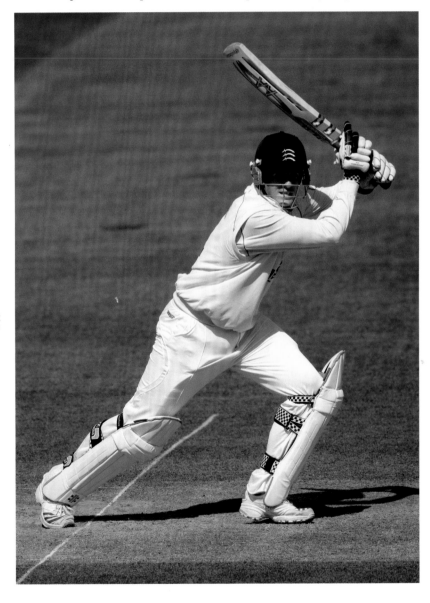

Neil Dexter, who was appointed Middlesex captain following Shaun Udal's resignation, responded by leading the side well and also scoring more than his share of runs.

Middlesex Ambition Will Fire Me
by Chris Rogers

The end of the 2010 season marks the end of an enjoyable three years in my life. I've been given the opportunity to experience something different with Middlesex for the next couple of years and, much as I'm looking forward to that challenge, I'll take a lot of good memories of my time with Derbyshire. As well as the good wins we've had and the celebrations that have followed – most recently that amazing game we had against Gloucestershire in Bristol – I'll also be able to look back on being part of the development of the careers of a few guys like Greg Smith, Wayne Madsen and now Chesney Hughes.

Chesney, in particular, is someone whose progress I will be following with interest. He is a cricketer that England should be getting very excited about. I know he's got a while to go before – as an Anguillan – he qualifies through residency, but for me England should be getting him into their system now. It certainly wouldn't be too early for him.

As for me, I'm in the latter stages of my career and the opportunity to end it with Middlesex was one I couldn't turn down. I've only ever played in the Midlands over here, with Northants, Derbyshire and briefly Leicestershire, so Middlesex is a very different challenge. The club has been in the second division for too long but Angus Fraser has explained to me that he's very ambitious, and there are a lot of good things happening down there. I'm looking forward to playing a part in helping them to bounce back where they belong. To play at Lord's regularly is also something to relish.

start by looking to do the right things as individuals. It's easy to talk about it, but there is a lot of hard work ahead of us.'

Middlesex have started that process already, having released Danny Evans and Shah, recruited former Derbyshire skipper Chris Rogers, West Indies all-rounder Corey Collymore from Sussex and Gloucestershire seamer Anthony Ireland to bolster their options. A six-week winter training camp before Christmas was also inked in to their schedule for the first time at Fraser's instigation. In full support of the plan, Dexter said the team needed to work on their fitness and one-day skills and he expects his players to return after Christmas to face an even tougher training schedule.

Mid-table mediocrity will no longer be tolerated at Middlesex, it would seem. Not on Neil Dexter's watch at least.

Right Adam Gilchrist, the former Australia wicketkeeper–batsman, was a popular Twenty20 Cup signing for Middlesex in 2010.

Steven Finn (second left) celebrates winning the 2010 Young Cricketer of the Year award with former winners (from left) Mike Atherton (1990), James Whitaker (1986) and Nasser Hussain (1989).

PLAYER OF THE SEASON

Neil Dexter shook off a back injury and courageously took on the mantle of captaincy. He scored 900-plus runs and topped the club's Championship averages.

YOUNG PLAYER OF THE SEASON

Steven Finn took 36 wickets costing 23.44 apiece in his seven Championship appearance before England whisked him away.

A YEAR TO REMEMBER

- Scott Newman recovered from an inconsistent start to score 1,485 runs in all formats
- John Simpson played in all 16 four-day games taking 44 victims and scoring 657 runs
- Dawid Malan was the only Middlesex batsman to pass 1,000 Championship runs

A YEAR TO FORGET

- Owais Shah mustered 804 Championship runs and read of his sacking in a local paper
- Iain O'Brien managed seven four-day starts, but performed well summarising on BBC Radio London
- Shaun Udal stood down from the captaincy and bagged only 27 first-class wickets

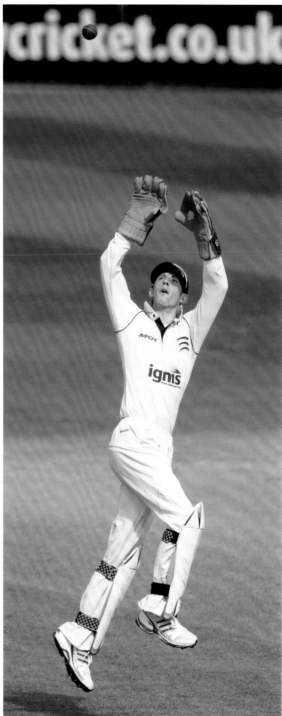

John Simpson, who turned 22 in July, enjoyed a solid first full season as Middlesex wicketkeeper and also opened the innings in County Championship cricket on many occasions.

MIDDLESEX CCC

FIRST-CLASS MATCHES
BATTING

	DJ Malan	JA Simpson	GK Berg	TJ Murtagh	SA Newman	SD Udal	OA Shah	NJ Dexter	PT Collins	SD Robson	AJ Strauss	TS Roland-Jones	ST Finn	IE O'Brien	AB London	D Evans	TMJ Smith	JH Davey	DM Housego	TRG Hampton	RH Patel	SW Poynter	AM Rossington	KS Toor	EJG Morgan	Extras	Total	Wickets	Result	Points
v. Worcestershire (Worcester) 9-11 April	1	20	13*	8	8	11			32	1		0	5	9												18	126	10		
	69	0	22	0*	1	13			17	15		1	5	15												11	169	10	L	3
v. Glamorgan (Lord's) 15-18 April	17	32	14	13	7	15			0	44		0*	0	6												12	160	10		
	115	12	28	9*	0	23			0	69		0	13	13												14	296	10	L	3
v. Northamptonshire (Northampton) 21-24 April	1	101*	41	5	44	25			52	25		2*		77	-											69	442	8		
	56*	-	37*	-	112	-			10	32		-		-	-											11	258	3	L	6
v. Gloucestershire (Lord's) 27-30 April	25	43	4	10*	1	55	20		17	18			0		1											9	203	10		
	60	0	24	9	42	12*	16		4	9			2		0											7	185	10	L	4
v. Sussex (Hove) 5-8 May	0	45	60	13*	13		24	80	0	13			0				24									24	296	10		
	100*	0	49	9*	5		4	8	-	23			-				8									37	243	7	W	21
v. Derbyshire (Lord's) 10-12 May	37	11	125	14*	0	14	21	112		13			6	0												21	374	10		
																													W	23
v. Surrey (The Oval) 17-20 May	27	2	45*	0	91	13	3	9	1	92			18													23	324	10		
	30	-	-	-	43	-	40*	5*	-	61																10	189	3	D	7
v. Oxford UCCE (Oxford) 25-27 May										204			7*				72	102*	-	-	-	-		15		14	399	2		
										18	15		10	0			54	6	1*	19*	42	1		15		5	186	9	W	
v. Leicestershire (Leicester) 29 May-1 June	5	34*	7*	-	14	-	156	118	-	7			-													15	356	5		
																													D	8
v. Northamptonshire (Lord's) 4-7 June	28	65	83	9	11	3	5	61	10	59							3*									10	347	10		
	44	32	11	8	0	4	77	37	2	42							19*									9	285	10	L	3
v. Gloucestershire (Bristol) 28-30 June	29	9		17	25		4	0	1*	39	19						7	61								25	236	10		
	13	23		8	5		32	54	7*	12	21						18	9								26	228	10	L	3
v. Sussex (Uxbridge) 21-24 July	51	58	26			8	38	43		8	15	3	14*												58	28	350	10		
	5	14	0			2	14	46		37	1	0*	-												58*	27	204	8	D	10
v. Surrey (Lord's) 29-31 July	107	36	45	25*	54	0	63	24	1		26						13									29	423	10	W	24
v. Leicestershire (Lord's) 9-12 August	0	13	53	50*	13	0	1	47	13		8						11									10	219	10		
	4	44	21	8*	70	9	55	18	1		13						0									12	255	10	D	7
v. Glamorgan (Cardiff) 16-19 August	31	11	0	1*	99	3	1	4	0	0*							18									13	181	10		
	84*	14	30*	-	64	-	47	11	-	-																3	253	4	W	19
v. Derbyshire (Derby) 25-28 August	41	21	4	6	126	0	12	20	0								2*									28	263	10		
	10	8	9	11*	7	6	29	92*	-								33									16	221	7	D	8
v. Worcestershire (Lord's) 7-10 September	9	9	10	8	78		117	97	0*	2	3										32					27	392	10		
	2	0	0	0	12		25	21	0*	1	1										4						66	10	L	7

	DJ Malan	JA Simpson	GK Berg	TJ Murtagh	SA Newman	SD Udal	OA Shah	NJ Dexter	PT Collins	SD Robson	AJ Strauss	TS Roland-Jones	ST Finn	IE O'Brien	AB London	D Evans	TMJ Smith	JH Davey	DM Housego	TRG Hampton	RH Patel	SW Poynter	AM Rossington	KS Toor	EJG Morgan
Matches	16	16	15	15	15	13	13	12	10	8	8	8	7	7	4	4	4	4	2	1	1	1	1	1	1
Innings	29	27	26	23	27	19	23	21	13	15	15	12	11	7	5	7	7	4	1	1	1	1	1	1	2
Not Out	3	2	5	10	0	1	1	2	4	0	0	1	3	1	1	2	1	0	1	1	1	0	0	0	1
Highest Score	115	101*	125	50*	126	55	156	118	13	204	92	26	18	14*	77	19*	33	72	102*	1*	19*	42	1	15	58*
Runs	1001	657	761	241	945	216	804	907	36	513	460	124	34	39	137	23	110	220	144	1	19	42	1	15	116
Average	38.50	26.28	36.23	18.53	35.00	12.00	36.54	47.73	4.00	34.20	30.66	11.27	4.25	4.87	22.83	7.66	18.33	31.42	48.00	-	-	42.00	1.00	15.00	116.00
100s	3	1	1	0	2	0	2	2	0	1	0	0	0	0	0	0	0	0	1	0	0	0	0	0	0
50s	5	2	3	1	6	1	3	5	0	2	3	0	0	1	0	0	3	0	0	0	0	0	0	0	2
Catches/Stumpings	19/0	42/2	7/0	4/0	8/0	6/0	10/0	10/0	0/0	8/0	16/0	3/0	1/0	1/0	3/0	1/0	3/0	3/0	1/0	0/0	0/0	3/0	1/0	0/0	0/0

Home Ground: Lord's
Address: Lord's Cricket Ground, London, NW8 8QN
Tel: 0207 289 1300
Fax: 0207 289 5831
Email: enquiries@middlesexccc.com
Directions: *By underground:* St John's Wood on Jubilee Line. *By bus:* 13, 82, 113 stop along east side of ground; 139 at south-west corner; 274 at top of Regent's Park.
Capacity: 30,000
Other grounds used: Southgate, Uxbridge, Richmond
Year formed: 1864

Chief Executive: Vinny Codrington
Head Coach: Richard Scott
Captains: Shaun Udal, Neil Dexter
County colours: Pink and navy blue

Website:
www.middlesexccc.com

Honours
County Championship
1903, 1920, 1921, 1947, 1976, 1980, 1982, 1985, 1990, 1993. Joint Champions 1949, 1977
Sunday League/NCL/Pro40
1992
Benson & Hedges Cup
1983, 1986
Gillette Cup/NatWest/C&G Trophy
1977, 1980, 1984, 1988, 1989
Twenty20 Cup
2008

FIRST-CLASS MATCHES
BOWLING

	TS Roland-Jones	TJ Murtagh	ST Finn	PT Collins	SD Udal	GK Berg	IE O'Brien	NJ Dexter	D Evans	DJ Mala	RH Patel	OA Shah	JH Davey	TMJ Smith	AB London	TRG Hampton	KS Toor	SD Robson	Overs	Total	Byes/Leg-byes	Wickets	Run outs
v. Worcestershire		17-5-34-0	22-4-89-5		11-1-45-1	17.3-3-62-3	18-4-47-1				2-0-10-0								87.3	287	20	10	
(Worcester) 9-11 April		7-1-20-0	15.4-5-37-9		4-0-10-0	6-1-21-0	10-1-27-1												42.4	119	4	10	
v. Glamorgan		24-7-57-2	22.2-5-69-2		10-2-33-0	17-4-59-3	20-2-59-2				4-0-25-0								97.2	315	13	10	
(Lord's) 15-18 April		19-3-53-3	18-4-45-1		4-1-6-1	18-1-72-4	14-2-40-1												73	219	3	10	
v. Northamptonshire		16-4-52-1	18-3-75-2		12-2-30-1	17-1-54-1				20.4-0-87-5	10-0-63-0								83.4	307	9	10	
(Northampton) 21-24 April		23-4-63-1	18.1-1-81-2		16-1-80-0	14-0-60-0					8-0-29-1								89.1	395	19	4	
v. Gloucestershire		20-3-81-0			10-1-24-1	7-1-47-0	21.2-6-48-7		12-3-45-2		1-0-7-0								71.2	268	16	10	
(Lord's) 27-30 April		19-6-53-2			6.4-1-10-1	15-3-57-1			10-4-22-2										70.4	223	7	10	
v. Sussex		19-7-32-3		12-2-39-2		13.3-1-45-3	17-2-50-0	1-0-5-0						7-1-30-1					69.3	217	16	10	1
(Hove) 5-8 May		21-5-91-5		15.5-3-50-2		18-1-49-0	24-3-65-3		2-1-11-0					12-1-45-0					92.5	321	10	10	
v. Derbyshire		18-7-36-2	21-6-45-3		5-0-14-0	18-4-47-1	23-6-47-3	2-1-3-1											87	196	4	10	
(Lord's) 10-12 May		10.4-2-35-2	9-4-19-4		1-0-7-1	10-2-49-2	10-5-25-1												40.4	143	8	10	
v. Surrey		22-13-97-1	28-9-62-0	22-3-67-1	39.2-7-128-5	21-6-62-1					12-0-51-2	3-0-17-0							157.2	490	6	10	
(The Oval) 17-20 May		8-2-25-0	10-2-40-1	5.3-0-17-1	15-2-59-0	2-0-20-0					6-0-28-0	4-0-16-1							50.3	207	2	3	
v. Oxford UCCE	14-3-46-0								13-3-59-1		25-7-52-3	5-0-24-0		8-3-15-1	7-1-27-0	16-2-48-0			88	277	6	1	
(Oxford) 25-27 May	10-4-11-2								7.5-2-14-1		22-1-82-2	9-0-41-2		7-2-15-1	9-0-36-1				64.5	207	8	10	1
v. Leicestershire		23-8-82-0		15-1-86-0	13-0-60-0	15-1-78-1	10-0-51-0	11-0-43-0				9-0-48-0					1-0-6-0		97	464	10	3	1
(Leicester) 29 May-1 June																			–	–			
v. Northamptonshire		27-7-86-0		33.1-5-122-3	36.1-3-112-3	14-3-35-1			2-0-9-0	28-7-99-0	20-0-87-0		5.5-2-9-0						167.1	581	11	7	
(Lord's) 4-7 June		3-1-16-0			3.3-0-28-1					1-0-8-0								1-0-11-0	7.3	53	1	1	
v. Gloucestershire	26.3-4-88-2		22-6-85-0	21-6-55-2					19-3-64-3		4-1-7-1			8-2-20-0	29-7-84-1				129.3	420	17	10	
(Bristol) 28-30 June	4-0-18-0										2.1-0-7-0			2-0-7-0	5-1-13-0				13.1	45	0	0	
v. Sussex	28-3-100-4		30-3-134-3		15-1-45-1	7-0-43-0	20-2-104-2	3-0-16-0											103	452	10	10	
(Uxbridge) 21-24 July	21.1-3-54-2		23-1-83-3		6.2-1-28-2	2.5-0-8-0	20-4-48-2		1-0-8-0										74.2	240	11	9	
v. Surrey	5-1-19-1				18-4-68-4	13.4-3-63-2	12-1-47-2		9-3-23-0										46.3	167	5	10	
(Lord's) 29-31 July	11-2-41-5				14-4-55-1														50.4	212	6	10	
v. Leicestershire		22.5-5-52-4	22-4-59-1		28-5-76-4	19-7-37-0			5-0-28-0		1-0-5-1	3-0-15-0							100.5	282	10	10	
(Lord's) 9-12 August		6-1-16-0	8-6-7-2		10.3-1-56-1	15-2-37-1							8-1-17-1						47.3	139	6	5	
v. Glamorgan	14-4-43-1	17.1-7-34-3			19.5-5-54-4	2-0-7-0			16.5-6-40-2						4-0-14-0				72.1	198	5	10	
(Cardiff) 16-19 August	12.2-0-54-4	17-2-64-3			19-2-51-1				12-3-31-2						5-0-28-0				65.2	232	4	10	
v. Derbyshire	6-0-27-1	9-1-41-1			17.3-3-46-4	12-2-37-4			5-2-16-0						2-0-8-0				51.3	182	7	10	
(Derby) 25-28 August	14-1-42-3	4-0-22-0			4-2-7-0	20-3-61-3						2-0-5-0			8-2-40-0				52	189	12	6	
v. Worcestershire	16.2-2-51-4	17-4-47-0	17-5-40-1		14-4-50-1				13-3-50-3	2-0-16-0		13-1-51-1							92.2	313	8	10	
(Lord's) 7-10 September	19.1-1-83-5	8-3-26-0	9-2-45-0		13-2-63-3				2-1-2-0			8-1-18-1							59.1	256	19	10	1

	TS Roland-Jones	TJ Murtagh	ST Finn	PT Collins	SD Udal	GK Berg	IE O'Brien	NJ Dexter	D Evans	DJ Mala	RH Patel	OA Shah	JH Davey	TMJ Smith	AB London	TRG Hampton	KS Toor	SD Robson
Overs	230.2	459.2	261.1	284.4	284.3	235	205.1	120	102.3	74.1	47	43.5	27	72	8	14	25	2
Maidens	34	127	54	51	38	32	36	25	19	2	8	5	2	12	3	3	2	0
Runs	745	1405	844	999	917	877	628	378	397	339	134	133	107	262	15	42	84	17
Wickets	38	38	36	36	27	24	23	13	11	6	5	4	2	2	1	1	1	0
Average	19.61	36.97	23.44	27.75	33.96	36.54	27.30	29.08	36.09	56.50	26.80	33.25	53.50	131.00	15.00	42.00	84.00	–

FIELDING

44	JA Simpson (42 ct, 2 st)
19	DJ Malan
16	AJ Strauss
10	NJ Dexter
10	OA Shah
8	SA Newman
8	SD Robson
7	GK Berg
6	SD Udal
4	TJ Murtagh
3	JH Davey
3	AB London
3	SW Poynter (3 ct)
3	TS Roland-Jones
3	TMJ Smith
1	D Evans
1	ST Finn
1	DM Housego
1	IE O'Brien
1	AM Rossington

Division Two – Final Table

	P	W	L	D	Bat	Bowl	Pens	Pts
Sussex	16	8	3	5	45	47	0	235
Worcestershire	16	7	4	5	39	42	0	208
Glamorgan	16	7	4	5	33	43	0	203
Leicestershire	16	7	5	4	31	44	0	199
Gloucestershire	16	6	9	1	28	47	-2	172
Northamptonshire	16	6	7	3	28	34	0	167
Surrey	16	4	6	6	43	36	-2	159
Middlesex	16	4	7	5	37	41	-2	155
Derbyshire	16	3	7	6	30	42	0	138

CB40   FPt20

Limited overs nickname:
MIDDLESEX PANTHERS

NORTHAMPTONSHIRE

by Paul Bolton

During the dark days of the Kepler Wessels reign, when Afrikaans was the preferred language of the Wantage Road dressing room, Northamptonshire were known throughout the county circuit as Kolpakshire.

It has taken time for Northamptonshire to lose the South African influence but there were signs of a home-grown policy beginning to bear fruit during a season that offered more encouragement than bare results might suggest.

With Riki Wessels and Johan van der Wath denied work permits before the start of the season and Nicky Boje, who stepped down as captain early in the campaign, injured in mid-season, Northamptonshire played much of the season with new skipper Andrew Hall as their only Kolpak.

When Hall and Elton Chigumbura, a moderate overseas signing, were injured for the final match of the season against Leicestershire, Northamptonshire took the field with a side comprised entirely of Englishmen, a notable rarity in the increasingly cosmopolitan world of county cricket.

The new youth policy was partly forced on Northamptonshire by a chronic injury list that meant that 24 players were used during their County

Rob Newton, Northamptonshire's batting find of the season, is pictured during his maiden first-class hundred scored against Leicestershire at Wantage Road.

Alex Wakely, the 21-year-old batsman, made solid progress for Northants in 2010.

Championship campaign and there was only a brief flirtation with promotion. The injuries were frequent and serious restricting David Lucas, the leading wicket-taker in 2009, to 11 appearances and preventing David Wigley, who was released at the end of the season, from bowling a ball in the Championship. Boje, who will not be returning in 2011, broke a hand and was restricted to just nine matches and Ireland wicketkeeper Niall O'Brien returned from the ICC World Twenty20 with a damaged finger which meant that he played only three four-day matches. O'Brien's absence meant there were plenty of opportunities for David Murphy, a capable wicketkeeper-batsman from Loughborough University, whose promise was rewarded with a new two-year contract.

Other opportunities were created for youngsters because Mal Loye, back after seven years with Lancashire, David Sales and Rob White were out of form. Loye managed to make 164 against Surrey without ever looking in form but he passed 50 only once more in 18 innings. Sales, who missed the 2009 season with a knee problem, struggled to recapture his form though he made a century against Glamorgan. There were also 11 single-figure scores in Sales's 28 Championship innings. White had an even leaner time, with just two half-centuries and 363 runs in 19 innings, and he spent time in the seconds alongside Loye.

Alex Wakely helped to compensate for Loye and White's failure but the big breakthrough came from Rob Newton, a chunky right-hander from Norfolk, who looked at ease in six Championship matches and ended the season with a maiden first-class century against Leicestershire. Rob Keogh, who made his Clydesdale Bank 40 debut against Yorkshire, was another who was given first team exposure, recognition that the county academy under former captain David Ripley is producing some talented youngsters.

'If we look at some of the key personnel that were missing we could easily have got disappointed, but what we did see was a flash of hope for the future. We had Rob Newton coming in and showing he is capable of getting runs at this level, and that was just one example

Light at the End of the Tunnel

Northamptonshire submitted retrospective planning permission in 2010 for the new floodlights at Wantage Road. Three of the six pylons for the impressive lights were originally put in the wrong place after the contractors made an error in their positioning. The club then had to re-apply to the planners for permission to move them. 'We have been very pleased with the positive comments received about how the ground looked last summer and with all the improvements made our visitor experience has increased significantly,' said Northamptonshire chief executive Mark Tagg. 'However, it was, of course, very frustrating to have to go through the planning process for a second time. One of the main reasons for installing new lights is to maintain the club's position among the professional ranks with much talk of franchises and the parlous state of Test match ground finances. It is important that we maintain our position in the game both locally and nationally and remain a pinnacle of the sport for the many thousands of youngsters that we introduce to the game and develop each year. I am very comforted that as a direct result of having floodlights we appeared live on television more often in 2010, which has brought profile to the club, to Northampton and the county which it would not otherwise have received.'

by Paul Bolton

Stephen Peters made more of a mark with the bat during the summer, but here he saves runs in the field.

Peters Awards Cap Productive Year
by Paul Bolton

Northamptonshire opening batsman Stephen Peters capped a productive season by winning two of the county's major awards. The former Essex and Worcestershire player ended the season with almost 1300 runs in the County Championship and was voted Northamptonshire's Player of the Year and Players' County Championship Player of the Year. Both prizes were presented to Peters at Northamptonshire's end-of-season awards dinner.

Peters, 31, joined Northamptonshire from Worcestershire four years ago and has enjoyed his most productive season so far. He twice achieved his career-best score, 183 not out against Middlesex at Wantage Road in April and then surpassed it in the return fixture at Lord's in June when Peters made 199.

Northamptonshire's other awards winners included Sri Lanka all-rounder Chaminda Vaas, who was named as the Players' Friends Provident t20 Player of the Year. Batsman David Sales won the Players' Clydesdale Bank 40 Player of the Year prize with Paul Taylor, head groundsman at Wantage Road, being honoured with the Clubman of the Year prize for his unstinting efforts in producing quality pitches in all weather conditions.

of numerous breakthrough stories,' said head coach David Capel.

There is still room for experience, though, and Stephen Peters was the obvious choice as player of the season after his Indian summer. The former Essex and Worcestershire batsman had his most productive summer with 1320 runs, including two centuries and a career-best 199 at Lord's. James Middlebrook, signed on an initial one-year contract, impressed as a replacement for Monty Panesar by bowling tidily in all cricket and scoring valuable lower-order runs. The former Essex and Yorkshire off-spinner was rewarded with a new two-year deal.

Chigumbura was a gamble that did not quite pay off for Capel, even though the Zimbabwe all-rounder took five expensive wickets at Chesterfield. Chaminda Vaas, signed as a locum while Chigumbura was on international duty, impressed sufficiently in the Friends Provident t20 to be contracted for all cricket in 2011 as overseas player.

Hall was the leading Championship wicket-taker with solid support from former Warwickshire seamer Lee Daggett and youngster Jack Brooks, who took 67 wickets between them.

Northamptonshire's chronic injury list stretched a small squad to its limits and Capel occasionally had to look outside of his immediate playing staff to get a side on the field. Gavin Baker, a seamer from Loughborough University, was drafted in to face Derbyshire, Luke Evans was signed on loan from Durham and David Burton, the former Gloucestershire and Middlesex seamer, made a

Right An old dog with a new trick: Chaminda Vaas emerged in 2010 as a Twenty20 pinch hitter for Northants.

Below James Middlebrook made the move from Essex to Wantage Road at the end of the 2009 season, and had a steady summer for his new county.

surprise debut against Leicestershire in September. Burton received a late call-up when Hall turned an ankle in the warm-up and took one of Northamptonshire's three five-wicket hauls.

In the Friends Provident t20 Northamptonshire were competitive until they faced Somerset in the quarter-finals at Taunton when a target of 113 proved hopelessly inadequate. Four early defeats in the CB40 meant interest in that competition soon waned, which gave Capel the opportunity to assess the potential of his emerging youngsters in the second half of the season.

PLAYER OF THE SEASON

Stephen Peters enjoyed his best summer at the age of 31 and twice topped his career-best score.

YOUNG PLAYER OF THE SEASON

Rob Newton emerged from club cricket in Norfolk and the Northamptonshire Academy to play a series of eye-catching late-season innings.

A YEAR TO REMEMBER

- Lee Daggett – steady performer, who is successfully rebuilding his career after being released by Warwickshire in 2008
- James Middlebrook looked like he was on the scrapheap when he was released by Essex in 2009 but Monty Panesar's departure gave him the chance to resurrect his career
- Alex Wakely made the most of his opportunities as Mal Loye and Rob White struggled for runs

A YEAR TO FORGET

- David Wigley was unable to build on a successful 2009 because of persistent injuries, which prevented him from making a Championship appearance. He was released at the end of season
- Mal Loye rarely looked in touch on his return from Lancashire and flitted in and out of the first team
- Rob White was out-of-form and out of the side for the final two months of the season.

NORTHAMPTONSHIRE CCC

FIRST-CLASS MATCHES
BATTING

Match	SD Peters	AJ Hall	DJG Sales	JA Brooks	AG Wakely	LM Daggett	JD Middlebrook	DS Lucas	MB Loye	RA White	N Boje	D Murphy	BHN Howgego	E Chigumbura	RI Newton	PW Harrison	V Tripathi	DJ Willey	NJ O'Brien	L Evans	WPUJC Vaas	T Brett	GC Baker	DA Burton	Extras	Total	Wickets	Result	Points
v. Oxford UCCE (Oxford) 3-5 April	24		-	13	-		-		42*	2					11	55*	-					-			21	168	4		
																												D	
v. Leicestershire (Leicester) 9-12 April	9	26*	39	2	7		13	44	4	20					0	8									18	190	10		
	28	4	24	2	28		40*	8	68	8					16	28									15	269	10	L	2
v. Gloucestershire (Bristol) 15-17 April	23	14	2	0			3	4		95	11				20	2			0*						12	186	10		
	1	19	39	53			31		0	10	4				44	19			8*						15	243	10	W	19
v. Middlesex (Northampton) 21-24 April	62	39	55	1	24		16	13	0	61*					8				8						20	307	10		
	183*	15*	30	-	87		-	19	40	-					-				-						21	395	4	W	20
v. Derbyshire (Northampton) 27-30 April	32	33	33	0			26*	13		0	54				6	13									10	220	10		
	14	27	2	5*	39		4	16		5	12				32*	71									10	237	9	D	4
v. Glamorgan (Cardiff) 10-13 May	72	56	25	0*	7	10	13	0	5	11							49								5	253	10		
	48	1	27	7	0	8*	32	9	14	6							33								8	193	10	L	3
v. Sussex (Northampton) 18-20 May	136	2	1	4	17	13*	25		15	1						11	22								27	274	10		
	4	0	12	-	51	-	3*		9	42						9*	24								17	171	7	W	21
v. Surrey (Northampton) 24-27 May	61	5	0		4*	1			164	8	88					3	44			0					19	397	10		
	9	32	0		2	5			20	29	18					18*	44				17				35	229	10	L	7
v. Middlesex (Lord's) 4-7 June	199	133	-	108	-				0	12	37	50*	23						-						19	581	7		
	2								-	31*			13*						-						7	53	1	W	23
v. Glamorgan (Northampton) 5-7 July	76	84*	127	0	16		11	8			98		18	44											12	494	10		
	17*	-	-		-		-			-	-		23*												0	40	0	W	24
v. Surrey (The Oval) 20-22 July	41	0	7	36	50		13	13	16				18*	12	23										11	240	10		
	50	2	0	6*	7		36	14	0				8	45	25										12	205	10	L	3
v. Worcestershire (Worcester) 29-31 July	0	28	0		20	0*	2	24						26	8	0	23								27	158	10		
	37	9	46		68									10*	3	7*	33								13	226	6	W	19
v. Derbyshire (Chesterfield) 9-12 August		29	36		13	9*	16		3		0	35	26	0							14				20	201	10		
		7	92		10	14*	84		4		7	80	33	82							35				21	469	10	D	7
v. Gloucestershire (Northampton) 16-18 August	1	23	25	4	21	0	1						8*	17	8	10									6	124	10		
	25	13	19	1	8	0*	81							55	11	14	6								19	252	10	L	3
v. Worcestershire (Northampton) 25-28 August	75	65	4	34	48	6*	40						36*	4	9	56									8	385	9		
	-				-								-												0	0	0	D	6
v. Sussex (Hove) 7-9 September	10	10	15	1	4	0	2	10	2				47*		8										16	125	10		
	22	20	6	5	8	7	26	28*	73				0		19										23	237	10	L	3
v. Leicestershire (Northampton) 13-16 September	55		5	9	9	22*	3	31		0					5	102								0	9	250	10		
	4		9	7	6	48	62	11		15					6	18								2*	10	198	10	L	3
Matches	16	15	15	14	13	12	12	11	10	10	9	9	7	6	6	5	4	3	3	2	2	1	1	1					
Innings	30	27	28	20	22	17	21	17	18	19	15	15	13	10	11	8	7	4	6	3	2	0	2	2					
Not Out	2	3	0	3	0	8	3	2	1	1	1	6	2	1	0	1	1	2	0	2	0	0	0	1					
Highest Score	199	133	127	53	108	48	84	40*	164	95	98	55	80	44	102	44	71	18*	49	8*	17	0	35	2*					
Runs	1320	696	680	177	627	167	459	316	420	363	471	276	292	189	357	137	196	41	216	16	17	0	49	2					
Average	47.14	29.00	24.28	10.41	28.50	18.55	25.50	21.06	24.70	20.16	33.64	30.66	26.54	21.00	32.45	19.57	32.66	20.50	36.00	16.00	8.50	-	24.50	2.00					
100s	3	1	1	0	1	0	0	0	1	0	0	0	0	0	1	0	0	0	0	0	0	0	0	0					
50s	7	3	2	1	4	0	3	0	1	2	4	2	1	0	2	0	0	0	0	0	0	0	0	0					
Catches/Stumpings	16/0	21/0	20/0	2/0	6/0	3/0	6/0	1/0	0/0	3/0	3/0	26/0	3/0	0/0	1/0	7/2	3/0	1/0	7/1	1/0	1/0	0/0	0/0	1/0					

Home Ground: County Ground
Address: Abington Avenue, Northampton, NN1 4PR
Tel: 01604 514455/514444
Fax: 01604 609288
Email: commercial@nccc.co.uk
Directions: Junction 15 from M1 onto A508 (A45) towards Northampton. Follow the dual carriageway for approx. 3 miles. Keeping in left-hand lane, take next exit from dual carriageway marked A428 Bedford and Town Centre. Move into middle lane approaching the roundabout at bottom of slip road. Take second exit following signs for Abington/Kingsthorpe on to Rushmere Road. Follow Rushmere Road (A5095) across the junction with Billing Road and continue straight on through Abington Park to traffic lights at main junction with Wellingborough Road.

Capacity: 6,500
Other grounds used: Campbell Park, Milton Keynes
Year formed: 1878

Chief Executive: Mark Tagg
First XI Coach: David Capel
Captains: Nicky Boje, Andrew Hall
County colours: Claret and navy

Honours
Benson & Hedges Cup
1980
Gillette Cup/NatWest/C&G Trophy
1976, 1992

Website:
www.northantscricket.com

FIRST-CLASS MATCHES
BOWLING

	JA Brooks	AJ Hall	DS Lucas	LM Daggett	E Chigumbura	JD Middlebrook	N Boje	WPUJC Vaas	DJ Willey	L Evans	AG Wakely	RA White	DJG Sales	BHN Howgego	RI Newton	DA Burton	V Tripathi	T Brett	GC Baker	Overs	Total	Byes/Leg-byes	Wickets	Run outs
v. Oxford UCCE (Oxford) 3-5 April	22-7-33-3		18-5-45-1	18-1-49-0				15-5-47-1									4-0-17-0	17-6-38-0		94	244	15	5	
																				-	-	-	-	
v. Leicestershire (Leicester) 9-12 April	30-5-103-2	26.1-7-66-1		28-7-64-5	25-3-107-2		16-3-41-0													125.1	395	14	10	
	9.5-3-28-2			10-2-33-2																19.5	65	4	4	
v. Gloucestershire (Bristol) 15-17 April	6-1-21-1	5-0-17-3	7.5-3-21-4								6-1-24-1									24.5	86	3	10	1
	18.2-4-55-3	11-1-46-1		19-4-68-2			7-1-12-1				15-5-53-3									70.2	249	15	10	
v. Middlesex (Northampton) 21-24 April	30-7-89-3	28.4-8-76-1		28-3-86-1			31-8-72-2				25-4-73-1									142.4	442	46	8	
	12-2-49-0	5-0-14-0		10-1-54-1			13-1-87-2				11-0-51-0									51	258	3	3	
v. Derbyshire (Northampton) 27-30 April	29-8-83-1	18-1-49-0	24.1-0-77-0			38-4-126-2	27-2-111-2										2-0-11-0			138.1	480	23	5	
																				-	-	-	-	
v. Glamorgan (Cardiff) 10-13 May	24.1-5-86-1	24-2-93-4	22.1-3-72-2		28.5-7-80-2	8-1-36-0	18-1-62-1													125.1	450	21	10	
																				-	-	-	-	
v. Sussex (Northampton) 18-20 May	8-0-31-0	7-2-19-3		15-3-38-3		3-1-16-1	12-2-14-0	12-2-47-2												52	175	10	10	1
	19.3-4-45-3	14-3-35-0		20-5-50-3		9.2-3-42-1	9.4-2-80-0	14.5-0-57-2												85.5	269	17	10	
v. Surrey (Northampton) 24-27 May		15-1-65-2		28-5-119-3		16-3-51-1	23.3-8-47-2	22-5-37-2	11-1-53-0											115.3	386	14	10	
		4-0-10-0		11-1-45-0		13.4-3-40-1	18-4-88-1	7-2-28-0	4-0-14-1			1-0-7-0								58.4	241	9	3	
v. Middlesex (Lord's) 4-7 June	21-5-74-2	20-6-57-1		20-2-87-2			17-2-72-0	21.2-6-48-4			1-0-4-1									100.2	347	4	10	
	18-4-78-1	13.1-3-44-4		14-2-49-3			22.5-6-62-2	23-7-47-0												90.1	285	5	10	
v. Glamorgan (Northampton) 5-7 July	11-5-32-2	9-2-22-0	13-3-48-3	8-0-67-4			9-1-31-1													50	207	7	10	
	12-3-43-1	16-4-48-4	13-5-54-1	7-0-45-1		16.2-3-57-1	13-0-69-1													77.2	325	8	10	1
v. Surrey (The Oval) 20-22 July	20-1-116-1	21-1-81-1	30-5-146-1	29-4-100-4		32-3-132-0							2-0-28-0							134	620	17	7	
																				-	-	-	-	
v. Worcestershire (Worcester) 29-31 July		17-5-53-1	23.3-9-68-4	19-6-66-0	19-5-53-3	9-2-36-1														87.3	287	11	10	
		9-6-10-2	10-3-20-1	10-4-25-4		9.2-3-23-3														38.2	93	15	10	
v. Derbyshire (Chesterfield) 9-12 August			16.5-1-78-2	20-3-70-2	15-0-92-5	3-0-19-0												10-1-52-0		64.5	319	8	10	1
			4.1-0-13-0	15-5-35-0	9-3-17-0	2-0-4-0												3-2-2-0		33.1	76	5	0	
v. Gloucestershire (Northampton) 16-18 August	21-10-63-3	12-2-42-1		19.5-4-57-4	18-5-63-1	21-2-62-1														91.5	302	15	10	
	8-2-45-2			6-2-17-0	3-0-13-1															17	76	1	3	
v. Worcestershire (Northampton) 25-28 August														1-0-10-0	2-0-16-0	2-0-19-0				5.1	45	0	0	
	11-3-30-1	12-2-47-2		11-5-20-1	6-0-32-1	12-1-45-1														52	182	8	6	
v. Sussex (Hove) 7-9 September	19.1-1-88-4	10-0-61-0	16-2-74-3	4-3-87-1		21-4-62-2														89.1	381	9	10	
																				-	-	-	-	
v. Leicestershire (Northampton) 13-16 September		24-7-68-1		28-4-108-1	18-3-57-0	38-8-117-2				20-4-75-5	6-0-21-0									134	448	2	9	
											0.1-0-4-0									0.1	4	0	0	

	JA Brooks	AJ Hall	DS Lucas	LM Daggett	E Chigumbura	JD Middlebrook	N Boje	WPUJC Vaas	DJ Willey	L Evans	AG Wakely	RA White	DJG Sales	BHN Howgego	RI Newton	DA Burton	V Tripathi	T Brett	GC Baker
Overs	373.3	318	300.4	321.4	114	251.2	230.3	73.2	56.5	20	57	9.1	1	1	2	2.1	6	17	13
Maidens	86	57	59	65	17	40	42	20	8	4	10	0	0	0	0	0	0	6	3
Runs	1260	1047	1038	1058	482	863	796	161	218	75	201	57	7	10	16	19	28	38	54
Wickets	37	33	32	30	20	18	15	6	6	5	5	1	0	0	0	0	0	0	0
Average	34.05	31.73	32.44	35.27	24.10	47.94	53.07	26.83	36.33	15.00	40.20	57.00	-	-	-	-	-	-	-

FIELDING

26	D Murphy (26 ct)
21	AJ Hall
20	DJG Sales
16	SD Peters
9	PW Harrison (7 ct, 2 st)
8	NJ O'Brien (7 ct, 1 st)
6	JD Middlebrook
6	AG Wakely
3	N Boje
3	LM Daggett
3	BHN Howgego
3	V Tripathi
3	RA White
2	JA Brooks
1	DA Burton
1	L Evans
1	DS Lucas
1	RI Newton
1	WPUJC Vaas
1	DJ Willey

Division Two – Final Table

	P	W	L	D	Bat	Bowl	Pens	Pts
Sussex	16	8	3	5	45	47	0	235
Worcestershire	16	7	4	5	39	42	0	208
Glamorgan	16	7	4	5	33	43	0	203
Leicestershire	16	7	5	4	31	44	0	199
Gloucestershire	16	6	9	1	28	47	-2	172
Northamptonshire	16	6	7	3	28	34	0	167
Surrey	16	4	6	6	43	36	-2	159
Middlesex	16	4	7	5	37	41	-2	155
Derbyshire	16	3	7	6	30	42	0	138

CB40 & FPt20

Limited overs nickname:
STEELBACKS

NOTTINGHAMSHIRE

by Andy Wilson

The County Championship has never had a finish quite like it. Nottinghamshire have never celebrated a draw with such enthusiasm. Adam Voges and Samit Patel will rarely, if ever, play such valuable innings. And the 10 runs eked out by Ryan Sidebottom and Darren Pattinson will be remembered by Notts team-mates and supporters as the most painstakingly precious for many seasons.

That was the story of a suitably dramatic last day of a 2010 campaign that had lurched from triumph to disaster from start to finish, with little in between. 'It's been an incredible day, and an incredible rollercoaster way to end the season,' said Chris Read at Old Trafford, champagne still dripping from his cap, after becoming his adopted county's sixth Championship-winning captain.

The title had been teasingly within reach for three weeks, after victory over Lancashire – the seventh of the season, and the fifth in seven matches at Trent Bridge – had established a 16-point lead over Yorkshire, who had played a game more.

But to say that Notts then wobbled would be a major understatement. They collapsed feebly against the innocuous medium pace of Ben Harmison on the last day at Durham to slump to a 210-run defeat against the 2008 and 2009 champions, and then crumbled to the lowest Division One total of the season – 59 – after losing a crucial toss at home to Yorkshire.

The moment that Nottinghamshire's players knew that the 2010 county title was theirs: Andre Adams has just dismissed Lancashire's Shivnarine Chanderpaul for the all-important third bowling bonus point.

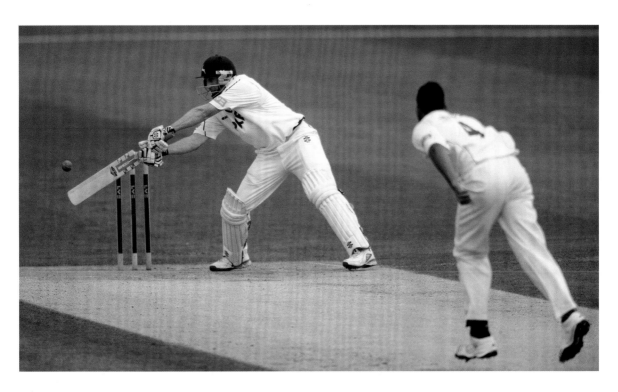

Above David Hussey tries to give himself room against the pace of Ajmal Shahzad in the County Championship fixture against Yorkshire.

Right Chris Read, the Nottinghamshire captain, was an inspirational leader for the county during 2010 as well as keeping up his usual high standards with the gloves and the bat.

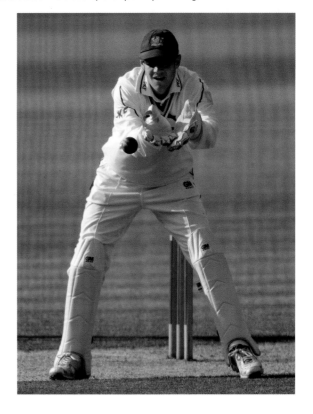

That left a three-horse race going into the last round of matches, and although Notts retained a narrow lead over Somerset and Yorkshire, they suffered the further agony of watching it disappear as persistent Mancunian rain – and even, briefly and surreally, a burst of bright sunshine glinting off a shiny roof at the Stretford End on the second evening – kept them in the Old Trafford pavilion for almost all of the first three days.

The general assumption was that Read would have to offer Lancashire a last-day target even more generous than the 260 in two sessions that Notts had successfully chased when they held all the cards at Trent Bridge three weeks earlier. But at a team dinner in Manchester that Wednesday night, Read and the director of cricket Mick Newell – both survivors of the county's last Championship season of 2005 – decided on a different approach.

They would play proper cricket, try to secure the six bonus points necessary to pull level with Somerset, and gamble that neither the Westcountrymen nor Yorkshire were able to win their games against Durham and Kent respectively. But with an overnight score of 89 for 2 from

Notts Heroes Reserve Special Praise for Patel
by Andy Wilson

There were heroes everywhere as Nottinghamshire celebrated their dramatic Championship triumph, but captain Chris Read and coach Mick Newell had special praise for the contribution of Samit Patel. It was Patel's brilliant innings of 96 from only 91 balls against Lancashire that brought the distant possibility of pulling level with Somerset on bonus points into view, with Adam Voges providing equally intelligent support in a fifth-wicket stand of 153 in 28 overs.

'I couldn't be more pleased for him,' Read said of Patel, the 24-year-old all-rounder. 'He's had a really difficult year in red ball cricket. People have seen that he's been a fantastic one-day asset to us, scoring runs consistently and also bowling exceptionally well with the white ball. But he's had to battle for runs and wickets in the red ball game. To show his class on such a big occasion shows what he's made of.'

Newell agreed, saying that, 'Samit played the best knock he's played this season by a mile'. But he also saluted Voges, who admits to having felt under pressure following the outstanding performances of Hashim Amla and David Hussey as Nottinghamshire's overseas players for the bulk of the season. 'Adam is probably the least fashionable and least well known of the three,' added Newell of the Australian, whose 126 also came at the decent rate required, from 183 balls. 'So for him to pull it off, I'm very pleased for him.'

'It's been an interesting day,' continued the unshaven Newell with deliberate understatement after a title-clinching sixth bonus point was secured in the final session of their rain-wrecked last match against Lancashire at Old Trafford. 'I'm pleased that we won it in that way. We went out and scored at five an over for a long time and took three wickets. I don't think anyone can begrudge us that.'

It would be impossible to begrudge Newell his second title in six years. While the players were celebrating, he wandered quietly over to the Old Trafford groundstaff to thank them for their efforts on the thoroughly miserable three days that preceded the euphoric climax. Like his captain, Newell is a class act.

Samit Patel, one of the most naturally gifted cricketers in England, played perhaps the most important innings of his career on the crucial final day of the County Championship season. Currently out of favour with the national selectors, he remains central to Nottinghamshire's success on the field in all formats of the game.

Right Graeme Swann, in a rare appearance in 2010 for Nottinghamshire, catches Somerset's James Hildreth off his own bowling during the Friends Provident t20 semi-final at the Rose Bowl.

Below Hashim Amla enjoyed a successful stint as Nottinghamshire's overseas player.

28 overs, it was a seriously tall order. 'To be honest, when we first came up with the idea of trying to get 400 and then taking three wickets, it felt like a bit of fun,' the young opener Alex Hales later admitted in his *testmatchextra.com* column. 'I don't think anyone believed we could actually do it. We were almost resigned to coming second.'

It was only when Patel joined Voges, and scored 96 from 91 balls in a fifth-wicket stand of 153 in 28 overs, that Notts' audacious plan became apparent. But then those wobbles surfaced again, with Patel's dismissal the first of five wickets to fall for 65 – leaving Pattinson and Sidebottom, in his last match for the county, under unimaginable pressure.

'The important thing was not to panic, and to stay calm,' said Sidebottom, although that was way beyond Read. 'Watching that from the dressing room was the most nervous I've been all season,' he said. 'One wicket then and your dreams are pretty much shattered. Adam [Voges] was kicking the walls after getting out. We were all just praying that the big bowling guys could get us over the line.'

They did, leaving 18 overs to take the three Lancashire wickets now necessary. Fewer than five were required, as Sidebottom struck a first blow before Andre Adams took two in four balls, a fitting climax to an outstanding season for the previously low-profile New Zealander. He hadn't managed a five-wicket haul in his first three summers with the county, but after breaking that duck in an otherwise forgettable draw against Kent at Tunbridge Wells in June, he repeated the feat three times in the remaining nine matches.

It was the seamers who laid the foundations for the title push as Notts began the season with four consecutive wins by mid-May, their best start for 88

NOTTINGHAMSHIRE CCC

FIRST-CLASS MATCHES

BATTING

Opponent / Venue & Date	AD Brown	SR Patel	CMW Read	PJ Franks	MA Wagh	AR Adams	DJ Pattinson	AD Hales	SJ Mullaney	RJ Sidebottom	NJ Edwards	BM Shafayat	LJ Fletcher	HM Amla	CE Shreck	DJ Hussey	MJ Wood	AC Voges	SCJ Broad	GG White	GP Swann	Extras	Total	Wickets	Result	Points
v. Durham UCCE	37*	72	16*	-	100	-			-		23	159	-	86								12	505	5		
(Durham) 10-12 April	21*	37	13	114	-		8		22*		43	-	15	-								18	291	6	D	
v. Kent	18	15	62	73	0	19			8*		85	4	13	129								30	456	10		
(Trent Bridge) 15-17 April																									W	24
v. Somerset	2	33	29	61	16	10					2	1	5*						1			32	250	10		
(Trent Bridge) 21-23 April	16	10	0	12	70	0*					1	49	-	64*					6			22	250	8	W	21
v. Hampshire	81	41	9	48	11	1			100*		3	2	5		0							27	328	10		
(Rose Bowl) 4-7 May	14	1	7*	-	131*	-			-		8	12	54		-							19	246	5	W	22
v. Durham	134	4	124*	64	44				24		33	16	67		-							49	559	8		
(Trent Bridge) 10-13 May																									W	24
v. Hampshire	42	11	22	57*	8	8		0	97		4	14			0							7	270	10		
(Trent Bridge) 17-20 May	15	0	27	45	26*	7		136	7		23	14			0							15	315	10	L	5
v. Essex	0	12	52	23	10	1	2	6	53	0*	30											28	217	10		
(Trent Bridge) 29 May-1 June																									D	7
v. Kent	39	10	112*	17	44	35	5	95	1							52				29		23	462	10		
(Tunbridge Wells) 4-7 June	-	76*	-	-	34	-	-	13	48*							22				-		17	210	3	D	9
v. Essex	50*	25	32	4	20	10	9	1			1	12			7*							16	180	10		
(Chelmsford) 5-7 July	62	4	20	0	26	0	7	12			5	9			7*							7	159	10	L	3
v. Warwickshire	1	1	83	-	139	37		53	31	6*						8		0			1	29	389	10		
(Edgbaston) 20-22 July	-	10*	-	-	-			10*	-	-					7*			-			-	5	25	0	W	23
v. Somerset	2	104	80	15	4	20	7*	6							0	4	72					25	339	10		
(Taunton) 29-31 July	47	1	4	1	45	10	7*	28							3	30	0					14	190	10	L	3
v. Yorkshire	2	96	42	61	4	13*	-	2	-							251*	59					15	545	7		
(Headingley) 3-6 August																									D	11
v. Warwickshire	76	34	45	17	54	6	6	9	18*							32	15					16	328	10		
(Trent Bridge) 16-17 August																									W	22
v. Lancashire	28	10	49*	-	6	-	-	98	0*	-							0					12	203	5		
(Trent Bridge) 24-27 August	65	37	2	0	3	8*	-	93	34*	-							2					17	261	7	W	20
v. Durham	52	4	56	26	30	10	19	13	25	5*			23*					48				32	343	10		
(Chester-le-Street) 31 Aug-3 Sept	29	2	0	8	18	9	0*	36	64				5					0				9	180	10	L	3
v. Yorkshire	16	0	0	0	22	3	0	3	0		6*						8					1	59	10		
(Trent Bridge) 7-9 September	4	4	47	79	90	0*	27	24	15		8						72					43	413	10	L	3
v. Lancashire	10	96	12	40	32	15	4*	36	0	7*								126				22	400	9		
(Old Trafford) 13-16 September																									D	9
Matches	17	17	17	16	16	14	13	12	11	9	7	7	6	5	5	5	4	3	2	1	1					
Innings	26	28	26	22	24	20	14	20	17	7	11	11	9	7	7	7	6	5	3	1	1					
Not Out	3	2	5	1	1	5	4	1	4	7	0	0	3	1	1	1	0	0	0	0	0					
Highest Score	134	104	124*	114	139	37	27	136	100*	22*	85	159	23*	129	7*	251*	72	126	6	29	1					
Runs	863	750	945	765	953	240	101	677	512	66	255	277	96	463	10	399	148	254	7	29	1					
Average	37.52	28.84	45.00	36.42	41.43	16.00	10.10	35.63	39.38	-	23.18	25.18	16.00	77.16	1.66	66.50	24.66	50.80	2.33	29.00	1.00					
100s	1	1	2	1	3	0	0	1	1	0	0	1	0	1	0	1	0	1	0	0	0					
50s	6	4	5	6	3	0	0	4	1	0	1	0	0	5	0	1	2	1	0	0	0					
Catches/Stumpings	12/0	9/0	60/4	1/0	8/0	13/0	0/0	12/0	6/0	3/0	17/0	7/0	2/0	1/0	4/0	7/0	1/0	1/0	0/0	1/0	0/0					

Home Ground: Trent Bridge
Address: Trent Bridge, Nottingham, NG2 6AG
Tel: 0115 982 3000
Fax: 0115 945 5730
Email: administration@nottsccc.co.uk
Directions: By road: Follow signs from ring road towards city centre.
Capacity: 17,000
Year formed: 1841

Chief Executive: Derek Brewer
Director of Cricket: Mick Newell
Captain: Chris Read
County colours: Green and gold

Website:
www.nottsccc.co.uk

Honours
County Championship
1883, 1884, 1885, 1886, 1907, 1929, 1981,
1987, 2005, 2010
Sunday League/NCL/Pro40
1991
Benson & Hedges Cup
1976, 1989
Gillette Cup/NatWest/C&G Trophy
1987

FIRST-CLASS MATCHES
BOWLING

	AR Adams	PJ Franks	DJ Pattinson	RJ Sidebottom	SR Patel	SCJ Broad	CE Shreck	LJ Fletcher	SJ Mullaney	GP Swann	GG White	AC Voges	MJ Wood	AD Hales	AD Brown	DJ Hussey	Overs	Total	Byes/Leg-byes	Wickets	Run outs
v. Durham UCCE (Durham) 10-12 April		18-3-59-0	16-5-52-2	18-4-48-3	29-8-77-2		20-8-39-3								2-0-4-0		103	291	12	10	
		6-1-24-1			5-1-13-0		5-1-16-0										16	53	0	1	
v. Kent (Trent Bridge) 15-17 April	18-3-63-4	11-2-35-2		16-6-31-3	4-1-17-0			13-2-47-1									62	200	7	10	
	18-1-78-3	11.4-4-33-0		14-6-35-1	6.4-1-24-3			15.2-8-43-3									65.4	224	11	10	
v. Somerset (Trent Bridge) 21-23 April	19.1-4-68-2	16-6-45-3			6-0-25-0	19-1-79-3	16-5-48-2										76.1	272	7	10	
	14-5-59-1	6.5-0-22-3			3-1-3-0	15-2-89-5	10-1-49-1										48.5	227	5	10	
v. Hampshire (Rose Bowl) 4-7 May		21-4-58-2	20.1-1-85-3		15-3-40-2		24-4-74-2		12-1-30-1								92.1	300	13	10	
		22-4-63-1	21-5-66-2		36.2-14-55-4		23-6-70-3		7-1-12-0								109.2	273	2	10	
v. Durham (Trent Bridge) 10-13 May		15.4-4-38-3	17-2-63-2		7-3-17-2		23-6-73-3		5-1-21-0								67.4	218	6	10	
		21-8-58-3	21-3-95-4		12-3-56-0		19-5-30-1		12-6-35-2								85	279	5	10	
v. Hampshire (Trent Bridge) 17-20 May	25.5-8-56-4	20-5-57-2	24-7-58-3		4-1-22-0		26-9-70-1		5-1-15-0								104.5	305	27	10	
	29.5-5-118-3	16-3-41-2	21-4-51-2		15-7-23-1		16-6-38-0										97.5	281	10	8	
v. Essex (Trent Bridge) 29 May-1 June	24-6-82-2	17-6-45-1	22-2-60-2	22-4-48-1	4-0-26-0					13.5-5-31-4							102.5	329	36	10	
	9-2-34-1	8-1-13-1	10-1-33-0	5-1-24-0	8-0-30-0					3-0-17-0							43	152	1	2	
v. Kent (Tunbridge Wells) 4-7 June	31-2-106-5	28.1-6-75-2		15-5-89-1	37-6-129-1					5-0-33-0	23-3-104-1					3-0-19-0	148.1	570	15	10	
v. Essex (Chelmsford) 5-7 July	14-4-26-2	12-7-20-3			3-0-13-0		16-5-40-3	16-1-50-0	0.5-0-1-1								61.5	154	4	10	1
	25.1-4-57-4	17-5-37-1			24-7-71-1		23-4-81-4	19-7-57-0	4-1-14-0								112.1	328	11	10	
v. Warwickshire (Edgbaston) 20-22 July	17.4-7-35-3			20-3-81-1		19-1-79-3		4-1-13-0		26-5-88-2							86.4	313	17	10	1
	4.3-0-33-1			8-4-14-0		13-3-52-8											25.3	100	1	10	1
v. Somerset (Taunton) 29-31 July	26-4-121-1	15-2-50-0	20-3-95-5		18.3-0-93-3		29-5-101-1					0.5-0-5-0			10-1-44-0		118.3	517	13	10	
															1-0-8-0		1.5	13	0	0	
v. Yorkshire (Headingley) 3-6 August	14-3-44-2	13-3-40-2	12-1-61-1	15-6-25-2	3.3-1-2-2												58.3	178	6	10	1
	29-11-68-0	26-11-61-1	24-3-78-3	29-9-66-3	41-6-104-1										4-0-11-0		153	406	18	8	
v. Warwickshire (Trent Bridge) 16-17 August	13.1-9-14-4	11-6-15-3	12-3-35-0	18-5-37-3	4-2-16-0												54.1	121	20	10	
	16-7-37-3	11-3-20-2	5-1-34-0	16-4-35-5	4-2-16-0												52	152	10	10	
v. Lancashire (Trent Bridge) 24-27 August	26-6-79-6	17-4-40-0	16-3-61-0	26-7-79-4	8-1-33-0			8-2-16-0					1-0-11-0	5-1-21-0	7-0-53-0		100	319	11	10	
			3-1-11-0					8-0-45-1									24	143	2	1	
v. Durham (Chester-le-Street) 31 Aug-3 Sept	27.5-6-92-5	18-4-48-1			27-3-100-3			22-4-85-1	2-0-17-0								103.5	372	15	10	
	15.5-1-76-2	13-1-51-0	2.1-0-26-0		30-3-113-3			20-3-67-1	4-0-21-0			1-0-2-0					86	361	5	6	
v. Yorkshire (Trent Bridge) 7-9 September	20.1-3-82-6	15-3-58-3	10-2-58-0		9-1-19-1			8-0-39-0									62.1	264	8	10	
	16-0-77-2	3-0-23-0	13-2-67-3		5.3-2-8-0			5-0-23-0									42.3	209	11	5	
v. Lancashire (Old Trafford) 13-16 September	1.4-0-3-2		1-0-2-0	2-0-6-1													4.4	11	0	3	

	AR Adams	PJ Franks	DJ Pattinson	RJ Sidebottom	SR Patel	SCJ Broad	CE Shreck	LJ Fletcher	SJ Mullaney	GP Swann	GG White	AC Voges	MJ Wood	AD Hales	AD Brown	DJ Hussey
Overs	455.5	410.2	310.2	236	345.3	66	199	169.2	93.4	26	23	1	1	5.5	9	18
Maidens	101	106	54	62	73	7	50	40	19	5	3	0	0	1	0	1
Runs	1508	1129	1180	630	1044	299	577	563	321	88	104	2	11	26	57	82
Wickets	68	42	33	30	26	19	18	12	9	2	1	0	0	0	0	0
Average	22.18	26.88	35.76	21.00	40.15	15.74	32.06	46.92	35.67	44.00	104.00	–	–	–	–	–

FIELDING

64	CMW Read (60 ct, 4 st)
17	NJ Edwards
13	AR Adams
12	AD Brown
12	AD Hales
9	SR Patel
8	MA Wagh
7	DJ Hussey
7	BM Shafayat
6	SJ Mullaney
4	CE Shreck
3	RJ Sidebottom
2	LJ Fletcher
1	HM Amla
1	PJ Franks
1	AC Voges
1	GG White
1	MJ Wood

Division One – Final Table

	P	W	L	D	Bat	Bowl	Pens	Pts
Nottinghamshire	16	7	5	4	47	43	0	214
Somerset	16	6	2	8	53	41	0	214
Yorkshire	16	6	2	8	41	42	0	203
Lancashire	16	5	3	8	35	43	0	182
Durham	16	5	3	8	30	39	0	173
Warwickshire	16	6	9	1	20	47	0	166
Hampshire	16	3	6	7	47	41	0	157
Kent	16	3	7	6	42	44	-1	151
Essex	16	2	6	8	29	43	-2	126

CB40 FPt20

OUTLAWS

Limited overs nickname:
NOTTS OUTLAWS

Steven Mullaney came to Trent Bridge from Lancashire after the 2009 season and held down an all-round role for his new county.

years. Three came at Trent Bridge, as the strategy of requesting early home games when the pitches would be at their juiciest worked perfectly – although it took one of several crucial innings by Hashim Amla to secure a tense two-wicket victory against Somerset, a result that was to prove so important come September.

Stuart Broad took eight wickets in that match and another 11, including career-best figures of 8 for 52, at Edgbaston in his only other Championship appearance in one of two crushing victories over Warwickshire that kept the title bid on track in mid-summer, despite heavy defeats to struggling Essex at Chelmsford and in the return match against Somerset in Taunton.

The other outstanding individual performance of the season came from David Hussey against Yorkshire at Headingley, an unbeaten 251 that was his third double-century in exactly 100 first-class innings for the county.

Other commitments restricted Hussey to five Championship appearances but he played a key role, with Twenty20 specialist Dirk Nannes, in the county's commanding progress to Finals Day at the Rose Bowl – only for a brilliant catch by Kieron Pollard, and some badly-timed rain, to condemn the Outlaws to a cruel three-run Duckworth Lewis defeat against Somerset in the second semi-final. However, they were to claim ample consolation for that as the scramble to the tape in the Championship between the same two counties reached a climax that no one involved will ever forget.

PLAYER OF THE SEASON

Andre Adams was the leading wicket-taker in the first division with 68 at an average of 22 – appropriately including Shivnarine Chanderpaul edging to third slip to clinch the Championship title.

YOUNG PLAYER OF THE SEASON

Steven Mullaney – from the fringes at Lancashire to winning the Championship at Old Trafford for the all-rounder from Leigh.

A YEAR TO REMEMBER

- Chris Read had another excellent season with bat and gloves, and now has the honour of being a Championship-winning captain
- Paul Franks – county stalwart justified the faith shown in him by director of cricket Mick Newell to take on extra responsibility following the retirement of Mark Ealham
- Alex Hales had a slow start, but after spectacular success in Twenty20, he went on to establish himself in the Championship team

A YEAR TO FORGET

- Charlie Shreck – a series of injuries restricted the Cornish seamer to a bit-part role
- Neil Edwards – life was little better for the county's other son of Truro, as he became the latest opener to find things tough on the Trent Bridge pitches
- Bilal Shafayat – a popular local lad whose second stint with the club was ended after he also struggled for runs

SOMERSET

by Richard Latham

Somerset vowed to go one better in 2010, having finished runners-up in both limited-overs competitions the previous season. In a sense they achieved that aim, but in a manner that offered no greater satisfaction and even more frustration.

Incredibly, the Cider county contrived to come second in all three tournaments under the new leadership of Marcus Trescothick, coming so close to a historic first-ever County Championship pennant on a day of almost unbearable tension at Chester-le-Street in their final match that there were tears in the eyes of long-standing members and former players when Nottinghamshire grabbed it by virtue of more wins, both teams having amassed 214 points.

Somerset narrowly failed to bowl out Durham in time to clinch the victory they needed and, when the game ended in a draw, players and supporters alike could only watch and suffer as television pictures from Old Trafford showed Nottinghamshire taking the three Lancashire wickets they required for the crucial extra bonus point to draw level with their West Country rivals at the top of the table.

Alfonso Thomas had good reason to bowl, and field, well during the season as captain Marcus Trescothick offered him one of his bats if he took 100 wickets – he responded with 109 in all competitions.

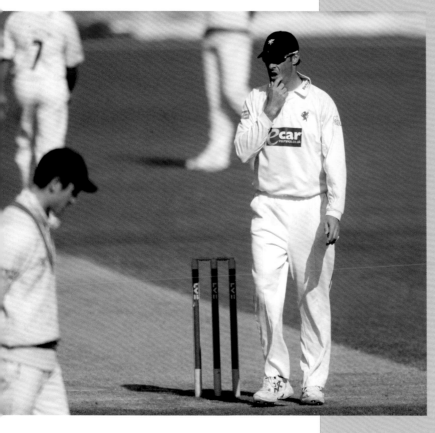

Marcus Trescothick proved a hugely popular captain at the County Ground, encouraging the players to return to the pitch after each one-dayer to sign autographs and greet the fans.

Still in Search of 'Holy Grail'

Brian Rose described losing out to Nottinghamshire by the narrowest of margins in the County Championship race as the most disappointing experience of his cricketing life. Somerset's director of cricket also faced the frustration of seeing the club finish as runners-up in the Friends Provident t20 and the Clydesdale Bank 40 in 2010.

But he has always described winning the Championship for the first time in the club's history as the 'Holy Grail' and coming second to Nottinghamshire, having secured the same number of points, was a devastating blow.

Rose, who captained Somerset in the glory years of Botham, Richards and Garner, and also played for England, said, 'Everyone who knows me will tell you that bringing the title to Taunton for the first time is what I live for as far as my job is concerned and the emotions at Chester-le-Street will stay with me for a long time.

'That I am sure applies to everyone who made the long trip to the North East from the West Country and thousands of others around England and further afield who have Somerset County Cricket Club in their blood… It was an extraordinary day of almost unbearable tension as we kept a close eye on events at Headingley and Old Trafford, where the sort of drama top-level sport provides was also being witnessed.

'I know it is not too strong to say that many of our supporters were heartbroken when Notts took that third Lancashire wicket at Old Trafford to condemn us to the runners-up spot, even though we had the same number of points.

'My own feeling was one of desperate disappointment. I wouldn't say I felt heartbroken because somewhere deep down there was consolation in the fact that the team had performed fantastically well over the course of a long season. The players have competed strongly in virtually every session of every match in each competition and I know from experience how hard that is to do, particularly with a relatively small squad.'

by Richard Latham

That heartbreak followed a bizarre end to the Friends Provident t20 final at the Rose Bowl when Hampshire celebrated an unlikely success. This time the scores were tied and Somerset would have won had they spotted that the injured Dan Christian had left his crease, along with his runner, to complete the leg bye off the final ball that won the hosts the competition because they had lost fewer wickets. Christian actually passed the stumps at the other end and would have been run out comfortably by a simple throw to wicketkeeper Craig Kieswetter.

Trescothick was only informed of his team's oversight as he left the field. It was an error that was to give the former England player plenty of sleepless nights in the weeks ahead, but Somerset had also suffered major misfortune in the final when a ball from Dominic Cork penetrated the grille of Kieron Pollard's helmet at the end of their innings, causing a fearful eye injury, which prevented the charismatic all-rounder from fielding and, more importantly, bowling.

Above left James Hildreth scored freely in all competitions this season, top scoring in each and hitting seven Championship centuries.
Above right All-rounder Peter Trego enjoyed a successful season for the cider county with both ball and bat – averaging 33 with the willow and taking 22 Championship wickets at 33.14.

It was always going to take a massive effort for Trescothick and his men to lift themselves for the Clydesdale Bank 40 final just 48 hours after the Championship drama at Durham. This time a late order batting collapse to the leg-spin of Imran Tahir gave Warwickshire an opportunity that Ian Bell's brilliant century ensured they accepted. Yet again Somerset looked on as their opponents celebrated.

Still, there was much to celebrate in the style of cricket played under director of cricket Brian Rose and coach Andy Hurry and in the individual achievements of several players. Trescothick proved an immensely popular captain, encouraging his side to forge closer links with supporters by returning to the pitch as a group after each one-day home game to sign autographs and have photographs taken. While the experienced opener may not have scaled the heights of the previous season with the bat, he still managed nearly 1,400 Championship runs at an average of 58, hitting 228 not out, the second highest score of his career, against Essex at Colchester.

James Hildreth matured into the player good judges, including Trescothick, have long thought he would be. At the age of 25 and having worked to simplify his technique, he excelled in all competitions. Of his seven Championship centuries, the most satisfying came at the Rose Bowl, Canterbury and Chester-le-Street, silencing suggestions that he was not the same force away from the plumb batting strips at Somerset's own County Ground and no doubt going some way to earning him a place alongside team-mate Kieswetter with the England Performance Programme in Australia during the winter of 2010-11.

Jos Buttler began the season having made only one first-class appearance, but with a dream opportunity to make his mark as a wicketkeeper-batsman through Craig Kieswetter's absence with the England Twenty20 World Cup squad. By the end of the summer the 19-year-old was being talked about as the most exciting batting prospect in the country, having thrilled not only Somerset fans but large television audiences with a series of audacious one-day innings that saw top bowlers dispatched over the ropes with a mixture of deceptive power and impudent shot selection.

With the big-hitting potential of Trescothick, Kieswetter, Hildreth, Pollard, Buttler and all-rounder Peter Trego, who was to almost double his previous best one-day score when making 147 in a 40-over game with Glamorgan at Taunton, it was little wonder Somerset issued hard hats to spectators at home games as a marketing ploy when Twenty20 cricket began. Emerging West Indies star Pollard, in particular, had packed crowds diving for cover, blasting 29 sixes in his 17 games, including some of the biggest ever seen at the County Ground, having been signed specifically for the competition. 'Danger! Batsmen At Work' read the posters advertising matches.

At the start of the season Trescothick offered Alfonso Thomas one of his bats if he could take 100 wickets. The 33-year-old South African, delighted to be made vice-captain, was quick to claim his prize after claiming 109 victims in all forms of the game, including 33 in the t20, the most by any bowler in the tournament. Fellow countryman Charl Willoughby was again a model of consistency, taking more than 50 Championship wickets, just as he had done in every one of his previous four seasons with Somerset.

Ben Phillips enjoyed some overdue good luck with fitness to be a key member of the bowling attack. But it was the shrewd signing of Murali Kartik from Middlesex that gave Somerset a potent extra weapon with which to pursue their Championship ambitions. Having missed the first five matches because of Indian Premier League commitments, the wily left-arm spinner soon felt at home on pitches Somerset had done their best to ensure suited his immense talent and finished top of the club's bowling averages, a reward for subtle changes in flight and pace that were a joy to watch.

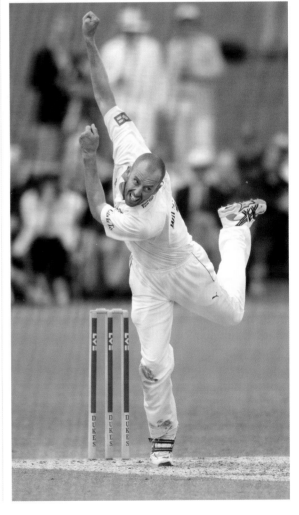

Top 'Danger! Batsmen at Work!' said the posters – Jos Buttler (left) and Kieron Pollard make their way to the wicket.

Right The evergreen Charl Willoughby took more than 50 first-class wickets for Somerset for the fifth season in a row.

SOMERSET CCC

FIRST-CLASS MATCHES
BATTING

	JC Hildreth	AV Suppiah	PD Trego	ME Trescothick	CM Willoughby	AC Thomas	Z de Bruyn	JC Buttler	C. Kieswetter	NRD Compton	BJ Phillips	M Kartik	DG Wright	MK Munday	DA Stiff	CR Jones	Extras	Total	Wickets	Result	Points
v. Yorkshire (Headingley) 15-18 April	30	5	45	117	4	8	4		7	6			21		12*		13	272	10		
	4	71	10	16	4*	44	83		17	21			25		40		9	344	10	L	4
v. Nottinghamshire (Trent Bridge) 21-23 April	14	10	66	22	8	40*	1		1	42			43		14		11	272	10		
	0	11	3	98	4	12	0		0	1			78		5*		15	227	10	L	5
v. Essex (Taunton) 27-30 April	73	7	71*	19	9	8	73	36		72			0	0			19	387	10		
	-	47*	-	42*	-	-	-	-		-			-	-			11	100	0	D	10
v. Lancashire (Old Trafford) 4-7 May	99	10	108	56	0*	9	48	20		0			18	0			15	383	10		
																				D	10
v. Hampshire (Rose Bowl) 10-13 May	106	27	35	41	0		21	144		49	10		51	0*			40	524	10		
																				D	8
v. Yorkshire (Taunton) 17-20 May	31	99	22	39	10	14	47	52		5	16	15*					27	377	10		
	102*	16	-	53	-	-	93	31*		65	-	-					4	364	4	W	21
v. Warwickshire (Taunton) 24-26 May	131	64	1	3	0	15*	34	24	4	0	0						14	290	10		
	-	15*	-	30	-	-	-	0*		-	-						0	45	1	W	21
v. Warwickshire (Edgbaston) 4-6 June	52	2	25	53	4	27	25	1	40		9	11*					19	268	10		
	14	8	0	4	0*	12	24	19	5		55	32					10	183	10	W	21
v. Kent (Taunton) 20-23 July	0	34	3	27	11*	17	44	20	6		0	15					28	205	10		
	48	24	4	80	-	30	43	42	9*		2*	-					19	301	7	D	7
v. Nottinghamshire (Taunton) 29-31 July	142	30	54	0	5	30*	44	88	73	17		7					27	517	10		
	-	-	-	4*	-	-	-	-	-	5*		-					4	13	0	W	24
v. Kent (Canterbury) 3-6 August	151	125	8	5	4	11	23	0	26		14	2*					11	380	10		
	32	28	37	188*	-	0*	14	0	58		14	-					16	387	7	D	10
v. Hampshire (Taunton) 9-12 August	130	37	32	7	5	5	95	20	43		11*	2					25	412	10		
																				D	11
v. Essex (Colchester) 18-20 August	84	4	27	0	0*	12	34	21	10		10	0					13	215	10		
	59	0	2	228*	-	0	10	6	0		0	52*					10	367	8	W	20
v. Durham (Taunton) 24-27 August	7	54	18*	128	-	-	54		75	45	8*						11	400	6		
																				D	8
v. Lancashire (Taunton) 7-9 September	26	13	51	33	16	8		0	84	49	30	52*				-	20	382	10		
	-	12*	-	8	-	-		-	-	26*	-	-					2	48	1	W	23
v. Durham (Chester-le-Street) 13-16 September	105	18	69	75	1*	26		39	10	46	0	11					26	426	10		
	-	-	2	21	-			6*	3	12*	-	-					4	48	3	D	11

	JC Hildreth	AV Suppiah	PD Trego	ME Trescothick	CM Willoughby	AC Thomas	Z de Bruyn	JC Buttler	C. Kieswetter	NRD Compton	BJ Phillips	M Kartik	DG Wright	MK Munday	DA Stiff	CR Jones
Matches	16	16	16	16	16	15	14	13	12	11	11	11	5	3	2	1
Innings	23	26	23	28	18	20	21	20	18	17	15	12	7	3	4	0
Not Out	1	3	2	4	6	4	0	3	1	3	3	5	0	1	2	0
Highest Score	151	125	108	228*	16	44	95	144	84	72	55	52*	78	0*	40	-
Runs	1440	771	693	1397	85	328	814	569	467	465	179	199	236	0	71	-
Average	65.45	33.52	33.00	58.20	7.08	20.50	38.76	33.47	27.47	33.21	14.91	28.42	33.71	0.00	35.50	-
100s	7	1	1	4	0	0	0	1	0	0	0	0	0	0	0	0
50s	5	4	5	6	0	0	5	2	4	1	2	2	0	0	0	
Catches/Stumpings	7/0	5/0	12/0	26/0	1/0	1/0	10/0	23/0	29/0	5/0	5/0	9/0	4/0	1/0	0/0	0/0

Home Ground: Taunton
Address: County Ground, St James Street, Taunton, Somerset, TA1 1JT
Tel: 0845 337 1875
Fax: 01823 332395
Email: info@somersetcountycc.co.uk
Directions: By road: M5 junction 25, follow A358 to town centre. Signposted from there.
Capacity: 6,500

Other grounds used: Bath
Year formed: 1875

Chief Executive: Richard Gould
Director of Cricket: Brian Rose
Head Coach: Andy Hurry
Captain: Marcus Trescothick
County colours: Brown and red

Honours
Sunday League/NCL/Pro40
1979
Benson & Hedges Cup
1981, 1982
Gillette Cup/NatWest/C&G Trophy
1979, 1983, 2001
Twenty20 Cup
2005

Website:
www.somersetcricketclub.co.uk

FIRST-CLASS MATCHES
BOWLING

	CM Willoughby	AC Thomas	M Kartik	BJ Phillips	PD Trego	DG Wright	Z de Bruyn	MK Munday	AV Suppiah	NRD Compton	DA Stiff	JC Hildreth	Overs	Total	Byes/Leg-byes	Wickets	Run outs
v. Yorkshire (Headingley) 15-18 April	29-6-105-2	22-5-52-1			14.1-4-26-4	26-8-63-2	10-1-30-1		23-2-55-0		18-2-77-0		142.1	419	11	10	
	7-2-17-0	8-2-27-1			7-0-35-0	6-1-23-1	7-1-30-1		5-0-24-0		5.5-0-42-1		45.5	199	1	4	
v. Nottinghamshire (Trent Bridge) 21-23 April	23-8-40-4	17-7-34-2			7-2-22-1	19-10-41-2	6-1-31-0		3-0-12-0		12-1-52-1		87	250	18	10	
	22-5-83-3	15.5-3-54-2			13-4-30-1	10-1-30-1	2-0-8-1		4-2-3-0		5-0-36-0		71.5	250	6	8	
v. Essex (Taunton) 27-30 April	24-7-87-2	11-2-35-0			14-3-53-1	17-6-41-2		30.1-6-105-4	9-1-29-1				105.1	353	3	10	
v. Lancashire (Old Trafford) 4-7 May	14-6-30-0	23-5-84-3			13-4-41-0	18.1-5-41-5	10-0-40-1	4-0-27-0	3-0-16-0				85.1	292	13	10	1
	20-3-70-0	19-7-33-4			12-5-18-0	26-8-48-1	5-1-18-0	6-2-28-1	5-1-6-0				90	221	5	6	
v. Hampshire (Rose Bowl) 10-13 May	43-18-83-3			33-10-75-4	17-0-69-1	26-1-81-0	14-0-70-0	12-1-78-1	11-2-42-0	0.2-0-1-1			156.2	512	13	10	
	7-3-7-2				2-0-7-0	6-1-9-0	2-0-14-0						17	37	0	2	
v. Yorkshire (Taunton) 17-20 May	29-8-95-0	18-6-60-2	35.5-8-106-3	36-13-76-4	7-0-40-0		2-1-9-1		3-1-3-0	1-0-2-0		13-0-95-1	131.5	405	14	10	
	10-1-35-0	8-1-20-1	18-2-48-1	6-1-14-0			6-0-29-0			13-0-84-1			74	333	8	4	
v. Warwickshire (Taunton) 24-26 May	15.3-3-51-3	13-1-41-5	2-2-0-0	11-1-25-2	6-3-9-0				3-1-4-0				47.3	127	1	10	
	14-6-41-2	19-3-51-1	29-7-61-6	11-2-23-1	2-1-4-0		4-1-5-0						82	207	18	10	
v. Warwickshire (Edgbaston) 4-6 June	11-4-20-2	13.1-3-37-2	20-8-30-5	14-4-32-1	1-0-3-0				2-1-9-0				61.1	140	9	10	
	10-3-20-2	12-3-36-1	18.3-3-42-6	7-4-14-1					2-1-5-0				49.3	130	13	10	
v. Kent (Taunton) 20-23 July	12-1-46-2	8-3-21-3	14-4-50-5	9-2-33-0	2-0-16-0								45	172	6	10	
	13-3-22-1	16-2-53-1	31-13-57-5	8-1-21-0	2-1-1-0				4.4-1-14-0				74.4	191	23	7	
v. Nottinghamshire (Taunton) 29-31 July	22.3-3-101-6	13-3-68-1	33-15-59-1		6-1-17-1		7-1-33-0		11-2-48-1				92.3	339	13	10	
	13-1-52-1	14.4-4-40-5	26-3-64-2				5-1-24-2						58.4	190	10	10	
v. Kent (Canterbury) 3-6 August	27-2-93-1	13.2-2-72-1	18-4-50-2	28-8-72-5	11-1-58-1		1-0-2-0						98.2	372	25	10	
v. Hampshire (Taunton) 9-12 August	23.3-4-80-4	21-4-69-2	23-7-51-3	13-7-33-0	9-3-27-1		3-0-8-0			7.2-2-21-1			92.3	284	16	10	
	12-2-44-1	5-0-28-0	20-5-50-1	6.4-1-12-0	10-1-35-0		6-2-17-1						67	224	17	4	
v. Essex (Colchester) 18-20 August	15-1-67-4	13-3-44-4	3-1-6-0	7-2-13-2	7-3-20-0			7.2-1-23-4					45	151	1	10	
	11-0-38-1	13-2-37-0	8-1-21-1	17-4-51-1	11-3-27-3								67.2	212	15	10	
v. Durham (Taunton) 24-27 August	8-1-26-0		3-0-4-0	4-3-2-0									15	37	5	0	
v. Lancashire (Taunton) 7-9 September	20-3-60-4	16-3-69-1	24-8-65-3	13-5-21-1	10-3-30-0								83	259	14	10	1
	14-4-37-3	15.5-4-53-3	14-3-33-0	8-3-17-2	8-3-20-2								59.5	170	10	10	
v. Durham (Chester-le-Street) 13-16 September	20-5-81-3	13-3-32-1	11-2-28-0	23.5-5-60-4	19-3-60-2				3-1-9-0				89.5	286	11	10	
	22.4-5-51-2	17-4-52-2	32-11-57-1	22-3-67-1	17-2-61-4								110.4	320	32	10	

	CM Willoughby	AC Thomas	M Kartik	BJ Phillips	PD Trego	DG Wright	Z de Bruyn	MK Munday	AV Suppiah	NRD Compton	DA Stiff	JC Hildreth
Overs	512.1	377.5	383.2	277.3	227.1	154.1	94.2	52.1	99	14.2	40.5	13
Maidens	118	85	107	79	50	41	10	9	18	0	3	0
Runs	1582	1202	882	661	729	377	386	238	300	87	207	95
Wickets	58	49	45	29	22	14	12	6	3	2	2	1
Average	27.28	24.53	19.60	22.79	33.14	26.93	32.17	39.67	100.00	43.50	103.50	95.00

FIELDING

29	C Kieswetter (29 ct)
26	ME Trescothick
23	JC Buttler (23 ct)
12	PD Trego
10	Z de Bruyn
9	M Kartik
7	JC Hildreth
5	NRD Compton
5	BJ Phillips
5	AV Suppiah
4	DG Wright
1	MK Munday
1	AC Thomas
1	CM Willoughby

Division One – Final Table

	P	W	L	D	Bat	Bowl	Pens	Pts
Nottinghamshire	16	7	5	4	47	43	0	214
Somerset	16	6	2	8	53	41	0	214
Yorkshire	16	6	2	8	41	42	0	203
Lancashire	16	5	3	8	35	43	0	182
Durham	16	5	3	8	30	39	0	173
Warwickshire	16	6	9	1	20	47	0	166
Hampshire	16	3	6	7	47	41	0	157
Kent	16	3	7	6	42	44	-1	151
Essex	16	2	6	8	29	43	-2	126

CB40

FPt20

Limited overs name:
SOMERSET

England Ambitions Fire Hussain and Kirby
by Richard Latham

Gemaal Hussain believes he can go on to play for England after signing a three-year contract with Somerset, while his fellow former Gloucestershire pace bowler Steve Kirby expressed similar sentiments when he penned his own three-year deal.

The 27-year-old Hussain said, 'My aim is to become a successful England bowler and I believe that the challenge of playing first division cricket, plus the experience of competing to win trophies on all fronts, will bring the best out of me… The pitches at Taunton have the reputation of being batsmen-friendly, but I like the County Ground and I think the challenge of taking wickets in such conditions will enhance my ability to become a future Test bowler.'

Hussain had played in only one Championship game prior to last summer, but took Division Two by storm in 2010, claiming 67 wickets for Gloucestershire with his ability to swing the ball as well as nip it about off the seam. Somerset put in a 28 days' notice of approach for him and director of cricket Brian Rose is delighted to have got his man. He said, 'We faced competition from a number of counties and it is an indication of the way Somerset have evolved as a club in recent years that players of the calibre of Steve and Gemaal want to join us.'

Kirby, meanwhile, is excited about the challenge of helping Somerset to be the strongest side in the country. At the age of 32, insists he is still fired by ambition and desperation to win trophies. 'Somerset are putting together the nucleus of a side who can be consistent contenders in all forms of cricket,' said Kirby. 'I am looking forward to competing for a place at Taunton because competition is what sport is all about for me.

Pace bowlers Gemaal Hussain (top) and Steve Kirby both made the short journey from Gloucestershire to Taunton at the end of the 2010 season to add firepower to the Somerset attack.

'The club has a great infrastructure as well as a very good team. I can assure their supporters that I have plenty of fire left in my belly and I am looking for a new challenge. Of course, there were financial considerations in losing a benefit at Gloucestershire, but I believe they are for players reaching the end and I don't feel that way at all.

'I'll be running in and giving it everything for Somerset next summer and if I take wickets in Division One I hope England will take notice.'

PLAYER OF THE SEASON

James Hildreth finished top of the club's batting averages in all three competitions and hit seven Championship centuries, including three on opposing grounds to dispel the theory that he could only make significant scores consistently on the batsmen-friendly Taunton pitches.

YOUNG PLAYER OF THE SEASON

Jos Buttler recorded his maiden first-class century against Hampshire at the Rose Bowl and produced some spectacular innings in limited-overs cricket that marked him as an outstanding talent, also keeping wicket tidily when Craig Kieswetter was away with the England one-day squad.

A YEAR TO REMEMBER

- Murali Kartik took 45 Championship wickets in 11 matches at an average of 19.6
- Alfonso Thomas took 109 wickets in all competitions
- Charl Willoughby's 58 first-class wickets meant it was the fifth time he had passed 50 in as many seasons with Somerset

A YEAR TO FORGET

- Craig Kieswetter made only 467 first-class runs at an average of 27.47
- David Stiff made just two Championship appearances in the first two fixtures, both defeats
- Michael Munday took only six first-class wickets at an average of 39.67

We are Somerset

Consistently the best team in England in 2010

SOMERSET CRICKET CLUB

SURREY

by Mark Pennell

Having spent much of 2009 demolishing a dysfunctional and underachieving squad, Surrey's cricket manager Chris Adams is at last beginning to enjoy the fruits of his major rebuilding programme in SE11.

Though the former Sussex captain admits to sporadic bouts of 'extreme frustration' when his younger Surrey wards reveal their inexperience, he does overall appear to be making headway toward achieving his remit of transforming Surrey into a leading force in county cricket. Or, as Adams puts it, turning Surrey into 'the team of the decade'.

Thus far, last year's four close-season signings have proved the cornerstones of Adams's plan. Chris Tremlett, Gareth Batty, Steven Davies and the new captain, Rory Hamilton-Brown, all bedded in quickly to play huge roles at the start of Surrey's latest renaissance. Recruited from Sussex and first appointed skipper at the tender age of 22, Hamilton-Brown has taken to his leadership task manfully. Handling experienced, yet occasionally prickly players with aplomb, he also contributed more than 1,600 runs in all forms of cricket.

The player-of-the-season battle proved a near three-way photo finish between wicketkeeper-batsman Davies, run machine Mark Ramprakash and rejuvenated strike bowler Tremlett. Newly installed behind the stumps, Davies handled the expectations that came with his big-money move from Worcestershire as deftly as he would a Chris Schofield googly and, by mid-season, had

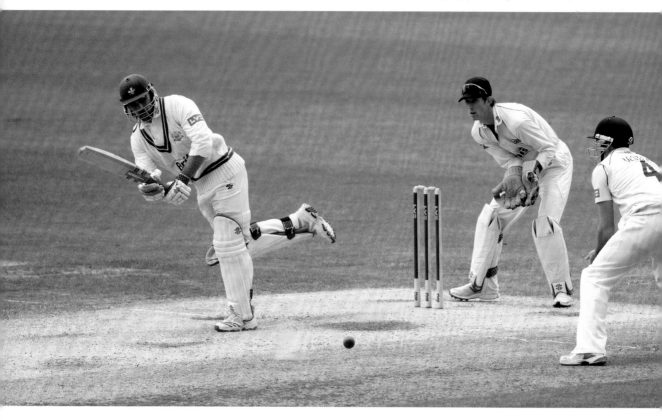

'Mr Irreplaceable': Mark Ramprakash hits a ball from Middlesex's Shaun Udal to the midwicket boundary at The Oval – a match in which the prolific right-hander scored two of his five Championship centuries.

already fully deserved England recognition. He claimed more than 50 victims in all cricket and bettered Hamilton-Brown's contribution by topping 1,700 runs with his flamboyant, left-handed batting.

Tremlett, who joined from Hampshire with an unwanted, if understandable, reputation for fitness fragility, also overcame his doubters to reclaim his England spot and an Ashes tour berth. An early-season groin problem prompted another bout of nay saying, but Tremlett progressed to carry Surrey's pace attack on his strapping shoulders and finish as their leading County Championship wicket-taker with 48 from 12 appearances costing 20 runs apiece.

With hitherto unseen stamina and resilience to injury, Tremlett regularly extracted pace and bounce from Oval pitches to win Adams's vote as the club's outstanding performer for 2010. Adams said, 'For Chris to bowl the overs he did and to lead the attack in such a positive way would probably lead me to making him our player of the season. Much to the frustration of us all he picked up a groin injury in the gym that put him out for five weeks. That wasn't a good time, but since then he's blown those perceptions of himself out of the window and bowled quite superbly.'

As for finishing seventh in Division Two of the Championship and Surrey's moderate limited overs displays, Adams added, 'My satisfaction in our new players fitting in so well was tainted a little by us not qualifying for the latter stages of the one-day competitions and not doing better than our four wins out of 16 four-day starts. But I think we were a cat's whisker away from a place in the last eight of the Friends Provident t20 and, had there been a quarter-final stage in the Clydesdale Bank 40, I believe we'd have kicked on to reach that too. We aren't far off being a very competitive unit.'

Batty, the second of Adams's New Road recruits, was another star bowling turn. After the club's abortive bid to sign Indian mystery spinner Piyush Chawla, Batty was promoted from an anticipated support role to number one spinner, and duly lived up to the billing. The 33-year-old returned for a second stint in Kennington to chip in with 41 Championship wickets, almost 500 runs and merit another big tick in the box as far as Adams was concerned.

Yet few Surrey supporters would deny the player of the season claims of Ramprakash, who

Chris Tremlett overcame the doubters with a series of excellent displays of pace bowling, ending his first season at The Oval as the county's leading wicket taker.

CHRIS ADAMS, the Surrey cricket manager, explains why the loan of Kevin Pietersen at the end of the 2010 season should be the start of something new…

KP and England Stars Need More County Time

Having Kevin Pietersen with us at Surrey for the last two weeks of the season was a win-win situation for all concerned. KP is England's best batsman, but found himself in a situation where he needed to rediscover the rhythm and flow of his batting.

We wanted to help Kevin and the England management in their preparations for the winter's Ashes series, and in only his second match for us – against Sussex at Hove in the Clydesdale Bank 40 – he duly made his first hundred for 18 months. He looked fantastic and proved just what a quality player he is.

Andy Flower and Andrew Strauss have made some big calls in terms of England in the last two years. They have got it right most times and I believe they did again with KP. He was great in the Surrey dressing room and was happy to help the other guys, particularly the youngsters, who wanted to tap into his knowledge and experience in trying to improve their own games. You could see just how much Jason Roy, for instance, benefitted from batting with Kevin.

Then there are the commercial benefits. When he made his debut in the CB40 The Oval crowd was double our normal gate for those games and at Hove his presence helped swell the attendance to 5,000. Sussex also sold two corporate boxes as soon as it was confirmed that he was playing. I strongly believe that the ECB need to make their England players more available to their counties.

I realise that once again our domestic schedule is under scrutiny but at the moment where is the value in any county having a centrally contracted player on their books? If we had someone like KP available for six weeks of the season, even if it was in three or four blocks, then each of our domestic competitions would be a much more appealing product, especially T20, for the public and sponsors. That applies whether it's KP, Andrew Strauss, Stuart Broad, Eoin Morgan, James Anderson or any other regular England stars.

They become totally different entities if you know that there will be certain times of the season when they are available. All the county coaches and chief executives I speak too on the circuit feel the same – these guys are box office and we need to see more of them. They might enjoy it too – as I know KP did with us.

It would be great for everyone if occasionally you could sprinkle a bit of stardust on the county programme by including our top centrally contracted players because, frankly, there is no cricket value in the situation as it stands at the moment.

Kevin Pietersen, whose loan spell at Surrey at the end of the season was regarded as a success by county officials but was less popular with supporters keen for the club to support home-grown players.

New skipper Rory Hamilton-Brown coped well with his new responsibilities, scoring over 1,600 runs in all competitions and forging a great opening partnership in one-day matches with Steven Davies.

continues to churn out runs well beyond his 40th birthday. The classy right-hander made more than 650 runs in 20 limited-overs appearances and amassed 1,595 at an average of 61.34 in the Championship's second tier. County bowlers will be upset to read that Ramprakash intends to play on for at least one more season, possibly longer. Adams, who simply refers to the veteran as 'Mr Irreplaceable', is, of course, delighted.

Sadly, Surrey's overseas players Andrew Symonds, Iftikhar Anjum and Younis Khan did not fare as well as their domestic recruits and the decision to accept the ECB's offer of locum batsman, Kevin Pietersen – who needed 'centre practice' ahead of the Ashes – also backfired somewhat as far as some of the county's supporters were concerned. A faction of Surrey members, preferring to support home-grown players, voiced their disapproval and although Pietersen hit one hundred he only showed glimmers of his talent when performing at The Oval.

Senior batsman Michael Brown and aspiring all-rounder Chris Jordan picked up injuries that sidelined them all season, but that led to opportunities for others. Whitgift School prodigy Jason Roy became the first Surrey batsman to score a Twenty20 Cup century when still a teenager. His eye-catching 57-ball innings against Kent at Beckenham included five sixes.

Languid off-spinning all-rounder Matt Spriegel hit hundreds against Bangladesh and Northamptonshire and Jade Dernbach's steady progress merited a place in the ECB's winter Performance Programme squad. Bustling paceman Stuart Meaker improved as the summer progressed and closed with 28 Championship wickets, and opening batsman Arun Harinath revealed admirable concentration without enjoying much luck.

Individually, performances improved but sometimes, as a team, Surrey misfired. Losing their way during a session, they would often toss away their match advantage in the space of a few overs. On these occasional exasperations Adams added, 'We've started from scratch and at times the results are terrifically exciting, like when Jason spanked our first Twenty20 hundred. What you also get with it is a good deal of frustration when the youngsters don't quite understand what's required of them through naivety. Like the final

Tremlett Earns Ashes Tour Place
by Mark Pennell

Surrey cricket manager Chris Adams believes the county's 29-year-old paceman Chris Tremlett deserves his place in England's party to contest this winter's Ashes series. Nicknamed 'Twiggy' by his former Hampshire team-mates – as much for his fragile injury record than his strapping 6 foot 7 inch-frame – Tremlett responded to the rigours of leading Surrey's attack so well that England's selectors came calling once more almost three years since his previous international appearance.

Tremlett finished the LV County Championship campaign as Surrey's leading wicket-taker with 48 wickets costing barely 20 runs apiece, albeit in the second division. Adams said, 'Chris has surpassed and surprised everyone's expectations, probably even his own. He's been able to play so much cricket consistently well, which, given our gruelling schedule, has been fantastic. For Chris to arrive at a new county with a concern surrounding him over how much cricket he could actually play and to bowl the overs he did, and to lead the attack, has been a revelation.'

day at Worcestershire, for example, when we were bowled out within an hour.

'We've now identified who will be with us for the long haul and a lot of players have left inside two years. I'm afraid that had to happen. We are looking to build something that will be strong for many years, rather than a side that enjoys short-term success through a lot of Kolpak signings.'

PLAYERS OF THE SEASON

Mark Ramprakash – 1,595 County Championship runs and five more centuries. Irreplaceable, the ageless master continues to defy time by churning out runs.

Chris Tremlett – a career rejuvenated, he led the attack with pace, bounce and stamina.

YOUNG PLAYER OF THE SEASON

Rory Hamilton-Brown – coped superbly with the pressure and expectation and led from the front. Forged a superb one-day opening partnership with Davies and contributed more than 800 Championship runs.

A YEAR TO REMEMBER

- Steven Davies earned the right to understudy Matt Prior in Australia
- Jason Roy will never forget his Friends Provident t20 savaging of Kent

A YEAR TO FORGET

- Stewart Walters, deposed as captain, he mustered only 242 first-class runs and one half-century
- Usman Afzaal was released after three years having failed to reach 500 Championship runs
- Michael Brown and Chris Jordan – both will want to forget an injury-ravaged summer

Above left Teenager Jason Roy pulls another boundary on his way to a 57-ball century against Kent in the Friends Provident t20 match at Beckenham.

Left Gareth Batty was another successful new recruit for Surrey in 2010 – bowling almost 500 overs in the Championship and taking 42 wicket at 40.38.

MARK RAMPRAKASH, Surrey's former England batsman, says he has never before had a county summer like 2010…

Why 2010 Season Was a New Experience

In all my 24 seasons as a professional cricketer I don't think I have ever played in a county team like the one we had at Surrey last season. With Usman Afzaal out of the team due to lack of form, Andre Nel injured and Michael Brown unfortunately unable to shake off a chronic arm injury, which needed an operation and cost him a whole season, the Surrey team which represented the club towards the end of the season was incredibly inexperienced.

Of course, a number of players were deliberately moved on last year as part of Chris Adams's strategy to revitalise Surrey, and in many areas – especially in terms of our one-day cricket – there were real signs of progress last summer. However, in the County Championship match at Leicestershire in August, for example, I found myself playing in the most inexperienced and youthful team I have ever been a part of. Of the Surrey XI in that match, only Gareth Batty, Chris Tremlett and myself could be described as senior players, although Steven Davies is an exceptional young player who deservedly attracted the interest of the England selectors for the limited-overs matches against Pakistan in September and then won himself an Ashes tour place.

Tremlett, in particular, bowled magnificently this season and, when Nel was fit, we were really looking like we had a bowling unit to take us forward with Batty's off-spin and the youthful pace of both Jade Dernbach and Stuart Meaker to add to the mix. Our young batsmen prepare very well and very thoroughly for the challenge of trying to make their way as professionals, but it is very difficult for them. A lot of them have yet to play 15 first-class matches, and are being thrown in to a team with only Steve Davies and myself as what you would call established batsmen at this level.

When I came into the Middlesex team as a young player I was batted down at No. 6. I had established Test batsmen coming in above me, and I was able to make my mistakes with the comforting knowledge that others were there to make the big scores when they were needed. In other words, I was allowed time to grow even in a hard school like the Middlesex dressing room of the late 1980s and early 1990s.

In 2010, Surrey regularly fielded the youngest and least experienced XIs in the county's history.

Now, I find myself in a Surrey team with hardly another capped player around me and for someone like me – someone who believes, in cricket, that experience is very important – that has been a big challenge for me to embrace. But I am also welcoming the added responsibility and it was nice for me not only to score 179 on the first day of that same game at Leicester, my 113th first-class hundred, but also to see Gary Wilson put together a top-class and very mature century at the other end as we built a big first innings total.

I am trying my very best to provide the leadership on the field – and also, if asked, off the field with advice and help – that Surrey needs from me, but I will also be honest and say that I have always enjoyed winning. I was hoping that we would be challenging for promotion from Division Two of the Championship last season and not still scrapping it out near the bottom.

At the moment, a lot of our younger players are far more comfortable in one-day cricket, which is only natural. In the longer game, you need to piece together an innings and you need to know when to attack and when to defend, when to absorb pressure as a batsman, and how to build an innings with all its ebbs and flows. You need to learn to hit in the 'V', especially early on, and the value of playing the ball late. Again, in my own early days, I was helped enormously by the example of players like Mike Gatting and Desmond Haynes. Everyone at Middlesex used to talk cricket in the evenings, and I'd hang on every word they said about how to play different bowlers in different conditions.

SURREY CCC

FIRST-CLASS MATCHES
BATTING

	RJ Hamilton-Brown	MR Ramprakash	GJ Batty	JW Dernbach	A Harinath	U Afzaal	SM Davies	CT Tremlett	SC Meaker	MNW Spriegel	CP Schofield	TJ Lancefield	TE Linley	A Nel	SJ Walters	GC Wilson	TM Jewel	Iftikhar Anjum	Younus Khan	JJ Roy	LJ Evans	KP Pietersen	MJ Brown	MP Dunn	SJ King	SP Cheetham	Extras	Total	Wickets	Result	Points
v. Cambridge UCCE (Cambridge) 3-5 April	36	67	–	3	66	122*	18	35	–						4*								17				17	385	7		
	–	–	–	50*	–	–	–	–	–						–								47				8	105	1	D	
v. Derbyshire (The Oval) 9-12 April	9	102	65	0*	16	4	55	6	27				10	37													21	352	10		
	8	0	12	1	5	3	56	21	28				1*	15													15	165	10	L	6
v. Sussex (Hove) 15-18 April	36	5	23	1*	62	0	1			4	46			1		0											26	205	10		
	11	14	9	1	17	87	37			0	13			0		16*											38	243	10	L	3
v. Worcestershire (Croydon) 21-24 April	125	40	47	8*	45	0	137				23			28	0	12											28	493	10		
	9	82	0	–	1	9	69*				21			4	19	–											25	239	8	D	9
v. Gloucestershire (The Oval) 4-6 May	0	12	31	16	51	19	23*	1	2		6				4												13	178	10		
	13	7	8	13*	38	16	54	31	0		6					29											7	222	10	L	3
v. Bangladeshis (The Oval) 9-11 May							19	6	94	108*	5	47	0	–					22	–	–						17	318	7		
					20	159*				11	10*								–	–	98		–	–			15	313	3		
v. Middlesex (The Oval) 17-20 May	55	223	13	2*	39	42	13				12		3	62					10								16	490	10		
	29	103*	–	–	63	–	–				–		–	–					7								5	207	3	D	9
v. Northamptonshire (Northampton) 24-27 May	30	70	56*	0	12	33	43				29		0	96	1												16	386	10		
	45	79*	–	48	33*	25	–				–		–	–	1												11	241	3	W	22
v. Glamorgan (Cardiff) 29 May-1 June	0	73	32	2	31	49	83	7*	4				6*						0								16	303	9	D	9
v. Leicestershire (The Oval) 4-6 June	13	30	0	0	4	54	69	7*	13					29					3								14	236	10		
	8	20	4	16	15	0	5	12	1					7					77*								18	183	10	L	2
v. Derbyshire (Chesterfield) 28 June-1 July	24	99	4	16	73	29*	15	0	53	6	45																27	391	10		
	4	30	26	25	26	10*	7	35	15	28	30																17	253	10	W	23
v. Northamptonshire (The Oval) 20-22 July	103	248	48*	7	5	–	–			103	31	–				31											44	620	7	W	24
v. Middlesex (Lord's) 29-31 July	0	44	15	12	11	24	2	25	15	0*	14																5	167	10		
	1	6	12	15	6	43	53*	0	24	0	43																9	212	10	L	3
v. Sussex (Guildford) 9-12 August	22	21	19	0	20	62	28	9*	1	37	45																28	292	10	D	8
v. Worcestershire (Worcester) 16-19 August	1	20	30	0*	8	68	10	1	4			74				21											22	259	10		
	34	0	6	4*	21	19	6	1	1			35				1											2	130	10	L	5
v. Leicestershire (Leicester) 24-27 August	36	179	13	0	4	19	1								5	125				76						0*	25	483	10		
	–	–	–	–	–	–	–				–				–	–				–							0	0	0	D	8
v. Glamorgan (The Oval) 7-10 September	96	40	34	2*	15	1	63	18	39											69		0					3	380	10		
	6	0	32*	–	0*	–	90	6	45											8		1					18	206	7	D	10
v. Gloucestershire (Bristol) 13-16 September	40	15	5	5	4	3	11	0*	34							11						40					18	186	10		
	50*	33	–	–	–	67*	16	–								6						–					8	180	3	W	17
Matches	17	16	15	15	14	13	13	12	11	10	8	8	7	7	6	6	3	3	3	3	2	2	1	1	1	1					
Innings	29	28	24	20	25	22	21	17	14	14	13	13	10	10	10	9	2	5	5	5	4	3	2	0	0	1					
Not Out	1	2	2	9	1	2	3	6	1	1	0	1	4	0	0	1	1	1	1	1	0	0	0	0	0	1					
Highest Score	125	248	67	56*	63	159*	137	53*	94	108*	90	74	16	96	53	125	4*	29	77*	76	98	40	47	–	–	0*					
Runs	844	1595	550	154	621	682	1009	230	175	391	341	381	55	219	242	349	5	61	155	170	137	41	64	–	–	0					
Average	30.14	61.34	25.00	14.00	25.87	34.10	56.05	20.90	13.46	30.07	26.23	31.75	9.16	21.90	24.20	43.62	5.00	15.25	38.75	34.00	34.25	13.66	32.00	–	–	–					
100s	2	5	0	0	0	1	2	0	0	2	0	0	0	0	0	1	0	0	0	0	0	0	0	0	0	0					
50s	3	5	2	1	4	4	8	1	1	0	2	2	0	1	1	1	0	0	1	2	1	0	0	0	0	0					
Catches/Stumpings	11/0	5/0	12/0	1/0	3/0	4/0	30/0	1/0	3/0	10/0	5/0	3/0	4/0	4/0	8/0	14/0	0/0	0/0	2/0	0/0	1/0	0/0	0/0	0/0	0/0	0/0					

Home Ground: The Oval
Address: The Oval, Kennington, London, SE11 5SS
Tel: 08712 461 100
Fax: 020 7820 5601
Email: enquiries@surreycricket.com
Directions: *By road:* The Oval is located south of the Thames in Kennington on the A202, near the junction with the A3 and A24, just south of Vauxhall Bridge and 10 minutes from Victoria and Waterloo stations. *By rail:* Take South West Trains to Vauxhall which is a short walk from the ground. The station is well served by trains from throughout Surrey and Hampshire as well as from the Greater London area. Connections include Clapham Junction and Waterloo.

Capacity: 23,000
Other grounds used: Croydon, Guildford, Whitgift School
Year formed: 1845

Chief Executive: Paul Sheldon
Cricket Manager: Chris Adams
Captain: Rory Hamilton-Brown
County colours: Gold and brown

Website:
www.surreycricket.com

Honours
County Championship
1890, 1891, 1892, 1894, 1895, 1899, 1914, 1952, 1953, 1954, 1955, 1956, 1957, 1958, 1971, 1999, 2000, 2002
Joint Champions 1950
Sunday League/NCL/Pro40
1996, 2003
Benson & Hedges Cup
1974, 1997, 2001
Gillette Cup/NatWest/C&G Trophy
1982, 1992
Twenty20 Cup
2003

FIRST-CLASS MATCHES
BOWLING

Match	JW Dernbach	CT Tremlett	GJ Batty	SC Meaker	A Nel	TE Linley	CP Schofield	U Afzaal	Iftikhar Anjum	MNW Spriegel	MP Dunn	TM Jewell	SP Cheetham	LJ Evans	SJ King	RJ Hamilton-Brown	MR Ramprakash	TJ Lancefield	A Harinath	SJ Walters	JJ Roy	GC Wilson	Younis Khan	Overs	Total	Byes/Leg-byes	Wickets	Run outs
v. Cambridge UCCE (Cambridge) 3-5 April	21-6-42-4	14.2-3-44-1	18-3-58-1			23-9-41-2							10-2-31-1		5-0-17-1									91.2	247	14	10	
	5-3-4-1	4-1-14-0	4-1-29-0			5-3-5-0	1-0-5-0																	19	58	1	1	1
v. Derbyshire (The Oval) 9-12 April	24-4-82-0		34-3-115-3	14.5-4-58-2	29-8-94-2	20-3-53-1	8-0-26-2			12-1-35-1						2-0-8-0								131.5	451	15	10	
	9-1-48-1		16.5-2-82-2	3-1-15-0	6-1-21-0	6-0-28-1	4-0-19-1									4-1-20-0								60.5	274	6	6	
v. Sussex (Hove) 15-18 April	29-11-65-4		16-0-90-1		28-9-79-1	19-3-78-1		24-4-87-2	1.3-0-5-1															117.3	416	12	10	
	3.4-0-20-0		3-1-9-0																					6.4	33	4	0	
v. Worcestershire (Croydon) 21-24 April	24-3-85-3		33.4-4-121-1		22-8-41-3		33-6-120-2	12-2-26-0	14-4-57-1							1-0-6-0								143.4	465	9	10	
	5.5-0-16-1		23-3-75-3		5-1-17-1		18-9-42-2	5-4-4-1								1-0-13-0								57.5	170	3	8	
v. Gloucestershire (The Oval) 4-6 May	16-2-45-0	18-7-35-4	10-3-17-1	12-4-33-1			10-1-38-2	10-0-53-2																80	229	8	10	
	18.2-3-81-3	14-4-36-1	5-1-11-0	20-2-48-5			9-1-23-0	9-0-43-1																75.2	248	26	10	
v. Bangladeshis (The Oval) 9-11 May			6-3-15-0				21-1-65-0	3-0-11-0		8-0-32-0	14.5-7-48-3	16-7-22-1			6-0-30-1	28-1-134-1								102.5	372	15	6	
v. Middlesex (The Oval) 17-20 May	17-3-68-5	15-1-36-1	34.4-5-113-2			17-3-71-2	2-0-5-0			4-0-18-0														89.4	324	13	10	
	12-2-33-1	9-2-28-0	22-4-65-1			5-4-5-0	14-0-42-1			3-0-8-0														65	189	8	3	
v. Northamptonshire (Northampton) 24-27 May	24-5-84-2					26-7-79-1	34.4-11-105-5	6-0-27-0		2-0-4-0	8-0-19-0		11-0-56-1		4-0-11-0									115.4	397	12	10	1
	17.5-7-40-3					17-4-68-4	21-9-43-1	1-0-4-0					3-1-18-0		3-0-5-0									74.5	229	18	10	1
v. Glamorgan (Cardiff) 29 May-1 June	24-7-78-4	24-8-55-3	13-2-51-0	22.5-2-83-3		22-2-71-0										3-0-8-0								108.5	372	26	10	
	2-0-5-0	1-0-2-0																						3	7	0	0	
v. Leicestershire (The Oval) 4-6 June	32-7-87-5	28-6-69-1	35.2-4-122-3			19-2-69-1	4-0-12-0									1-0-3-0						7-0-17-0		142.2	479	13	10	
			16-1-87-0																									
v. Derbyshire (Chesterfield) 28 June-1 July		18.4-5-64-2	13.1-1-50-3	19-3-63-1		10.2-4-13-4										6-0-16-0			3-0-15-0			5-0-22-0		69.1	237	10	10	
		32.5-7-94-4	38-9-99-1	30-9-74-3			10-1-33-2															6-0-25-0		117.5	365	24	10	
v. Northamptonshire (The Oval) 20-22 July		15-3-38-2	20.5-4-78-5	21-6-95-1	11-6-23-2		1-1-0-0																	68.5	240	10	10	
		17-6-34-3	13-3-47-1	13-2-59-4	17-7-36-1		7.3-1-19-1																	67.3	205	10	10	
v. Middlesex (Lord's) 29-31 July	21-4-87-2	29.2-6-90-4	22-3-87-1			25-9-96-2	1-0-7-0			8-0-23-1						2-0-11-0								108.2	423	22	10	
v. Sussex (Guildford) 9-12 August	12.1-2-34-2	18-5-32-4	22-2-81-3	17-3-42-0										7-0-18-1										76.1	217	10	10	
	19.1-4-48-0	16-5-45-1	16-3-42-1	26-5-86-4										7-0-23-0		2.5-0-8-0	1-0-9-0							88	275	13	6	
v. Worcestershire (Worcester) 16-19 August	25-4-78-3	19.1-5-46-4	23-3-68-3		18-5-76-0		4-2-11-0									1-0-7-0								90.1	308	23	10	
	18.5-3-76-1	19-7-42-4	25-1-116-3		11-1-53-1		3-0-15-1																	76.5	319	17	10	
v. Leicestershire (Leicester) 24-27 August	6-1-12-0	7-1-18-0											16-1-71-2		5.4-0-28-0	1-0-6-0	2-0-12-0	1-0-6-0				9-0-44-0		30.4	123	3	0	
	14.5-0-64-1	21-0-87-2	22-3-78-3												1-0-12-0			1-0-6-0						75.5	338	20	8	
v. Glamorgan (The Oval) 7-10 September	20-7-46-1	17-4-53-3	9-2-23-0	24-1-97-5			10-1-30-1																2-0-12-0	82	276	15	10	
v. Gloucestershire (Bristol) 13-16 September	9-4-24-0	9.5-3-29-4	9-2-18-1				7-1-20-0	2-0-8-0																36.5	106	7	5	
	16.2-5-55-4	13-3-37-1	14-2-46-1				5-1-20-0	16-1-63-4								5-0-11-0								69.2	250	18	10	

	JW Dernbach	CT Tremlett	GJ Batty	SC Meaker	A Nel	TE Linley	CP Schofield	U Afzaal	Iftikhar Anjum	MNW Spriegel	MP Dunn	TM Jewell	SP Cheetham	LJ Evans	SJ King	RJ Hamilton-Brown	MR Ramprakash	TJ Lancefield	A Harinath	SJ Walters	JJ Roy	GC Wilson	Younis Khan
Overs	447	361.5	488.5	269.4	227	170	184	75.3	65	65.3	14.5	40	16	6	28	47.3	1	1	2	3	3	9	18
Maidens	98	88	70	48	67	46	34	9	8	3	7	10	1	0	1	1	0	0	0	0	0	0	0
Runs	1390	969	1696	998	671	483	606	217	240	207	48	127	71	30	134	184	6	9	12	15	18	44	64
Wickets	51	48	42	29	21	14	14	8	6	5	3	3	2	1	1	1	0	0	0	0	0	0	0
Average	27.25	20.19	40.38	34.41	31.95	30.19	43.29	27.12	40.00	41.40	16.00	42.33	35.50	30.00	134.00	184.00	-	-	-	-	-	-	-

FIELDING

30	SM Davies (30 ct)
14	GC Wilson (14 ct)
12	GJ Batty
11	RJ Hamilton-Brown
10	MNW Spriegel
8	SJ Walters
5	MR Ramprakash
5	CP Schofield
4	U Afzaal
4	TE Linley
4	A Nel
3	A Harinath
3	TJ Lancefield
3	SC Meaker
2	Younis Khan
1	JW Dernbach
1	LJ Evans
1	CT Tremlett

Division Two – Final Table

	P	W	L	D	Bat	Bowl	Pens	Pts
Sussex	16	8	3	5	45	47	0	235
Worcestershire	16	7	4	5	39	42	0	208
Glamorgan	16	7	4	5	33	43	0	203
Leicestershire	16	7	5	4	31	44	0	199
Gloucestershire	16	6	9	1	28	47	-2	172
Northamptonshire	16	6	7	3	28	34	0	167
Surrey	16	4	6	6	43	36	-2	159
Middlesex	16	4	7	5	37	41	-2	155
Derbyshire	16	3	7	6	30	42	0	138

CB40   FPt20

SURREY CRICKET

Limited overs nickname:
SURREY LIONS

SUSSEX

by Bruce Talbot

If Murray Goodwin appeared slightly reluctant to spray champagne around at New Road, when Sussex's acting captain received the second division trophy on the penultimate day of the season, it was understandable. Sussex effectively came tenth out of 18 counties, their lowest finish since coming bottom of the pile in 2000.

However, they had achieved what everyone – themselves, their supporters and even the bookies – had expected back in April by winning the second division

title. Mission accomplished, then. And while coach Mark Robinson was correct when he said that Sussex have no right to be a first division county, they have only spent two seasons since 2000 in Division Two. A county with their recent track record of success should be in the top flight.

What no one, least of all Robinson, could have predicted was that his side would go up despite the sparing contributions of four of their most influential players. Skipper Mike Yardy, Luke Wright and Ed Joyce only played in nine of the 16 Championship games and Matt Prior seven, and although Prior and Wright's England absences were expected, no one could have foreseen that the other two, both cornerstones of the top five, would only make modest contributions.

For the second season running only two players passed 1,000 runs – Goodwin (1,201) and Chris Nash (1,029, including three scores of 150-plus). Goodwin

All-rounder Robin Martin-Jenkins' 15-year career at Sussex ended in July 2010. He signed off with a series of superb performances with both ball and bat and left the pitch at Hove to a standing ovation from the members after victory over Worcestershire in their CB40 match.

rediscovered his form after a lean 2009 when he was distracted by his benefit while Nash came good in the second half of the season. It was gratifying to see less experienced players, particularly Ben Brown, emerge too but Sussex may recruit an experienced batsman for 2011 with Yardy likely to be a regular absentee on England one-day duty and Goodwin perhaps only a year or two away from retirement.

When the top order was exposed, Sussex's lower end consistently got them out of trouble, which is a sure indicator of a strong dressing room. The division's best partnerships for the seventh, eighth and ninth wickets were posted by a combination of Murray Goodwin, Rana Naved-ul-Hasan, who outperformed Yasir Arafat in the overseas role, and Robin Martin-Jenkins, whose de-mob happy form before retirement in July was the most consistent of his 15-year career.

Sussex's inability in the post-Mushtaq Ahmed era to bowl out teams had been the root cause of relegation. That was not a problem in 2010. In fact, the enduring consistency of their attack proved crucial to their success even though it took their quickest bowler, Arafat, until the last month to produce his consistent best. In 30 innings, the opposition was bowled out 23 times, 15 times for under 250, while Sussex only conceded 350 or more twice. Compare that to 2009 when their opponents passed 350 fourteen times.

It was a great summer for seam bowlers everywhere but Monty Panesar, in his first year at Hove following his move from Northamptonshire,

rediscovered his mojo. He took 52 wickets, the second highest by an English-qualified spinner, despite opponents trying to negate what they perceived as Sussex's biggest strength. One of the sights of a bone-dry mid-summer was the verdant pitch Middlesex prepared at Uxbridge to counter Monty – a green oasis amid a sun-baked brown outfield. The over-riding impression as far as Panesar was concerned was

Corey Collymore was Sussex's player of the season, with 56 Championship wickets at 19.88. His move to Middlesex will leave a big hole in the Sussex attack next season.

Kirtley Reflects on His Cricket Career
by Bruce Talbot

James Kirtley insists he has headed into cricketing retirement 'totally fulfilled' after a 15-year career with Sussex and England.

It was at Lord's that Kirtley says he enjoyed his finest moment when he took 5 for 28 in the 2006 C&G Trophy final against Lancashire, a few months after he had re-modelled his bowling action for the second time.

He said, 'Playing for England was an ambition and I achieved that, but the 2006 C&G final felt like redemption what with everything that had gone on during the previous winter with my bowling action.

It is a game which is still talked about because it is such a good final. I wasn't particularly fired up that afternoon – I have always regarded myself as a big-match player – but I guess it was my day.'

Kirtley now admits he thought about walking away from the game a few months earlier when 'chucker' jibes resurfaced five years after he had been reported by the match referee for a suspect action during his first England tour in Zimbabwe. 'That winter of 2005–06 was the lowest ebb,' he said. 'I think my own stubbornness made me determined not to leave the game with the stigma of being labelled a chucker. I just didn't want to give up even though taking a one-way ticket out of cricket would have been the easy option.'

Kirtley played four Tests and 11 ODIs and was Man of the Match on his Test debut when he took 6 for 34 against South Africa in 2003. A few weeks later he was helping Sussex win the first of three County Championships during a decade of success in which Kirtley played a massive part, but he felt his international career should have been prolonged. 'I came at a time when Caddick and Gough had just finished and Duncan Fletcher was still looking at the likes of Hoggard, Jones and Anderson,' he said. 'I was always just on the outside and felt it was hard to be judged in four Tests. I also only played 11 ODIs and that is perhaps harder to accept. I think my ability to adapt to different pitches is greater now than back then and my t20 skills are far better than when I got the opportunity to go to the World Cup in 2007. But just being part of it was outstanding. I was always around and went on six trips but I never quite nailed it. However, I can't have many regrets about my career, especially the three Championships and one-day trophies I won with Sussex. I leave fulfilled.'

Kirtley is to devote time to his sports clothing business in retirement but will also complete his Level 3 coaching course this winter and hopes his county might use his experience in future to mentor the next generation of Sussex bowlers.

Go to *www.cricketarchive.com* for James Kirtley's final career records.

James Kirtley celebrates one of his five wickets in the 2006 C&G final against Lancashire – a match that he rightly regards as one of the highlights of his career.

Right Monty's back. In his first season at Hove, Monty Panesar proved that he still has the talent to take wickets, with 52 victims in the Championship.

Below right Lively with bat and ball, overseas player Rana Naved-ul-Hasan was missed when his short-term contract ended in late May.

that he remains a work in progress, his rehabilitation far from complete.

Sussex, though, had an attack for all seasons. The earliest ever start to a season suited the likes of Corey Collymore, whose nagging consistency brought him 57 wickets. He would have had considerably more had the slip catching been less fallible and his departure to Middlesex leaves a gaping hole in the attack although Amjad Khan looks an ideal replacement. Martin-Jenkins (with 30 wickets), Arafat (36 with 26 in the last five games), James Anyon (26) and Wright (23) all chipped in, while the emergence of left-armer Lewis Hatchett was a welcome if unexpected bonus.

Sussex wobbled briefly after winning their first four games, but re-grouped in the second half of the season and won four more times. They didn't always look a cut above their opponents but in certain games the gulf between the two divisions looked like a chasm.

Where the absence of Yardy, Wright and Prior was most keenly felt was in one-day cricket. Sussex started their Twenty20 Cup defence in unstoppable form but, as they knew from previous campaigns, momentum in that competition can be lost as quickly as it is gained. Only two of the 2009 finalists were missing when Sussex limply bowed out in the quarter-finals, but the absence of Rory Hamilton-Brown and Dwayne Smith proved significant.

The Clydesdale Bank 40 competition has been widely criticised and rightly so. The absence of a quarter-final round left little room for error in the group stage and Sussex were always struggling after losing to the part-time Unicorns and only taking one point out of four from Glamorgan.

Still, ten trophies in ten years is a fantastic achievement for a so-called 'smaller' county and off the field Sussex are beginning to match progress made on it. The second phase of the redevelopment of the County Ground began almost as soon as the final game had finished. The £5m scheme will see the sea end transformed with new stands and media facilities while a refurbishment of the pavilion and improvement to the players' dressing rooms will also take place before the new season.

And when the 2011 campaign starts Sussex should have a side capable of competing in Division One and, with the right recruitment, perhaps challenging for a fourth title in eight years. Their run of success shows no signs of ending just yet.

SUSSEX CCC

FIRST-CLASS MATCHES
BATTING

Match	CD Nash	MW Goodwin	MS Panesar	CD Collymore	MA Thornely	JE Anyon	AJ Hodd	EC Joyce	RSC Martin-Jenkins	LJ Wright	MH Yardy	BC Brown	Yasir Arafat	JS Gatting	MJ Prior	OP Rayner	Naved-ul-Hasan	LJ Hatchett	RG Aga	WAT Beer	MS Chadwick	MW Machan	WA Adkin	LWP Wells	Extras	Total	Wickets	Result	Points
v. Glamorgan	8	30	0	19*	3	13	37		65	34	43			15											17	284	10		
(Cardiff) 9-12 April	36	83	4	6*	46	11	18		33*	0	34			21											19	311	9	W	21
v. Surrey	1	74	0	0	32		7		64	63	68			15		68*									24	416	10		
(Hove) 15-18 April	12*	-	-	-	-				-	-	17*			-		-									4	33	0	W	23
v. Gloucestershire	47	24	7*	0	25	8	1		2			14	2			10									12	152	10		
(Bristol) 21-23 April	35	14	0*	1	64	25	2		102			0	20			13									26	302	10	W	19
v. Leicestershire	4	142	14	7*	9	32	0		15			21	8			101									39	392	10		
(Hove) 27-29 April	27*	-	-	-	29*	-			-			-													8	64	0	W	23
v. Middlesex	0	17	7	0	5	6	9		0			14	123*	6											30	217	10		
(Hove) 5-8 May	42	0	46*	13	15	19	109		17			0	49	1											10	321	10	L	4
v. Cambridge UCCE	4				-			135*			1		0			54	-		66*	-	-	6			11	277	5	W	
(Cambridge) 12-14 May	18							13			110*		31			67*	-		-	-		5			9	253	4	W	
v. Northamptonshire	78	30		0	6	0	7		14	2							23	3	2*						10	175	10		
(Northampton) 18-20 May	32	39		5	51	1	5		30	55*							0	27	7						17	269	10	L	3
v. Worcestershire	4	111	0	0	4	-		67	66*	14†	3#	0	40	-											19	328	10		
(Hove) 24-27 May																												D	8
v. Derbyshire	5	121	0		8	34		9	130	20	8	5	34*												55	429	10		
(Derby) 5-8 June	18	6			4	1		20	-	0	8	2*													12	71	7	D	11
v. Gloucestershire	49	44	5	1*	7			43	78				58	24	37	20									23	389	10		
(Arundel) 7-9 July	0	26*	-	-	6			17*	-				-	-	-	-									3	52	2	W	23
v. Middlesex	46	80	9	12*	10			85		134	5			30	1	20									21	452	10		
(Uxbridge) 21-24 July	14	35	9*	-	53			7		62	21			4	18	6									11	240	9	D	11
v. Leicestershire	184	19	0	12*				14		36	2	38	58			0	0								16	379	10		
(Leicester) 29-31 July																												W	23
v. Surrey	21	0	20*	2	1			0		18	18	23			47								45		22	217	10		
(Guildford) 9-12 August	22	23	0	-	0			40		100*	52	23*			-								-		15	275	6	D	7
v. Derbyshire	156	100*	-	-	-			164	-	-	-	-	112	-		4*									40	576	3		
(Horsham) 18-20 August																												W	24
v. Glamorgan	19	28	17	0*		8	26	56		8	18	59	0												11	250	10		
(Hove) 27-30 August	0	58*	-	-		-	-	24*		-	-	10	-												1	93	2	D	8
v. Northamptonshire	169	0	16	0*	89	0	7						39	18		0	16								27	381	10		
(Hove) 7-9 September																												W	23
v. Worcestershire	0	34	0		0	52			0			32	1			4				37*				62	15	237	10		
(Worcester) 13-16 September	-	63	-		16	39*			94*			37	-			-				-				8	7	264	4	L	4

	CD Nash	MW Goodwin	MS Panesar	CD Collymore	MA Thornely	JE Anyon	AJ Hodd	EC Joyce	RSC Martin-Jenkins	LJ Wright	MH Yardy	BC Brown	Yasir Arafat	JS Gatting	MJ Prior	OP Rayner	Naved-ul-Hasan	LJ Hatchett	RG Aga	WAT Beer	MS Chadwick	MW Machan	WA Adkin	LWP Wells
Matches	17	16	15	14	12	11	10	10	9	9	9	9	9	8	7	7	5	4	2	2	1	1	1	1
Innings	29	26	19	17	21	15	14	17	13	12	13	14	9	11	11	10	8	4	2	1	0	2	1	2
Not Out	2	3	5	8	1	0	1	3	3	1	2	2	2	0	1	2	2	0	1	1	0	0	0	0
Highest Score	184	142	46*	19*	89	34	109	164	130	134	100*	112	58	31	123*	67*	101	20	66*	37*	0	6	45	62
Runs	1051	1201	154	78	467	174	319	738	629	465	345	515	255	155	296	256	208	30	66	37	0	11	45	70
Average	38.92	52.21	11.00	8.66	23.35	11.60	24.53	52.71	62.90	42.27	31.36	42.91	36.42	14.09	29.60	32.00	34.66	7.50	66.00	-	-	5.50	45.00	35.00
100s	3	4	0	0	0	0	1	2	2	1	1	2	0	0	1	0	1	0	0	0	0	0	0	0
50s	1	5	0	0	4	0	1	3	5	3	1	2	2	0	0	2	1	0	1	0	0	0	0	1
Catches/Stumpings	12/0	5/0	1/0	3/0	8/0	3/0	29/1	17/0	4/0	3/0	12/0	9/2	1/0	4/0	19/0	10/0	0/0	1/0	1/0	1/0	0/0	0/0	0/0	0/0

Key: † replaced by JE Anyon
replaced by JS Gatting

Home Ground: Hove
Address: County Ground, Eaton Road, Hove, BN3 3AN
Tel: 08712 461100
Fax: 01273 771549
Email: simon.dyke@sussexcricket.co.uk
Directions: *By rail:* Hove station is a 10-minute walk. *By road:* Follow AA signs. Street parking at no cost.
Capacity: 5,500

Other grounds used: Arundel Castle, Horsham
Year formed: 1839

Chief Executive: David Brooks
Cricket Manager: Mark Robinson
Captain: Mike Yardy
County colours: Black and white

Honours
County Championship
2003, 2006, 2007
Sunday League/NCL/Pro40
1982, 2008, 2009
Gillette Cup/NatWest/C&G Trophy
1963, 1964, 1978, 1986, 2006
Twenty20 Cup
2009

Website:
www.sussexcricket.co.uk

FIRST-CLASS MATCHES
BOWLING

	CD Collymore	MS Panesar	Yasir Arafat	RSC Martin-Jenkins	JE Anyon	LJ Wright	Naved-ul-Hasan	OP Rayner	LJ Hatchett	CD Nash	WAT Beer	MA Thornely	RG Aga	JS Gatting	WA Adkin	MS Chadwick	LWP Wells	Overs	Total	Byes/Leg-byes	Wickets	Run outs
v. Glamorgan (Cardiff) 9-12 April	12-3-42-1	13.5-5-20-3		16-3-34-3	12-2-32-1	15-3-52-2				1-1-0-0								69.5	191	11	10	
	17-6-25-2	22-5-46-1		11-1-32-2	12-4-37-0	12-3-41-1				9.3-3-12-4								83.3	203	10	10	
v. Surrey (Hove) 15-18 April	19-7-27-0		23-8-44-1		19.1-4-45-5	16-4-48-0	20-8-28-4			2-1-2-0								99.1	205	11	10	
	10-4-16-2		25.4-7-54-2		5-1-18-0	15-1-44-3	18-3-89-3			4-0-13-0								77.4	243	9	10	
v. Gloucestershire (Bristol) 21-23 April	11-6-15-3				7-0-16-2	11-2-44-1	15.4-2-49-4											44.4	128	4	10	
	12-1-30-3				10-1-34-2	7.1-1-29-3	10-4-24-2											39.1	119	2	10	
v. Leicestershire (Hove) 27-29 April	9.3-2-32-2				8-4-15-2	7-2-16-2	11-2-49-4											35.3	114	2	10	
	19.1-3-37-2		29-6-77-3		17-5-35-0	17-3-63-3	24-6-95-1			5-0-13-1								111.1	338	16	10	
v. Middlesex (Hove) 5-8 May	15.2-1-67-5		25-7-65-2		14-3-31-2	7-0-41-0	18-6-68-1			4-2-7-0								83.2	296	17	10	
	15-0-68-2		13.2-2-52-0		9-1-46-4	4-0-12-1	20-6-49-0											61.2	243	11	7	
v. Cambridge UCCE (Cambridge) 12-14 May				15-2-40-1			5.5-1-16-2	10-3-28-2	7-2-11-1	5-0-15-2			13-4-29-2				9-1-41-1	57.5	181	12	10	
				20-10-31-2			24-5-62-4	4.2-1-21-2	13-4-35-0				14-5-32-0	5-2-19-1			10-1-33-0	97.2	265	21	10	
v. Northamptonshire (Northampton) 18-20 May	22.5-6-56-3			14-2-36-2	14-2-53-2		19-5-62-0	12-5-45-3		4-1-7-0								88.5	274	15	10	
	7-1-24-1			6-0-30-0	10-1-37-1		7-2-19-1	14-3-34-2		4.3-0-16-2								48.3	171	11	7	
v. Worcestershire (Hove) 24-27 May	23-7-66-2	44.3-14-98-2	24-3-112-2	21-5-59-2	18-2-62-1	9-0-31-0				4-0-21-0		7-1-14-2						143.3	464	15	10	1
	12-5-29-1	16.4-4-47-2	9-1-31-0	12-2-40-1		6-0-12-0				4-0-8-0								66	205	24	6	
v. Derbyshire (Derby) 5-8 June			30-6-71-2	17-3-54-1	11-1-38-1	21-3-74-1	20.5-2-65-5			2-0-2-0								101.5	337	33	10	
	–	–	–	–	–	–	–			–												
v. Gloucestershire (Arundel) 7-9 July	18-4-58-2	31-8-70-3		21.5-6-55-3	13-2-66-2		12-4-33-0						2-0-10-0					102.5	307	15	10	
	5-2-9-1	15-3-44-5		7-2-24-1	3-0-18-0		10.3-3-24-3											40.3	131	12	10	
v. Middlesex (Uxbridge) 21-24 July	19-6-66-4	19-6-60-1			15-3-47-1		18-2-84-1	16.1-5-62-2					6-1-19-1					93.1	350	12	10	
	16-4-42-0	30-11-89-5					16-6-30-2	2-1-13-0					2-0-11-1					66	204	19	8	
v. Leicestershire (Leicester) 29-31 July	18-8-42-2	9-4-13-1	13-2-47-1					14.1-2-47-5					7-1-38-0					61.1	204	17	10	1
	13.1-5-48-6	14-1-15-1	11-1-42-2					8-0-45-1										43.1	156	6	10	
v. Surrey (Guildford) 9-12 August	25-8-54-1	24-8-50-2	21.1-3-81-5					13-2-33-1	1-0-8-0				3-0-15-0		11-2-38-1			98.1	292	13	10	
	–	–	–					–	–				–		–							
v. Derbyshire (Horsham) 18-20 August	14-4-37-2	13-2-55-3	18-5-57-3			9-1-60-2	7-3-19-0											61	242	14	10	
	23-7-50-4	24-5-67-4	18-0-66-1			6-1-30-1	2-2-0-0											73	225	12	10	
v. Glamorgan (Hove) 27-30 August	18-4-57-2		22-3-70-1	15-0-67-2	15.2-3-52-3	6-0-41-1				4-0-6-0								80.2	300	7	9	
	13-2-52-1		13-3-38-0	21-6-64-3	10.5-2-19-2	7-2-24-4												64.5	210	13	10	
v. Northamptonshire (Hove) 7-9 September	12-5-39-1	10-4-14-2	15-4-43-4		8-1-23-3							1-0-6-0						46	125	0	10	
	15-4-45-2	17.5-5-36-2	21-1-74-5		7-1-35-1		11-5-32-0											71.5	237	15	10	
v. Worcestershire (Worcester) 13-16 September		14-2-48-1	12-4-29-1	3-0-11-0	15-2-48-3		9-3-25-0					8.4-2-31-3						61.4	201	9	9	1
		21.1-3-85-3	12-2-50-2	8-0-56-1	3-0-30-0		3-0-15-0					6-1-30-0					2-0-16-0	55.1	306	24	6	

	CD Collymore	MS Panesar	Yasir Arafat	RSC Martin-Jenkins	JE Anyon	LJ Wright	Naved-ul-Hasan	OP Rayner	LJ Hatchett	CD Nash	WAT Beer	MA Thornely	RG Aga	JS Gatting	WA Adkin	MS Chadwick	LWP Wells
Overs	414	516.2	256	201.1	227.2	154.5	162.4	148.2	66.4	56	32.4	21	34	5	11	19	2
Maidens	115	135	43	35	41	22	44	38	15	10	7	2	10	2	2	2	0
Runs	1133	1328	896	593	767	573	532	412	256	126	111	75	99	19	38	74	16
Wickets	57	52	36	30	29	23	20	18	12	8	5	4	2	1	1	1	0
Average	19.88	25.54	24.89	19.77	26.45	24.91	26.60	22.89	21.33	15.75	22.20	18.75	49.50	19.00	38.00	74.00	–

FIELDING

30	AJ Hodd (29 ct, 1 st)
19	MJ Prior
17	EC Joyce
12	CD Nash
12	MH Yardy
11	BC Brown (9 ct, 2 st)
10	OP Rayner
8	MA Thornely
5	MW Goodwin
4	JS Gatting
4	RSC Martin-Jenkins
3	JE Anyon
3	CD Collymore
3	LJ Wright
1	RG Aga
1	WAT Beer
1	LJ Hatchett
1	MS Panesar
1	Yasir Arafat

Division Two – Final Table

	P	W	L	D	Bat	Bowl	Pens	Pts
Sussex	16	8	3	5	45	47	0	235
Worcestershire	16	7	4	5	39	42	0	208
Glamorgan	16	7	4	5	33	43	0	203
Leicestershire	16	7	5	4	31	44	0	199
Gloucestershire	16	6	9	1	28	47	-2	172
Northamptonshire	16	6	4	6	28	34	0	167
Surrey	16	4	6	6	43	36	-2	159
Middlesex	16	4	7	5	37	41	-2	155
Derbyshire	16	3	7	6	30	42	0	138

CB40   FPt20

SSE SHARKS

Limited overs nickname:
SUSSEX SHARKS

Amjad Recalls Day Sussex Turned Him Down
by Bruce Talbot

Sussex's new recruit Amjad Khan has revealed how the county missed the chance to sign him when he was a teenager. Amjad, who has joined the county on a three-year contract from Kent, was 17 when he was recommended to former Sussex coach Peter Moores and arrived at Hove for a trial. Nothing came of it, and he enjoyed nine years at Canterbury instead.

PLAYER OF THE SEASON

Corey Collymore: Not playing one-day cricket enabled the Bajan paceman to produce consistent performances. Sussex supporters were stunned to hear in September that he was heading to Middlesex because he wanted to base his family in London. He will be a big loss.

YOUNG PLAYER OF THE SEASON

Lewis Hatchett's emergence as a genuine replacement for Jason Lewry was a reward for his hard work two years after he wasn't considered good enough to play in the second team. A five-wicket haul in his second Championship game amply showcased his potential.

A YEAR TO REMEMBER

- Robin Martin-Jenkins retired, after 15 seasons, in the form of his life
- James Kirtley: Kevin Pietersen's wicket in the CB 40 match against Surrey in September marked the perfect end to a stellar county career
- Ben Brown: Wicketkeeper-batsman who looked at home in the top three by the end of the season

A YEAR TO FORGET

- Michael Thornely 12 Championship games but averaged only 23 and was released at the end of the season
- Chris Liddle second successive season badly affected by an ankle injury
- Ed Joyce injury and family illness restricted his appearances

Pace bowler Amjad Khan was signed by Sussex from Kent at the end of the summer 2010. He will lead the attack next season, replacing Corey Collymore who has moved to Middlesex for family reasons.

Now aged 28, Khan believes the best years of a career interrupted by knee surgery are ahead of him thanks to a tailor-made fitness programme he undertook for the first time 12 months ago. His cricket-specific training involved lots of sprint work rather than conventional running. It sounds obvious – after all quick bowlers only run in for ten seconds at a time – and it has certainly been working for Khan. 'My body feels really strong,' he said. 'What I am doing now fitness-wise has made a massive difference … I took 38 wickets in 12 games in 2010 and could have had 50. More importantly I was able to bowl long spells.'

Amjad is planning to go to Port Elizabeth after Christmas to step up his preparations for the 2011 season in the South African sunshine. 'I'm delighted with the move,' he added. 'Sussex have won ten trophies in ten years and they are not afraid of winning. I have long been an admirer of the environment they have created for their players and I also look upon it as an opportunity to get back into the England picture … I played once [against West Indies in 2009], which was a fantastic experience, and I'm determined not to be a one-cap wonder.'

Sussex County Cricket Club, LV=CC Division Two Winners 2010

Sussex Women, County Championship Winners 2010

FROM MAJOR SPONSORS...

Family Club Formula is the Secret of Sussex Success

by Bruce Talbot

The most successful county club of the last decade seems to have developed a winning formula when it comes to the integration of their professional and recreational cricket structures.

Sussex's Dave Brooks is the only chief executive in the first-class game who also heads up his county's Cricket Board. 'It was part of the job specification when I applied for the position and I have really enjoyed forming our vision for developing the game at all levels in Sussex,' said Brooks, who celebrates two years in his job in January 2011. Brooks has his hands full with the county club so Andy Hobbs, who heads up a development and community cricket team that has

Sussex players, including James Kirtley (middle), help out with some sightscreen renovation work during a NatWest CricketForce day at Hailsham Cricket Club in April.

doubled in size to six and is based at Hove, is responsible for the day-to-day decision-making.

Brooks has played club cricket for his village side Cookham Dean in Berkshire for many years and knows the sorts of problems that crop up at grass-roots level, whether it is finding a suitably qualified coach for the colts or getting advice on preparing better pitches.

He is a visible presence on the club scene in Sussex. 'I make sure I am,' said Brooks. 'For instance, I will go to a league's pre-season AGM and be in contact with 40 or so clubs straight away. It is nice to meet people, listen to what they have to say and I think the clubs appreciate it as well.'

He and his team have instigated several schemes designed to forge closer links between the professional and recreational games that have been well received. Brooks said, 'We have Reward Days where we celebrate outstanding achievements by our clubs by hosting them at a day's county cricket. Last summer we entertained Glynde and Beddingham for winning the National Village Knockout Cup and the under-13s and under-15s girls teams at a small club called Bells Yew Green, who won their respective Lady Taverners competitions.

'At the end of the season we staged the Sussex OSCAs which celebrate the work and achievements of the volunteers who are the lifeblood of our clubs. And a new initiative we are considering for 2011 is to invite any club cricketer who gets a hundred or takes seven wickets in a match to come along to a day's cricket as our guest.'

Sussex also hosted their over-50s, 60s and 70s teams last year and even invited the county's wandering teams – Brighton Brunswick, Sussex Martlets, Armadillos and Harry Baldwin's XI – to a get-together during a County Championship game.

There aren't many counties where the professionals are so closely integrated to the club game. It is hardly surprising considering nearly two-thirds of the current Sussex professional playing staff were nurtured by the county's clubs.

It has a two-way benefit. Last season, when he wasn't selected for the Twenty20 Cup, Monty Panesar had five games for Bexhill in the Sussex League and made a tremendous impression on his new club. Sussex were delighted as well. When Monty returned to the county side he took his first five-wicket innings haul for the

Dave Brooks,
the Sussex chief executive.

two grass pitches in 2011. Two nomadic clubs will be based there with colts sections, and promising youngsters who emerge from initiatives such as Street20 will then be funnelled through the county's existing Academy set-up.

Brooks is proud of what has been achieved but is always looking to improve. He added, 'What is important is to spread the message of the county club throughout Sussex. We don't want just to be regarded as just a Hove or Brighton club. Andy Hobbs and his team have done a magnificent job. They are all club cricketers who know what is needed and have made delivery of our initiatives much easier due to the excellent relationships they have forged.

'It is all part of the ethos of Sussex. We are a family club where everyone pulls together. It has underpinned the success of the team in the past ten years and continues to be the basis of everything we do.'

Street20 is a Sussex cricket programme which takes the game into parts of the county where there are no proper facilities to play the game. It is proving very popular with youngsters, besides offering clear social benefits.

county in a Championship win over Gloucestershire, and Sussex coach Mark Robinson credits much of his improvement in the second half of the season with that stint at the Polegrove. Where possible, players are made available to present prizes at end-of-season awards nights and will turn out at weekends if they are available.

Sussex has a special membership category for its hundreds of affiliated clubs which has proved popular too. The community development arm of the club also comes under its recreational wing and they are particularly proud of the Street20 initiative which gets cricket played in the less affluent areas of the county.

The new £28m Academy, which opened at Falmer on the outskirts of Brighton last September, has a non-grass cricket pitch with Sussex hoping to put down

National Achievements by Sussex Clubs, 2010
Ocklynge, National Runners-up, Asda Kwik Cricket Girls
Greenway, National Finalists, Asda Kwik Cricket Year 6
Helenswood, National Runners-up, Lady Taverners indoor
Bells Yew Green, National Runners-up, U-13 Lady Taverners

Participation in Cricket in Sussex, 2010*
Overall Participation: +13%
Women and Girls Participation: +26%
Club Membership: +2%
Volunteers: +19%
16–25-year-old volunteers: +40%
*compared with 2009

SUSSEX WOMEN, COUNTY CHAMPIONSHIP WINNERS 2010

Sussex claimed the LV Women's County Championship by beating holders Kent by six wickets in the deciding match of the season at Horsham. Kent, the 2009 domestic champions, took a slender lead into the final round of games with Sussex needing to beat their rivals to regain the crown they last held two years ago.

Izi Noakes was the pick of the bowling attack for Sussex after they put Kent in to bat, taking 4 for 24 in her ten-over spell including the prized wicket of Kent and England captain Charlotte Edwards for seven. Susie Rowe (52) top-scored for the visitors before she was trapped lbw by Caroline Atkins, but no one else topped fifty as the visitors were bowled out for a modest 132.

Sussex then rarely looked troubled as they chased down their victory target with Atkins (52) making a half-century before Alexia Walker hit a quickfire 15 off 13 balls to seal a win for the home side.

Sussex's Charlotte Burton said, 'It's a great feeling winning the Championship again, and it was an outstanding performance from the team – not just today but throughout the season. The standard of cricket has improved and we have been really tested this year.'

WARWICKSHIRE

by Paul Bolton

When Ashley Giles, Warwickshire's director of cricket, faced the press after his side had been demolished in two days by Nottinghamshire in mid-August he could not have imagined that within five weeks he would be doused in champagne on the Lord's outfield as he celebrated victory in the Clydesdale Bank 40.

Giles was a man under pressure at Trent Bridge, unsure of his future and uncertain whether his players had the character to recover from surrendering 20 wickets in a day, ten in the final session.

It proved to be both the low point and the turning point of Warwickshire's season. They avoided relegation by winning their last three County Championship matches, all against fellow strugglers, and produced three nerveless performances under pressure in their last three one-day games to win the revamped 40-over competition.

That winning feeling! Imran Tahir (centre) celebrates with his delighted teammates having taken the wicket of Somerset's Murali Kartik during the Clydesdale Bank 40 final at Lord's.

Neil Carter was in the form of his career in 2010 – wickets and runs in all three competitions saw him rightly rewarded with the PCA Player of the Year award.

PCA Winner Carter Enjoying a Golden Career Autumn

Neil Carter capped a memorable season at the age of 35 by collecting the NatWest Professional Cricketers' Association Player of the Year Award at a glittering ceremony at London's Hurlingham Club.

Besides becoming the first Warwickshire seamer in eight years to take 50 Championship wickets, and being their third-highest run-scorer, he also helped the county to win the Clydesdale Bank 40 final at Lord's. Moreover, his efforts in all forms of cricket secured him top spot in the PCA's Most Valued Player rankings, a remarkable turnaround for a player who Warwickshire career has twice been on the point of ending as the club has encouraged him to consider moving away.

'Those weren't easy times [2004 and 2007] though there were other counties interested in me, but I backed myself, things went my way and Warwickshire changed their mind about me,' Carter said.

'I've performed better than my stats suggest over the last couple of seasons but things went well for me in the first game against Yorkshire and they got better and better. But the MVP award suggests that statistics don't lie. The Player of the Year Award is a great accolade because it means that your efforts are recognised and appreciated by your fellow professionals.

'My first ball of the season was creamed for four by Jacques Rudolph of Yorkshire and I thought it was going to be a long hard season. But it has turned out much better than that and these awards are a great way to round things off.'

by Paul Bolton

Warwickshire's CB40 success, Giles's third trophy in as many seasons but his first major honour, should not have been a surprise. Their one-day and t20 form was consistent throughout the season but it was often overshadowed by some abject batting collapses in the Championship.

'I think we slipped in under the radar a bit,' said Giles. 'People thought we had a rough season all round, but we topped our groups in both the t20 and CB40 having not lost a 40-over game in 2009. So our one-day stats were very good but to go back to Lord's and win a trophy brought a bit of history back to the

Seamer Chris Woakes has a right to smile – his efforts with the new ball won him accolades at Edgbaston and helped him keep his place in the England Lions side.

but Ian Westwood, Darren Maddy, Jim Troughton and Tim Ambrose failed to muster a Championship century between them and Varun Chopra, a winter recruit from Essex, fared little better with just one half-century from 18 innings.

Westwood did manage a series of nuggety innings and finished as leading run-scorer with 726, but it was usually left to the middle- and lower-order batsmen to dig Warwickshire out of trouble. Warwickshire's meagre haul of 20 batting bonus points was the lowest in the Championship.

Neil Carter and Chris Woakes, the new ball bowlers, had little opportunity to put their feet up as Warwickshire wickets tumbled and they were required to launch the counter-attack. Carter also made 617 runs, missing out on a century when last man Boyd Rankin was run out against Nottinghamshire at Edgbaston, and Woakes 431.

club. People like Bob Woolmer coached us to success in Lord's finals in the past so it's a great honour to be following him. But it's all about this group of players leaving their own legacy.'

Victory at Lord's enabled Giles to finish the season in relaxed mood and to plan for the future with more confidence, but he is not blind to the weaknesses that had threatened his side with Championship relegation all season.

The former England spinner expected Ian Bell and Jonathan Trott to be away on England duty for most of the season but he could not have predicted that his senior batsmen would fail so spectacularly and so often. The England batsmen managed two centuries and five fifties between them in 12 Championship appearances,

Woakes finished the season with 54 wickets, taking a career-best match haul of eleven in the win against Kent, which virtually assured Warwickshire of safety. But Carter beat Woakes to 50 Championship wickets and became the first Warwickshire seamer to that milestone in eight years.

Carter capped an outstanding season by being voted the NatWest Professional Cricketers' Association Player of the Year and also agreeing a new two-year contract. Warwickshire told Carter in 2004 and 2007 that he was free to talk to other counties but he stayed loyal and, at the age of 35, found himself in a strong bargaining position.

Leg-spinner Imran Tahir finished as leading wicket-taker in his only season at Edgbaston. Imran was

Giles Given Cash to Strengthen the Side
by Paul Bolton

Warwickshire's director of cricket Ashley Giles has been given more money to strengthen his squad for 2011. With Ian Bell and Jonathan Trott expected to miss most of next season because of England commitments, Giles's priority is to bring in two or three quality batsmen and he will have extra money in his budget to do so after a request to the county's power-brokers.

'Clearly the playing performances this season in the Championship with the absence of Jonathan Trott and Ian Bell have highlighted that we need to reinforce,' said Norman Gascoigne, who has succeeded Neil Houghton as Warwickshire chairman. 'It has really been up to Ashley to come up with a plan. He's put it to the club and we have said that we'll support him.'

Gascoigne is a native of Nottinghamshire who played club cricket for Newark before his work commitments in banking brought him to Birmingham 17 years ago. A former chairman of the Lord's Taverners in the West Midlands, he retired from banking in 2001 but has kept himself busy running a loan fund for the regional development agency Advantage West Midlands.

The 60-year-old will have a higher profile than Houghton and has already become a regular at Warwickshire matches home and away. He describes himself as 'first and foremost a Warwickshire fan' which will come as good news to those who fear that the club is in danger of becoming Edgbaston PLC with the construction of a new £30 million pavilion.

'Since I came to Birmingham 17 years ago I have been a Warwickshire fan and there is nothing more I lose sleep over than seeing Warwickshire struggling. I want to see us competing in all competitions. So the success of Warwickshire cricket comes first and foremost for me.

'The ground development is another issue. Apart from being a cricket club, we also have an international stadium to run as a business. Let's not be under any illusions. With the facilities we had we would have struggled to attract major matches to Edgbaston. The new development will put us in a prime slot to be able to compete for those matches.'

Success on the pitch has ensured that England's former 'King of Spain', Ashley Giles, will get money to strengthen the Warwickshire line-up for next season.

Young Pair Offered Warwickshire Contracts
by Paul Bolton

Warwickshire have offered contracts to Devon slow left-arm Chris Metters and former Surrey batsman Laurie Evans.

Warwickshire have been monitoring Metters' progress for three years, since he was first recommended to the club by former county manager Bob Cottam. The youngster has since switched from seam to spin with considerable success and has been a prolific wicket-taker with Devon in the Minor Counties Championship over the last two seasons.

He played in Warwickshire's second team at the end of the season and impressed sufficiently to be offered a seven-month contract, which will begin when he returns from spending the winter playing grade cricket in Australia.

Evans, who was released by Surrey, joined Warwickshire on loan for the final month of the season and made his County Championship debut in the victory over Kent at Edgbaston. He also made a second team century against Northamptonshire at Milton Keynes and has now been offered a full contract for 2011.

Meanwhile, wicketkeeper Richard Johnson is spending the winter in Australia on an ECB scholarship. The highly rated Johnson was recommended for the scholarship by ECB wicketkeeping coach Bruce French.

popular with his teammates and members but Warwickshire's lack of first-innings runs meant that his best efforts were usually in a lost cause.

Imran, who will return to Hampshire in 2011, signed off his Warwickshire career in style with a five-wicket burst which turned the CB40 final against Somerset. He was unfortunate to miss out on the man of the match award to Ian Bell whose brilliant century rounded off a consistent if injury-interrupted season in one-day cricket.

Bell also had the honour of captaining Warwickshire in their last three CB40 matches, leading them for the first time in their winner-takes-all group match against Nottinghamshire. He replaced Westwood, who struggled for runs in one-day cricket and who also stood down from the t20 side to allow Troughton to captain and to improve the balance of the side.

There were reminders of Rikki Clarke's potential with a superb century in a defeat at Headingley and his maiden five-wicket haul in the win at Canterbury. But little was seen of Naqqash Tahir who played only three early season matches before succumbing to an ankle injury.

The second team, coached by Dougie Brown, were beaten finalists in the Second XI Championship but the back-up batsmen also struggled for runs and failed to

press for first-team places. But Richard Johnson, a highly regarded wicketkeeper, showed glimpses of promise when Giles lost patience with Ambrose who was twice dropped from the side with a batting average of barely 13, a sad fall from grace for the former England wicketkeeper.

Giles summed up his side's season succinctly, 'We are thrilled that we won a one-day trophy but we know that our batting in the Championship wasn't good enough and that is an area we are looking to improve. But what pleased me is that we won our last three Championship games largely because we wanted to win more than the opposition. That shows the character and spirit of the side.

'When we lost in two days at Trent Bridge it was the lowest point of the season and I wasn't sure which way we would go, but I was delighted with the way we responded.'

PLAYER OF THE SEASON

Neil Carter for his efforts in the County Championship with 617 runs and 51 wickets. The Professional Cricketers' Association Player of the Year Award was a deserved accolade.

YOUNG PLAYER OF THE SEASON

Chris Woakes, an England Lions seamer, who took 50 wickets for the first time in a season and also contributed valuable lower-order runs.

A YEAR TO REMEMBER

- Rikki Clarke, who took a maiden five-wicket haul against Kent at Canterbury
- Imran Tahir, the leg-spinner, who enjoyed his most productive Championship season
- Richard Johnson – it was a breakthrough season for the 22-year-old wicketkeeper

A YEAR TO FORGET

- Jim Troughton scored just one Championship fifty in 30 innings
- Tim Ambrose was dropped by the county barely a year after he lost his England place
- Naqaash Tahir who topped the bowling averages in 2009 but was injured for most of 2010

Above Warwickshire's leading run-scorer, Ian Westwood, played a series of important innings for the county but failed to make even a single Championship century.

Opposite page Ian Bell leads the celebrations as Warwickshire receive the Clydesdale Bank 40 trophy at Lord's in September.

WARWICKSHIRE CCC

FIRST-CLASS MATCHES
BATTING

Match	Imran Tahir	JO Troughton	IJ Westwood	R Clarke	DL Maddy	CR Woakes	TR Ambrose	NM Carter	V Chopra	WB Rankin	AG Botha	AS Miller	IR Bell	IJL Trott	RM Johnson	KHD Barker	A Javid	NS Tahir	SA Piolet	JE Ord	LJ Evans	Extras	Total	Wickets	Result	Points
v. Yorkshire (Edgbaston) 9-12 April	12	39	39			9	5	41	4			0*	31	7				23				7	217	10		
	3	78	0			2	0	9	45			11*	54	88				34				23	347	10	L	4
v. Lancashire (Old Trafford) 15-18 April	8*	44	15	43		29	9	19	1				47	0			4					35	254	10		
	36	39	82*	7		0	0	0	6				9	6			0					12	197	10	L	5
v. Hampshire (Edgbaston) 27-30 April	40	13	0	1	22	136*	54	62			13		17	0								24	382	10		
	-	-	21*	-	24	-	-	24			-		10*									1	80	2	W	23
v. Kent (Canterbury) 4-7 May	17*	1	18	8	39	11	14	43					10	67			8					14	250	10		
	0	24	68	4	3	11	14	37*					94	66			0					6	327	10	W	21
v. Lancashire (Edgbaston) 17-20 May	9	4	1	0	5		2	69*	5			0	5	6								7	113	10		
	4	41	13	42	11		22	73	0*			0	0	150								19	375	10	L	3
v. Somerset (Taunton) 24-26 May	0	22	4	7	13	28	0		45	1	4	1*										2	127	10		
	28	6	1	17	61	10	8		31	12	9	2*										22	207	10	L	3
v. Durham (Edgbaston) 29 May-1 June	0	1	16	5	0	5			1		20	35			9	0*						8	100	10		
	-	9	86*	66	16				6		-	-			20*	-						26	229	4	D	6
v. Somerset (Edgbaston) 4-6 June	0	27	2	17	3	21			27	1	19	2*			12							9	140	10		
	2	7	22	1	3	21			46	0*	0	3			10							15	130	10	L	3
v. Durham (Chester-le-Street) 28 June-1 July	10	44	11	68	8		31	2		10*	19	2					6					13	224	10		
	0	43	0	8*	6		0	3		0	33	4					30					7	134	10	L	4
v. Yorkshire (Headingley) 5-8 July	1	22	66	46*	35		30	15		0	19					1		6				12	253	10		
	41	17	42	127*	16		16	21		0	24					48		4				15	371	10	L	4
v. Nottinghamshire (Edgbaston) 20-22 July	29	25	17	27	21	13	34	99*		5	1				21							21	313	10		
	17	9	0	0	8	0	22	27		8*	4				4							1	100	10	L	6
v. Essex (Southend-on-Sea) 4-6 August	13	10	7	36	39	1	6	13		1*						22			1			6	155	10		
	-	18*	61	22*	39		-	-		-						-			6			9	155	3	W	19
v. Nottinghamshire (Trent Bridge) 16-17 August	1	0	19	15	8	19*	0		15	13						4	5					22	121	10		
	11	13	14	4	11	20	0		54	0*						10	1					14	152	10	L	3
v. Essex (Edgbaston) 25-28 August	4	5	4	24	7	0		28	14	7*					39		0					23	155	10		
	-	4	40	16*	50*	-		-	36						-		-					9	155	3	W	19
v. Kent (Edgbaston) 31 August-2 September	69*	9	14	10	11	30		6	24		76				18					15		12	294	10		
	9*	9	7	0	0	51		26	9		7				10					3		9	140	10	W	21
v. Hampshire (Rose Bowl) 13-16 September	20	2	9	52	40	14*			27			5	104	0	21							9	303	10		
	-	-	27*	-	-	-			18*			-	104	-	-							6	51	0	W	22
Matches	16	16	16	15	14	13	11	11	9	9	8	7	6	6	5	4	4	3	1	1	1					
Innings	27	30	32	28	27	21	20	20	18	16	14	12	11	11	8	5	7	6	2	2	2					
Not Out	0	3	5	3	3	3	4	2	3	1	1	2	1	2	0	0	2	2	0	0	0					
Highest Score	69*	78	86*	127*	61	136*	54	99*	54	13	76	35	104	150	39	22	48	34	6	6	15					
Runs	384	585	726	673	499	431	267	617	409	63	248	65	381	415	118	57	91	69	10	7	18					
Average	16.69	20.17	25.92	29.26	19.19	23.94	13.35	36.29	24.05	7.00	17.71	9.28	38.10	37.72	16.85	14.25	13.00	11.50	5.00	3.50	9.00					
100s	0	0	0	1	0	1	0	0	0	0	0	0	1	1	0	0	0	0	0	0	0					
50s	1	1	5	3	2	1	1	4	1	0	1	0	2	3	0	0	0	0	0	0	0					
Catches/Stumpings	4/0	5/0	6/0	23/0	16/0	6/0	33/3	0/0	9/0	3/0	7/0	4/0	10/0	10/0	12/2	1/0	3/0	2/0	2/0	1/0	1/0					

Home Ground: Edgbaston
Address: County Ground, Edgbaston, Birmingham, B5 7QU
Tel: 0870 0621902
Fax: 0121 4464544
Email: info@edgbaston.com
Directions: *By rail:* New Street station, Birmingham.
By road: M6 to A38(M) to city centre, then follow signs to County Ground.
Capacity: 21,000

Other grounds used: Stratford upon Avon
Year formed: 1882

Chief Executive: Colin Povey
Director of Coaching: Ashley Giles
Captain: Ian Westwood
County colours: Blue and yellow

Honours
County Championship
1911, 1951, 1972, 1994, 1995, 2004
Sunday League/NCL/Pro40/CB40
1980, 1994, 1997, 2010
Benson & Hedges Cup
1994, 2002
Gillette Cup/NatWest/C&G Trophy
1989, 1993, 1995

Website:
www.thebears.co.uk

FIRST-CLASS MATCHES

BOWLING

	Imran Tahir	CR Woakes	NM Carter	R Clarke	WB Rankin	DL Maddy	AS Miller	NS Tahir	IJL Trott	AG Botha	KHD Barker	SA Piolet	Overs	Total	Byes/Leg-byes	Wickets	Run outs
v. Yorkshire (Edgbaston) 9-12 April	28.2-6-67-3 / 26-1-81-2	22-10-43-2 / 15-5-57-0	18-9-37-2 / 13.5-3-50-3				19-6-57-0 / 10-1-48-0	19-5-49-2 / 14-2-31-1	2-1-4-1 / 1-0-12-0				108.2 / 79.5	274 / 291	17 / 12	10 / 6	
v. Lancashire (Old Trafford) 15-18 April	23-4-66-1 / 25.5-2-95-2	20-7-44-3 / 25-7-73-2	19.4-2-64-3 / 26-10-79-5					16-4-57-1 / 14-2-45-1	7-2-20-2 / 1-0-6-0				85.4 / 91.5	253 / 319	2 / 21	10 / 10	
v. Hampshire (Edgbaston) 27-30 April	8-0-23-2 / 7-1-8-1	16.5-4-60-2 / 26-7-75-4	23-6-59-4 / 23.3-2-71-5	6-0-32-0		17-3-53-1 / 4-1-20-0			8-1-29-1	2-0-13-0			80.5 / 60.3	283 / 176	14 / 2	10 / 10	
v. Kent (Canterbury) 4-7 May	19-3-55-2 / 16-5-27-4	25-4-82-1 / 18.3-3-43-3	20-2-76-0 / 7-1-22-0	15.3-1-63-6 / 9-0-28-1		13-5-22-1 / 6-1-20-2		17-2-45-0 / 3-0-11-0					109.3 / 59.3	377 / 156	34 / 5	10 / 10	
v. Lancashire (Edgbaston) 17-20 May	33-7-93-3 / 4-0-25-0		20.5-5-60-1 / 8-0-20-1	8-0-26-0 / 9.2-0-28-2	18-1-90-2 / 5-1-28-0	7-3-19-1 / 13-5-25-2	16-5-45-3 / 14-2-58-5						102.5 / 53.2	354 / 199	21 / 15	10 / 10	
v. Somerset (Taunton) 24-26 May	16-0-70-1 / 5-0-27-1	22-3-63-0		9-2-22-1	9-1-27-1	14-3-24-2	22-8-72-5 / 4-3-8-0			2-1-2-0 / 1.4-0-10-0			94 / 10.4	290 / 45	10 / 0	10 / 1	
v. Durham (Edgbaston) 29 May-1 June	30.3-5-114-8	20-5-39-1		8-2-31-0			2.5-1-8-0	17-7-39-0		19-4-49-1	13-2-68-0		110.2 / -	379 / -	31	10	
v. Somerset (Edgbaston) 4-6 June	19-2-54-1 / 17.4-2-58-6	15.5-5-44-3 / 10-2-37-2		12-4-35-3	9-3-33-0 / 2-0-15-0	10-5-12-0	12-5-24-0 / 7-0-23-1			13-5-50-3 / 3-0-14-0			90.5 / 46.4	268 / 183	16 / 8	10 / 10	
v. Durham (Chester-le-Street) 28 June-1 July	19-3-57-2 / 24.1-1-69-6		15-1-36-3 / 18-3-62-1	12-0-51-2 / 10-0-43-1	10-2-44-1 / 19-2-58-2	13-3-35-1 / 3-0-23-0	14.4-0-55-1 / 4-2-18-0						83.4 / 78.1	288 / 289	10 / 16	10 / 10	
v. Yorkshire (Headingley) 5-8 July	21.5-3-73-1 / 11.4-2-71-1		30-7-87-4 / 5-0-29-0	24-8-63-2	20-4-73-1 / 8-1-33-2	10-4-18-0 / 7-0-38-0				4-0-15-0 / 1-0-7-0		15-3-67-1 / 2-0-13-0	124.5 / 34.4	425 / 200	29 / 9	10 / 4	1 / 1
v. Nottinghamshire (Edgbaston) 20-22 July	26-5-79-1	18-5-59-2 / 2-0-15-0	27.4-3-116-5 / 1-0-10-0	7-0-25-0		10-2-49-2	12-4-22-0			5-1-15-0			105.4 / 3	389 / 25	24 / 0	10 / 0	
v. Essex (Southend-on-Sea) 4-6 August	8.4-3-20-4	13-2-39-2 / 15-5-36-1	15-3-48-3 / 10.2-4-18-2	9.3-2-27-4 / 12-2-27-1	7-0-22-1 / 7-1-32-2	6-2-9-0					6.4-1-10-0		44.3 / 65.4	150 / 159	14 / 7	10 / 10	
v. Nottinghamshire (Trent Bridge) 16-17 August	18-1-55-1	18-4-59-3		11-1-53-1	14.5-0-66-3	17-3-52-2					9-1-35-0		87.5 / -	328 / -	8	10	
v. Essex (Edgbaston) 25-28 August	1-0-7-0	14-6-37-3 / 16-2-69-3	7-2-25-0 / 16.2-2-54-1	5-1-24-1 / 13-5-20-3	5.4-1-16-5 / 1-0-8-0		4-2-7-1 / 10-4-24-2						35.4 / 57.2	114 / 193	5 / 11	10 / 10	1
v. Kent (Edgbaston) 31 August-2 September	2-1-5-0 / 10-0-41-0	14-3-52-6 / 15-3-45-5	15-3-46-3 / 16.1-2-60-5	0.3-0-4-1 / 6-0-30-0			13-3-39-0						31.3 / 60.1	111 / 228	4 / 13	10 / 10	
v. Hampshire (Rose Bowl) 13-16 September	4-0-15-1 / 6-1-21-2	20-3-60-1 / 15.1-5-34-5		15-2-47-2 / 4-0-36-0			18-8-37-4 / 7-2-16-2	9-3-21-0 / 6-0-20-1				7.3-0-22-2	73.3 / 38.1	218 / 132	16 / 5	10 / 10	
Overs	430.4	396.2	356.2	212.5	145.3	206.5	154.4	83	19	50.4	36.1	17					
Maidens	58	100	70	31	19	62	42	15	4	11	4	3					
Runs	1376	1165	1129	743	594	523	488	238	71	175	135	80					
Wickets	56	54	51	32	22	21	16	5	4	4	2	1					
Average	24.57	21.57	22.14	23.22	27.00	24.90	30.50	47.60	17.75	43.75	67.50	80.00					

FIELDING

- 36 TR Ambrose (33 ct, 3 st)
- 23 R Clarke
- 16 DL Maddy
- 14 RM Johnson (12 ct, 2 st)
- 10 IR Bell
- 10 IJL Trott
- 9 V Chopra
- 7 AG Botha
- 6 IJ Westwood
- 6 CR Woakes
- 5 JO Troughton
- 4 Imran Tahir
- 4 AS Miller
- 3 A Javid
- 3 WB Rankin
- 2 SA Piolet
- 2 NS Tahir
- 1 KHD Barker
- 1 LJ Evans
- 1 JE Ord

Division One – Final Table

	P	W	L	D	Bat	Bowl	Pens	Pts
Nottinghamshire	16	7	5	4	47	43	0	214
Somerset	16	6	2	8	53	41	0	214
Yorkshire	16	6	2	8	41	42	0	203
Lancashire	16	5	3	8	35	43	0	182
Durham	16	5	3	8	30	39	0	173
Warwickshire	16	6	9	1	20	47	0	166
Hampshire	16	3	6	7	47	41	0	157
Kent	16	3	7	6	42	44	-1	151
Essex	16	2	6	8	29	43	-2	126

CB40   FPt20

Limited overs nickname:
THE BEARS

WORCESTERSHIRE

by Paul Bolton

Worcestershire defied the sceptics, including the bookmakers, by winning a swift return to the County Championship first division.

They were favourites for the wooden spoon in April after they were relegated without winning a game and suffered an exodus of senior players, including four with international experience in Kabir Ali, Steve Davies, Gareth Batty and Simon Jones. Director of cricket Steve Rhodes was also forced to slash £300,000 from his playing budget because of serious cash-flow problems at New Road, which appeared another cause for pessimism. But Rhodes's small squad demonstrated tremendous character and spirit to pip Glamorgan to the second promotion place by staging a thrilling last-day run chase against already-crowned second division champions Sussex at New Road.

Like neighbours Warwickshire, Worcestershire were a transformed side in the final five weeks of the season with the resignation of Vikram Solanki after six seasons

Giving up the captaincy has taken the pressure off Vikram Solanki, allowing him to enjoy his cricket more and to rediscover his batting form.

Daryl Mitchell has risen through the ranks at New Road – from schoolboy to county captain.

Mitchell Relishing Captaincy Role

Daryl Mitchell was an immediate success as Worcestershire captain, leading them to promotion and to a run of victories in the Clydesdale Bank 40 after his appointment in mid-August. The 26-year-old batsman took charge of his native county after Vikram Solanki stepped down. Mitchell's appointment came after he replaced Gareth Batty as vice-captain at the start of the season and his impressive start to captaincy soon led to him being confirmed in the job for the 2011 season.

'I've played for Worcestershire from the age of 11, right through the academy system, through the second team and into the firsts,' said Mitchell. 'Captaining the side wasn't something I thought about seriously until Vikram asked me to be his vice-captain.

'When Vikram resigned I had a range of emotions. It was a very sad day because Vikram was the only captain I have played under at Worcestershire and I worked very closely with him as vice-captain. Like everyone in the dressing room at Colwyn Bay, at the end of our Championship game against Glamorgan, it came as a bit of a shock when Vikram came in and told us that he was resigning. But it was a great honour to be asked to captain the side and to know that the powers-that-be at the club thought that I could do the job.'

Mitchell, who was educated at Worcester University on a scholarship that allowed him to continue playing cricket when a student, also enjoyed a successful 2010 season with the bat.

by Paul Bolton

Alan Richardson had a fine first season at Worcestershire, showing a tremendous work ethic and taking 55 Championship wickets.

Zimbabwean, was playing club cricket in Perth when he was spotted by Worcestershire's bowling coach Matt Mason. Rhodes took a punt and Cameron, an aggressive left-hander, responded with 576 Championship runs including a maiden century in the Sussex run chase.

Moeen Ali and Alexei Kervezee showed consistency and maturity to reach 1,000 first-class runs for the first time and Shakib Al Hasan proved an inspired choice as overseas player. The all-rounder was the first Bangladeshi to play county cricket and he improved the future employment prospects for his compatriots by taking 35 wickets in eight matches including a match-winning 7 for 32 against Middlesex at Lord's, the best figures by a Worcestershire spinner since 1974.

There were useful middle-order runs from Gareth Andrew, who impressed more as a hard-hitting left-hander than a right arm seamer.

in charge as captain. Solanki stepped down to concentrate on his batting after a season of moderate form, which meant that the inexperienced Daryl Mitchell was promoted from vice-captain.

Mitchell showed an immediate aptitude for captaincy and Worcestershire won seven of their nine matches under him, including four consecutive Clydesdale Bank 40 matches, a competition in which they had previously floundered. 'Daryl managed to get a different tune out of the boys,' Rhodes said.

Mitchell had some raw material to work with, very raw in some cases. James Cameron, an English-qualified

Sussex made an approach but Andrew opted to stay at New Road. Matt Mason's season was blighted by injuries but Alan Richardson, who arrived from Middlesex with a dodgy fitness record, proved a revelation in his first season with his fourth county by taking 55 wickets in 14 matches. 'He is a great role model for the younger bowlers to follow and he has been unbelievably professional in the way he has gone about his business,' Rhodes said.

Opposite Moeen Ali scores six more – v. Surrey – on his way to a best ever 1,260 Championship runs.

Rhodes made Richardson his player of the year but Worcestershire's success was based on a strong team ethic and spirit. 'At the start of the season, everyone was tipping us to finish bottom,' Rhodes said. 'So this was a great effort and I'm very proud of them. A good spirit in the dressing room is massive. It's your 12th man. Now we have lads who enjoy each other's company and enjoy playing together.'

As Worcestershire know from painful experience, winning promotion is one thing but staying in the top flight is a different matter altogether. Three times before they have been promoted but spent only one season in Division One. Financial constraints mean that Rhodes is unlikely to be allowed to bring in reinforce-ments and avoiding relegation will be the sole concern in 2011.

Improving their one-day and t20 form will also be a priority. Until Mitchell took the reins Worcestershire had not won a CB40 match, with a humiliating defeat by the Unicorns part-timers at Kidderminster the low point. They have yet to successfully master Twenty20 cricket and finished bottom of the Friends Provident

Cash Boost Follows Hotel All-Clear
by Paul Bolton

Worcestershire have cleared a major hurdle in their attempt to build a hotel at New Road. The club reached an agreement with the Chapter and Dean of Worcester Cathedral to lift a covenant on the land on the River Severn side of the ground which has cleared the way for work to commence. The county hopes to start work on the hotel, which will be a Premier Inn, on 11 January 2011, and Worcestershire will receive £1 million in staged payments when the work begins. That should help ease their cash flow difficulties after another difficult financial year.

Worcestershire reported only a slight increase in revenue – £15,841 – from their Friends Provident t20 programme this year despite staging three additional home games. Indifferent weather, clashes with the football World Cup and Worcestershire's own poor form in the competition produced an aggregate t20 attendance of 18,259 in eight matches compared with 16,319 from five games in 2009.

Andrew Rejects Sussex to Stay at New Road
by Paul Bolton

Worcestershire beat off competition from Sussex to retain the services of all-rounder Gareth Andrew. Andrew, 26, joined Worcestershire from Somerset three years ago and his aggressive lower-order batting attracted the interest of Division Two champions Sussex, who made a 28-day approach for him. But Andrew has now decided to commit himself to Worcestershire by signing a new contract, which will keep him at New Road until the end of the 2012 season.

'Gareth showed what he can achieve with his excellent 60-ball century against Surrey in the Clydesdale Bank 40 league and with some further progression with the ball he has the potential to be a quality all-rounder,' said Worcestershire's director of cricket Steve Rhodes.

Worcestershire have also secured the services of seamer Chris Russell on a two-year contract. The 21-year-old, who hails from the Isle of Wight, was introduced to first-team cricket in August when he made his debut in the CB40 victory over the Unicorns at New Road. He also played in the floodlit CB40 match against Surrey at The Oval when Worcestershire's crushing victory was rather overshadowed by the debut of England batsman Kevin Pietersen at the start of his loan spell with the Lions.

Gareth Andrew clubs another boundary during his quick-fire century in the Clydesdale Bank 40 match against Surrey at The Oval.

Namibian-born Dutchman, Alexei Kervezee, is developing into a fine strokemaker, dependable and able to score runs quickly when required.

t20 North Group with just five wins and some depressingly mediocre performances. The crowds also stayed away, a clash with football's World Cup not helping to make the competition any more attractive to prospective spectators and putting further pressure on the finances.

There was better off-the-field news as the season closed, however, as Worcestershire managed to secure agreement for a new hotel complex to be built on the River Severn side of New Road. Work on the hotel was due to start early in 2011, providing a valuable new source of revenue for a club that has struggled to stay afloat since the calamitous floods of 2007 and 2008.

Mark Newton, the chief executive during those dark days, departed the county at the end of the season after nine years in office. David Leatherdale, the popular former county all-rounder, was promoted to replace Newton, coupling his new responsibilities to those of his existing job as commercial director.

PLAYER OF THE SEASON

Alan Richardson. The season saw outstanding effort from the veteran seamer who stayed fit, passed 50 first-class wickets and proved a perfect role model for the youngsters.

YOUNG PLAYER OF THE SEASON

Moeen Ali was the leading run-scorer and is starting to add maturity and judgment to his undoubted talent.

A YEAR TO REMEMBER

- Daryl Mitchell took to the captaincy and continued to be a solid contributor at the top of the order
- Shakib Al Hasan – important runs and wickets for the Bangladeshi pioneer
- James Cameron was signed from grade cricket in Perth but adapted quickly to county cricket

A YEAR TO FORGET

- Imran Arif took five wickets on his debut in 2008 but failed to follow it up and was released after a poor campaign
- Chris Whelan turned an ankle in the opening match against Middlesex and missed the rest of the Championship campaign
- Phil Jaques the former Australian opener got six ducks in 15 innings

WORCESTERSHIRE CCC

FIRST-CLASS MATCHES
BATTING

	AN Kervezee	DKH Mitchell	MM Ali	VS Solanki	A Richardson	RA Jones	JD Shantry	JG Cameron	GM Andrew	OB Cox	PA Jaques	BF Smith	MS Mason	Shakib Al Hasan	BJM Scott	DA Wheeldon	Imran Arif	CD Whelan	SH Choudhry	Extras	Total	Wickets	Result	Points
v. Middlesex	44	85	7	8	1*	16			0		47	46			0			5		28	287	10		
(Worcester) 9-11 April	43	1	0	5	4*	3			12		41	2			3			0		5	119	10	W	21
v. Surrey	68	0	126	114	2	3*	0				0	80			55	0				17	465	10		
(Croydon) 21-24 April	14	5	70*	44	0*	0	0				0	10			19	-				8	170	8	D	9
v. Glamorgan	6	5	85*	1	2	3	0				0	15			5		4			8	134	10		
(Worcester) 27-28 April	27	19	58	18	0	3	0				25	6			1		4*			10	171	10	L	3
v. Leicestershire	32	56	80	9	6	21*	7		53		0	8			5					31	308	10		
(Leicester) 4-7 May	99	23	42	5	10*	0	8		1		0	51*			16					22	277	9	W	22
v. Derbyshire	130	148		42		0	-	25	33		92	14			40*					35	559	8		
(Worcester) 17-20 May	4*	5		18*	-	-	-	-	-		94	-			-					5	126	2	W	24
v. Sussex	50	9	22	70	0*	5			21		80	17			98				63	29	464	10		
(Hove) 24-27 May	15	15	21	61	-	11			-		40	7*			4*				-	31	205	6	D	10
v. Gloucestershire	57	29	106	27	5	1	13*				38	3	27		67					15	388	10		
(Worcester) 29 May-1 June																							D	10
v. Leicestershire	1	0	33			0	1	15	53*	42	8	14	1							7	175	10		
(Worcester) 28-30 June	8	77	24			4	5*	75	79	22	0	9	3							9	315	10	L	3
v. Derbyshire	8	14	2	22	0*	3		89		17			1	90		20				13	279	10		
(Derby) 21-24 July	155	71	29	3	-	-		9*		6*				21		14				20	328	6	D	10
v. Northamptonshire	28	23	0	17	11	8		7		59			51*	9		50				24	287	10		
(Worcester) 29-31 July	24	7	9	0	0*	7		7		0			8	0		14				17	93	10	L	5
v. Gloucestershire	8	104	59	9	4*		6	26		4			1	19		16				22	278	10		
(Cheltenham) 4-7 August	17*	134*	94	64			-	-		-			-	10		2				18	339	4	W	19
v. Glamorgan	72	165*	10	9	-	12		0		2			25*	47	0					8	350	8		
(Colwyn Bay) 9-12 August	45	45	0	10	1*	0		12		1			3	25	26					7	175	10	L	7
v. Surrey	0	5	13	37			4*	95	24	18			4	18		65				25	308	10		
(Worcester) 16-19 August	144	16	22	0			1*	17	34	13			8	34		7				23	319	10	W	22
v. Northamptonshire	-	31*	-	-	-		-	-		-				-			12*			2	45	0		
(Northampton) 25-28 August	52	3	62	27	-		-	0		10*				9*			7			12	182	6	D	5
v. Middlesex	5	47	66	39	11		10*	28	36	4				34		14				19	313	10		
(Lord's) 7-10 September	0	19	81	2	10*		0	17	73	0				10		22				22	256	10	W	21
v. Sussex	10	3	24	52	4*		0	49	5	18*			5	18						13	201	9		
(Worcester) 13-16 September	24*	16	115	4			-	105	1	2*			-	14						25	306	6	W	20
Matches	16	16	15	15	14	11	11	10	9	9	8	8	8	8	7	7	2	1	1					
Innings	30	31	28	28	18	19	15	17	14	16	15	14	12	15	12	14	3	2	1					
Not Out	3	3	2	1	11	2	5	1	1	4	0	2	2	1	2	1	1	0	0					
Highest Score	155	165*	126	114	11	21*	13*	105	79	59	94	80	51*	90	98	65	4*	5	63					
Runs	1190	1180	1260	717	71	100	55	576	425	218	465	282	137	358	313	269	8	5	63					
Average	44.07	42.14	48.46	26.55	10.14	5.88	5.50	36.00	32.69	18.16	31.00	23.50	13.70	25.57	31.30	20.69	4.00	2.50	63.00					
100s	3	4	3	1	0	0	0	1	0	0	0	0	0	0	0	0	0	0	0					
50s	6	4	9	4	0	0	0	3	4	1	3	2	1	1	3	2	0	0	1					
Catches/Stumpings	14/0	32/0	9/0	18/0	5/0	7/0	3/0	7/0	2/0	18/1	9/0	9/0	6/0	3/0	30/1	2/0	1/0	1/0	1/0					

Home Ground: New Road, Worcester
Address: County Ground, New Road, Worcester, WR2 4QQ
Tel: 01905 748474
Fax: 01905 748005
Email: admin@wccc.co.uk
Directions: From the M5 junction 7, follow the brown 'broken stumps' logos to WCCC.
Capacity: 4,500

Other grounds used: Kidderminster, RGS Worcester
Year formed: 1865

Chief Executive: Mark Newton
Director of Cricket: Steve Rhodes
Captain: Vikram Solanki, Daryl Mitchell
County colours: Green, black and white

Honours
County Championship
1964, 1965, 1974, 1988, 1989
Sunday League/NCL/Pro40
1971, 1987, 1988, 2007
Benson & Hedges Cup
1991
Gillette Cup/NatWest/C&G Trophy
1994

Website:
www.wccc.co.uk

FIRST-CLASS MATCHES
BOWLING

	A Richardson	RA Jones	Shakib Al Hasan	MS Mason	JD Shantry	GM Andrew	MM Ali	JG Cameron	Imran Arif	SH Choudhry	CD Whelan	VS Solanki	AN Kervezee	DKH Mitchell	Overs	Total	Byes/Leg-byes	Wickets	Run outs
v. Middlesex	20-7-41-2	17.2-5-37-6			8-2-21-0						4-0-21-1				49.2	126	6	10	1
(Worcester) 9-11 April	19-9-35-4	15-1-68-2			13.3-1-40-3						5-1-13-0			2-0-7-0	54.3	169	6	10	1
v. Surrey	27-9-69-1	22-5-119-2			27-2-98-2		24-3-107-2		14-2-63-2					3-1-13-0	117	493	24	10	1
(Croydon) 21-24 April	13-2-48-1	3-1-18-0			20.3-7-52-2		24-5-59-2		3-0-17-1			5-0-22-1			68.3	239	23	8	1
v. Glamorgan	26.2-10-86-5	17-2-82-1			12-2-48-3				12-0-44-1						67.2	267	7	10	
(Worcester) 27-28 April					3.4-0-24-1				4-0-17-0						7.4	41	0	10	
v. Leicestershire	21-10-45-2	18-3-49-3				22.1-9-49-5	9-0-32-0								70.1	181	6	10	
(Leicester) 4-7 May	25-9-44-5	18-4-70-2				17-3-62-1	16-6-35-1	2-1-1-0						1-0-3-0	79	231	16	9	
v. Derbyshire	27-6-72-4	28-9-93-3				18-4-51-1	12.3-1-57-2					1-0-10-0			86.3	295	12	10	
(Worcester) 17-20 May	31-9-82-2	22-2-108-3				19-4-57-2	19-0-61-3	12-1-29-0				18-3-40-0			121	389	12	10	
v. Sussex	22-5-80-1	26-3-115-7					16-1-42-1	8-0-40-0		10-3-32-1					82	328	19	10	
(Hove) 24-27 May															-	-	-	-	
v. Gloucestershire	21-3-58-2	17-3-69-2		17-7-42-2	14.4-4-48-2		8-2-20-2								77.4	245	8	10	
(Worcester) 29 May-1 June	28-8-68-4	11-1-54-0		19-4-53-1	20-7-39-2		5-1-11-0								83	243	18	7	
v. Leicestershire		19-0-96-2		25-9-56-3	11-0-42-1		19.2-4-68-3	5-1-25-1							79.2	309	22	10	
(Worcester) 28-30 June		4-1-26-0		14-4-52-0	10-3-35-1		10-3-24-2	6-2-20-0	1.5-0-10-0						45.5	182	15	3	
v. Derbyshire	30-7-64-1	24-4-83-3	37.5-9-94-3		29-8-80-2			16-3-43-1							135.5	405	41	10	
(Derby) 21-24 July															-	-	-	-	
v. Northamptonshire	20.4-12-28-3	11-2-36-0	3-0-15-0	20-9-34-3						6-1-18-2					60.4	158	27	10	2
(Worcester) 29-31 July	17-3-50-1	6-1-33-0	10-2-35-0	15-4-62-1					3-0-12-1	7-0-25-1					58	226	9	6	2
v. Gloucestershire	29-6-89-0		25-2-85-2	32-3-92-4	13-1-65-1		26.1-5-83-1	8-0-37-0							133.1	480	29	10	2
(Cheltenham) 4-7 August	15-0-57-4		12.4-3-23-5	5-1-12-1	2-0-13-0		5-0-22-0								39.4	136	9	10	
v. Glamorgan	27-12-59-2	18-1-105-2	23.4-9-38-3	29-9-82-2			7-1-36-0		5-1-27-1						109.4	369	22	10	
(Colwyn Bay) 9-12 August	4-0-17-0	3-0-20-0	31-3-147-3	20-4-87-4			7-0-42-1		11-1-50-0					7-1-28-0	83	397	6	8	
v. Surrey			20-4-60-2	23-5-60-3	20-7-57-1		11-4-38-1	2-1-4-0							90	259	10	10	1
(Worcester) 16-19 August			11.4-0-42-6	12-0-60-3	5-1-16-0		5-1-10-1	14-6-30-2							33.4	130	2	10	
v. Northamptonshire	29-7-83-4		29-9-75-3		26-7-61-1		16-3-57-1	14-3-38-0	14-2-58-0			4-1-5-0			132	385	8	9	
(Northampton) 25-28 August															-	-	-	-	
v. Middlesex	19-3-68-0		35-2-112-1		25-7-58-1		14-0-63-0	10.3-0-36-5	10-3-29-1					1-1-0-0	114.3	392	26	10	2
(Lord's) 7-10 September	13-3-20-2		11.1-3-32-7		4-1-11-0			3-1-3-1							31.1	66	0	10	
v. Sussex	27-7-47-3		5-2-13-0	17-5-63-2	14-4-37-0		16.2-4-45-4	4-0-24-0	4-2-18-1			1-0-19-0			83.2	237	14	10	
(Worcester) 13-16 September	13-6-32-2		4-0-12-0	1-0-14-0	4-0-22-0		11-2-63-1		1-0-1-0				4.3-0-63-0	1-0-13-0	44.3	264	1	4	1

	A Richardson	RA Jones	Shakib Al Hasan	MS Mason	JD Shantry	GM Andrew	MM Ali	JG Cameron	Imran Arif	SH Choudhry	CD Whelan	VS Solanki	AN Kervezee	DKH Mitchell
Overs	524	298.2	259	278	308	196.4	179.4	93.5	33	10	9	29	4.3	15
Maidens	153	48	48	72	73	32	29	17	2	3	1	4	0	3
Runs	1342	1281	783	849	945	656	626	332	141	32	34	96	63	64
Wickets	55	38	35	31	27	23	17	8	4	1	1	1	0	0
Average	24.40	33.71	22.37	27.39	35.00	28.52	36.82	41.50	35.25	32.00	34.00	96.00	-	-

FIELDING

32	DKH Mitchell
31	BJM Scott (30 ct, 1 st)
19	OB Cox (18 ct, 1 st)
18	VS Solanki
14	AN Kervezee
9	MM Ali
9	PA Jaques
9	BF Smith
7	JG Cameron
7	RA Jones
6	MS Mason
5	A Richardson
3	Shakib Al Hasan
3	JD Shantry
2	GM Andrew
2	DA Wheeldon
1	SH Choudhry
1	Imran Arif
1	CD Whelan

Division Two – Final Table

	P	W	L	D	Bat	Bowl	Pens	Pts
Sussex	16	8	3	5	45	47	0	235
Worcestershire	16	7	4	5	39	42	0	208
Glamorgan	16	7	4	5	33	43	0	203
Leicestershire	16	7	5	4	31	44	0	199
Gloucestershire	16	6	9	1	28	47	-2	172
Northamptonshire	16	6	7	3	28	34	0	167
Surrey	16	4	6	6	43	36	-2	159
Middlesex	16	4	7	5	37	41	-2	155
Derbyshire	16	3	7	6	30	42	0	138

CB40　　FPt20

Limited overs nickname:
WORCESTERSHIRE ROYALS

YORKSHIRE

by Tim Wellock

It was predicted in these pages last year that Yorkshire would be title contenders in 2010 and, despite being the book-makers' favourites for relegation, they would actually have been champions but for 45 minutes of madness on the final day of the season.

In 55 balls they squandered all the hard work of the previous five months as they lost nine wickets for 37 runs and left Kent with a victory target of 90. The visitors lost six wickets, indicating that an extra 50 runs may well have been beyond them.

Victory would have given Yorkshire a title for which they will be well placed to challenge for the next few years, quite possibly with a fully home-grown team. The return of Ryan Sidebottom should negate the need to risk a repeat of the setbacks suffered in trying to sign an overseas paceman, while the departure of Jacques Rudolph need not be a disaster if other young batsmen, such as Joe Root, emerge in the slipstream of Adam Lyth, Jonnie Bairstow and the captain, Andrew Gale.

The success of those with an Asian background also bodes well. Adil Rashid had a superb season with bat and ball, Ajmal Shahzad shot to prominence and 18-year-old seamer Moin Ashraf took nine wickets at 11.77 in the last two games. The only blot came from Azeem Rafiq's foul-mouthed Twittering, which earned him a suspension. Assuming Rafiq is unharmed by the

The imposing new pavilion at Headingley – venue for the second Test between Pakistan and Australia in July.

Right Left-hander Adam Lyth's promotion to opener saw him reveling in his new found responsibility, and scoring over 1,500 Championship runs.

Bottom right Oliver Hannon-Dalby burst onto the scene in 2010 with five wickets in each of the county's first two matches, against Warwickshire and Somerset.

incident and David Wainwright regains the form that deserted him while struggling with an injury, then Yorkshire will have depth in the spin as well as seam departments.

The departure of Matthew Hoggard, the retirement of Deon Kruis and the England calls upon Tim Bresnan and Shahzad were cited as reasons why Yorkshire might be relegated. But Steve Patterson and Oliver Hannon-Dalby proved their worth. What Patterson lacks in pace he made up for in accuracy, offering the control that enabled Yorkshire to attack from the other end. He also stayed fit, being almost ever-present in all forms of the game. The 6ft 7in Hannon-Dalby burst on to the scene with five-wicket hauls in the first two games and, although his form tailed off, he played in all 16 Championship matches.

Yorkshire's initial choice as their overseas player, Australian seamer Ryan Harris, was unable to take up his contract, and then plans to bring in New Zealander Daryl Tuffey on a temporary basis also fell flat. Other than Rudolph and Twenty20 signings Herschelle Gibbs and Clint McKay, plus the sporadic appearances of the disappointing Tino Best, the only semi-regular player not born in Yorkshire was Gerard Brophy. He could not initially get into the side, but a viral infection suffered by Joe Sayers gave him the opportunity to bat at No. 6 and keep wicket instead of Bairstow.

Until Sayers fell ill there was no reason to change the side as Yorkshire won three and drew two of their first five games, being thwarted partly by the weather after amassing 610 for 6 at home to Durham. Gale was on England Lions duty when Rudolph declared on 333 for 4 in the second innings at Taunton, only to see Somerset reach their target of 364 with only four wickets down. But there was no reason to believe Gale would have been more cautious as he stressed from the outset his intention to play attacking cricket.

Still on the fringes of the England set-up, Adil Rashid was able to concentrate fully on county cricket this summer. In tremendous form with bat and ball, it seems only a matter of time before he returns to the international fold.

Anthony McGrath responded to the loss of the captaincy with some magnificent performances, perhaps his best being the century on a tricky pitch at Durham, which turned the game in Yorkshire's favour. He totalled 1,219 runs in the Championship and over 2,000 in all matches. Rudolph bettered those figures and the fact that he initially preferred the middle order opened the door for Lyth. The stroke-playing left-hander from Whitby was given the chance to open the innings with Sayers and proved a revelation as he

amassed 1,509 Championship runs at an average of 52.03.

As the son of the late David 'Bluey' Bairstow, the much-loved former captain, Jonnie is a favourite of many Yorkshire members and has inherited his dad's fighting spirit. When the going got tough, Jonnie got going, most notably when his thrilling counter-attack against Nottinghamshire won the match at Trent Bridge. His 918 runs came at an average of 41.72. At the helm of a dynamic young team, Gale's captaincy

Moxon Delighted at Sidebottom Return
by Tim Wellock

Martyn Moxon has finally got his man. During his time as Durham coach he thought he had succeeded in signing Ryan Sidebottom and he is delighted to have persuaded the 32-year-old left-arm bowler to return to Yorkshire. But when Sidebottom left Yorkshire in 2004 he preferred Nottinghamshire to Durham and was a key part of the County Championship winning sides of 2005 and 2010. The former England seamer has put the lure of his home county before the offers of bigger wages from other counties and has signed a three-year deal.

Moxon, Yorkshire's director of professional cricket, said, 'I am delighted that Ryan has chosen us ahead of many other counties. I think that proves his Yorkshire pride. He will provide us with proven consistency and wicket-taking ability and will provide Andrew Gale with a senior bowler of real quality to turn to.'

Sidebottom, who has now retired from international cricket, played 54 first-class games for Yorkshire between 1997 and 2003, capturing 163 wickets at 25.12. He left for Trent Bridge under a cloud, citing a lack of first-team opportunities and hinting at personality clashes. But the Huddersfield-born player remains a popular figure in Yorkshire, especially as his father, Arnie, also played for the county. 'Ryan is in his 30s but he's still a very good performer,' said Moxon. 'The fact that he's not going to play international cricket again is important because it means he will be available for the whole season, and he also provides variety with his left-arm pace. I've got the utmost respect and admiration for him and I know he is desperately keen to finish his career on a high.'

Sidebottom made his England Test debut in 2001 against Pakistan, but after a wicketless performance and two ODIs against Zimbabwe he seemed destined to be a one-cap wonder, like his father. But in 2007 he was recalled to England's attack and responded with eight wickets against West Indies at Headingley. He was England's Player of the Year in 2008 and played a crucial role in the 2010 World Twenty20 triumph.

Sidebottom said, 'I have enjoyed my time at Trent Bridge and with England enormously, but I'm a Yorkshire lad and the opportunity to return to Headingley to end my career was something I couldn't ignore. The Yorkshire side has some real quality and under Martyn Moxon and Andrew Gale made real strides forward. I want to give the county everything I can over the next three years and if we can reward the Yorkshire public with a trophy or two that would be fantastic.'

Having won the 2010 County Championship with Nottinghamshire, Ryan Sidebottom delighted many Yorkshire supporters by returning to Headingley for the last few years of his career.

Brophy Awarded Benefit for 2011
by Tim Wellock

Yorkshire have rewarded two of their lesser lights by awarding Gerard Brophy a benefit season in 2011 and handing Richard Pyrah a new contract and his county cap. Brophy's benefit has come after five seasons at Headingley, instead of the normal ten, and is believed to be in lieu of an improved contract. He was unable to get into the team at the start of this season, when Jonnie Bairstow kept wicket, but came in when opening batsman Joe Sayers was ruled out by a virus that exacerbated his asthma. Though he was born in South Africa, his parents are from Northern Ireland, entitling him to a British passport, and he has played English domestic cricket since he joined Northamptonshire in 2002.

Brophy has scored over 4,000 runs in all competitions for Yorkshire and claimed more than 250 victims behind the stumps. He was awarded his county cap in 2008.

He said, 'It is a great honour to be awarded a benefit season. The players, coaches, staff and supporters have all made me so welcome since I joined the club. To play for Yorkshire with its history and stature, to receive my county cap and now to get a benefit is beyond my wildest dreams.'

was highly regarded and he also scored vital runs. His 151 not out against Nottinghamshire in the first innings of the penultimate match was an outstanding, match-winning effort after the hosts had been dismissed for 59.

That victory took them into the final week with high hopes of a double, but silverware eluded them. First, after topping their Clydesdale Bank 40 group with nine wins from 11, they had to play the home semi-final at Scarborough because it clashed with the one-day international at Headingley. After a flying start their innings was briefly interrupted by a shower and, despite scoring 257 for 5 in 36 overs, they lost by four wickets to Warwickshire, who got home with seven balls to spare. Rudolph's 106 in that match took his aggregate from 13 CB 40 innings to 861 at an average of 95.66, while Patterson took 21 wickets at 22.38.

Yorkshire were much less successful at Twenty20, finishing sixth in their group with the only notable achievements being a century by Gibbs and 26 wickets for Rashid at 16.46. Five days after the Scarborough defeat came the crushing disappointment of the final day collapse against Kent. But, at the end of the match, Yorkshire received a rousing round of applause from

fans who are notoriously frugal with their praise.

Not all the supporters are impressed, however, by the monstrous new Carnegie Pavilion, which opened in mid-season, nor are they be happy about reports of £18m debts. But they are clearly happy with their team, recognising that a bright future lies ahead for a young, home-grown side.

Right Jacques Rudolph acknowledges the applause after reaching his century against Nottinghamshire at Headingley. Released from his contract a year early for personal reasons, he will be sorely missed by Yorkshire supporters.

Opposite Keeper Gerard Brophy fought hard to get a place in the starting line-up this season. His reward was a regular berth behind the stumps and a benefit season in 2011.

PLAYER OF THE SEASON

Adil Rashid – left alone by England, he benefited from regular cricket and scored valuable runs as well as taking stacks of wickets in all forms of the game.

YOUNG PLAYER OF THE SEASON

Adam Lyth. Previously considered a middle-order man, he responded magnificently to the challenge of opening. To score 1,509 Championship runs was an outstanding effort.

A YEAR TO REMEMBER

- Andrew Gale challenged for silverware on two fronts in his first season as captain
- Jacques Rudolph ended his four-year stint at the club with batting of remarkable consistency
- Oliver Hannon-Dalby began a Championship campaign in which he was ever-present with two five-wicket hauls

A YEAR TO FORGET

- Joe Sayers missed the last two thirds of the season with a viral infection
- David Wainwright – injury and tinkering with action left him struggling for form

Yorkshire Agree to Release Rudolph
by Tim Wellock

At the end of the 2010 season Yorkshire agreed to release South African batsman Jacques Rudolph from the final year of his contract. Rudolph was at Headingley for four seasons after joining as a Kolpak player in 2007. He scored more than 1,000 first-class runs every year, while amassing 8,629 runs in all competitions.

While Rudolph has thoroughly enjoyed his time with the club, he and his wife Elna found it difficult adjusting to life in England. Jacques spent each winter with his family in South Africa and although Elna moved to Leeds in an attempt to find suitable employment as a doctor, it did not work out as they both would have liked. A club statement said, 'They are both very keen to start a family and, with an unsettled lifestyle, felt it was impossible to put down roots and make plans for the future. As such, they formally requested to be released from the final year of Jacques' contract and the Board of Directors granted this wish.'

YORKSHIRE CCC

FIRST–CLASS MATCHES
BATTING

	OJ Hannon-Dalby	JM Bairstow	A Lyth	A McGrath	AU Rashid	JA Rudolph	SA Patterson	AW Gale	JJ Sayers	A Shahzad	TL Best	GL Brophy	DJ Wainwright	RM Pyrah	TT Bresnan	MA Ashraf	Azeem Rafiq	GS Ballance	LJ Hodgson	JE Root	JAR Blain	CJ Geldart	BW Sanderson	AZ Lees	JR Lowe	CG Roebuck	Extras	Total	Wickets	Result	Points
v. Warwickshire (Edgbaston) 9-12 April	1	2	6	13	44	75	0	23	50	30*				10													20	274	10		
	-	81	67	16	-	69*		0	12	11				11*													24	291	6	W	21
v. Somerset (Headingley) 15-18 April	1*	11	0	21	63	33	101	51	45			0		61													32	419	10		
	-	6*	90	4	-	27	64*	0	-			-		-													8	199	4	W	22
v. Kent (Canterbury) 21-24 April	0	70	8	40	59	38		13	0	14		16*			0												25	283	10		
	-	6*	84	55	-	3		2*	61	-					70												19	300	5	D	8
v. Durham (Headingley) 27-30 April	-	9	85	105	43	228*	-	41	63	-				14*													22	610	6		
																														D	9
v. Essex (Scarborough) 4-6 May	1*	62	47	112	16	45	5	135	5		4			61													23	516	10		
																														W	23
v. Loughborough UCCE (Headingley) 10-12 May												89	-	134*	-	-		43	33	14	-	17	-				18	348	5		
												-		-	-	-	6*		-	20*	-	-	-				3	29	0	D	
v. Somerset (Taunton) 17-20 May	2*	17	142	73	1	11	25	50		15			39		4												26	405	10		
	-	29*	93	83	-	66	-	12					31*														19	333	4	L	6
v. Hampshire (Rose Bowl) 24-27 May	0	4	133	64	51	3	3*	56	49	6				8													38	415	10		
	-	36*	98	64	11*	28	-	12	13	-				-													30	292	5	D	9
v. Lancashire (Headingley) 29 May-1 June	-	29	0	4	65	30	0*	9	10	38*	12																2	199	8	D	5
v. India A (Headingley) 5-7 June	8*							19		40		19			5		0		34	4				38	5	23	24	219	10	D	
v. Lancashire (Old Trafford) 28 June-1 July	11*	47	100	61	13	83	27			1	35		32		4												33	447	10		
	-	11	29	57	42*	4	-			6	23		16				13*										14	215	7	D	10
v. Warwickshire (Headingley) 5-8 July	0	44	84	57	29	0	14			2		103	45*		12												35	425	10		
	-	64*	1	15	16*	80	-			-	14	-															10	200	4	W	23
v. Essex (Chelmsford) 20-23 July	1	18	75	11	52*	32	16	47		0		33			5												34	324	10		
	-	62	42	16	19*	106	0*	41		-		28			1												18	333	7	D	8
v. Nottinghamshire (Headingley) 3-6 August	2	45	0	29	13	1	10	24		17	5	20*															12	178	10		
	-	7	37	80	34*	141	26	14		3	37	-															27	406	8	D	5
v. Durham (Chester-le-Street) 16-19 August	-	18	6	124*	17	7	7	0		15	4				8	25											24	255	10		
	-	13	48	29	15*	100	3	70*			0				-												21	299	6	W	21
v. Hampshire (Scarborough) 23-26 August	1*	5	63	21	76	34	7	3		21*	44				20												27	322	9		
	-	50*	44	20	-	54	-	24		10*					-												23	225	4	D	7
v. Nottinghamshire (Trent Bridge) 7-9 September	0	36	19	10	11	10	0	151*		7	5			0													15	264	10		
	-	63*	45	4	9*	29	-	5		-	41			-													13	209	5	W	21
v. Kent (Headingley) 13-16 September	1	64	17	1	29	25	39*	39		21	1			10													14	261	10		
	0*	9	46	30	4	13	2	2		16	0			0													8	130	10	L	5
Matches	17	16	16	16	16	16	14	13	9	9	9	9	7	7	6	4	3	3	2	2	1	1	1	1	1	1					
Innings	15	29	29	29	24	29	17	23	14	12	9	17	6	7	9	4	3	5	2	3	0	1	0	1	1	1					
Not Out	7	7	0	1	8	2	4	4	0	3	0	1	3	2	1	0	1	2	0	1	0	0	0	0	0	0					
Highest Score	11*	81	142	124*	76	228*	39*	151*	63	45	40	103	39	134*	70	10	13*	43	34	20*	-	17	-	38	5	23					
Runs	29	918	1509	1219	732	1375	184	876	395	238	86	472	108	304	203	15	29	84	67	38	-	17	-	38	5	23					
Average	3.62	41.72	52.03	43.53	45.75	50.92	14.15	46.10	28.21	26.44	9.55	29.50	36.00	60.80	25.37	3.75	14.50	28.00	33.50	19.00	-	17.00	-	38.00	5.00	23.00					
100s	0	0	3	3	0	4	0	3	0	0	0	1	0	1	0	0	0	0	0	0	0	0	0	0	0	0					
50s	0	8	9	9	6	6	0	3	5	0	0	1	0	2	0	0	0	0	0	0	0	0	0	0	0	0					
Catches/Stumpings	1/0	29/5	9/0	9/0	14/0	20/0	3/0	2/0	3/0	1/0	4/0	20/0	4/0	2/0	1/0	0/0	1/0	1/0	1/0	0/0	0/0	0/0	0/0	0/0	0/0	0/0					

Home Ground: Headingley
Address: Headingley Carnegie Cricket Ground, Leeds, LS6 3BU
Tel: 0871 971 1222
Fax: 0113 2784099
Email: cricket@yorkshireccc.com
Directions: From M1 South leave at junction 43 to M621 as far as junction 2. From M62 West leave at junction 27 to take M621 as far as junction 2. From M62 East leave at junction 29 to join M1 northbound to junction 2 of M621. At junction 2 of the M621 follow the signs for Headingley stadium along A643. Follow Leeds Inner Ring Road (A58(M)) to A660 which is signposted to Headingley stadium. Signs along this route will indicate when you have reached the Headingley area and on Test match days additional temporary signing will direct you to the free Park & Ride car park to the north of Headingley at Beckett Park.
Capacity: 20,000
Other grounds used: Scarborough
Year formed: 1863

Chief Executive: Stewart Regan
Operations Director: Ian Dews
Director of Cricket: Martyn Moxon
Captain: Andrew Gale
County colours: Gold and black

Website:
www.yorkshireccc.com

Honours
County Championship
1867, 1869, 1870, 1893, 1896, 1898, 1901, 1902, 1905, 1908, 1912, 1919, 1922, 1923, 1924, 1925, 1931, 1932, 1933, 1935, 1937, 1938, 1939, 1946, 1959, 1960, 1962, 1963, 1966, 1967, 1968, 2001
Joint Champions 1949
Sunday League/NCL/Pro40
1983
Benson & Hedges Cup
1987
Gillette Cup/NatWest/C&G Trophy
1965, 1969, 2002

FIRST-CLASS MATCHES
BOWLING

	AU Rashid	SA Patterson	OJ Hannon-Dalby	A Shahzad	TL Best	TT Bresnan	DJ Wainwright	MA Ashraf	RM Pyrah	BW Sanderson	Azeem Rafiq	LJ Hodgson	A Lyth	JAR Blain	E Root	JA Rudolph	JJ Sayers	A McGrath	Overs	Total	Byes/Leg-byes	Wickets	Run outs
v. Warwickshire (Edgbaston) 9–12 April	4-1-11-1	14-1-51-3	13.2-3-40-3	8-2-35-1		19-3-71-2												1-0-2-0	59.2	217	7	10	
	10-1-24-0	20-5-68-2	19-1-72-2	17-1-68-5		23-5-74-1												9-1-18-0	98	347	22	10	
v. Somerset (Headingley) 15–18 April	9-1-41-2			14-3-54-1	17-3-54-2	17-3-48-3	13.4-0-42-2											5-1-22-0	75.4	272	11	10	
	9-2-27-0			16-2-63-2	18.2-1-68-5	23-5-78-1	27-4-99-1												93.2	344	9	10	1
v. Kent (Canterbury) 21–24 April	11-1-39-0		26-3-65-3	18-3-59-0		24.2-7-52-5	14-4-49-2									1-0-1-0		3-0-18-0	97.2	317	34	10	
	20-2-80-2		15-2-55-1	9-1-37-1		18-5-33-2	26-1-112-2											4-1-14-0	92	357	26	8	
v. Durham (Headingley) 27–30 April	27-4-83-2	15-6-41-2		17-4-50-0	22-2-86-4	16-3-50-1											1-0-3-0		98	330	17	9	
	7-0-20-0	5-2-6-0		4-0-13-0	3-2-6-0	3-3-0-0													22	46	1	0	
v. Essex (Scarborough) 4–6 May	9-0-42-1	19.5-7-50-5		11-1-38-1	15-2-54-3				3-1-21-0										57.5	206	1	10	
	25.5-2-98-3	10-6-19-2		10-3-26-2	13-0-51-1				6-2-8-2								3-1-5-0		67.5	214	7	10	
v. Loughborough UCCE (Headingley) 10–12 May							21-6-47-2	17-7-35-1			18-3-50-5	12-1-46-1	14.4-4-42-1		14-7-20-0				96.4	253	13	10	
v. Somerset (Taunton) 17–20 May	19-0-85-4	22-7-54-1		20-3-50-2	19-2-95-0			15.4-3-48-3										9-2-25-0	104.4	377	20	10	
	20.4-0-123-2	19-2-96-1		12-2-47-0	2-0-16-0			12-1-78-1											65.4	364	4	4	
v. Hampshire (Rose Bowl) 24–27 May	18.4-3-62-4	22-7-60-0		21-3-70-1	21-4-91-2				14-1-50-1									1-0-2-0	97.4	351	16	9	1
	6-3-3-0												1-0-3-0	1-1-0-0				6-1-6-0	14	12	0	0	
v. Lancashire (Headingley) 29 May–1 June	36.2-6-121-4	20-8-48-2		29-3-87-2	16-1-52-1			14-1-49-0									13-1-45-0		128.2	416	14	9	
v. India A (Headingley) 5–7 June				17-3-73-0	14-1-66-1		25-1-134-1	16-1-71-1				16-2-86-1		7-0-27-0					95	473	16	3	
v. Lancashire (Old Trafford) 28 June–1 July	38.5-6-90-5	9-0-31-0		15-4-52-0	15-2-45-1				6-2-15-0		35-5-92-4			3-0-11-0					121.5	358	22	10	
	20.4-8-46-3	9-4-14-1		4-1-15-0	10-0-40-3				20-3-66-0										63.4	192	11	7	
v. Warwickshire (Headingley) 5–8 July	29-5-71-4	22-6-57-4		13-5-42-1	7-0-32-1				6-1-24-0		5-0-15-0								82	253	12	10	
	39-3-137-5	15.3-4-25-3		18-3-54-0	18-3-54-0				14-5-35-1		16-4-49-0							5-3-3-0	125.3	371	14	10	1
v. Essex (Chelmsford) 20–23 July	25.5-7-87-5	23-5-89-2		14-3-54-1	16-1-63-2	28-8-73-0											10-4-17-0		116.5	399	16	10	
	16.2-7-6-2	7.5-2-30-2		6-0-35-0	9-0-45-0	18-2-44-2										5-1-26-0			67.5	293	16	6	
v. Nottinghamshire (Headingley) 3–6 August	23-0-104-1	29-3-110-3	21-1-115-2	22-1-104-1			11-1-57-0					1-0-13-0						10-1-32-0	117	545	10	7	
v. Durham (Chester-le-Street) 16–19 August		13.2-5-44-1	16-2-51-5				16-4-58-1		11-2-40-2									1-0-5-0	57.2	213	15	10	1
	9-2-28-0	25.3-4-87-4	26-6-81-2	23-1-73-4					11-2-53-0										92.3	340	18	10	
v. Hampshire (Scarborough) 23–26 August	25-1-114-1		27-6-77-2	26-9-05-1	20-4-78-0	2-0-7-0			13.4-0-80-1							1-0-5-0		7-0-27-0	121.4	498	20	6	1
	–																		–	–			
v. Nottinghamshire (Trent Bridge) 7–9 September		7-2-8-0		11-4-21-4	9.2-4-18-4			6-4-11-2											33.2	59	1	10	
	17-4-48-2	21-2-83-2		26-9-100-4	18-2-71-1			14-1-50-1										3-0-18-0	102	413	43	10	
v. Kent (Headingley) 13–16 September	21-2-83-2	10.5-1-42-1		25-4-102-1	7-0-36-1			18-7-32-5											81.5	302	7	10	
	7.5-1-41-2	6-1-10-2		6-2-17-1	7-0-36-1			4-0-13-1										1-0-4-0	24.5	90	5	6	

	AU Rashid	SA Patterson	OJ Hannon-Dalby	A Shahzad	TL Best	TT Bresnan	DJ Wainwright	MA Ashraf	RM Pyrah	BW Sanderson	Azeem Rafiq	LJ Hodgson	A Lyth	JAR Blain	E Root	JA Rudolph	JJ Sayers	A McGrath
Overs	504.4	392.5	292.2	382.4	198	188.2	184.2	75	84.4	18	88	30.4	2	14	7	11	24	74
Maidens	67	96	47	61	20	42	27	20	16	3	13	6	0	7	0	2	3	13
Runs	1784	1201	1013	1372	793	538	716	212	326	50	268	128	16	20	27	43	61	226
Wickets	57	45	34	34	18	17	14	11	7	5	5	2	0	0	0	0	0	0
Average	31.30	26.69	29.79	40.35	44.06	31.65	51.14	19.27	46.57	10.00	53.60	64.00	–	–	–	–	–	–

FIELDING

34	JM Bairstow (29 ct, 5 st)
20	GL Brophy (20 ct)
20	JA Rudolph
14	AU Rashid
9	A Lyth
9	A McGrath
4	TL Best
4	RM Pyrah
3	SA Patterson
3	JJ Sayers
2	TT Bresnan
2	AW Gale
1	MA Ashraf
1	GS Ballance
1	OJ Hannon-Dalby
1	LJ Hodgson
1	JE Root
1	A Shahzad
1	DJ Wainwright

Division One – Final Table

	P	W	L	D	Bat	Bowl	Pens	Pts
Nottinghamshire	16	7	5	4	47	43	0	214
Somerset	16	6	2	8	53	41	0	214
Yorkshire	16	6	2	8	41	42	0	203
Lancashire	16	6	3	8	35	43	0	182
Durham	16	5	3	8	30	39	0	173
Warwickshire	16	6	9	1	20	47	0	166
Hampshire	16	3	6	7	47	41	0	157
Kent	16	3	7	6	42	44	-1	151
Essex	16	2	6	8	29	43	-2	126

CB40   FPt20

Limited overs nickname:
YORKSHIRE CARNEGIE

MARTYN MOXON, the former England batsman and director of cricket at Yorkshire, urges caution in the domestic cricket scheduling debate…

Yorkshire: Doing it Our Way

It was reported during the 2010 season that I have a radical plan for the restructuring of the County Championship, but I would like to stress that my preference would be to leave well alone. If they're going to change it – and at the time of writing it seems as if the present two-division structure will be retained for 2011 – then I don't like any of the ideas that were suggested a few months ago.

My alternative isn't radical, it's a simple variation on the idea of three conferences and ensures the groups have an even spread of standard. For example, Group A would involve the teams finishing first, fourth, seventh, twelfth, fifteenth

and eighteenth with the rest divided similarly between the two other groups. That would avoid splitting the counties at random – a system which could produce a really tough division or a really weak division.

I certainly don't like the idea of a regionalised tournament. I wouldn't want to see any fewer than 14 Championship games being played, so the teams finishing first, second, third etc in each group would play off against each other, home and away. Every team would then have a finishing position, which would determine the following season's groups. Prize money would be available to all, increasing the incentive.

We have to get it sorted properly. I have always said that for players to develop properly we need a template that reads: prepare, play, recover. At the moment we play, play, play. If we continue to play the amount of one-day cricket we saw in 2010 then we are in danger of killing the golden goose. For example, like many other counties, Yorkshire had three home Twenty20 games in a week during the Friends Provident t20 group stage, and we have to ask whether people can afford either the time or the money to come to them all. Everyone agrees Test cricket is the ultimate, so we have to play enough of the longer form of the game to produce Test cricketers.

We have already had so many reviews that we have to get it right this time from both a cricketing and financial point of view. Continually chopping and changing is not doing anyone any good. We need sensible cricketing people having a big input rather than simply allowing the financial aspects to take precedence, otherwise the England team will not be successful and we will lose revenue.

A good example of how the system in place last season wasn't satisfactory was our 40-over Clydesdale Bank league match against Holland in Rotterdam, which was scheduled on a Sunday. We travelled to Holland from Cheltenham and had to be back for a Championship game that began

Jonathan Bairstow, one of Yorkshire's current crop of immensely talented young cricketers, keeps wicket during the County Championship fixture against Warwickshire at Edgbaston.

David Wainwright, the Yorkshire slow left-arm spinner, appeals in vain for the run out of Kent's James Hockley at Canterbury. The umpire is Nick Cook.

the following Tuesday. We struggled to find flights, so we took the coach over on Eurostar and then drove to Rotterdam. After the match, which we had to start early so we could catch the overnight ferry from Rotterdam to Hull, we slept on the boat and arrived back in Yorkshire mid-morning on the Monday. It was not the best way of preparing for the following day's Championship fixture!

On the plus side, last season at Yorkshire was a good one – in terms of the way we played – because we had a lot of our own, home-grown players in the team.

I was the county captain when we abandoned our Yorkshiremen-only policy in the early 1990s because we felt we were operating with one hand tied behind our backs. Given that we have won only one County Championship since, it could be argued that bringing in outsiders has not been a great success!

This is a club with strong traditions, however, in which the members take great pride in seeing local lads doing well. We're trying to build a side that will be competitive over

a number of years and, although the average age of the team is only 24, a lot of them have already been around for some time.

Andrew Gale, Tim Bresnan, Joe Sayers, Adil Rashid, David Wainwright and Adam Lyth have all played a lot of first-team cricket now. We've brought in Jonathan Bairstow and Oliver Hannon-Dalby, who has been a real bonus, and there are others in their age group showing a lot of potential such as Azeem Rafiq, James Lee, Joe Root and Ben Sanderson.

The work ethic among them is tremendous and they have a genuine desire to be successful.

We have been working for three years on getting them to understand how the game works and to know their own games, and we seem to be succeeding in that if last season's performances are anything to go by. We invest a lot of money in our academy and players have to be given opportunities. Some counties recruit well, but for me the greatest pleasure comes from being able to produce players of our own.

WEATHER WATCH

by Andrew Hignell

'Somerset stay on course for title with a hand from the weather gods' – this was the headline in *The Times* on Thursday 16 September, as the final day of the County Championship season dawned with the West Country team on top of the table and seemingly poised to become champions for the first time in their history. But as the notes and statistics below show, the weather throughout the season had not been so kind to Somerset.

Somerset had certainly enjoyed far more luck with the weather in their match with Durham at Chester-le-Street compared with Nottinghamshire, who had started the

final round of matches on top of the table, but had seen 16.25 hours of play lost on the first three days of their match against Lancashire at Old Trafford. Throughout the season Nottinghamshire had lost just 6.75 hours of play in their previous seven away matches, and their visit to Manchester looked like literally dampening their aspirations of lifting the county title. But on a remarkable final day of the season – as declaration bowling occurred elsewhere – Nottinghamshire opted to go for maximum batting points and then one bowling point in order to finish level with Somerset on top of the table, but becoming champions by virtue of having won seven games compared with Somerset's six.

But the weather gods, which appeared to be smiling on Somerset at Chester-le-Street, had been less kind during the season, with the West Country side losing more time to the weather than Nottinghamshire. Whereas the latter lost 48 hours, split evenly between home and away games, Somerset lost a total of 54.75

Rain did not help Somerset's cause in their final County Championship match of the season against Durham, at Chester-le-Street. This hold-up did not last long, but in the end Somerset ran out of time as they attempted to chase down a modest fourth-innings target when a win would have clinched them a historic first title.

hours' play – 38.50 at home and 16.25 hours when away from home. Their match with Durham at Taunton in late August saw 17 hours of play lost, while their game with Kent in mid-July saw the loss of 10 hours' play and the contest with Essex in late April saw nine hours lost. All three of these rain-affected games ended in draws and had Somerset been able to clinch one more bonus point, or one more victory, the LV County Championship pennant would be flying proudly next year at their Taunton ground.

The statistics below show that, once again, Lancashire were the 'raining' champions, losing a total of 74.50 hours of play during the first-class season. In all, they lost 40.75 hours at their home games – the only side to lose more time at home than Somerset – while Essex and Kent in the drier south-east lost just 7.25 and 9.25 hours respectively.

Many might suggest a west-east split in these rainfall statistics, prompting calls for a variant of the Duckworth-Lewis Method (perhaps called McCaskill-Fish) in rewarding county sides for performances in the rain-affected Championship matches. Somerset might well have benefitted from such a system, but on the basis of the statistics below there might not have been such a sharp west-east split in rainfall patterns in 2010, as Somerset's West Country neighbours Gloucestershire lost just 26 playing hours throughout the season – less than any other county side in the country – with just 10.25 playing hours lost in matches at Bristol, and all of this in their final Championship match of the season against Surrey.

The table below shows the breakdown of time lost in each division of the LV County Championship in 2010.

TIME LOST (IN HOURS) IN COUNTY CHAMPIONSHIP			
Division One		Division Two	
Durham	60.00	Derbyshire	45.00
Essex	46.00	Glamorgan	42.75
Hampshire	45.00	Gloucestershire	26.00
Kent	37.00	Leicestershire	41.75
Lancashire	74.50	Middlesex	35.00
Nottinghamshire	48.00	Northamptonshire	32.25
Somerset	54.75	Surrey	46.00
Warwickshire	39.00	Sussex	41.75
Yorkshire	36.50	Worcestershire	42.00

While Lancashire were the wettest county in first-class cricket in 2010, it was Durham – the former winners of Division One of the LV County Championship – who were the county side most affected by rain in one-day cricket, losing almost 17 per cent of their playing time in limited-overs contests. In contrast, Lancashire were one of the sides to lose very little time in one-day matches

Bad weather cost Nottinghamshire dear when they lost their Friends Provident t20 semi-final against Somerset on Duckworth-Lewis.

last summer, with the Red Rose county losing a mere 1.95 per cent of playing time. Only Sussex lost fewer overs in 2010, with South Coast neighbours Hampshire – the winners of the Friends Provident t20 competition – also losing just 2.44 per cent of playing time. Somerset, who were the runners-up in both the 20 and 40-overs competitions, also lost a mere 2.23 per cent of time, but across the Severn Estuary, Glamorgan faired worse with 12.13 per cent of time being lost – both at home and away – with their total of lost time only being surpassed by Durham, Kent and Nottinghamshire. The table below shows the percentage of time lost by each county in one-day cricket in 2010.

TIME LOST (IN PERCENTAGE TERMS) IN ONE-DAY CRICKET			
Derbyshire	3.83	Middlesex	8.25
Durham	16.94	Northamptonshire	4.94
Essex	8.18	Nottinghamshire	13.04
Glamorgan	12.13	Somerset	2.23
Gloucestershire	5.13	Surrey	8.06
Hampshire	2.44	Sussex	1.64
Kent	13.38	Warwickshire	4.89
Lancashire	1.95	Wocrestershire	4.06
Leicestershire	6.56	Yorkshire	3.98

Andrew Hignell writes regular Weather Watch columns for testmatchextra.com.

A FUNNY THING HAPPENED...

by Andrew Hignell

With a number of unusual and funny events happening during the course of the 2010 county season, it seemed rather fitting that events should begin under the lights of Abu Dhabi rather than in a chill wind at Derby.

The unusual setting for the traditional curtain-raiser as Durham met the MCC was the precursor to some bizarre happenings around the county circuit, such as the time when fragments from a small meteorite fell onto the outfield at Uxbridge during the County Championship match between Middlesex and Sussex, while in a game at Northampton a fire alarm halted play for ten minutes as the pavilion complex was evacuated and the two match scorers hastily relocated on to the dressing room balcony.

As it was one of the driest seasons in recent times, however, at least we were spared the sight of the covers being on for prolonged periods of time at many county grounds, but there was still the instance of sunshine stopping play, such as at Old Trafford in September for over quarter of an hour as the reflections dazzled the batsmen and fielders who ironically had already spent much of the game cooped up in the Manchester pavilion because of rain!

Headline writers were also nearly given a treat back in May, the day after the General Election, when Glamorgan met Worcestershire in a one-day match at Cardiff. The home side boasted David Brown in their side while the visitors had James Cameron in their ranks but, unlike events on the political stage, Cameron failed to dismiss Brown when the Worcestershire all-rounder bowled at the Glamorgan man.

During the course of the summer, there were some unusual and funny sights as well, such as at Grace Road where on several occasions Will Jefferson at 6 foot 10 inches – the tallest man in the county game – batted for Leicestershire with one of the shortest, James Taylor at 5 foot 4 inches, with their mid-pitch chats in-between overs causing plenty of mirth as Jefferson bent down to have a chat with his diminutive colleague. A far less humorous, but equally bizarre, incident took place at Chesterfield during Derbyshire's match with Surrey when a fierce drive from the home side's Steffan Jones struck Tom Lungley standing at the other end, with the non-striker having to briefly retire hurt as his arm was broken by the blow. Sadly, it proved to be Lungley's final season with Derbyshire and few players could surely have bowed out of the first-class game (if he doesn't find another county) in such a manner.

Gloucestershire's James Franklin took a career best 7 for 14 against Derbyshire at Bristol in late August and still ended up on the losing side!

Derbyshire were also involved in the most unusual and remarkable game of the season as they were dismissed on the opening morning of their Championship match against Gloucestershire at Bristol for just 44, yet went on to win the game the following afternoon, much to the delight of recently appointed captain Greg Smith, who himself had been involved in a strange occurrence a few weeks before in the match at Grace Road when he had dismissed his Leicestershire namesake in the home side's first innings.

But while the announcement of 'Greg Smith was bowled by Greg Smith' might have brought a few smiles to the hardy spectators at Leicester, it was nothing compared to the laughs across the country when the public address announcers have tried in vain to grapple with the name of Eric Szwarczynski, Holland's regular opening batsman in the Clydesdale Bank40 competition. Over the years, it's been bad enough for some of the announcers when trying to correctly say that 'the new Essex batsman is Ryan ten Doeschate', but saying the name of that particular Dutchman is a piece of cake compared with Szwarczynski whose surname spans a dozen letters with only two vowels – another new county record set in 2010!

They say it's never over until the fat lady sings, but not even the most diehard of Derbyshire supporters could have thought that their team held much of a chance of defeating Gloucestershire in their LV County Championship match at Bristol as the Peakites were dismissed for 44 in their first innings in the space of just an hour and a quarter, with James Franklin taking career-best figures of 7 for 14.

But then after dismissing Gloucestershire for 156 – on a remarkable opening day when 24 wickets fell – Derbyshire made a rally as they amassed 236 in their second innings, thanks to an unbeaten 96 from Chesney Hughes. With the home side needing 125 to win in the two and a half days remaining, the Derbyshire seamers scythed through the Gloucestershire batting, dismissing them for 70 with Tim Groenewald taking 4 for 22 and Graham Wagg 3 for 31 to seriously dent Gloucestershire's hopes of promotion into Division One.

Derbyshire's first innings total of 44 was the third lowest recorded by a team batting first in the County Championship who then went on to win the game, with their total only surpassed by Yorkshire's 42 against Sussex at Hove in 1922 and Gloucestershire's 31 against Middlesex at the Packer's Ground in Bristol in 1924.

The latter was a truly remarkable contest with Middlesex arriving at the Bristol ground knowing that victory would assure them of the county title. When they dismissed Gloucestershire for 31 in the space of 23 overs

29 March–1 April 2010
MCC v. Durham at Sheikh Zayed Stadium, Abu Dhabi

Durham 459 for 9 dec (KJ Coetzer 172, MJ Di Venuto 131, BA Stokes 51, DJ Malan 4 for 20)
& 228 for 6 dec (CD Thorp 79*, KJ Coetzer 52*, P Mustard 50)
MCC 162 (SG Borthwick 4 for 27) & 214 (TJ Murtagh 55*, ID Blackwell 4 for 70, SG Borthwick 4 for 57)
Durham won by 311 runs

Above Captains Alex Gidman of MCC (left) and Will Smith of Durham toss up before the opening match of the season. It was the first ever first-class, day/night match played with a pink ball.
Below MCC take the field in an almost empty Sheikh Zayed Stadium.

– and without a single member of the home side getting into double figures – they must have felt as if the title was theirs.

But they had reckoned without two of Gloucestershire's greatest-ever players, as firstly spinner Charlie Parker took 7 for 30 including a hat-trick to dismiss Middlesex for 74. Then Wally Hammond struck a sublime 174 not out, allowing Gloucestershire to declare on 294 for 9 and leave the visitors with a target of 250 to win on the final afternoon. It proved too much as Parker claimed a further seven wickets, and his second hat-trick of the game, as Middlesex were bowled out for 190, thereby ending their aspirations of the Championship title.

To see a more detailed listing of the lowest-ever totals in the first innings of a game by teams who ended up winning the game, please visit: http://cricketarchive.com/Archive/Records/Firstclass/Overall/Lowest_Innings_and_Win.html

The County Championship match between Sussex and Derbyshire at Horsham in August 2010 saw a rare batting feat being achieved when the first four batsmen in the Sussex line-up all scored hundreds in Sussex's first innings. Ed Joyce (164), Chris Nash (156), Ben Brown (112) and Murray Goodwin (100*) all reached three figures as Sussex amassed a mammoth total of 576 for 3 declared en route to a comprehensive innings victory which consolidated their lead at the top of Division Two. It was only the fourth time in the history of Championship cricket that the first four batsmen of a side had all scored a century in an innings, with the previous occasions being in the following games:

Middlesex v. **Sussex** at Lord's, 1920
(PF Warner 139, HW Lee 119, JW Hearne 116*, NF Haig 131)

Middlesex v. **Hampshire** at Southampton, 1923
(HL Dales 103, HW Lee 107, JW Hearne 232, EH Hendren 177*)

Somerset v. **Leicestershire** at Taunton, 2007
(ME Trescothick 182, NJ Edwards 133, JC Hildreth 163, CL White 114)

There had been a previous occasion when four Sussex batsmen had scored a century in an innings – that was in July 1938 when they played at Northampton, and in reply to the home side's first innings total of 377, the South Coast club amassed 631 for 4. Their run spree began with John Langridge and Jim Parks Snr adding 192 for the first wicket, before Parks departed for 106. His brother Henry then came in at No. 3, but he was dismissed for just a single. However, No. 4 George Cox and No. 5 Hugh Bartlett subsequently scored hundreds, with Langridge completing a double-century before Sussex declared. For the record, the recent Horsham match was the 21st time in the history of the competition

that four batsmen have scored a century for the same side in an innings in a Championship match – to see a list of these, please visit: http://www.cricketarchive.com/Archive/Records/Firstclass/Overall/Most_Hundreds_in_Innings.html

Glamorgan's County Championship match against Leicestershire at Swansea saw a moment of cricket history as Robert Croft, the veteran Glamorgan all-rounder, became the Welsh county's first-ever player and the first for any county since 1972 to achieve the fantastic career double of 1,000 first-class wickets and 10,000 first-class runs for a single club. The 40-year-old achieved this magnificent milestone when he claimed his 1,000th first-class wicket for Glamorgan by dismissing Wayne White to become the first county cricketer since Hampshire's Peter Sainsbury in May 1972 to complete the feat. Only eight other players have achieved this since the end of the Second World War:

Player	County/Season	Runs	Wickets
Trevor Bailey	Essex 1946–1967	21,460	1,593
Tony Brown	Gloucestershire 1953–1976	12,684	1,223
Tom Cartwright	Warwickshire 1952–1969	10,781	1,058
Ray Illingworth	Yorkshire 1951–1983	14,986	1,431
Derek Morgan	Derbyshire 1950–1969	17,842	1,216
John Mortimore	Gloucestershire 1950–1975	14,918	1,696
Peter Sainsbury	Hampshire 1954–1976	19,576	1,245
Fred Titmus	Middlesex 1949–1982	17,320	2,361

Croft also became the first county bowler to take 1,000 wickets for one club since Martin Bicknell achieved the feat for Surrey, taking his milestone wicket during their Championship match with Glamorgan at The Oval in May 2005 – ironically when Croft was leading the Welsh county (although the off-spinner was not one of Bicknell's eight wickets in the contest).

The late Phil Carrick narrowly missed out on achieving the feat for Yorkshire for whom he took 1,018 wickets and scored 9,994 runs between 1970 and 1993. He had gone into Yorkshire's final match of the 1993 season, against Surrey at The Oval, needing 20 runs to reach the 1,000-run mark. Rain washed out the first two day's play before Surrey batted first when play finally got underway on the third day. After the home side had been dismissed shortly before the close of play, Carrick was promoted to open the batting and ended the day 14 not out, just six runs short of his target. But the rains returned the following day, washing out the final day of the contest and preventing Carrick from reaching his goal.

Fortunately, the weather gods have smiled more favourably on Croft, and given the changes which have been talked about taking place to the county calendar in the future, the 40-year-old might also be the last-ever player the reach this milestone for a single club.

Sussex all-rounder Robin Martin-Jenkins certainly went out on a high this summer. He left halfway through the season to start work as a geography teacher with a batting average in the County Championship of 62.90 (Sussex's highest) and 30 wickets at 19.76.

stellar performance with either bat or ball. They were not to be disappointed as he made an important 78 in Sussex's first innings, which allowed them to amass what proved to be a match-winning lead as they defeated Gloucestershire to return to the top of the Division Two table.

Indeed, Martin-Jenkins had been in decent form with the bat in Sussex's last few Championship matches, with the all-rounder passing fifty each time in what proved to be his last four innings in the competition. An unbeaten 55 against Northamptonshire was followed by another unbeaten 66 against Worcestershire, then a superb 130 against Derbyshire and 78 in his final match at Arundel – giving the 34 year-old a tally of 329 runs at a remarkable average of 164.50.

These impressive statistics prompted the question what is the best performance by a batsman in their final appearance in the County Championship. That honour lies with Fred Bakewell who scored an unbeaten and chanceless 241 for Northamptonshire against Derbyshire at Chesterfield in 1936 – the only instance of a batsman making a double-century in their last innings in the competition. To see the scorecard for this match, please visit:

http://www.cricketarchive.com/Archive/Scorecards/15/15991.html

However, at the time when he walked off the field, Bakewell and the rest of the Northants team were unaware that it would be the right-hander's final innings. Tragically, on his return journey home from Chesterfield, Bakewell and his opening partner Reg Northway were involved in a serious car accident near Kibworth in Leicestershire. Northway was killed, and Bakewell's arm was so severely injured that he never played first-class cricket again. At the time, he was just 27 years old.

Andrew Hignell writes regular 'Stats Man' columns for the *testmatchextra.com* website

It's always sad when an honest county trooper makes his final appearance. Indeed, end-of-season games are often littered with fine valedictory performances as a batsman or bowler bows out of the county game. Some though have called it a day mid-season, often through injury, but this was not definitely not the case when Robin Martin-Jenkins made his final appearance in the LV County Championship for Sussex, against Gloucestershire at Arundel, in July 2010 before taking up a teaching appointment.

The all-rounder has been a stalwart figure in Sussex's highly successful team of the past few years, which won the County Championship in 2003, 2006 and 2007 besides a series of one-day titles. His supporters were therefore hoping that he would bow out with another

CHAMPIONS LEAGUE

by Mark Baldwin

A competition which should also have featured Hampshire and Somerset was eventually won by Chennai Super Kings who, under the captaincy of Mahendra Singh Dhoni, thus completed a 2010 double of Indian Premier League and Champions League titles.

The two English counties, finalists in the Friends Provident t20, were shamefully denied their place at the second Champions League tournament – held this time in South Africa – by political posturing.

Originally, the Champions League was due to start in late September, and the England and Wales Cricket Board dutifully moved the end of the English domestic programme forward by a week and a half (the 2009 season had finished on 27 September) to accommodate it. Sussex and Somerset had participated in the inaugural Champions League, which was staged in India between 8 and 23 October in 2009, and had returned home highly enthusiastic about the standard of the Twenty20 cricket played and the format of the event – even though neither county made much of a mark on the competition.

When the Champions League organisers altered the scheduling of the 2010 tournament, however, bringing it forward to the middle of September in order to avoid a clash with the start of Australia's tour to India, the ECB merely decided to withdraw its two qualifiers. Some claimed the Indian authorities had deliberately changed the dates of the incoming Australia tour to cause

Players from the Chennai Super Kings franchise celebrate winning the 2010 Champions League after beating South African side Warriors in the final at the Wanderers Stadium in Johannesburg. The Super Kings also won the Indian Premier League earlier in the year.

problems for England's administrators, and the ECB initially lobbied to have the dates changed back.

What they said they would not do, though, was allow the end of the English domestic season to be disrupted by two counties flying off to play Champions League cricket. And, while this sounded suitably strong and principled, the bottom line meant that – for the second time – English influence on the world game's newest competition was wastefully compromised.

Even before the event was launched, remember, England's inflexible approach had cost them a place at the Champions League top table alongside India, Australia and South Africa. The ECB were offered a share in the organisation of the event, but declined it due to a falling out with India.

Now, in 2010, the players and coaching staff of Hampshire and Somerset were being denied the opportunity of competing and learning alongside some of the game's leading performers. It would have been fascinating, for instance, to see how Somerset might have fared in their second attempt at success in the competition, having had their eyes opened by their 2009 experience.

Of course, it would have been impossible – given the already overcrowded nature of the English domestic fixture list – to have re-arranged both Hampshire and Somerset's final County Championship matches on 13–16 September any earlier. Somerset, too, as it turned out, were also involved in the Clydesdale Bank 40 final at Lord's on 18 September, the final day of the domestic season. If those matches had been delayed until after the Champions League (in other words, until the last week of September) it would also have taken a huge amount of drama away from what was a thrilling finale to the Championship season in particular.

But it still seems a nonsense cricket-wise that England should not have had its two leading Twenty20 representatives at the tournament, let alone with regards to the financial implications that were denied both Hampshire and Somerset. Surely something should have been sorted out, because it is the ECB's duty to maximise opportunities for its member counties to improve themselves – both on and off the field. It is to be hoped that nothing is allowed to stand in the way of the two 2011 Twenty20 Cup finalists going to the next Champions League.

The sad reality of the 2010 stand-off was that the young guns of Hampshire and Somerset, such as Danny Briggs, James Vince and Jos Buttler, were prevented from playing against world stars like Dhoni, Sachin Tendulkar, Dale Steyn, Muttiah Muralitharan and Suresh Raina. The lamentable performances of Central Districts, of New Zealand, and Guyana, the West Indies

qualifier, indeed, made it even more galling that some of England's best young players – and crusty old pros like Dominic Cork, the Hampshire captain – were not able to compete in South Africa.

Chennai, meanwhile, made the most of a gilded path through the competition to beat South African side Warriors in the final. Dhoni's team had the advantage of playing two of the weakest sides at the start of their campaign and they reached the semi-final by beating Warriors in a match in which the South Africans, who had already all but qualified, were only focused on scoring the 109 that they needed to make sure of their last four spot.

Then, in the semi-final itself, Bangalore's feared South Africa fast bowler Dale Steyn suffered concussion in a freak fielding accident and could not bowl in the Chennai innings. Against Warriors in the final, the Chennai spinners Muralitharan and Ravichandran Ashwin both bowled beautifully as the host country's side were restricted to a below-par total.

Muralitharan and Ashwin were the best slow bowlers in the tournament, with statistics to back it up. They took 31 of the 54 wickets that Chennai claimed, at an average of little more than 11 runs per wicket and at an economy rate of just above six runs per over.

Doug Bollinger, the Australian left-arm paceman, was alongside his Chennai spin-bowling teammates in the top three bowlers, while Murali Vijay was the highest run-scorer in the competition with 294 runs from six innings at an average of 49, and Raina fourth with 203 runs at a strike rate of more than one and a half runs scored per ball faced.

It was an emotional success for Chennai, as the IPL champions are a team of players who will never all play together again due to the expansion and re-drafting of the franchises planned for 2011.

Group A
(Central Districts, Chennai Super Kings, Victoria, Warriors, Wayamba)

11 September 2010 at Port Elizabeth
Wayamba 153 for 9 (20 overs) (HGJM Kulatunga 59, J Theron 3 for 23)
Warriors 156 for 3 (18.2 overs) (MV Boucher 40*)
Warriors won by 7 wickets

11 September 2010 Day/Night at Durban
Chennai Super Kings 151 for 4 (20 overs) (S Badrinath 52*, A Srikkanth 42)
Central Districts 94 all out (18.1 overs) (L Balaji 3 for 20)
Chennai Super Kings won by 57 runs

13 September 2010 Day/Night at Port Elizabeth
Warriors 158 for 6 (20 overs) (DJ Jacobs 59)
Victoria 130 for 9 (20 overs) (J Theron 3 for 22)
Warriors won by 28 runs

15 September 2010 at Centurion
Central Districts 165 for 5 (20 overs) (JM How 77*)
Victoria 166 for 3 (19.4 overs) (AJ Finch 93*)
Victoria won by 7 wickets

15 September 2010 Day/Night at Centurion
Chennai Super Kings 200 for 3 (20 overs) (M Vijay 68,
SK Raina 87)
Wayamba 103 all out (17.1 overs) (JA Morkel 3 for 22,
R Ashwin 4 for 18)
Chennai Super Kings won by 97 runs

18 September 2010 at Port Elizabeth
Central Districts 175 for 3 (20 overs) (JM How 88*,
K Noema-Barnett 53*)
Warriors 181 for 4 (19.1 overs) (DJ Jacobs 74, AG Prince 64)
Warriors won by 6 wickets

18 September 2010 Day/Night at Port Elizabeth
Chennai Super Kings 162 for 6 (20 overs) (M Vijay 73)
Victoria 162 all out (20 overs) (AJ Finch 41, DJ Hussey 51,
SK Raina 4 for 26)
Match tied – Victoria won one-over eliminator

20 September 2010 Day/Night at Centurion
Wayamba 106 all out (16.3 overs) (DPMD Jayawardene 51,
J Mubarak 44, PM Siddle 4 for 29)
Victoria 108 for 2 (13.2 overs) (DJ Hussey 47*)
Victoria won by 8 wickets

22 September 2010 at Port Elizabeth
Wayamba 144 for 6 (20 overs)
Central Districts 70 all out (15.3 overs) (I Udana 3 for 22,
BAW Mendis 3 for 14)
Wayamba won by 74 runs

22 September 2010 Day/Night at Port Elizabeth
Chennai Super Kings 136 for 6 (20 overs) (MEK Hussey 50,
JP Kreusch 3 for 19)
Warriors 126 for 8 (20 overs) (R Ashwin 3 for 24)
Chennai Super Kings won by 10 runs

	P	W	L	N/R	NetRR	Pts
Chennai SK	4	3	1	0	+2.050	6
Warriors	4	3	1	0	+0.588	6
Victoria	4	3	1	0	+0.366	6
Wayamba	4	1	3	0	-1.126	2
Central Districts	4	0	4	0	-1.844	0

Group B

(Guyana, Lions, Mumbai Indians, Royal Challengers Bangalore,
South Australia)

10 September 2010 Day/Night at Johannesburg
Lions 186 for 5 (20 overs) (JD Vandiar 71, ND McKenzie 56*,
SL Malinga 3 for 33)
Mumbai Indians 177 for 6 (20 overs) (SR Tendulkar 69)
Lions won by 9 runs

12 September 2010 at Centurion
South Australia 178 for 6 (20 overs) (M Klinger 78,
CJ Ferguson 47)
Lions 167 for 8 (20 overs) (AN Petersen 56, SW Tait 3 for 36)
South Australia won by 11 runs

12 September 2010 Day/Night at Centurion
Guyana 103 all out (20 overs) (JH Kallis 3 for 16)
Royal Challengers Bangalore 106 for 1 (12.2 overs)
(JH Kallis 43*)
Royal Challengers Bangalore won by 9 wickets

14 September 2010 Day/Night at Durban
Mumbai Indians 180 for 7 (20 overs) (SS Tiwary 44)
South Australia 182 for 5 (19.3 overs) (M Klinger 50,
DJ Harris 56)
South Australia won by 5 wickets

16 September 2010 Day/Night at Durban
Mumbai Indians 184 for 4 (20 overs) (SR Tendulkar 48,
KA Pollard 72*, D Bishoo 3 for 34)
Guyana 153 for 6 (20 overs) (RR Sarwan 46)
Mumbai Indians won by 31 runs

17 September 2010 Day/Night at Durban
Royal Challengers Bangalore 154 all out (19.5 overs)
(LRPL Taylor 46, D du Preez 46, DT Christian 4 for 23)
South Australia 155 for 2 (18.3 overs) (DJ Harris 57,
M Klinger 69*)
South Australia won by 8 wickets

19 September 2010 at Johannesburg
Guyana 148 for 9 (20 overs) (E O'Reilly 4 for 27)
Lions 149 for 1 (15.1 overs) (AN Petersen 57*,
R Cameron 78*)
Lions won by 9 wickets

19 September 2010 Day/Night at Durban
Mumbai Indians 165 for 7 (20 overs) (S Dhawan 41,
DW Steyn 3 for 26)
Royal Challengers Bangalore 163 for 5 (20 overs)
(RS Dravid 71*, V Kohli 47)
Mumbai Indians won by 2 runs

21 September 2010 at Johannesburg
South Australia 191 for 6 (20 overs) (CJ Ferguson 55, CJ Borgas 48)
Guyana 176 for 7 (20 overs) (RR Sarwan 70, DJ Harris 3 for 33)
South Australia won by 15 runs

21 September 2010 Day/Night at Johannesburg
Lions 159 for 6 (20 overs) (AN Petersen 45)
Royal Challengers Bangalore 160 for 4 (19 overs) (MK Pandey 44, V Kohli 49*)
Royal Challengers Bangalore won by 6 wickets

	P	W	L	N/R	NetRR	Pts
South Australia	4	4	0	0	+0.589	8
RC Bangalore	4	2	2	0	+0.759	4
Lions	4	2	2	0	+0.401	4
Mumbai Indians	4	2	2	0	+0.221	4
Guyana	4	0	4	0	-2.083	0

Semi-finals

24 September 2010 Day/Night at Durban
Chennai Super Kings 174 for 4 (17 overs) (M Vijay 41, SK Raina 94*)
Royal Challengers Bangalore 123 all out (16.2 overs) (MK Pandey 52, DE Bollinger 3 for 27)
Chennai Super Kings won by 52 runs

25 September 2010 Day/Night at Centurion
Warriors 175 for 6 (20 overs) (DJ Jacobs 61, CA Ingram 46, DJ Harris 3 for 18)
South Australia 145 for 7 (20 overs) (CJ Ferguson 71)
Warriors won by 30 runs

FINAL – CHENNAI SUPER KINGS v. WARRIORS
26 September 2010 at Johannesburg

WARRIORS

DJ Jacobs (capt)	lbw b Ashwin	34
AG Prince	b Bollinger	6
CA Ingram	c Raina b Morkel	16
JP Kreusch	c Raina b Muralitharan	17
*MV Boucher	b Muralitharan	5
J Botha	c Srikkanth b Ashwin	7
CA Thyssen	c Srikkanth b Muralitharan	25
N Boje	not out	8
J Theron	not out	2
M Ntini		
LL Tsotsobe		
Extras	lb 4, w 4	8
	(7 wkts 20 overs)	128

	O	M	R	W
Bollinger	4	0	33	1
Morkel	4	0	31	1
Ashwin	4	0	16	2
Balaji	4	0	28	0
Muralitharan	4	0	16	3

Fall of Wickets
1-39, 2-45, 3-73, 4-81, 5-82, 6-111, 7-125

CHENNAI SUPER KINGS

MEK Hussey	not out	51
M Vijay	c Kreusch b Boje	58
SK Raina	c Botha b Ntini	2
*MS Dhoni (capt)	not out	17
S Badrinath		
A Srikkanth		
JA Morkel		
R Ashwin		
L Balaji		
DE Bollinger		
M Muralitharan		
Extras	lb 1, w 3	4
	(2 wkts 19 overs)	132

	O	M	R	W
Ntini	4	0	30	1
Tsotsobe	3	0	14	0
Theron	4	0	40	0
Botha	4	0	18	0
Boje	4	0	29	1

Fall of Wickets
1-103, 2-107

Umpires: Aleem Dar (Pakistan) & RE Koertzen (South Africa)
Toss: Warriors
Man of the Match: M Vijay

Chennai Super Kings won by 8 wickets

GULU EZEKIEL, a senior sports journalist and author based in New Delhi, explains why India rules the cricket world…

The turnabout in the fortunes of the Board of Control for Cricket in India (BCCI) – currently said to be controlling 70 per cent or more of the cricket world's finances – was not only due to the marketing skills of some of its bigwigs. It was also because the Indian cricket team pulled off two of cricket's most stunning upsets a quarter of a century apart that changed the face of cricket forever. Whether for better of worse depends on which side of the cricketing fence one resides in.

Kapil Dev and his unheralded team turning things upside down on a glorious summer's day at Lord's in June 1983 in the final of the third Prudential World Cup set the ball rolling and resulted in the first sweet sound of cricket's cash registers ringing. It also led to a tectonic shift in the International Cricket Council with cricket's powerbase for the first time moving to Asia away from the traditional Anglo-Australian nexus that had ruled since its founding in 1910.

For the first time the World Cup was staged outside England when in 1987 it was jointly hosted by India and Pakistan. The money on offer to the participating teams from the hosts was simply irresistible. By 1996 the die was cast when India, Pakistan and Sri Lanka jointly hosted the Wills World Cup, followed a year later by the ascension of Jagmohan Dalmiya to the ICC presidency.

It was not always so. The Indian dressing room after the Lord's triumph was a chaotic scene of jubilation and celebrations. But even amid all the pandemonium, the players had appointed captain Kapil Dev and senior statesman Sunil Gavaskar to arm-twist the BCCI into handing over a rich purse to the team. Having fulfilled their task of getting then BCCI president (and Union Minister) NKP Salve happily high on champagne, the canny duo pressed home their demands. Over and above the 500,000 rupees (approximately £12,000 at the time) the board had already promised the team, they also persuaded Salve to part with a further 100,000 rupees for each team member and the manager, that too minus the crippling 50 per cent tax it would have attracted back then. In the 1980s 100,000 rupees was a princely sum, enough to buy a flat, a car and with enough left over to invest.

Today the BCCI is one of the richest sporting bodies in the world, its net worth crossing the $1 billion mark. But in 1983 it did not have

Former India captain Sunil Gavaskar remains influential in Indian cricketing circles, often from inside the TV commentary box.

In 1992, the Indian state TV monopoly was broken, improving coverage for domestic supporters and increasing revenue from abroad.

Above Captain Rahul Dravid addresses the insatiable local media in a country whose population is cricket mad.

Below Jagmohan Dalmiya is widely acknowledged as the man most responsible for turning cricket into a global, multi-million dollar sport.

enough cash in its coffers for Salve to fulfil his drunken promise. The problem was solved when one of India's most famous singers was persuaded to give a free concert in a huge indoor stadium in New Delhi with all the gate-money and royalties on the subsequent LP going to the players.

The second seismic triumph came 24 years after the first at the inaugural ICC World Twenty20 in South Africa in 2007. Since the BCCI has been banking truckloads of money, this has not always translated into vision or common sense, as Indian cricket's many detractors will gleefully emphasise. So it was that the Indian board came close to boycotting the tournament – opposed as it was then to the whole concept of Twenty20 cricket – which their team would go on to win. And out of that triumph sprang the Indian Premier League in 2008 with its hitherto unheard of riches bringing in a permanent change in power equations.

If 1983 and 2007 were years that shook the cricket world, there was another major development that took place in 1991 that changed the entire nation and the world as well.

ISSUES SURROUND THIRD ASIAN WORLD CUP

The World Cup returns to Asia early in 2011, for the third time in 24 years. But as with 1987 and 1996, this time too it has been preceded by controversy.

When the tournament was staged in India and Pakistan for the first time, cricket was going through the South African crisis. England came close to boycotting as the Indian government objected to it choosing players who had plied their trade in the apartheid state. Many of the top stars such as Richard Hadlee, David Gower and Ian Botham also chose to stay away.

The subcontinent was not the favourite touring spot for most international sportspersons in those days. Now, of course, India is the land of silk and money as the world's cricketers flock here for the Indian Premier League and a myriad of business opportunities.

In 1996 it was a terror bomb attack in Colombo that led to the West Indies and Australia boycotting their matches in Sri Lanka when they were joint hosts with India and Pakistan. That led to a crisis on the eve of the event that almost saw it being scrapped.

Now, however, Pakistan finds itself out in the cold with the prevailing security situation there going from bad to worse. The last straw was the attack on the Sri Lankan team bus in Lahore in March 2009. International sporting events have since come to a grinding halt in Pakistan and they were stripped of their co-hosting rights with India, Sri Lanka and Bangladesh. Four nations had never before hosted a World Cup.

The political situation in Sri Lanka and Bangladesh, while calmer than in the past, is still unpredictable. In India it is security that is uppermost in the minds of those who run the game here. The trauma following the terrorist attacks on multiple targets in Mumbai in November 2008 has yet to heal and the threat of terror strikes hovers ominously over the tenth World Cup.

An India v Pakistan final in Mumbai on 2 April would be a dream match for the fans. But for the organisers it could turn out to be their worst nightmare. Here, the biggest threat comes from the right-wing Hindu political party, the Shiv Sena, which has vowed to prevent any Pakistan team from stepping on to Mumbai soil. It was for this reason that Mumbai's huge fan base was denied a quarter-final or semi-final in the 1996 Wills World Cup.

As far as the team prospects are concerned, Australia must always start as favourites. Having won every World Cup since losing the 1996 final to Sri Lanka in Lahore, theirs is a formidable record. India though will be itching to break the jinx of no host nation having ever lifted the cup – England came closest when they lost the 1979 final to the West Indies. It could also be Sachin Tendulkar's swansong, something he has hinted at for the last couple of years.

With the likes of Virender Sehwag, Suresh Raina, captain Mahendra Singh Dhoni, Zaheer Khan and Harbhajan Singh to support the master, who is to say the dream of countless millions of Indian fans does not come true come April 2011?

That year India's current Prime Minister Dr Manmohan Singh opened up India's markets to the world in his job as Union Finance Minister. A nation that had in place a Stalinist form of economy since its independence in 1947 and a miserable growth rate of barely two per cent, is today the world's second largest growing economy after China with the growth rate touching double figures. This has resulted in a massive middle-class that in numbers is more than double the population of Great Britain, enjoying loads of disposable income and a love for the good things of life.

With numbers such as these, a burgeoning economy and a population that is cricket mad, is it any surprise that India has the financial clout to repeatedly override the feeble ICC and lord over its member nations, most of who are happy to feed on the scraps thrown to them? It is what political pundits would describe as a unipolar world.

Dalmiya is widely credited in India at least with turning round the fortunes of cricket's economy in his role as first BCCI and then ICC president. When he took over as ICC presidency in 1997, a move bitterly opposed by cricket's traditional powers, the world body had about £16,000 in its kitty. By the time his term

Regarded by many as the best batsman ever, Sachin Tendulkar is likely to play in his final World Cup in 2011.

expired five years later, that had grown to $50 million, a figure that today has expanded manifold.

And the key to these riches lay in TV rights. With Rupert Murdoch's STAR TV network invading the Indian airwaves in 1992, the monopoly enjoyed by the state broadcaster Doordarshan finally came to an end. Much to the relief, it must be said, of countless millions of long-suffering Indian TV viewers.

It also gave Dalmiya, and his then comrade-in-arms (later *bête noir*) and board secretary Inderjit Singh Bindra, their golden opportunity. The BCCI had for years been in the ridiculous situation of having to pay Doordarshan to telecast cricket in India. But when in 1992 Mark McCormack's London-based TV production company Transworld International made an offer the Indian board could not refuse, Dalmiya and Bindra fought a bitter battle against the Indian government to free cricket coverage from the state's clutches. In the Supreme Court they were even accused of

being unpatriotic by the Indian government. But the doughty pair did not back down and won the day.

Today, the 10-year telecast deals for the IPL and its offshoot, the Champions League, run into the billions with current and former players around the world flocking to India for lucrative playing and endorsement contrast. This financial clout, it is alleged, allowed Indian cricket's bad boy Harbhajan Singh to escape with a slap on the wrist after his run-in with Andrew Symonds in the infamous 2008 Sydney Test. It also enabled India alone to oppose the Umpires Decision Review System (UDRS), which the ICC would have made compulsory but for the BCCI's cussedness.

Now early next year the World Cup (50 overs) returns to India (plus Sri Lanka and Bangladesh) for the third time and the IPL is already expanding after just three years. There is no looking back for the BCCI. And as far as they and the (largely) jingoistic Indian fans are concerned, the rest of the cricket world can either like it or lump it.

INTERNATIONAL CRICKET: FACTS AND FIGURES 2010

by Mark Baldwin

The seismic shift of the past cricket year occurred just before this book went to press – Australia lost a two-match Test series 2-0 in India and dropped to fifth place in the ICC rankings – their lowest ever position. Furthermore, the defeats in Mohali and Bangalore meant that for the first time since 1988 the Australians had lost three Tests in a row.

Those previous three successive defeats had come against the West Indies who, two decades ago, were still near their peak but getting ever closer to relinquishing their status as the world's most powerful cricket force. Ironically, their time at the top from around 1977 to 1994 has been followed by an era of Australian domination that has lasted almost the same span of years.

Will the next global domination on the field be by India, currently on top of the Test rankings and with a home World Cup fast approaching in which to replicate that position in the ODI ranking list too? Or can England climb to the summit, with a pivotal Test series against India coming up in 2011, following on from an Ashes winter in which glory beckons. They are already ICC World Twenty20 champions, and are also approaching the 50-over World Cup with great optimism.

A glance at the Test and ODI rankings show how the balance of cricket power shifts. In October 2009 it was South Africa who were number one in the Test list, with Sri Lanka second and India in third place. Now India lead the world in the five-day game.

When the 28th edition of this book was published a year ago, the world leaders in 50-over international cricket were, as now, Australia, with India second. But Sri Lanka have moved up from seventh to third in just twelve months, and New Zealand have fallen from fourth to sixth. England, befitting their gradual improvement under Andy Flower and Andrew Strauss, have moved up one place in both the Test and ODI ranking lists.

In individual terms, the re-emergence of Sachin Tendulkar as the world's best Test batsman has been one of the wonders of the past cricketing year. Indeed, following the series win against the Australians, Tendulkar's Test rating of 891 was his highest since early February 2002, when he was rated at just seven points more. For someone who has been playing Test cricket for 21 years, and who will be 38 in April 2011, that is quite something.

From an English perspective, the rise in 2010 of Graeme Swann to second place in the Test bowling rankings (and third in the ODI version) is instructive of the massive impact he has had at international level. Yet the improvement made by Jimmy Anderson is not too

Graeme Swann's superb form with the ball in 2009-10 has put him second in the list of the world's top Test bowlers.

far behind that of the meteoric Swann; Anderson, fourth in the Test rankings and twelfth in the ODI list, is now unquestionably sitting at the table of the world's elite bowlers.

Stuart Broad, for one still young at 24, also has Test and ODI rankings worthy of the highest praise – and it is very possible to see the Englishman one day assuming the mantle of Jacques Kallis as the world's outstanding all-rounder. Both Daniel Vettori of New Zealand and the impressive young Bangladeshi, Shakib Al Hasan, might yet have something to say about that as the veteran Kallis's medium-term successor.

The ICC rankings reproduced here also reveal the quality of performances put in over the past year by some of the more unsung internationals operating on the world stage. What about New Zealand's Ross Taylor at number nine in the Test batting list, for instance, or Sri Lankan Thilan Samaraweera just two places below him? Or Doug Bollinger's rapid rise into the Test bowling top ten, or Sri Lankan seamer Nuwan Kulasekera's position at number four in the ODI bowling rankings, or Zimbabwean left-arm spinner Ray Price's presence at number eight, or Ireland's Trent Johnson making it into the top 20?

As ever, the statistical side of cricket is as fascinating as the characters behind the figures. And, if you want more and deeper information about the statistics of the world game, or fuller lists than are reproduced on these pages, please go to: *www.cricketarchive.com*.

* All figures correct as at 15 October 2010

RELIANCE MOBILE ICC TEST RANKINGS – TEAMS

Position	Team	Points
1	India	130
2	South Africa	119
3	Sri Lanka	115
4	England	112
5	Australia	110
6	Pakistan	83
7	West Indies	79
8	New Zealand	78
9	Bangladesh	7

TEST RECORD TABLE

Country	Matches	Won	Lost	Drawn	Wins %
Australia	10	8	1	1	80.00
England	12	8	2	2	66.67
India	10	6	2	2	60.00
South Africa	9	4	2	3	44.44
New Zealand	6	2	3	1	33.33
Pakistan	12	3	8	1	25.00
Sri Lanka	6	1	3	2	16.67
West Indies	6	0	4	2	0.00
Bangladesh	7	0	7	0	0.00

RELIANCE MOBILE ICC TEST RANKINGS – INDIVIDUAL

Position	Player	Points
	Batting	
1	Sachin Tendulkar (India)	891
2	Kumar Sangakkara (Sri Lanka)	874
3	Virender Sehwag (India)	819
4	Shivnarine Chanderpaul (West Indies)	807
	Mahela Jayawardene (Sri Lanka)	807
6	Jacques Kallis (South Africa)	791
7	Graeme Smith (South Africa)	787
8	VVS Laxman (India)	767
9	Ross Taylor (New Zealand)	766
10	AB de Villiers (South Africa)	762
11	Thilan Samaraweera (Sri Lanka)	748
12	Hashim Amla (South Africa)	745
13	Michael Clarke (Australia)	738
14	Simon Katich (Australia)	735
15	Jonathan Trott (England)	733
16	Ricky Ponting (Australia)	731
17	Gautam Gambhir (India)	717
	Mohammad Yousuf (Pakistan)	717
19	Younis Khan (Pakistan)	710
20	Tamim Iqbal (Bangladesh)	707
	Bowling	
1	Dale Steyn (South Africa)	887
2	Graeme Swann (England)	858
3	Mohammad Asif (Pakistan)	753
4	Zaheer Khan (India)	744
	Jimmy Anderson (England)	744
6	Morne Morkel (South Africa)	739
7	Mitchell Johnson (Australia)	735
8	Harbhajan Singh (India)	679
9	Doug Bollinger (Australia)	659
10	Mohammad Aamer (Pakistan)	658
11	Stuart Broad (England)	650
12	Shakib Al Hasan (Bangladesh)	640
13	Makhaya Ntini (South Africa)	638
14	Daniel Vettori (New Zealand)	609
15	Jerome Taylor (West Indies)	580
16	Paul Harris (South Africa)	576
17	Umar Gul (Pakistan)	572
18	Peter Siddle (Australia)	562
19	Ben Hilfenhaus (Australia)	560
20	Jacques Kallis (South Africa)	559
	All-Rounders	
1	Jacques Kallis (South Africa)	442
2	Daniel Vettori (New Zealand)	393
3	Shakib Al Hasan (Bangladesh)	334
4	Stuart Broad (England)	319
5	Graeme Swann (England)	287
6	Shane Watson (Australia)	285
7	Dwayne Bravo (West Indies)	268
8	Virender Sehwag (India)	245
9	Chris Gayle (West Indies)	234
10	Mitchell Johnson (Australia)	233

Pace, serious bounce, hostility and the ability to swing the ball make South Africa's Dale Steyn the world's top Test bowler. Chosen by the ICC as their Test Player of the Year in 2008, his bowling also saw South Africa at number one in the 2009 Test rankings.

BEST TEST BOWLING ANALYSES

Player	Analysis	For	Against	Venue
JM Anderson	6-17	England	Pakistan	Nottingham
SR Watson	6-33	Australia	Pakistan	Leeds
MJ North	6-55	Australia	Pakistan	Lord's
GP Swann	6-65	England	Pakistan	Birmingham
SJ Benn	6-81	West Indies	South Africa	Bridgetown
Mohammad Aamer	6-84	Pakistan	England	Lord's
DW Steyn	5-29	South Africa	West Indies	Port of Spain
SR Watson	5-40	Australia	Pakistan	Lord's
ST Finn	5-42	England	Bangladesh	Manchester
SL Malinga	5-50	Sri Lanka	India	Galle
Mohammad Aamer	5-52	Pakistan	England	The Oval
JM Anderson	5-54	England	Pakistan	Nottingham
GP Swann	5-62	England	Pakistan	Lord's
M Muralitharan	5-63	Sri Lanka	India	Galle
Wahab Riaz	5-63	Pakistan	England	The Oval

RELIANCE MOBILE ICC ODI RANKINGS – TEAMS

Position	Team	Points
1	Australia	132
2	India	115
3	Sri Lanka	115
4	South Africa	115
5	England	112
6	New Zealand	100
7	Pakistan	99
8	West Indies	67
9	Bangladesh	64
10	Ireland	39
11	Zimbabwe	38
12	Holland	17
13	Kenya	0

HIGHEST TEST SCORES

Player	Score	For	Against	Venue
V Sehwag	293	India	Sri Lanka	Mumbai
DPMD Jayawardene	275	Sri Lanka	India	Ahmedabad
HM Amla	253*	South Africa	India	Nagpur
IJL Trott	226	England	Bangladesh	Lord's
KC Sangakkara	219	Sri Lanka	India	Colombo
RT Ponting	209	Australia	Pakistan	Hobart
SR Tendulkar	203	India	Sri Lanka	Colombo
MJ Guptill	189	New Zealand	Bangladesh	Hamilton
BB McCullum	185	New Zealand	Bangladesh	Hamilton
IJL Trott	184	England	Pakistan	Lord's
GC Smith	183	South Africa	England	Cape Town
RS Dravid	177	India	Sri Lanka	Ahmedabad
DPMD Jayawardene	174	Sri Lanka	India	Colombo
AN Cook	173	England	Bangladesh	Chittagong
JH Kallis	173	South Africa	India	Nagpur

ODI RECORD TABLE

Team	Matches	Won	Lost	Drawn	Wins %
Australia	27	19	7	1	73.08
England	20	14	6	0	70.00
South Africa	13	9	4	0	69.23
Ireland	17	11	6	0	64.71
Sri Lanka	24	14	8	2	63.64
Afghanistan	10	6	4	0	60.00
New Zealand	15	8	6	1	57.14
India	32	16	15	1	51.61
Scotland	10	5	5	0	50.00
Zimbabwe	25	11	14	0	44.00
Netherlands	12	5	7	0	41.67
West Indies	17	6	10	1	37.50
Canada	11	4	7	0	36.36
Pakistan	16	4	12	0	25.00
Bangladesh	24	6	18	0	25.00
Kenya	13	2	11	0	15.38

Captain, economical left-arm spinner and dependable middle-order batsman – Bangladesh's Shakib Al Hasan, at 23 years old, is now one of the world's leading all-rounders.

RELIANCE MOBILE ICC ODI RANKINGS – INDIVIDUAL

Position	Player	Points
Batting		
1	AB de Villiers (South Africa)	805
2	Mahendra Singh Dhoni (India)	796
3	Mike Hussey (Australia)	791
4	Tillekeratne Dilshan (Sri Lanka)	751
	Hashim Amla (South Africa)	751
6	Chris Gayle (West Indies)	738
7	Jacques Kallis (South Africa)	721
8	Virender Sehwag (India)	717
9	Ricky Ponting (Australia)	715
10	Sachin Tendulkar (India)	714
11	Shivnarine Chanderpaul (West Indies)	710
12	Kumar Sangakkara (Sri Lanka)	697
13	Graeme Smith (South Africa)	691
14	Eoin Morgan (England)	676
15	Andrew Strauss (England)	670
16	Ross Taylor (New Zealand)	662
17	Michael Clarke (Australia)	659
18	Shane Watson (Australia)	658
19	Paul Collingwood (England)	655
20	Herschelle Gibbs (South Africa)	641
Bowling		
1	Daniel Vettori (New Zealand)	746
2	Shakib Al Hasan (Bangladesh)	679
3	Graeme Swann (England)	669
4	Nuwan Kulasekera (Sri Lanka)	666
5	Stuart Broad (England)	662
6	Kyle Mills (New Zealand)	660
7	Doug Bollinger (Australia)	658
8	Ray Price (Zimbabwe)	656
9	Jacob Oram (New Zealand)	645
10	Dale Steyn (South Africa)	640
11	Praveen Kumar (India)	636
12	Jimmy Anderson (England)	635
13	Saeed Ajmal (Pakistan)	622
14	Mitchell Johnson (Australia)	619
15	Ajantha Mendis (Sri Lanka)	613
16	Shahid Afridi (Pakistan)	612
17	Ryan Harris (Australia)	610
18	Harbhajan Singh (India)	609
19	Trent Johnson (Ireland)	602
20	Johan Botha (South Africa)	595
All-Rounders		
1	Shakib Al Hasan (Bangladesh)	382
2	Shane Watson (Australia)	367
3	Shahid Afridi (Pakistan)	364
4	Jacques Kallis (South Africa)	350
5	Daniel Vettori (New Zealand)	336
6	Jacob Oram (New Zealand)	330
7	Yuvraj Singh (India)	299
8	Paul Collingwood (England)	297
9	Chris Gayle (West Indies)	296
10	Ryan ten Doeschate (Holland)	276

MOST ODI BOUNDARIES

Player	Team	Matches	Fours	Sixes	Boundaries
TM Dilshan	Sri Lanka	22	163	12	175
SR Watson	Australia	24	118	16	134
V Sehwag	India	23	117	14	131
AJ Strauss	England	17	102	12	114
WU Tharanga	Sri Lanka	24	104	10	114
H Masakadza	Zimbabwe	25	91	18	109
RT Ponting	Australia	27	96	13	109
MS Dhoni	India	26	89	17	106
Tamim Iqbal	Bangladesh	24	94	11	105
PR Stirling	Ireland	17	87	17	104
KC Sangakkara	Sri Lanka	19	91	7	98
SR Tendulkar	India	12	87	8	95
CL White	Australia	27	65	21	86
V Kohli	India	25	81	2	83
EJG Morgan	England	20	71	10	81

MUTTIAH MURALITHARAN

Muttiah Muralitharan, one of the greats of the game, retired from Test cricket in 2010 – although he is aiming to play one-day internationals this winter and to appear in the 2011 World Cup on home soil.

The smiling assassin from Sri Lanka, since his Test debut in late August 1992, has at times almost single-handedly carried his country's attack, although the left-arm seam and swing of his contemporary Chaminda Vaas not only often gave him crucial support from the other end but also created the rough outside the right-handers' off stump which Murali exploited so ruthlessly.

His final Test came against India at Galle in July, and it was written in the stars that he should take the eight wickets he needed in the game to finish his Test career with exactly 800 victims.

Murali's controversial action always attracted criticism, and twice in Australia he was called for throwing – the first time by Darrell Hair in 1995 and then by his fellow Australian umpire Ross Emerson three years later. The ICC, however, relaxed the degree of tolerance they would allow in an arm bent on delivery as Murali – in scientific tests and with his arm in a cast to prevent any further flexing of it – showed that he could still bowl normally.

Yet a deformity meant that Murali could not naturally straighten his right arm, and the incredible amount of spin he put on the ball was actually the result of strong fingers and, in particular, a freakishly double-jointed wrist. He was, in truth, a wrist spinner rather than a true finger spinner, and his levels of skill and stamina throughout his long Test career were quite remarkable.

Left and below These two views of Murali in bowling action illustrate the incredible flexibility of his double-jointed wrist which allows him to hide the position of his fingers on the seam – and therefore the direction of spin – from the batsman.

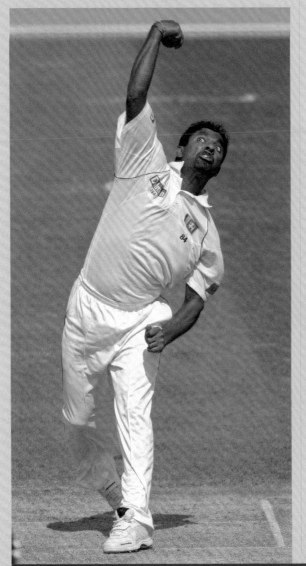

MURALITHARAN'S TEST CAREER IN FIGURES

M	Overs	Maidens	Runs	Wickets	Average	BB	5WI	10WM	SR	Econ
133	7,339.5	1,794	18,180	800	22.72	9–51	67	22	55.04	2.47

CHRISTOPHER MARTIN-JENKINS writes...

Test Championship Would Restore Balance of Bat and Ball

It is a toss-up, a matter of opinion, whether Brian Lara or Sachin Tendulkar is the greatest batsman of the last 25 years, but a softly spoken 33-year-old from Colombo has been building up records and a personal aggregate with an intensity that challenges them both.

In Ahmedabad in November 2009, at the start of a high-scoring three-match series won 2-0 by India, Sri Lanka's former captain Mahela Jayawardene made 275, his sixth Test double-century. When he came in Sri Lanka could have lost that Test to India, too. When he was out they had a chance of winning.

On a pitch so dead, flat and low bouncing that even Muttiah Muralitharan barely turned the ball, his effort was in vain but he had shared in the record sixth-wicket partnership in all Tests, putting on 351 with his namesake but not his relation, the wicketkeeper Prasanna Jayawardene.

There is a polished stone smoothness about Mahela Jayawardene's strokeplay and a poise that, at least on his own sort of pitches on the subcontinent, practically never fails him. He is no Lara, certainly, when it comes to excitement, nor does he have the panache of Sanath Jayasuriya or the wristy inventiveness of Aravinda de Silva. But, putting aside for a second the question of whether cricketing marathons still have a place in a world of sprints, we have to recognise a modern genius, especially the sort of genius that has been defined as infinite patience.

Only Lara (9), Bradman (12) and Wally Hammond (7) have managed more

Since his Test debut in 1997 Sri Lanka's Mahela Jayawardene has been quietly acquiring runs and a reputation as one of the world's finest Test match batsman. He has scored centuries against all other Test-playing nations, including five double and one treble century.

Brian Lara played his last Test match in 2006, retiring from international cricket the following year with almost 12,000 Test runs to his name. His top Test score was 400 not out against England in Antigua in 2004.

double-hundreds in Tests than Jayawardene. The 1930s, when Bradman and Hammond excelled, were, like this present era, years of too much plenty for batsmen. The ten-day Durban Test of 1939, supposedly timeless but finally concluded without a winner because of rain and the need for the England team to catch the boat home, might have been the final straw had not the Second World War put an end to that particular era and changed everyone's attitude.

Some similar watershed is needed now if Test cricket is to hold its place. Statistics may fascinate but it is close contests, the hope for a definite result and a proper balance between bat and ball that draws spectators, at least as much as famous names.

What is the point of long hours of accumulation by batsmen if the end product is just another high-scoring draw to measure against the quick-fire allure of Twenty20? The possibility of drawing a game that appears lost is actually one of Test (two innings) cricket's great advantages over the limited-overs versions, but only if there is some genuine suspense. The rolled mud pitches of India, Pakistan and Sri Lanka are mainly to blame but too many others are similar. England's early 2009 Test in Bridgetown, on a pitch once associated with pace like fire, was a case in point. The bowlers never had a chance.

Dull, batsman-friendly pitches have to be phased out quickly if Test cricket is to reverse a trend that is exacerbated by high ticket prices. Protective equipment that has taken some of the fear and danger out of facing fast bowling, more powerful bats, more muscular players and shorter boundaries have all counted against bowlers; but pitches remain the most serious problem.

The ICC has told match referees to mark as poor surfaces that offer 'limited carry, low bounce and no seam movement or turn... at any stage of the match'. But that means nothing if there is no real danger of international cricket being taken away from venues that get really bad marks. Not that it is always the groundsman's fault. If players really set out to win – which means scoring quickly in most cases and setting attacking fields – they can entertain even on bland surfaces.

To that end a Test Championship has to be tried, with Bangladesh and Zimbabwe starting in the second division alongside Ireland and others, and a points system that offers sufficient incentives to win. No doubt this will bring its own problems, not least perhaps on pitches that become a bit too sporting, but I dare say even Mahela Jayawardene and other great modern batsmen would agree that it is a better game when wickets are falling.

This article is taken from a column which first appeared on the testmatchextra.com *website.*

VIC MARKS, *Observer* cricket correspondent, former Somerset and England off spinner and long-serving *Test Match Special* summariser, bids farewell to another cricket year…

The year 2010 will never be recalled as one of the golden years (like 2005, 1981 or 1953 – if you know your Ashes history it does not take much to find a common thread there). It is, however, possible that 2010 will be remembered for quite some time since so many things went so spectacularly wrong.

At the start there were the hopelessly one-sided Tests against Bangladesh. Then it became apparent that there were so many international matches that it was becoming impossible for the harassed chief executives of our Test grounds to fill all their bright new bucket seats. ODI followed ODI and no one could quite remember who won what. Even worse, no one really cared.

Then came the England v Pakistan Test series, which was meant to be the saviour of the summer. Well, it certainly became the focal point of the season but for all the wrong reasons. How we had marvelled at the finesse of Mohammad Asif, the urbane, understated good sense of emergency captain Salman Butt and the unadulterated, youthful brilliance of Mohammad Aamer… until the last three days of the Lord's Test made us all think again. Those three no-balls threw the game into disarray, the sole consolation being that the spot-fixers were under the microscope again.

By the end of the summer there was paranoia all around. The ICC, alerted to some 'strange scoring patterns', wanted to call off the third ODI at The Oval just as the stands were filling up. At a midnight meeting the England team had to be persuaded to play the fourth ODI at Lord's after the fulminations (subsequently withdrawn) of Ijaz Butt, the chairman of the Pakistan Cricket Board. When the final international match of the season was completed at the Rose Bowl on 22 September, there was universal relief that a tempestuous summer, in which the cricket on the field had so often yielded to agonising off it, was finally over.

Nor was everything peace and light on the domestic front. County fans were bewildered by a new schedule, which had the Championship half-completed by the end of May while most of June was taken over by a constant diet of Twenty20 cricket. The Lord's cup final, the traditional pinnacle of the county season, was bizarrely played under lights on 18 September and attracted the smallest crowd (about 12,500) since it was first played back in 1963.

Around the counties the atmosphere was fraught and fractured. Those in possession of Test match grounds

Pakistan's superb Test victory against Australia at Headingley in late July was unhappily not a sign of things to come for the tourists.

Some things in cricket, however, have a timeless appeal – such as this scene at the Whitgift School ground in Croydon, the venue for Surrey's early-season County Championship game against Worcestershire.

(there are nine at the last count plus ODI specialists Gloucestershire) fretted about the bidding system for international matches and how they were going to generate enough income to pay for their grandiose building projects. The rest feared being marginalised by their big brothers. All 18 counties were perplexed that they were compelled to wait until 17 November (after this book went to press) before a clear idea (hopefully!) of the domestic structure for 2011 would be revealed.

So we have a picture of a game in turmoil. But there are some 'buts'. Despite all of the above shafts of light still shone through. The national team is not too bad and may be getting better. They are the world's Twenty20 champions; they were victorious in five of their six Tests and, just to remind you, they did win all three of those ODI series last summer.

Steven Finn is poking his head above the parapet (not so difficult for someone who is almost seven feet tall), Graeme Swann is the world's best spinner, Stuart Broad may be the world's best No. 9 – though not for long since he must surely return to No. 8 after that wonderful maiden Test hundred at Lord's.

While Andrew Strauss and Andy Flower are in charge we can anticipate England making the most of what they have got. And Kevin Pietersen is due (being sworn at by a

few Aussies may be just what he needs). So it is possible to view the Ashes campaign of 2010-11 with optimism although there is the caveat that every fourth October we usually manage to persuade ourselves that England will prevail in Australia.

Despite the headaches of finance and scheduling, somehow the domestic game produced much excitement and some young cricketers of talent, who may represent the new generation: Adam Lyth, James Hildreth, Andrew Gale, Ajmal Shahzad, Chris Woakes and Jonny Bairstow are all knocking on the door.

Moreover there appeared to be a renaissance of the County Championship. The last round of matches in both divisions fluctuated deliciously/horrendously depending on your provenance. And they provoked unusual interest. Oddly enough, amid all the talk of restructuring county cricket, by September it was no longer the automatic assumption that the Championship would be the first competition to be reduced.

Maybe the cricketing public sensed a rare purity about Championship cricket. Indeed, at the end of the frantic and often fractious summer of 2010, it became the epitome of the honest, unsung endeavour that seemed to have vanished from the international game.

AND FINALLY...

As 2010 draws to a close, it is time to look forward to another new cricket year. Deliberately, this annual now concentrates almost exclusively on what has happened over twelve months in English and England cricket at international and county level – there is simply too much going on now around the wider world of cricket to fit all of that into a single book in the time frame we have set ourselves.

In my twelve years as editor of *Cricket Year*, indeed, it is noticeable how much busier each year seems to become. Fixture lists, both internationally and domestically, are often bewildering in their complexity but – as my friend and colleague Vic Marks has pointed out on the previous pages to this one – there is happily much going right for England, and English cricket, at the moment.

We are currently involved, too, in one of the most exciting phases of the cricket calendar – an Ashes winter that also accommodates the tenth Cricket World Cup. Listeners of *Test Match Special* will themselves be as busy during these English winter months as they are every summer.

For cricket-lovers in England (and not forgetting Wales), moreover, there is much to look forward to in 2011. For a start, there are two very attractive teams touring England in our next summer – Sri Lanka, with cricketers of the stature of Kumar Sangakkara and Mahela Jayawardene, and India, bidding to maintain their current position as number one Test nation in the world.

What I will be looking forward to especially in 2011, however, is what is likely to be the great Sachin Tendulkar's final tour to England. Now back on top of the Test batting rankings, and – as I write this – fresh from a brilliant double-hundred (and unbeaten fifty in the second innings) as the Australians were beaten 2-0 in India, the Little Master is seemingly intent on marking the final years of his astonishing career with yet more bursts of heavy run-scoring.

So make sure you catch a live glimpse of Sachin in 2011 if you can, and also try to support county cricket as much as the international game. As Christopher Martin-Jenkins has written in these pages, the joy of county festival cricket in particular is woven into the very fabric of the English way of life.

Cricket Year 2010 has recorded matches memorable and moderate, and the deeds of cricketers magnificent to middling. There have also been, of course, all sorts of weird and wonderful happenings in the game besides major controversies and minor spats. And I don't suppose 2011 will be very much different...

Jonathan Agnew